T0237385

Learn Rails 6

Accelerated Web Development with Ruby on Rails

Adam Notodikromo

Apress®

Learn Rails 6: Accelerated Web Development with Ruby on Rails

Adam Notodikromo
Tokyo, Japan

ISBN-13 (pbk): 978-1-4842-6025-8   ISBN-13 (electronic): 978-1-4842-6026-5
https://doi.org/10.1007/978-1-4842-6026-5

Copyright © 2021 Adam Notodikromo

This work is subject to copyright. All rights are reserved by the Publisher, whether the whole or part of the material is concerned, specifically the rights of translation, reprinting, reuse of illustrations, recitation, broadcasting, reproduction on microfilms or in any other physical way, and transmission or information storage and retrieval, electronic adaptation, computer software, or by similar or dissimilar methodology now known or hereafter developed.

Trademarked names, logos, and images may appear in this book. Rather than use a trademark symbol with every occurrence of a trademarked name, logo, or image we use the names, logos, and images only in an editorial fashion and to the benefit of the trademark owner, with no intention of infringement of the trademark.

The use in this publication of trade names, trademarks, service marks, and similar terms, even if they are not identified as such, is not to be taken as an expression of opinion as to whether or not they are subject to proprietary rights.

While the advice and information in this book are believed to be true and accurate at the date of publication, neither the authors nor the editors nor the publisher can accept any legal responsibility for any errors or omissions that may be made. The publisher makes no warranty, express or implied, with respect to the material contained herein.

Managing Director, Apress Media LLC: Welmoed Spahr
Acquisitions Editor: Steve Anglin
Development Editor: Matthew Moodie
Coordinating Editor: Mark Powers

Cover designed by eStudioCalamar

Cover image by Taewoo Kimon on Unsplash (www.unsplash.com)

Distributed to the book trade worldwide by Apress Media, LLC, 1 New York Plaza, New York, NY 10004, U.S.A. Phone 1-800-SPRINGER, fax (201) 348-4505, e-mail orders-ny@springer-sbm.com, or visit www.springeronline.com. Apress Media, LLC is a California LLC and the sole member (owner) is Springer Science + Business Media Finance Inc (SSBM Finance Inc). SSBM Finance Inc is a **Delaware** corporation.

For information on translations, please e-mail booktranslations@springernature.com; for reprint, paperback, or audio rights, please e-mail bookpermissions@springernature.com.

Apress titles may be purchased in bulk for academic, corporate, or promotional use. eBook versions and licenses are also available for most titles. For more information, reference our Print and eBook Bulk Sales web page at www.apress.com/bulk-sales.

Any source code or other supplementary material referenced by the author in this book is available to readers on GitHub via the book's product page, located at www.apress.com/9781484260258. For more detailed information, please visit http://www.apress.com/source-code.

Printed on acid-free paper

for mom, dad, life

for more than life

Table of Contents

About the Author

Adam Notodikromo (formerly Adam Pahlevi Baihaqi) is a software engineer committed to creating working and technically well-written apps. With his colleagues in Indonesia and Germany, he is building their company together: Sonasign. He lives in Meguro, Tokyo to enjoy bowls of Yokohama-style ramen and also dry tantanmen. He works with kind teammates at Autify.

Acknowledgments

I would like to take this opportunity to express my gratitude toward Eldon Alameda, whose insightful voices have helped me on many occasions.

I also want to express my gratitude to everyone at Apress. In particular, thank you, Steve Anglin, for taking me on as an Apress author. Thanks also to Mark Powers for his help in getting this project started. Thank you, Matthew Moodie, for being a great sounding board for the book. To everyone at Apress, thank you for helping me to realize this book, one that I have long wanted to write.

Also thanks to my mom and dad. If not for my dad, I wouldn't have discovered the world of software engineering when I was 9. If not for my mom, I wouldn't be able to read. Thanks for being great parents.

I am also grateful to Zaenal Arifin, my first software engineering lecturer who taught me Microsoft Visual Basic 6.0 back in the day. Also, thanks to all the teachers who have taught me a lot, from Einstein's relativity theory to mitochondria to matrices to English. They are all interesting subjects!

Thank you to *you* too. I hope this book helps in advancing your career.

Introduction

Rails is a mature framework. In fact, Shopify, Airbnb, Twitter, Gojek, Groupon, Zendesk, GitHub, Kickstarter, Heroku, Intercom, Dribbble, SoundCloud, GitLab, Twitch, Etsy, and thousands of other innovations were built and run on it. Possibly yours will be next.

In this book, readers are taken on an adventure of building and deploying a social media application. Readers will learn how to get things done in Rails idiomatically.

As production-grade software demands rigorous testing processes to prevent quality regressions, the book also covers how to do automated testing, from unit testing to integration testing to end-to-end system testing. That will create a rapid feedback loop enabling teams to adopt modern development practices to be more productive, a topic we will explore in this book as well.

The source code for this book is available on GitHub at `https://github.com/adamnoto/learn-rails-6`. You may also reach out to the author on Twitter: `@adamnoto`.

Without further ado, let's get going!

CHAPTER 1

First Things Rails

At the risk of sounding glib, every piece of software really is a work of art.

We engineers make something out of nothing, sparking an idea into its own living universe. If we say, "Let there be a person!" lo and behold, we can have that.

This chapter is not a typical introductory chapter. The primary goal of this chapter is to acquaint you with the process of developing and deploying a Rails app. You will learn how to create a database and how to make use of it. We will also build a web interface for our app. Guesto will be born, and billions of Earthlings can have access to it. This chapter hopes to get you excited by walking through all of that.

Although you will experience a lot of things in this chapter, the goal is to demonstrate, not to overwhelm. Rails makes it incredibly easy to build a web app, and that's a feature this chapter highlights.

Let's go for it! But before we delve into coding, let's read some history.

The Web Chronicles

Have you ever used Airbnb? Airbnb is powered by Rails, as are many other modern applications on the Web such as GitHub, Twitch, and Zendesk. As we will create an application and deploy it on the Web, you may be wondering, "How does the web work?" or "How did it come to be?"

The Web was born in 1989 at CERN, a physics research facility in Geneva, Switzerland. Tim Berners-Lee, its creator, noticed a need for automated information-sharing. He created a proposal titled "Information Management: A Proposal"[1] to which his supervisor, Mike Sendall, marked it as being "vague but exciting" (see Figure 1-1).

---

[1] http://info.cern.ch/Proposal.html

© Adam Notodikromo 2021
A. Notodikromo, *Learn Rails 6*, https://doi.org/10.1007/978-1-4842-6026-5_1

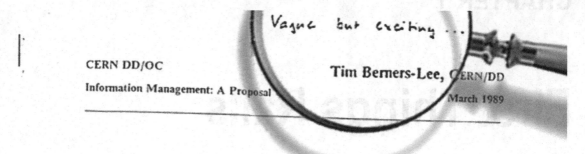

Figure 1-1. *Sendall's infamous commentary on the proposal*

Anyway, Berners-Lee was given some time to work on his project, and by October 1990, he put together three technologies that are still part of the Web as we know it today.

- HyperText Markup Language (HTML)

- Uniform Resource Identifiers (URIs)

- HyperText Transfer Protocol (HTTP)

By using these technologies, we can use a web browser to visit any web page using HTTP or the secure HTTPS protocol.

In those days, all web pages were static pages. That is, if you gave a browser an HTML file, the browser rendered the file the same way every single time. To change the content, one would need to change the file itself. Hence, this is called a *static* web page (see Figure 1-2).

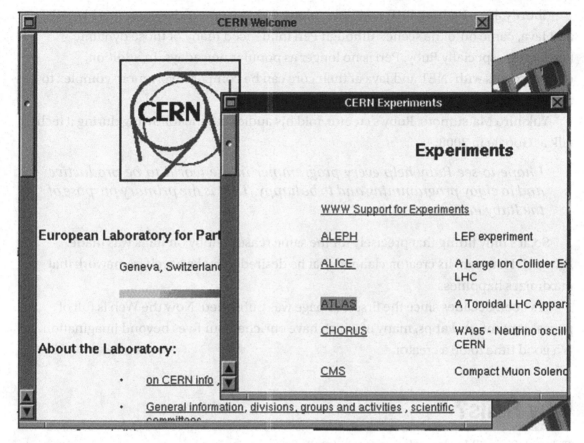

Figure 1-2. *One of the first web pages*

As web pages were all static, it wasn't possible, for example, to create a visitor hit counter, unless the counter was intended to display the same number every time. With the same token, it was not possible to update a researcher phone book page without re-uploading the HTML page. Dynamic page technology was needed!

In 1993, the folks at the National Center for Supercomputing Applications (NCSA) cooked up Common Gateway Interface (CGI), which allows for backend codes to generate an HTML document. In addition, the web server can pass along with it any user-specific data (such as cookies), allowing the resource not only to become dynamic but also customized for its visitors. Think of Twitter, for instance, where your timeline and mine are not the same.

CGI employs mostly Perl code, a language dubbed as the Swiss army knife of programming languages. Although a great programming language, Perl is relatively difficult to master. For one, it has many cryptic sigils.

Shortly after, Python, PHP, and Ruby, along with the enterprise solutions like .NET and Java, came onto the scene. Although Perl influenced many of those dynamic languages, especially Ruby, Perl is no longer as popular nowadays. In addition, environments with .NET and Java at their core can be comparatively more complex to use than Ruby.

Yukihiro Matsumoto, Ruby's creator, told his audiences the following during a tech talk at Google in 2008:

> *I hope to see Ruby help every programmer in the world to be productive and to enjoy programming and to be happy. That is the primary purpose of the Ruby language.*

So, it's only fitting that precisely for the same reason, Ruby on Rails was made. David H. Hansson, its creator, claimed that he desired to make a web framework that maximizes happiness.

It's been decades since the first web page was published. Now the Web is full of pages, content, and apps, many of which have enriched our lives beyond imagination. It is a good time to be a creator.

Why Rails?

This section will look at why we are using Rails.

Simplicity Through Conventions

Rails tries to eliminate as much of the plumbing code as possible, giving us a sane default that works satisfactorily. It is no coincidence that one of the productivity mottos of Rails is convention over configuration (CoC). Not only that, CoC lowers the barrier of entry for newcomers, since it becomes easier to be productive right away.

Increased Signal to Noise

Rails capitalizes on the fact that Ruby makes code read naturally like a human language. See whether you can understand what we are trying to do with the code shown in Listing 1-1.

Listing 1-1. Querying Data Using Rails' ActiveRecord

```
Article.where(category: ["Ruby", "Rails"])
  .or(Article.where(author: "Sam"))
```

The code in Listing 1-1 is so readable that no comments are required. It is self-explaining. Trying to do the same thing in another programming language or framework could be chaos.

MVC Architecture

Model-View-Controller (MVC) is a pattern allowing developers to modularize an application largely into three parts: the model, the view, and the controller (see Figure 1-3).

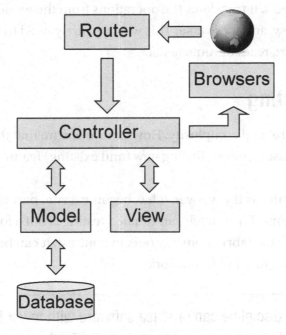

Figure 1-3. The MVC architecture in Rails

The part of the application the user sees is called the *view*. The view is responsible for displaying information based on the data it receives. The view may also contain user-interface components that can send a new request, thus starting the cycle all over again. The router then receives the request, which will then pass it to a controller.

Within each request, the controllers might need to retrieve data from a database or a storage service for display or data manipulation. Such a request is handled by the model.

Using this pattern, Rails code and workspaces become very structured from the get-go.

ActiveRecord

The majority of applications need to talk to a database. However, the way data is modeled with relational databases and object-oriented databases is not the same, as is self-evident from their names.

In a relational database, data is stored in a table made of rows and columns. Data in a table might be referenced by other tables through foreign key constraints.

ActiveRecord sought to bridge the two worlds by making a database look like a collection of Ruby objects. It translates the operations from the world of objects down to the relational worldview, and vice versa. This way, we rarely need to write any query and plumbing code to insert, read, or remove data.

Automated Testing

Software can grow in size and complexity. How can we ensure that the next feature we add won't break the existing ones? Testing new (and existing) features by hand would be a pain and error-prone.

Yep, automated testing is the answer. It has become a vital part of building software that stands the test of time. Fortunately, automated testing is not a foreign concept in Rails, as it is woven into the fabric from day one. In contrast, it can be a challenge just to set up automated testing in other frameworks.

Note   Good testing discipline can produce software with fewer bugs, which can make us feel great at programming. It is such a nice feeling to have!

Maximizing Developer Happiness

In Rails, there are many small things that are worth their weight in gold. For example, the error page during development is incredibly helpful. Rails is also known to be maintainable as its code is relatively stable and predictable. Those kinds of things not only make developers happy but are particularly valuable for long-term projects and startups so they can keep moving and delivering quickly.

Multiple Environments

In a production environment, we should not tolerate any major blowup as any issue can potentially result in a loss of revenue. The idea of multiple environments is then to keep errors separate. A typical workflow thus usually sports development, staging, and production environments to align with the development, test, and release processes. This environment separation is supported natively in Rails.

Rapid Application Development

Its flexibility and abundance of ready solutions to common problems have set Rails apart. In a blog post, GitLab CEO Sid commented as follows[2]:

> *Ruby on Rails has amazing shoulders to stand on and it would have been much slower to develop GitLab in any other framework.*

It is not a surprise that many startups started with Rails and keep on using it as they mature.

Open Source

Rails is open source. Rails is free both for individuals and for corporations alike. By going this path, Rails makes it possible for anyone to add features or fix bugs quickly.

There are many other reasons why Rails is such a great choice. Perhaps it will be easier to convince yourself once you give it a try.

---

[2]https://about.gitlab.com/blog/2018/10/29/why-we-use-rails-to-build-gitlab/

7

Preparing the Toolbox

For a smooth learning process, let's ensure we have the same software on our machines. The following software must be installed:

- asdf-vm version manager

- Node.js

- Ruby (preferably version 2.6)

- PostgreSQL

- Rails (preferably 6.0.2, a later 6.x release should be fine too)

This book uses asdf-vm, or asdf for short, to install Ruby and NodeJS. However, before installing asdf, we need to have git installed. To install git on an Ubuntu Linux, we can use the commands in Listing 1-2.

Listing 1-2. Installing git on Ubuntu

```
$ sudo apt-get update
$ sudo apt-get upgrade
$ sudo apt install make libssl-dev libghc-zlib-dev libcurl4-gnutls-dev
libexpat1-dev gettext unzip
$ sudo apt-get install git
```

macOS users can install command-line tools to install git; see Listing 1-3.

Listing 1-3. Installing Command-Line Tools for macOS Users

```
$ xcode-select --install
```

Let's double-check that git is there; see Listing 1-4.

Listing 1-4. Checking If git Is Installed

```
$ which git
/usr/bin/git
```

Next up, let's install asdf by cloning it into our system (see Listing 1-5).

Listing 1-5. Cloning asdf

```
$ git clone https://github.com/asdf-vm/asdf.git ~/.asdf --branch v0.7.4
```

The command in Listing 1-5 puts us in a detached head state so that we are using version 0.7.4, the same version we use in this book. After that, put asdf in the shell's source file. Bash users can use the code in Listing 1-6.

Listing 1-6. Adding Some Scripts into bashrc for Bash Users

```
$ echo $0 # check if you are using Bash
bash # if you see something else, you are not a Bash user
$ echo -e '\n. $HOME/.asdf/asdf.sh' >> ~/.bashrc
$ echo -e '\n. $HOME/.asdf/completions/asdf.bash' >> ~/.bashrc
```

Next, let's re-source the file. Or re-open the terminal window (see Listing 1-7).

Listing 1-7. Resourcing bashrc

```
$ source ~/.bashrc
```

Ensure that asdf is installed on our system using the code in Listing 1-8.

Listing 1-8. Ensuring asdf Is Installed

```
$ asdf --version
v0.7.4
```

Node.js

Rails uses Webpack to manage some JavaScript in Rails. For Webpack to work, we need to install a JavaScript runtime, such as NodeJS.

First, let's add NodeJS as a plugin by executing the command in Listing 1-9.

Listing 1-9. Adding NodeJS as a Plugin to asdf

```
$ asdf plugin-add nodejs
```

After that, let's import the Node.js release team's OpenPGP keys to the main keyring by executing the command in Listing 1-10.

Listing 1-10. Importing the Node.js Release Team's Keys into Main Keyring

```
$ bash ~/.asdf/plugins/nodejs/bin/import-release-team-keyring
```

After that, we are ready to install Node.js version 13.2.0 as used in this book. To do that, let's execute the commands in Listing 1-11.

Listing 1-11. Installing Node.js Version 13.2.0

```
$ asdf install nodejs 13.2.0
$ asdf global nodejs 13.2.0
```

Ruby 2.6.5

Ruby is needed to run Rails. We need to have Ruby 2.5.0 or greater installed on the machine, as Rails 6.0 requires Ruby 2.5.0 or greater. In this book, however, we are using Ruby 2.6.5.

To install the same version of Ruby as used in this book, let's run the commands in Listing 1-12.

Listing 1-12. Installing Ruby 2.6.5 Using asdf

```
$ asdf plugin-add ruby
$ asdf install ruby 2.6.5
$ asdf global ruby 2.6.5
```

After that, let's install Bundler, a dependency management tool for Ruby not unlike that of NPM in the JavaScript community, or Maven in Java. (See Listing 1-13.)

Listing 1-13. Installing Bundler

```
$ gem install bundler
Successfully installed bundler-2.1.4
Parsing documentation for bundler-2.1.4
Installing ri documentation for bundler-2.1.4
Done installing documentation for bundler after 3 seconds
1 gem installed
```

An Overview of the Project

Let's sketch out a brief summary of our application, which we will call Guesto. The application will be a guestbook application where anyone can send greetings. Formally, Guesto will do the following:

- Have a text editor for typing a greeting

- Let anyone send a greeting

- Let anyone see all greetings

Ready? Let's get started!

PostgreSQL 11 with PostGIS

Lots of web apps make use of a database to store their data. Rails apps are no exception. A popular database of choice is either PostgreSQL or MySQL/MariaDB.

Personally, I prefer to use PostgreSQL as it has richer data types, such as JSONB, which is missing in some database alternatives. It also has a lot of extremely advanced features such as window functions, PL/pgSQL, partitioned tables, and even inheritance. Not to mention, PostgreSQL is completely open source.

In addition, PostgreSQL is also very extensible. In fact, PostGIS, an extension we will use later in this book, has become the canonical example of how modular and extensible PostgreSQL is.

In this book, we will be using PostgreSQL 11 with the PostGIS extension. To install it on Ubuntu Linux and similar distros, we can use apt-get. But first, for Ubuntu users, let's add the PostgreSQL package repository by executing the commands from Listing 1-14 in the terminal.

Listing 1-14. Adding the PostgreSQL Package Repository for Ubuntu Users

```
$ sudo apt -y install gnupg2
$ wget --quiet -O - \
https://www.postgresql.org/media/keys/ACCC4CF8.asc | \
sudo apt-key add -
$ echo "deb http://apt.postgresql.org/pub/repos/apt/ \
`lsb_release -cs`-pgdg main" | \
sudo tee /etc/apt/sources.list.d/pgdg.list
$ sudo apt-get update
```

11

Then we can begin the installation process using the command in Listing 1-15.

Listing 1-15. Begin Installation Process for Ubuntu Users

```
$ sudo apt-get -y install postgis \
  postgresql-11-postgis-2.5 libpq-dev

[sudo] password for username: [password]
Reading package lists... Done
Building dependency tree
...
```

For macOS users, it might be easier to use a self-contained PostgreSQL binary such as Postgres.app. The binary should already contain the PostGIS extension that we will need in later chapters. You can download the app from https://postgresapp.com/.

Installing the PostgreSQL database doesn't mean that the database is running. On Ubuntu Linux, we can start the PostgreSQL server using the command in Listing 1-16.

Listing 1-16. Starting the PostgreSQL Server on Ubuntu

```
$ sudo service postgresql start
* Starting PostgreSQL 11 database server [OK]
* Starting PostgreSQL 12 database server [OK]
```

macOS users can start the server from within Postgres.app. There will be a clickable Start button under the blue, polite elephant (see Figure 1-4). Please start the database and choose PostgreSQL 11 when asked for the version.

PostgreSQL 9.3

⊗ Binaries not found

Server Settings...   ⟨?⟩   Stop   Start

▭   ☑ Show Postgres in menu bar

Figure 1-4. Starting PostgreSQL from within Postgres.app

If you are a macOS user and you are using `Postgres.app`, please proceed with installing the pg gem, as shown in Listing 1-17.

Listing 1-17. Installing pg gem for macOS Users

```
gem install pg -- --with-pg-config=/Applications/\
Postgres.app/Contents/Versions/11.0/bin/pg_config
```

Please note that you may need to adjust the version (11.0) to match yours if you decided to use a different version.

In some cases, macOS and Linux users also need to create a PostgreSQL account. We can skip this. But if you want to do this, let's create one where the account's username is equal to the system's username. (See Listing 1-18.)

Listing 1-18. Creating a PostgreSQL Username

```
$ whoami # to check the system's username
myuser123
$ sudo su - postgres -c "createuser myuser123 --superuser"
$ sudo -u postgres createdb `whoami`
```

13

That's it. Whatever method you choose to use to install PostgreSQL, please ensure that you install PostgreSQL 11 with the PostGIS extension. It may be possible to use other PostgreSQL versions, but it's not guaranteed that they will work the same.

Rails 6

The last thing we need to install is Rails itself. We can simply execute gem install rails to install it. Easy-peasy! However, we recommend you install a specific Rails version that is used throughout this book, that is, version 6.0.2.1. In that case, we can add the -v optional argument and specify the version to install. (See Listing 1-19.)

Listing 1-19. Installing Rails Version 6.0.2.1

```
$ gem install rails -v 6.0.2.1
Fetching thread_safe-0.3.6.gem
Fetching tzinfo-1.2.6.gem
....
38 gems installed
```

Since Rails comes with executable scripts (e.g., rails), we need to reshim our Ruby so that ASDF can recognize such scripts exist without having to restart the terminal. (See Listing 1-20.)

Listing 1-20. Reshim Ruby Apps

```
$ asdf reshim ruby
```

Let's double-check that Rails has now been installed; see Listing 1-21.

Listing 1-21. Checking the Installed Version of Rails

```
$ rails -v
Rails 6.0.2.1
$ rails _6.0.2.1_ -v
Rails 6.0.2.1
```

Integrated Development Environment

An integrated development environment (IDE) has unified features that a standard text editor is often lacking, such as code highlighting, code completion, debuggers, error checkers, terminals, and so on.

These are some of the best IDEs for developing Rails apps:

- *Vim*: Free. A very flexible IDE running on the terminal.

- *RubyMine*: Subscription-based. A cross-platform IDE specifically
  built for Ruby programming.

- *Visual Studio Code (VSCode)*: Free, extensible IDE. See Figure 1-5.

- *Sublime Text*: Shareware. Minimalist, extensible IDE.

- *AWS Cloud9*: Free, although credit card is required to sign up. An
  online, collaborative IDE.

Figure 1-5. *Visual Studio Code IDE*

If it is confusing which one to use, perhaps Sublime Text is the ideal choice. Sublime
Text supports Ruby out of the box; it is also very lightweight, it can be installed virtually
on any kind of (modern) machines, and it can be used for free. As for me, I am married
to VSCode.

Development

Just like any great software engineers, we begin the development process with finding
out what kind of software we would like to build. After that, we should be able to start
developing right away.

In the Beginning

The first step is to create a Rails project. Let's tell Rails that we want to use PostgreSQL as our database. See Listing 1-22.

Listing 1-22. Creating a New App with PostgreSQL as the Database

```
$ rails new guesto -d postgresql
```

The remainder of this chapter is going to assume that you will be inside the guesto folder. So, it's best to get oriented. See Listing 1-23.

Listing 1-23. Change the Working Directory to Guesto

```
$ cd guesto
```

Directory Structure

By default, a Rails app will have the directory structure shown in Listing 1-24.

Listing 1-24. Directory Structure of a Rails App

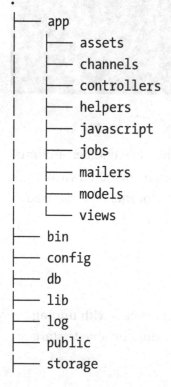

```
.
├── app
│   ├── assets
│   ├── channels
│   ├── controllers
│   ├── helpers
│   ├── javascript
│   ├── jobs
│   ├── mailers
│   ├── models
│   └── views
├── bin
├── config
├── db
├── lib
├── log
├── public
├── storage
```

```
├── test
├── tmp
└── vendor
```

To get accustomed with the directory structure, let's review what kind of files these folders generally contain (see Table 1-1).

Table 1-1. *Listing What Kind of Files Are in Each Subfolder*

File/Directory	What It Contains
app/assets	Files related to the front ends, such as CSS stylesheets, JavaScript code, and also images.
app/channels	Channels for ActionCable.
app/controllers	The *C* in MVC. Controllers of the app.
app/helpers	Utility methods accessible by the view.
app/javascript	JavaScript packs.
app/jobs	Background jobs.
app/mailboxes	Routers for incoming emails. This folder is not present on an app until we use the Action Mailbox feature of Rails.
app/mailers	Email senders.
app/models	The *M* in MVC. Models of the app.
app/views	The *V* in MVC. Usually written in embedded Ruby (erb), although it can also be written in another templating language such as Slim or Haml.
bin	Scripts to start/manage our Rails app.
config	Configuration files, such as database configurations, routings, localizations, etc.
db	Migration files for the tables, schema file, and database seeders. Database seeders are files that can be executed to prepare the database with some initial data.
lib	Rake files and independent codes.
log	Log files.
public	Static files, such as favicon, compiled assets, error pages.

(*continued*)

Table 1-1. (*continued*)

File/Directory	What It Contains
storage	Uploaded files for disk storage.
test	Test files. Many in the community prefer to use the RSpec framework for writing test codes; in that case, this folder will be deleted.
tmp	Temporary files.
vendor	Third-party front-end dependencies.

Typically, most of our work will be inside the app folder, where changes can take effect without a server restart in the dev (read: development) environment.

If for some reason you feel disoriented, please don't worry. You will get used to the structure quickly since all Rails applications will share this basic structure.

Starting the Server

Everything is in place, so let's fire up the web server! See Listing 1-25.

Listing 1-25. Starting a Rails Server

```
$ rails s
=> Booting Puma
=> Rails 6.0.2.1 application starting in development
Puma starting in single mode...
* Version 4.3.1 (ruby 2.7.0-p0), codename: Mysterious Traveller
* Min threads: 5, max threads: 5
* Environment: development
* Listening on tcp://127.0.0.1:3000
* Listening on tcp://[::1]:3000
Use Ctrl-C to stop
```

From the message in Listing 1-25, we can see that the server is listening on port 3000. However, if we hit http://localhost:3000, we would unfortunately see an error page (see Figure 1-6).

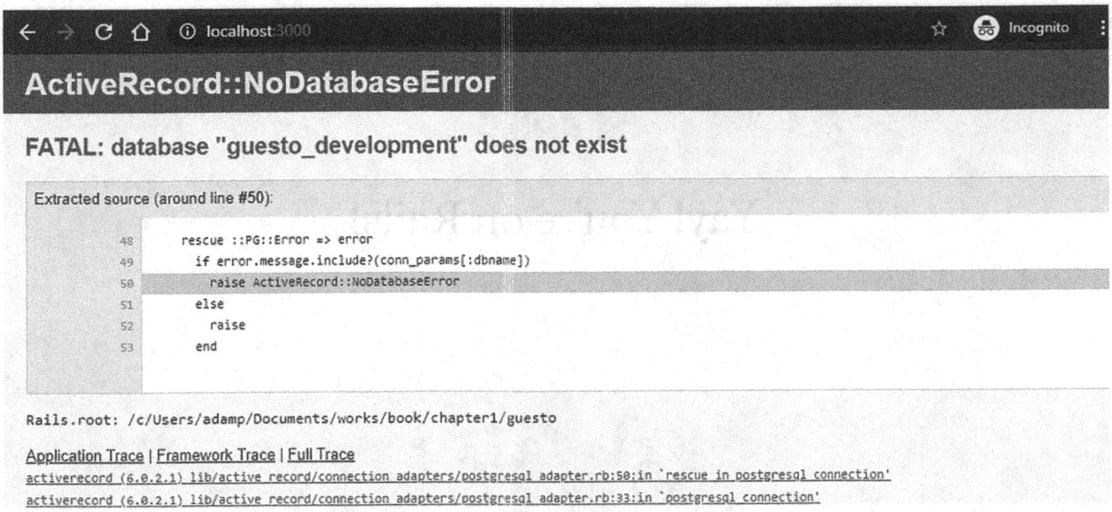

```
←  →  C  ⌂     ⓘ localhost:3000                                              ☆  😎 Incognito  ⋮

ActiveRecord::NoDatabaseError

FATAL: database "guesto_development" does not exist

Extracted source (around line #50):

    48        rescue ::PG::Error => error
    49          if error.message.include?(conn_params[:dbname])
    50            raise ActiveRecord::NoDatabaseError
    51          else
    52            raise
    53          end


Rails.root: /c/Users/adamp/Documents/works/book/chapter1/guesto

Application Trace | Framework Trace | Full Trace
activerecord (6.0.2.1) lib/active_record/connection_adapters/postgresql_adapter.rb:50:in `rescue in postgresql_connection'
activerecord (6.0.2.1) lib/active_record/connection_adapters/postgresql_adapter.rb:33:in `postgresql_connection'
```

Figure 1-6. *Error due to the database not existing yet*

It is not rocket science to understand what is going on. The app doesn't have a database! Let's create one by running the command in Listing 1-26.

Listing 1-26. Command to Create the Database

```
$ rails db:create
Created database 'guesto_development'
Created database 'guesto_test'
```

Note   Rails 4 and older uses Rake more extensively than later versions of Rails. Thus, in earlier versions of Rails, the following command is used instead of `rails db:create`:

```
$ rake db:create
```

If we reload our browser, we are now greeted by happy, smiling people brimming with positive energy. Look at them (see Figure 1-7): how welcoming.

Figure 1-7. *Yay! A page of a fresh Rails project*

Currently, there's not much we can do with our application. So, let's develop it further!

Note "What if I have another kind of error?" Don't be discouraged! You could ask your favorite search engine. Most of the time, other users may have experienced the same issue as you.

Committing to Version Control

In the old days, programmers kept different copies of their source code in different folders—and even on different floppy disks if you are like my father. So, it's not surprising to see directories with these kinds of inspiring names:

- `guesto_latest_app`

- `guest_prod_v3`

- `2020jan15_guesto`

- `2020jan15_guesto (copy 1)`

In the age of cloud computing, we have evolved past that point. Right now, everyone I know is using version control to manage their code. One of those tools is git.

With git, we are like time travelers. We can move back and forth between versions and *branches* (aka working copies). Different people can work on different branches simultaneously and merge their different edits gracefully into one. It makes git an essential tool for building 21st-century software. So, let's set up our git if you haven't done it (see Listing 1-27).

Listing 1-27. Configuring the User's Name and Email

```
$ git config --global user.name "Your Name"
$ git config --global user.email your.email@example.com
```

Now, inside the guesto folder, let's initialize a git repository (see Listing 1-28).

Listing 1-28. Initializing a git Repository

```
$ git init
```

To add all the trackable files in it, we use git add -A (see Listing 1-29).

Listing 1-29. Adding Files to Be Staged for Commit

```
$ git add -A
```

Now to commit our changes, we use git commit and pass in the commit's message so that others don't hate you (see Listing 1-30).

Listing 1-30. Committing with a Message

```
$ git commit -m "guesto project"
```

Instead of using the command line to stage files and make a commit, we can also use GUI tools such as Fork (see Figure 1-8), which is available for Windows and macOS users. Sublime Merge is another good choice, which is available for all major platforms including Linux.

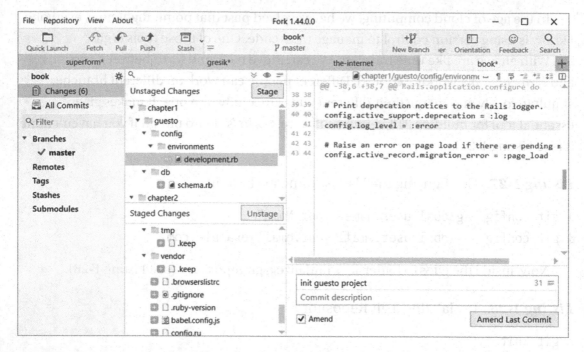

Figure 1-8. *Fork, a graphical git tool for Windows and macOS*

From now on, we will get into the habit of committing changes as our code evolves.

Scaffolding Greeting

Scaffolding is like magic. It prevents us from doing repetitive work such as generating a model and its associated migration when such a process can be automated. It aims to create the necessary structures so that we can save some time and begin working on the features immediately. Let's see it in action!

Let's do scaffolding for the greeting resource. Doing so will generate the model, views, and controller files for us, complete with the code. See Listing 1-31.

Listing 1-31. Scaffolding the Greeting Resource

```
$ rails g scaffold Greeting name message:text
Running via Spring preloader in process 8894
      invoke active_record
      create db/migrate/20200215071910_create_greetings.rb
```

```
create app/models/greeting.rb
invoke test_unit
...
```

Let's open the migration file: `create_greetings.rb`. A migration is a file describing changes we want to see in our database schema. It is used to evolve our database schema over time. For that reason, a migration file has numbers signifying the exact moment in time it was created.

Listing 1-32 shows the content of our `create_greetings.rb` migration file.

Listing 1-32. Content of the Migration File

```
class CreateGreetings < ActiveRecord::Migration[6.0]
  def change
    create_table :greetings do |t|
      t.string :name
      t.text :message

      t.timestamps
    end
  end
end
```

First, let's notice the method `change`. This method defines what changes we want to see when we migrate up. When we migrate down (roll back), Rails can figure out what needs to be done based on just the `change` method. This means, in most cases, we don't need to write any single line of code for rolling back!

Let's skim the `change` method for a while.

We can see that there's a `create_table` method, passed with an argument for the name of a table we want to create, and a block of code. Inside the block, we specify the columns of the table and its data type.

On its own, a migration file does nothing. It needs to be migrated for the changes to take effect. In fact, we will be given an error page if we visit an endpoint while there are pending migrations in the project (see Figure 1-9).

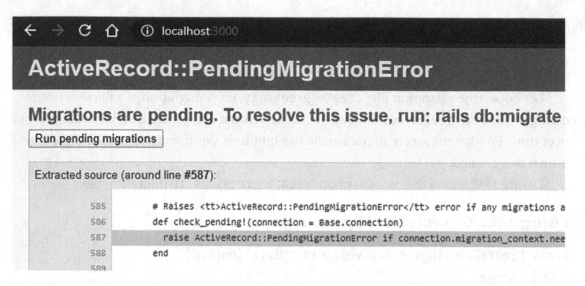

Figure 1-9. *Error due to pending migrations*

So, let's run the migrations!

```
$ rails db:migrate
== 20200215071910 CreateGreetings: migrating ==============
...
```

If all is well, we will have a greetings table in our database, just as what the output shown previously indicates. As a side effect, our schema.rb file will be updated as well.

Now, we can see our app is working just fine if we revisit the URL again. Let's not forget to commit the changes we have made so far.

```
$ git add -A
$ git commit -m "scaffolded greeting"
[master eca52d2] scaffolded greeting
...
```

Just for fun, we can try to roll back by executing the command in Listing 1-33. But please don't forget to rerun the migration command again.

Listing 1-33. Rolling Back Changes Using rails db:rollback

```
$ rails db:rollback
```

Tour of the Routes

Let's fire up a browser and visit http://localhost:3000/greetings. We will see the index page for Greetings, as shown in Figure 1-10.

Figure 1-10. *Greeting resource's index page*

Let's click the New Greeting link, which will take us into the new page (see Figure 1-11). Let's fill in the form and then click the Create Greeting button.

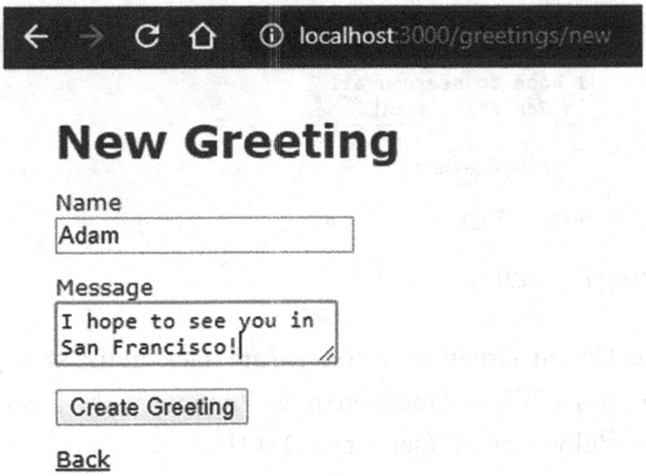

Figure 1-11. *New greeting form*

Upon submitting the form, we will be taken into the show page (see Figure 1-12).

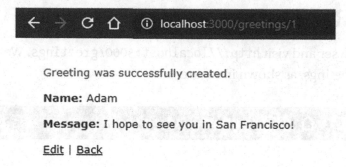

Figure 1-12. *Successfully created a new greeting*

We can also click the Edit link to make some changes (see Figure 1-13). Let's do that.

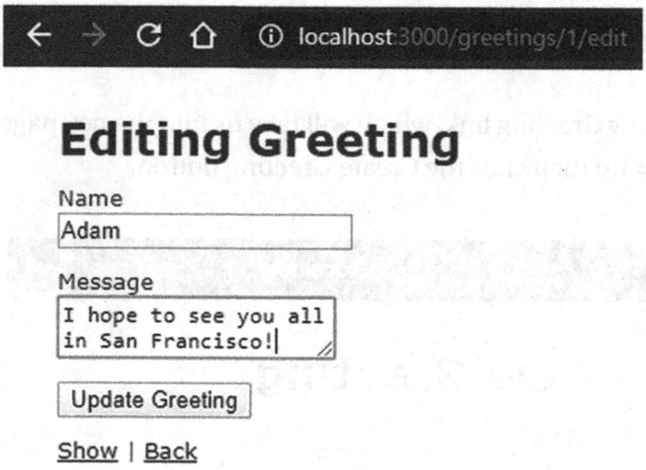

Editing Greeting

Name
Adam

Message
I hope to see you all
in San Francisco!

[Update Greeting]

Show | Back

Figure 1-13. *Editing a greeting*

After clicking the Update Greeting button, we are back on the show page. Notice how the flash notification has a different message now. Previously, the flash message was "Greeting was successfully created" (see Figure 1-14).

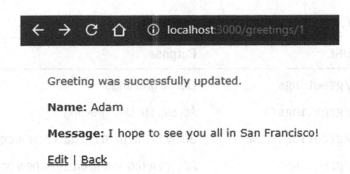

Greeting was successfully updated.

Name: Adam

Message: I hope to see you all in San Francisco!

Edit | Back

Figure 1-14. *The Greeting's show page*

If we click the Back button, we will back to the index page. That's it!

Isn't scaffolding cool? By using scaffolding, we are given an entire MVC set that works, without having to write any code.

As we've seen, scaffolding helps when we want to get something up and running quickly. It generates the necessary files and the wirings for us. However, it doesn't take us far in the real world, and eventually, we will end up replacing most, if not all, of the code.

In most scenarios, we use scaffolding only to generate file structures. The code is a bonus. As we will see later, we will change some of the scaffolded code.

Examining Actions

Rails follow the REST principle, which is an architectural style for developing a dynamic web app. In a RESTful app, components (such as greetings) are modeled as resources that can be created, read, updated, and deleted (CRUD), the basic building block of most applications.

A RESTful resource (take, for example, our greeting) can respond to some or all of the following requests, with 1 being the ID of the data, which of course can change. See Table 1-2.

Table 1-2. *RESTful Actions for Greeting*

Action	URL	Purpose
GET index	/greetings	List all greetings
GET show	/greetings/1	Access specific greeting
GET new	/greetings/new	Show the form to create a new greeting
POST create	/greetings	Accept a request to create a new greeting
GET edit	/greetings/1/edit	Show the form to edit a specific greeting
PATCH update	/greetings/1	Accept a request to update a specific greeting
DELETE destroy	/greetings/1	Accept a request to delete a specific greeting

Note   If our resource is a Student, the path will have /students instead of /greetings. Some resources might not be plural, such as /settings/user. The user is a resource that refers to the current user, and hence, no plural is needed. A resource that refers to the current user, or something like that, doesn't need to be pluralized, since the accessor cannot access other resources.

To check what routes we have in our app, we can run the command shown in Listing 1-34 in the terminal.

Listing 1-34. Listing All Routes in the App

```
$ rails routes
```

Those routes are defined in a config/routes.rb file. When Rails receives a request from, let's say, a browser, Rails parses the path, and then it tries to determine which definition in routes.rb is best to handle the request.

For example, if we ask Rails to recognize the index path, it will say that this path is best handled by the Rails::WelcomeController's index action (see Listing 1-35).

Listing 1-35. Trying to Recognize a Path

```
$ rails console
irb(main):001:0> Rails.application.routes.recognize_path("/")
=> {:controller=>"rails/welcome", :action=>"index"}
irb(main):002:0> exit
```

`rails console` is a tool we can use to interact with our app programmatically from a terminal. Another way to fire up the Rails console is by using `rails c`, with c being shorthand for "console."

Now, let's see what will happen if we change the router definition. Open the `routes.rb` file and add the code shown in Listing 1-36.

Listing 1-36. Snippet of the config/routes.rb File

```
Rails.application.routes.draw do
  root to: "greetings#index"
  resources :greetings
  # For details on the DSL available within this file ...
end
```

Now, we will notice that the root path will be handled by a different controller. Let's close the current console and fire up a new one (see Listing 1-37).

Listing 1-37. The Root Path Is Now Handled by a Different Controller and a Different Action

```
$ rails c
irb(main):001:0> Rails.application.routes.recognize_path("/")
=> {:controller=>"greetings", :action=>"index"}
```

So, if we hit `http://localhost:3000` (after restarting the web server), instead of seeing the Rails default welcome page, we will see the index page of the Greeting resource.

The `GreetingsController` has many actions. A method that handles HTTP(S) requests is called an *action* method. There are seven such action methods in the controller, namely:

- index

- show

- new

- edit

- create

- update

- destroy

To begin with, let's see the index action, which renders the index page for greetings. It has the following simple code:

```
def index
  @greetings = Greeting.all
end
```

The previous code basically retrieves a collection of greetings to be assigned to an instance variable @greetings, making it accessible in the view. The Greeting itself refers to the greeting model as defined in model/greetings.rb.

Note   Any instance variable, which is a variable that starts with @, will be made accessible in the view.

But, how does the view gets rendered, as we are only assigning an instance variable here? That is, we haven't done anything other than that.

By convention, Rails renders a view file with a name that matches the action. When the action is index, Rails will render an index.html.erb. In the case of GreetingsController, the view file will be the one in the app/views/greetings folder.

If we peek into index.html.erb, we can see that we are creating a table and iterating the data from @greetings, which we have defined earlier in the controller. Listing 1-38 shows a snippet.

Listing 1-38. Snippet (Not Complete Code) of greetings/index.html.erb

```
<table>
  <thead>
    <tr>
      <th>Name</th>
      <th>Message</th>
      <th colspan="3"></th>
    </tr>
  </thead>

  <tbody>
    <% @greetings.each do |greeting| %>
      <tr>
        <td><%= greeting.name %></td>
        ... more codes
```

This is MVC in action, where the controller can get data from models and then pass it into a view for rendering purposes, before returning the rendered view to the client.

However, not all actions need to render a view. If we take a look at the `create` action, we can see that upon successful saving, the user will be redirected to `@greeting`. That is an idiomatic way to say that we want to redirect to the `show` page of the resource.

Listing 1-39 shows the snippet for the create action.

Listing 1-39. Snippet for the create Action

```
def create
  @greeting = Greeting.new(greeting_params)

  respond_to do |format|
    if @greeting.save
      format.html { redirect_to @greeting, notice: 'Greeting was ...' }
      ...
```

We can also pass in a flash message such as a `notice` or `error` message while redirecting. The view can then render such a message by using `<%= notice %>` for a notice message and `<%= error %>` for an error message (see Listing 1-40).

Listing 1-40. Printing Notice in the Page

```
<p id="notice"><%= notice %></p>

<p>
  <strong>Name:</strong>
  ...
```

That is why we saw some messages such as the "Greeting was successfully created" when we created the record.

If we look again at the `create` action, we see code like this:

```
@greeting = Greeting.new(greeting_params)
```

It is a common pattern in Rails to filter only the necessary attributes that the browser sent. After all, we must remember the following Internet verse:

On the Internet, nobody knows you're a dog.

This means we can't really be sure if our user is a legitimate user or not. We should receive data from the Web with a grain of salt, and therefore, `greeting_params` is used instead of just `params` to filter only the allowed parameters to be processed. In other words, the `greeting_params` aims to protect us from the illegitimate addition of unwanted data. The method has the code shown in Listing 1-41.

Listing 1-41. Code for greeting_params

```
# Only allow a list of trusted parameters through.
def greeting_params
  params.require(:greeting).permit(:name, :message)
end
```

With this in place, even if the user (umm, maybe the hacker?) unlawfully edits the form's source code by adding some fields, those fields will be filtered out.

To give you some perspective, let's say someone would like to change the `user_id` of a record so that it will be theirs. They will add a hidden field and name it `user_id` in the form. But, if the `user_id` is not a permitted field, the `greeting_parms` will drop the field out.

Last but not least, a controller may have what are known as *filters*. An example of this is the `set_greeting` filter. A filter is essentially a method that is hooked in a `before_action` or an `after_action` callback (see Listing 1-42).

Listing 1-42. Making set_greeting as a Before Action Filter

```
class GreetingsController < ApplicationController
  before_action :set_greeting, only: [:show, :edit, :update, :destroy]
```

Filters are an excellent way to avoid doing repetitive works *before* or *after* we execute an action. They are meant to make our codebase follow the DRY principle (Don't Repeat Yourself).

In the previous example, we use the `set_greeting` filter to set the `@greeting` instance variable once and for all before hitting on actions where a reference to a greeting instance is needed, like in the update action, for example.

The code for `set_greeting` itself is simple and nothing out of the ordinary, as shown in Listing 1-43.

Listing 1-43. Code for set_greeting to Retrieve an Instance of Greeting Based on the ID Present in params (the Request's Parameters)

```
def set_greeting
  @greeting = Greeting.find(params[:id])
end
```

To sum up:

- A route file maps a path to an action method in a controller.

- Controllers can have many action methods.

- Controllers may render a view or do a redirection.

- Controllers may ask for data from models. The controller can make the data available in the view by assigning it (the data) to instance variables.

- To avoid doing repetitive work, we can define filters that are executed before or after an action.

- A controller can have other helper methods, and most of the time, those methods are marked as private (such as `greeting_params`).

As we have made some changes to our codebase, let's not forget to commit them. See Listing 1-44.

Listing 1-44. Committing Changes in Our Codebase

```
$ git add config/routes.rb
$ git commit -m "root to greetings' index"
[master 75740bb] root to greetings' index
 1 file changed, 1 insertion(+)
```

Rails Console

We have used the Rails console before, but let's explore it in a greater detail in this section. As we know it already, the Rails console functions like a back door into our own application. It is handy for testing some code, changing data on the server side without touching the website or the database directly, and generally just checking the system.

To start a console session, let's type the command shown in Listing 1-45.

Listing 1-45. Starting a Rails Console

```
$ rails c
```

Note   We can run the Rails console in sandbox mode, which will automatically roll back any changes made in the database. It is one of the safest ways to run `rails console` on a production machine. To run in sandbox mode, we can pass it the sandbox flag as follows:

```
$ rails c --sandbox
```

Let's ask how many greetings we have (see Listing 1-46).

Listing 1-46. Asking for the Number of Greetings in the Database

```
irb(main):001:0> Greeting.count
  (0.5ms)  SELECT COUNT(*) FROM "greetings"
=> 1
```

How about creating another greeting (see Listing 1-47)?

Listing 1-47. Creating a New Greeting from the Console

```
irb(main):002:0> Greeting.create(name: "Sam", message: "What's up?")
=> #<Greeting id: 3, name: "Sam", ...
```

Now, if we visit the greetings index page, we can see that the new greeting from Sam is there. See Figure 1-15.

Greetings

Name	Message			
Adam	I hope to see you all in San Francisco!	Show	Edit	Destroy

New Greeting

Figure 1-15. *Sam's greeting is recorded*

Now let's make a greeting instance and check its validity. See Listing 1-48.

Listing 1-48. Checking a Record's Validity Using Valid?

```
irb(main):003:0> g = Greeting.new(message: "I am anonymous")
irb(main):004:0> g.valid?
=> true
```

In Rails, a record can be persisted/updated into the database if it is in a valid state. That means this anonymous greeting can be saved into the database.

Doesn't that ring a bell?

Like, what good does it serve to have a greeting from a nameless sender?

So, let's make it necessary that a greeting must have both sender and message fields filled in. To do that, let's open the model and add some validations. See Listing 1-49.

Listing 1-49. Adding Validation into Greeting

```
class Greeting < ApplicationRecord
  validates :name, presence: true
  validates :message, presence: true
end
```

Let's go back to the command line and check the validity once more time (see Listing 1-50).

Listing 1-50. Checking Whether a Record Is Valid

```
irb(main):005:0> g = Greeting.new(message: "I am anonymous")
irb(main):006:0> g.valid?
=> true
```

Hmm...strangely, even with those validations in place, it doesn't seem to work out, except if you terminate the console and open a new one.

This issue happens because the Rails console does not automatically reload code when something changes. So, we need to reload it after making the changes. See Listing 1-51.

Listing 1-51. Reloading the Console

```
irb(main):007:0> reload!
Reloading...
=> true
```

Now, if we try to create an invalid record, Rails won't be happy (see Listing 1-52).

Listing 1-52. A Record Without a Name Is Invalid

```
irb(main):008:0> g = Greeting.new(message: "I am anonymous")
irb(main):009:0> g.valid?
=> false
irb(main):010:0> g = Greeting.new(name: "Mike")
irb(main):011:0> g.valid?
=> false
```

Similarly, our web app won't be happy either if the validations don't pass. See Figure 1-16.

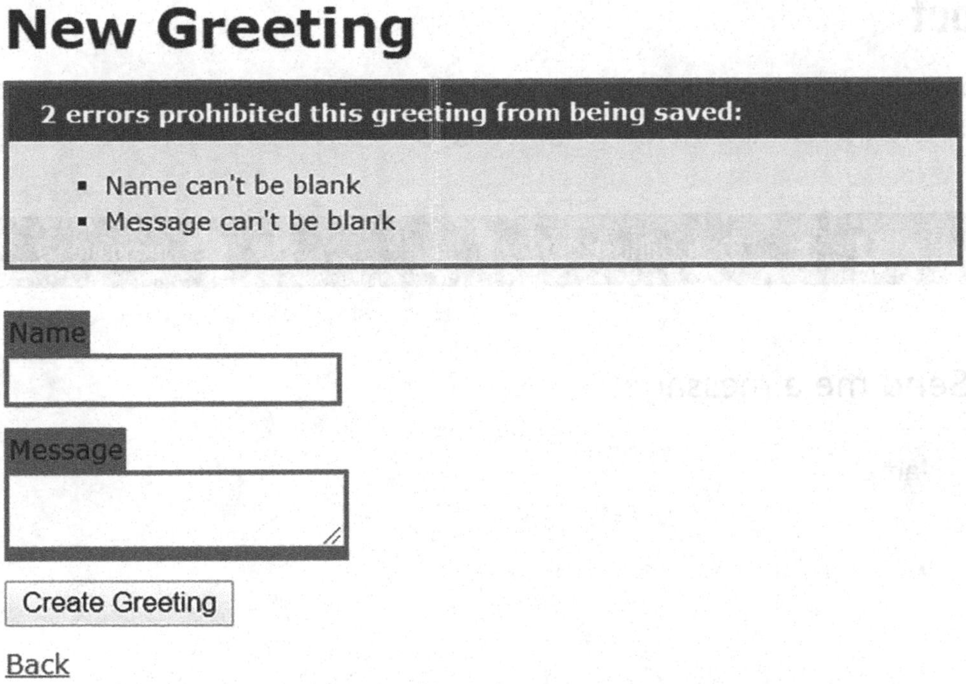

New Greeting

2 errors prohibited this greeting from being saved:

- Name can't be blank
- Message can't be blank

Name

Message

Create Greeting

Back

Figure 1-16. *Sending greeting failure when the record is invalid*

That's great! We have validations in place to prevent invalid data from being persisted.

To exit from the console, we can simply say exit (see Listing 1-53).

Listing 1-53. Terminating the Rails Console

```
irb(main):012:0> exit
$
```

Last but not least, let's commit those changes! (See Listing 1-54.)

Listing 1-54. Committing the Changes

```
$ git add app/models/greeting.rb
$ git commit -m "add validation to name and message"
[master 02551f3] add validation to name and message
 1 file changed, 2 insertions(+)
```

Layout

Let's make our app prettier before we let the world come and see it. By the end of this section, our app should look something like Figure 1-17.

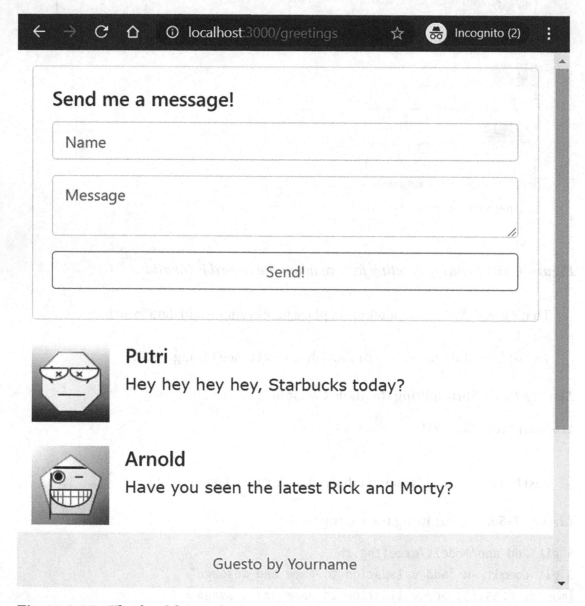

Figure 1-17. *The final form of Guesto*

First, let's add the bootstrap gem into our gemfile. Bootstrap is one of the most popular front-end frameworks developed by the folks at Twitter. What Bootstrap does, in a nutshell, is reduce the time needed to get a modern, fresh-looking, mobile-first website up and running. (See Listing 1-55.)

Listing 1-55. Adding Bootstrap into the Gemfile

```
# Reduces boot times through caching; required in config/boot.rb
gem 'bootsnap', '>= 1.4.2', require: false

gem 'bootstrap', '~> 4.4.1'
...
```

Then, let's run the command in Listing 1-56 to download any new dependencies we just added.

Listing 1-56. Running bundle install to Download the New Dependencies

```
$ bundle install
```

Then, let's import Bootstrap into our stylesheet. To do so, let's first rename app/assets/stylesheets/application.css to app/assets/stylesheets/application.scss. Then, add the code at the bottom of the file, as shown in Listing 1-57.

Listing 1-57. Importing Bootstrap Styles

```
@import "bootstrap";
```

Cool!

Now if we check out our app in the browser, we get an error page!

That's because Rails can't find the bootstrap styles, on top of the fact that it is not even aware of the gem. So, let's restart the server, and the error should be gone.

Now, let's add some custom stylings after the `import` statements. See Listing 1-58.

Listing 1-58. Additional Styling

```
@import "bootstrap";

main.container {
  width: auto;
  max-width: 680px;
```

```
  padding: 0 15px;
  padding-bottom: 60px;
}

footer {
  position: fixed;
  bottom: 0;
  width: 100%;
  height: 60px;
  line-height: 60px;
  background-color: #f5f5f5;
  text-align: center;
}

.media p {
  font-size: 16px;
}

a:hover {
  background: #f5f5f5;
}
```

Now we have all the styles! Let's change the views.

Let's begin with app/views/layouts/application.html.erb. It is the parent layout of basically all the templates that got rendered in the app. As such, it has a complete HTML structure from the head to the body. It also has yield, which will render a specific view template.

We want to enclose yield inside a new main tag. We will also add a static footer at the bottom of the page (see Listing 1-59).

Listing 1-59. Editing Made to application.html.erb Layout

```
<!DOCTYPE html>
<html>
  ... snippet
```

```
  <body>
    <main role="main" class="container">
      <%= yield %>
    </main>

    <footer class="footer">
      <div class="container">
        <span class="text-muted">
          Guesto by Yourname
        </span>
      </div>
    </footer>
  </body>
</html>
```

Now, let's replace app/views/greetings/index.html.erb to have its own style, with the code shown in Listing 1-60.

Listing 1-60. New Code for the greetings/index.html.erb View

```
<p id="notice"><%= notice %></p>

<br/>
<% @greetings.each do |greeting| %>
  <div class="media">
    <img src="<%= gravatarized_url(greeting.name) %>"
      class="align-self-start mr-3">
    <div class="media-body">
      <h5 class="mt-0"><%= greeting.name %></h5>
      <%= greeting.message %>
    </div>
  </div>
  <br/>
<% end %>
```

Let's define the gravatarized_url inside GreetingsHelper, and we will be done (see Listing 1-61). The file is at app/helpers/greetings_helper.rb.

Listing 1-61. Defining gravatarized_url Within the GreetingsHelper Module

```
module GreetingsHelper
  def gravatarized_url(name)
    hash = Digest::MD5.hexdigest(name)
    "https://www.gravatar.com/avatar/#{hash}?d=wavatar"
  end
end
```

We are done! Let's refresh our browser. Now we have a fresh-looking user interface. Fresh and crisp in an instant, isn't it? See Figure 1-18.

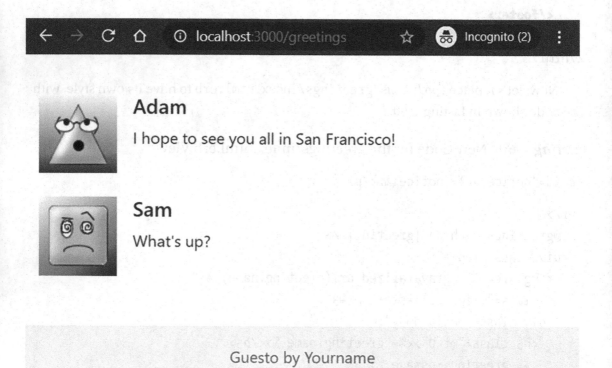

Figure 1-18. *New index*

Although this is taking shape now, it is useless if no one can send a message. So, for a better user experience, let's render the form on the index page. Add the following code into greetings/index.html.erb:

```
<p id="notice"><%= notice %></p>
```

<%= render("form", greeting: Greeting.new) %>

```
<br/>
<% @greetings.each do |greeting| %>
  <div class="media">
```

Then, change the form so that it looks prettier as well. Replace the content of greetings/_form.html.erb with the code in Listing 1-62.

Listing 1-62. New Code for the Form Partial for Greetings

```
<div class="card">
  <div class="card-body">
    <h5 class="card-title">Send me a message!</h5>

    <%= form_with(model: greeting, local: true) do |form| %>
      <% if greeting.errors.any? %>
        <div id="error_explanation">
          <h2>
            <%= pluralize(greeting.errors.count, "error") %>
            prohibited this greeting from being saved:
          </h2>

          <ul>
            <% greeting.errors.full_messages.each do |message| %>
              <li><%= message %></li>
            <% end %>
          </ul>
        </div>
      <% end %>

      <div class="form-group">
        <%= form.text_field :name,
          placeholder: "Name",
          class: "form-control" %>
      </div>
```

```
    <div class="form-group">
      <%= form.text_area :message,
        placeholder: "Message",
        class: "form-control" %>
    </div>

    <div class="actions">
      <%= form.submit "Send!",
        class: "btn btn-outline-primary btn-block" %>
    </div>
  <% end %>
  </div>
</div>
```

Now we have a form on the index page (see Figure 1-19). And it looks good!

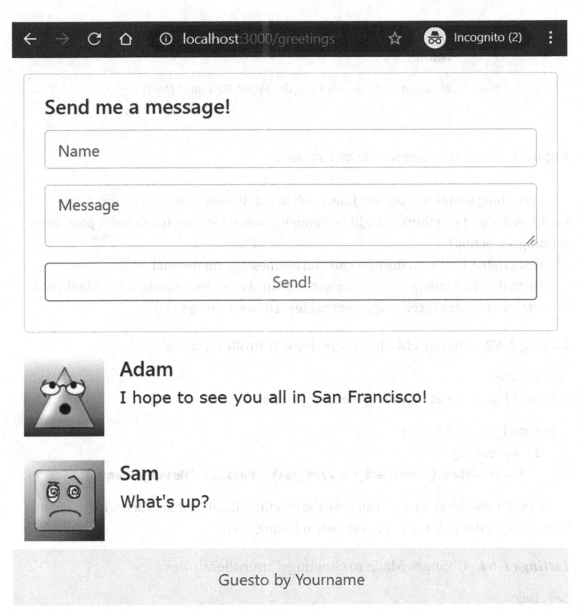

Figure 1-19. *Index page with the form*

Let's try to leave some greeting. Let's say Arnold wanted to ask you if you already watched the latest *Rick and Morty* episode. Don't worry, Arnold is always a polite user of the Internet (see Figure 1-20).

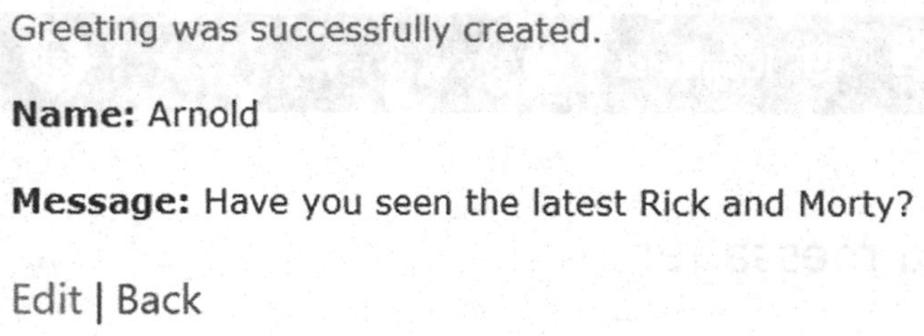

Greeting was successfully created.

Name: Arnold

Message: Have you seen the latest Rick and Morty?

Edit | Back

Figure 1-20. *Show page for the new message*

Everything seems to work just fine. Cool! But, although sending a new message works well, don't you think it might be better if a user was taken to the index page after sending a greeting?

Yeah, right? That way, the user can find his message on the wall.

To do this, let's change something in the controller's `create` action. The file should be app/controllers/greetings_controller.rb (see Listing 1-63).

Listing 1-63. Changes Made to GreetingsController#create

```
def create
  @greeting = Greeting.new(greeting_params)

  respond_to do |format|
    if @greeting.save
      format.html { redirect_to root_path, notice: 'Message sent.' }
```

It might also be great if we can have the greetings displayed in order. So, let's change something in the `index` action, as shown in Listing 1-64.

Listings 1-64. Changes Made to GreetingsController#index

```
def index
  @greetings = Greeting.all.order(created_at: :desc)
end
```

Cool! We made a lot of changes. Let's not forget to commit them. Sometimes using a GUI tool helps a lot when there are many changes. See Figure 1-21.

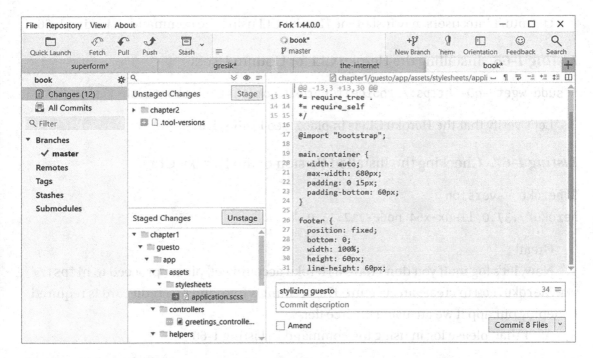

Figure 1-21. *Committing changes using Fork*

Deployment

Are you ready to deploy Guesto?

We will use Heroku as our web host, even though Heroku is *not* a web host. It is a platform-as-a-service. Using Heroku, we can deploy and manage our applications while all the backend infrastructures are managed for us behind the scenes. In a way, it enables us to focus on building features, not managing infrastructures.

First, let's install the Heroku command-line interface (CLI).

For macOS users, we can use Homebrew to install it. The first line in the code in Listing 1-65, to be executed on a terminal, will install Homebrew. The next command will install the Heroku CLI.

Listing 1-65. Installing Homebrew and Heroku CLI from Homebrew

```
$ /bin/bash -c "$(curl -fsSL https://raw.githubusercontent.com/\
Homebrew/install/master/install.sh)"
$ brew tap heroku/brew && brew install heroku
```

Ubuntu/Linux users may install the Heroku CLI using the command in Listing 1-66.

Listing 1-66. Installing the Heroku CLI for Ubuntu Users

```
$ sudo wget -qO- https://toolbelt.heroku.com/install-ubuntu.sh | sh
```

Let's verify that the Heroku CLI is in place (see Listing 1-67).

Listing 1-67. Checking the Installed Version of the Heroku CLI

```
$ heroku --version
heroku/7.37.0 linux-x64 node-v12.13.0
```

Great!

Now, let's log in. If you don't have a Heroku account yet, please proceed to https://www.heroku.com to create an account. The account is free, and no credit card is required to deploy our app if we are using the free tier.

After that, please log in using the command in Listing 1-68.

Listing 1-68. Logging In to Heroku on the CLI

```
$ heroku login/
heroku: Press any key to open up the browser to login or q to exit
 › Warning: If browser does not open, visit
 › https://cli-auth.heroku.com/auth/browser/***
heroku: Waiting for login...
Logging in... done
Logged in as youremail@example.org
```

If everything is OK, let's now create an app on Heroku. Please make sure you are in the project's root folder; then run the command in Listing 1-69 in the terminal.

Listing 1-69. Creating an App for Deployment

```
$ heroku create
Creating app... done, ⬢ frozen-ravine-67370
https://frozen-ravine-67370.herokuapp.com/ | https://git.heroku.com/frozen-
ravine-67370.git
```

The app is created, and it's named frozen-ravine-67370 by Heroku. Your app's name likely will be different. Please take note of the git repo URL, and let's run the command in Listing 1-70 to add the repo URL. This step might not be required for some macOS/Linux users.

Listing 1-70. Associating the git URL with Heroku

```
$ git remote add heroku <YOUR_GIT_URL>
```

What's required for both Linux and macOS users is to check that running git remote prints the git URL associated with our app on Heroku. If there's no such association, we will not be able to deploy our app on Heroku. In that case, please execute the previous command to associate Heroku with our app's repository on Heroku's server (see Listing 1-71).

Listing 1-71. Checking the Associated Repository Server

```
$ git remote -v
heroku   <YOUR_GIT_URL> (fetch)
heroku   <YOUR_GIT_URL> (push)
```

As we haven't deployed anything yet, if we visit the app in the browser, nothing but a minimalist welcome page will be rendered. (See Figure 1-22.)

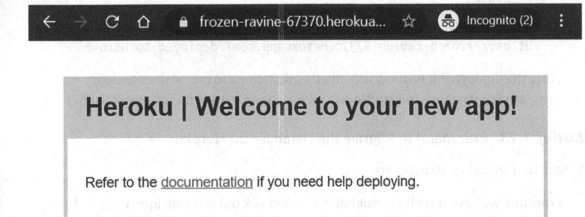

Figure 1-22. *Standard welcome page*

To deploy, we need to push our repo to the master branch of our app's repo on Heroku. Doing so will trigger the deployment process, which should take around five minutes to complete (see Listing 1-72).

Listing 1-72. Triggering the Deployment Using the git push Command

```
$ git push heroku master
Counting objects: 178, done.
Delta compression using up to 8 threads.
Compressing objects: 100% (147/147), done.
Writing objects: 100% (178/178), 155.67 KiB | 2.39 MiB/s, done.
Total 178 (delta 29), reused 0 (delta 0)
remote: Compressing source files... done.
remote: Building source:
remote:
remote: -----> Ruby app detected
remote: -----> Compiling Ruby/Rails
remote: -----> Using Ruby version: ruby-2.7.0
…
-----> Compressing...
       Done: 86.8M
-----> Launching...
       Released v6
       https://frozen-ravine-67370.herokuapp.com/ deployed to Heroku
```

After the deployment is done, let's run the migrations to create the necessary structures in our database (which Heroku set up automatically for us!). See Listing 1-73.

Listing 1-73. Command to Migrate the Database on Heroku

```
$ heroku run rails db:migrate
```

Now that we have run all the migrations, let's check out our web app! We can do so by running the command in Listing 1-74, which will open a browser for us or print the app's URL.

Listing 1-74. Command to Open Our App

```
$ heroku open
```

The domain generated by Heroku might not be what we want. Optionally, we can rename our app's subdomain on Heroku. To rename the subdomain, we can use the heroku rename command in Listing 1-75.

Listing 1-75. Renaming the App's Subdomain on Heroku

```
$ heroku rename adam-guest-book
Renaming frozen-ravine-67370 to adam-guest-book... done
https://adam-guest-book.herokuapp.com/ | https://git.heroku.com/adam-guest-
book.git
▶ Don't forget to update git remotes for all other local ...
```

Don't forget to re-associate the git repository, as shown in Listing 1-76.

Listing 1-76. Re-associating the Heroku Remote Repository

```
$ git remote remove heroku
$ git remote add heroku https://git.heroku.com/adam-guest-book.git
```

Congratulations, we have a working app on the Web!

Rails 6 vs. Rails 5: New Features

Before we close this chapter, let's discuss the new features in Rails 6. For a well-aged framework like Rails, it's great to know that the sixth incarnation of Rails still brings a lot of innovations to the table.

Note that this section is by no means comprehensive. Please feel free to refer to the Rails changelog for more comprehensive listings.

Database Read/Write Switch

As an application grows, it becomes necessary to help ease the cluster's workload by scaling horizontally (in example, adding more nodes). This applies not just for app servers but also for database servers.

A typical scenario has database nodes in a master-slave configuration. In this case, the database is replicated across multiple servers, with the master node receiving all the write operations. The changes in the master node are then propagated into the slaves, which is used only for reading the data back. This advanced technique is usually not required for early-stage startups; see Listing 1-77.

Listing 1-77. Example Syntax for Separating the Read/Write

```
class User < ApplicationRecord
  connects_to database: { writing: :primary, reading: :replica }
end
```

ActionMailbox

ActionMailbox adds the capability to route incoming emails to controller-like mailboxes for processing. With this feature, it is easy to directly process inbound emails, such as for support tickets, comment replies, order requests, and so on, from our app.

Zeitwerk

Zeitwerk is a code loader that can load classes and modules on demand (autoloading) or up front (eager loading) without writing any `require`. It allows us to streamline our code, knowing that our classes and modules are available everywhere we need them. Indeed, Rails has its own *classical* loading engine, but it has some quirks that are addressed by Zeitwerk.

For example, imagine the following scenario: we have `User`, `Admin::User`, and `Admin::UserManager` classes. The reference to the `User` class in Listing 1-78 may be interpreted differently depending on which `User` is loaded first, the global `::User` or the scoped `Admin::User`.

Listing 1-78. Hypothetical Code

```
# app/models/user.rb
class User < ApplicationRecord
end

# app/models/admin/user.rb
module Admin
```

```
  class User < ApplicationRecord
  end
end

# app/models/admin/user_manager.rb
module Admin
  class UserManager
    def self.all
      User.all # Want to load all admin users
    end
  end
end
```

If `Admin::User` has been loaded at the time `Admin::UserManager#all` is called, then the constant `User` will mean `Admin::User`.

However, if it's the global `User` (`::User`) that has been loaded, then the reference to `User` inside the `Admin` namespace will resolve to the global `::User`. That may be surprising (and not desired) since we are currently within the `Admin` namespace. Zeitwerk solved this kind of potential issue.

Note   Admittedly, I have never been bitten by the Rails classical engine for constant autoloading. That being said, Zeitwerk does use a better strategy than the classical engine, and since it is a gem, it can be used outside of Rails.

Replanting Seed (and Truncation)

Seeding is a process to populate a database with an initial set of data. The data might be dummy data, or it can be real, necessary data such as the admin account. To seed our database, we can use the command shown in Listing 1-79.

Listing 1-79. Command to Seed Our Database

```
$ rails db:seed
```

The problem is, seeding is best done when the database is in a clean state, that is, when there's no data on the tables. Rails 6 can remove all this data with this simple command so that we can seed it all over again. (See Listing 1-80.)

Listing 1-80. Command to Truncate All Data on All Tables

```
$ rails db:truncate_all
```

In the past, we must drop the database and rerun the migrations all before we can perfectly seed our data, which is tedious. That's not counting the fact that we have to stop a running server since we can't drop a database that is being used by another process.

If all we want is to truncate and then to seed it, Rails goes further by providing us with one command to do them all at once. (See Listing 1-81.)

Listing 1-81. Command to Truncate and Seed Our Database

```
$ rails db:seed:replant
```

How cool!

Action Text

Action Text makes it easy to have a what-you-see-is-what-you-get (WYSIWYG) editor, a type of editor where the post-editing final form as rendered on the Web should resemble the content during editing. This means we don't need to install third-party software if we ever have the need to manage textual content in such a fashion on our app. (See Figure 1-23.)

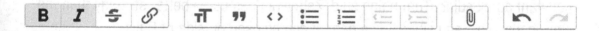

An awesome WYSIWYG editor, aka the "What You See, Is What You Get" editor

Wonderful!
I can also add ***images!!!***

Figure 1-23. *Action Text powered by the WYIWYG editor Trix*

Environment-Specific Credentials

Credentials are files that store sensitive information such as passwords and API keys in an encrypted format so that we can commit them. However, the master key used for decrypting the credentials should not be committed.

Until recently, Rails used the same credential file for all environments. This makes credentials less secure than it can be, since only one key is necessary to decrypt all of the credentials. We will talk about this in detail in a later chapter.

Webpacker

Webpack has become the de facto build tool in the front-end world, which Rails wraps as Webpacker to make it easier for us Rails engineers to use. As a build tool, Webpack can be used to combine various JavaScript files into one minified file. This process is called *assets compilation*. Before the introduction of Webpack into Rails, Rails relied on Sprockets for doing assets compilation.

Moving to Webpack makes sense because it makes front-end developers with little to no Rails knowledge feel more at home. In addition, Webpack, being a concerted effort by the JavaScript community, can easily outmaneuver Sprockets. It comes with features such as tree shaking, minification, and support for the latest ES syntax out of the box, to name a few.

As a Rails developer, integrating with Webpack also makes it incredibly easy to integrate JavaScript frameworks such as React, Vue, and Angular into Rails. To illustrate, integrating the Vue framework into Rails is now as easy as executing the command in Listing 1-82.

Listing 1-82. Command to Integrate Vue into Rails via Webpacker

```
$ bundle exec rails webpacker:install:vue
```

We will discuss this in detail in a later chapter.

Summary

Rails is a framework that keeps delivering and innovating. With it, countless early-stage startups can launch their products in record time, allowing them to reach customers as soon as possible. Just as how this chapter plays out, we made and deployed our app in one sitting!

Being more than 14 years old, Rails has grown into a huge ecosystem with a worldwide community of contributors actively trying to make it easier (than ever) to build a web app.

Please do not be discouraged if things look difficult initially. Most of the time, that means we just need to type more code, and repeat. Coding is, after all, pretty much like brainwashing in disguise.

Yet, just as expert carpenters must be thoroughly acquainted with their craft, competent software engineers must have a deep understanding of their toolings. In the next chapter, we will take a break from Rails and focus a little bit more on Ruby. That being said, this book is democratic, and as such, feel free to go straight to Chapter 4 if you would like to skip Chapter 2 and Chapter 3, where Ruby is discussed in greater detail in an introductory style.

CHAPTER 2

Fundamental Ruby

If you are new to Ruby, I would like to welcome you to this amazing community of awesome, easygoing engineers who uphold the MINASWAN principle, which states that "Matz is nice, and so we are nice."

In this chapter, you will learn various foundational concepts in Ruby, such as how to represent a number, how to create a string, and how to keep a collection of data.

There is also a unique data type in Ruby, known as Symbol, that does not exist in many other programming languages; we will discuss it in this chapter.

We will start this chapter with one of the most fundamental concepts all software engineers must know: the Boolean. While discussing Boolean logic, you will learn how to use logical statements such as the if statement, as well as how to use Booleans to do iteration/looping.

If you come from a language such as JavaScript or Python, you may want to simply skim this chapter or go straight to the next one where we will explore more advanced Ruby techniques.

In fact, both Chapter 2 and Chapter 3 are optional. If you would like to hit the ground running on learning Rails, Chapter 4 is for you.

For those who are here, let's start with the basics: irb.

Interactive Ruby (irb) and Variables

irb was first developed by Keiju Ishitsuka. It is a convenient tool allowing us to write instructions to be executed immediately so that we can experiment with our code in real time.

To start irb, open a console/terminal and type the following:

```
irb --simple-prompt
```

Windows users may search for *Interactive Ruby* in the Start menu.

57

© Adam Notodikromo 2021
A. Notodikromo, *Learn Rails 6*, https://doi.org/10.1007/978-1-4842-6026-5_2

After the shell's session starts, let's type "Hello World" in the shell and then press Enter. With that, we created a "Hello World" string! See Listing 2-1.

Listing 2-1. Evaluating a String in irb

```
>> "Hello World"
=> "Hello World"
```

In Ruby, we are allowed to call a method without parentheses, which is usually the preferred way. The calls in Listing 2-2 are equal to one another.

Listing 2-2. Passing a String Argument into puts

```
>> puts("Hello World")
Hello World
=> nil
>> puts "Hello World"
Hello World
=> nil
```

In the previous code, we created a "Hello World" string and passed it as an argument to Kernel#puts. The notation Kernel#puts means that the method puts is located within Kernel.

We can also ask irb to do some calculations for us. Let me calculate my daily salary using irb. See Listing 2-3.

Listing 2-3. Evaluating Calculation in irb

```
>> 10000000 / 30
=> 333333
```

Computers are great at remembering things. We can use variables to store some value to be retrieved later. Let's try assigning my monthly salary into a variable. See Listing 2-4.

Listing 2-4. Storing a Value in a Variablestoring value

```
>> monthly_salary = 10_000_000
```

The previous code is called an *expression*. Theoretically, a line of code can be classified either as an expression or as a statement. An expression produces something to be assigned to an identifier (e.g., variable). If there is no assignment, the line is a statement.

Now that we have declared a variable, we can refer to it without having to type the actual value every single time. See Listing 2-5.

Listing 2-5. Using a Variable

```
>> monthly_salary / 30
=> 333333
>> annual_bonus = (365/365) * monthly_salary
=> 10000000
```

irb is very much like the Ruby interpreter itself; as such, we can also define methods, modules, and classes, among other things. We will learn about creating our own methods, modules, and classes in the next chapter.

As we have demonstrated, irb is a handy tool to get Ruby to do what we want without having to create a file and then execute it. Indeed, the Rails console, which we used in the previous chapter, is an irb console.

nil

Some programming languages have the notion of nil, which is used to indicate that a value is neither available, specified, nor produced.

In the following example, we are trying to get the value of an instance variable named @city, which we have never defined; thus, the code returns nil. See Listing 2-6.

Listing 2-6. Accessing an Instance Variable

```
>> @city
=> nil
```

Similarly, when we retrieve nonexistent data from a collection such as a hash, nil is returned. See Listing 2-7.

Listing 2-7. Retrieving Undefined Data Returns nil

```
>> phone_numbers = { adam: 3953672, sam: 39019211 }
>> phone_numbers[:adam]
=> 3953672
>> phone_numbers[:steven]
=> nil
```

Therefore, we sometimes need to check whether the retrieved value is nil before calling a method on it. Otherwise, it might raise a NoMethodError, as demonstrated in Listing 2-8.

Listing 2-8. An Error Due to Calling an Unavailable Method on nil

```
>> name = { given: "Adam", family: "Notodikromo" }
>> name[:given]
=> "Adam"
>> name[:given].upcase
=> "ADAM"
>> name[:middle]
=> nil
>> name[:middle].upcase
Traceback (most recent call last):
        ...
        1: from (irb):6
NoMethodError (undefined method `upcase' for nil:NilClass)
Did you mean?  case
```

We can use the nil? method to check whether an object is nil. See Listing 2-9.

Listing 2-9. Checking for nil

```
>> phone_numbers[:steven].nil?
=> true
```

Sending nil objects a message is such a common mistake that its creator, Tony Hoare, calls nil his billion-dollar mistake.

Ruby's native way of helping us deal with nil is the safe navigation operator (&.). The safe navigation operator ensures that it won't call the message if nil is the immediate result. See Listing 2-10.

Listing 2-10. Using the Safe Navigation Operator

```
>> name[:middle]&.upcase
=> nil
```

The previous code is equivalent to the following longer form. See Listing 2-11.

Listing 2-11. Calling Upcase Only If the Value Is Not Nil

```
>> name[:middle].upcase unless name[:middle].nil?
=> nil
```

The Boolean System

The earliest computers were conceived as something like fancy calculating machines. Although their creators might have been aware that logic had something to do with it, it wasn't so clear how or why.

In 1847, George Boole entered the scene with his publication *The Mathematical Analysis of Logic*. Around 70 years later, Claude Shannon saw the relevance of Boole's symbolic logic, a system that would later make computer programming possible. *Booleans* are named after George Boole to recognize his work, and the rest is history.

Deep down, nonquantum computers are simple machines. The logic gates and transistors in the CPU can handle only 0s and 1s representing the on and off states of the electricity. The *law of excluded middle* ensures that it cannot be anything in between.

This primitive 0 and 1 forms the backbone of computer languages. In some standards of the C language, a Boolean is just an integer: 1 for true, and 0 for false. However, in a much higher language like Ruby, Python, Java, and many others, we have a dedicated true and false constant, or *keyword*.

But how do those 0s and 1s allow computers to do wonderful jobs, such as playing games, taking us to the moon, finding our life partners, scanning cancers, and anything in between?

The fact is, a computer program is a huge decision-making system. For instance, an operating system decides whether to turn on or off specific pixels to render a character on our screen. Those decisions stem from logical statements involving Booleans, handled by the logic gates inside a CPU, to produce yet another Boolean.

One of those gates is the AND gate. The AND gate calculates what the truthiness value is across two values when both are `true`. When both values are `true`, the output is `true`; else, it is `false`. In Ruby, the AND operator is the double ampersand (&&). See Listing 2-12.

Listing 2-12. Evaluating && on Boolean Values

```
>> true && true
=> true
>> true && false
=> false
>> false && true
=> false
>> false && false
=> false
```

Another important gate is the OR gate, which represents what the truthiness value is across two values when at least one input is `true`. In Ruby, the OR gate is represented by the double pipe (||) operator. See Listing 2-13.

Listing 2-13. Evaluating || on Boolean Values

```
>> false || false
=> false
>> true || false
=> true
>> false || true
=> true
>> true || true
=> true
```

It is interesting to note that, sometimes, when we say "or," we meant to say "either one but not both." For example, when we are ordering a burger, the staff might ask, "Would you like eating here *or* taking away, sir?" in which case, it is not expected for us to reply "Yes!" to mean both.

In that case, we need XOR, which is *exclusive OR*. True to its name, the output will be true if and only if one of the inputs is true. This gate seems to correspond the most to the English or.

It might be difficult to believe at first, but the not-equal-to (!=) logical operator is an exclusive OR, which is common to spot in any given source code. See Listing 2-14.

Listing 2-14. Evaluating the "Not-Equal-To" XOR Operator

```
>> true != true
=> false
>> true != false
=> true
>> false != true
=> true
>> false != false
=> false
```

However, the bitwise caret (^) XOR operator does exist for more complex calculations. Even then, this operator is hardly used except if we want to write a cryptography library or software. See Listing 2-15.

Listing 2-15. Evaluating the Caret XOR Bitwise Operator

```
=> true ^ false ^ true
>> false
=> true ^ true ^ true
>> true
=> true ^ true ^ true ^ true
>> false
```

Finally, there is the unary negation gate: the NOT gate. A NOT gate has just one input, and the output will always be the opposite of the input. In Ruby, the operator for NOT is the bang (!) operator. See Listing 2-16.

Listing 2-16. The NOT Operator

```
>> !true
=> false
>> !false
=> true
```

Another way to produce a Boolean other than by writing its literal is by using comparison operators, such as <, <=, ==, >=, >, !=. See Listing 2-17.

Listing 2-17. Comparison Operators in Ruby

```
>> a = 1
>> b = 2
>> a < b
=> true
>> a <= b
=> true
>> a == b
=> false
>> a >= b
=> false
>> a > b
=> false
>> a != b
=> true
```

Those Boolean values then can be used to model our reasoning. For example, we can say "If this is true, do that" using the if statement. See Listing 2-18.

Listing 2-18. Using the if Statement

```
>> hungry = true
?> if hungry
?>   puts "I am hungry"
>> end
I am hungry
=> nil
```

The program in Listing 2-18 will print "I am hungry" if hungry evaluates to true.

An if block may have elsif branches. It may also have an else branch, which will be executed only if the other branches have not yet. See Listing 2-19.

Listing 2-19. Using if-elsif-else Statements

```
>> score = 80
>>
?> if score > 90
?>   puts "A+"
?> elsif score > 80
?>   puts "A"
?> elsif score > 70
?>   puts "B"
?> elsif score > 60
?>   puts "C"
?> elsif score > 50
?>   puts "D"
?> else
?>   puts "F"
>> end
B
=> nil
```

If there are only two possible outcomes, we normally won't use an elsif, but an else branch instead. See Listing 2-20.

Listing 2-20. if-else Statements

```
>> hungry = false
>>
?> if hungry
?>   puts "I am hungry"
?> else
?>   puts "I am full"
>> end
```

```
I am full
=> nil
```

Ruby also has the unless statement, which is the same as if not (if !). The unless statement sometimes makes reading logical statements more natural. See Listing 2-21.

Listing 2-21. The unless Statement

```
>> hungry = false
?> unless hungry
?>   puts "I am full"
>> end
I am full
=> nil
```

However, unless is normally discouraged when logical operators are involved. For many people, using unless with logical operators makes the statement harder to understand. See Listing 2-22.

Listing 2-22. if-not versus unless with Logical Operators

```
do_something if !(a>0 && a<10)
do_something unless (a>0 && a<10)
```

Just like C, Ruby also has the ternary operator (?), which is like shorthand for an if-else block. It is really handy to be used either when we want to produce a value or when we want to make a statement. See Listing 2-23.

Listing 2-23. Ternary Operator

```
>> hungry = true
>> puts hungry ? "I am hungry" : "I am full"
I am hungry
=> nil
>> hungry ? eat : watch_youtube
```

There is also the case statement that bears resemblance to the switch statement of the C-family languages. See Listing 2-24.

Listing 2-24. The case-when Statement

```
>> grade = "A"
?> case grade
?> when "A" then
?>   puts "Exceptional Achievement"
?> when "B" then
?>   puts "Extensive Achievement"
?> when "C" then
?>   puts "Acceptable Achievement"
?> when "D" then
?>   puts "Minimal Achievement"
?> else
?>   puts "Inadequate Achievement"
>> end
Exceptional Achievement
=> nil
```

The condition in the when always refers to the case statement's value that is being examined.

The Boolean logic may also be used for doing repetitive works, or technically known as *looping*. The idea is something like, "If this is true, keep doing that."

One of the ways to express such an idea is by using the while block. When running the code in Listing 2-25, please enter any number. Otherwise, the block will keep looping for eternity.

Listing 2-25. Looping Using the while Statement

```
>> score = nil
?> while score.nil?
?>   score = gets.chomp.to_i
>> end
```

We can forcefully exit the block by using break. See Listing 2-26.

Listing 2-26. Using Break to Quit from an Infinite Loop

```
?> while true
?>   puts "I can be dangerous!"
?>   break
>> end
I can be dangerous!
```

Another last Boolean concept we must be aware of is that, in Ruby, there is a concept of truthy and falsey values. Those values are not Boolean per se, but the interpreter will work with them as if they are one.

For example, Ruby treats `nil` essentially as `false`, and other non-Boolean values essentially as `true`. It makes writing code easier and less brittle as we don't have to convert to Boolean. See Listing 2-27.

Listing 2-27. Boolean Coercion

```
>> data = nil
>> data = gets.chomp unless data
scan me!
=> "scan me!"
```

However, we can coerce any value into a truly Boolean value by using the `!!` operator, which is used only sparingly when returning a Boolean is a must. As such, it is normally used for expressing logical statements. See Listing 2-28.

Listing 2-28. Using `!!` to Coerce to Boolean Values

```
>> !!0
=> true
>> !![]
=> true
>> !!{}
=> true
>> !!nil
=> false
>> !!false
=> false
```

```
>> !!true
=> true
>> !!""
=> true
>> !!Object.new
=> true
```

Numeric

In Ruby, every numeric literal is a subtype of Numeric, as shown in Figure 2-1.

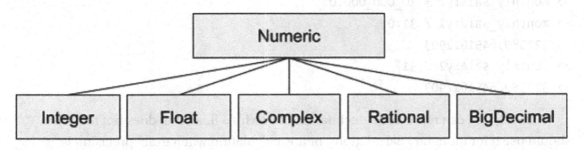

Figure 2-1. *Subclasses of Numeric*

One of the simplest numerical types in Ruby is the integer. An integer means whole number, without any denominator or parts. See Listing 2-29.

Listing 2-29. Expressing an Integer

```
>> 1
=> 1
>> 2
=> 2
>> 1_000_000
=> 1000000
```

Another commonly used numeric data type is Float, which can handle any decimal number. See Listing 2-30.

Listing 2-30. Expressing a Float

```
>> 10.1234567890
=> 10.123456789
>> 10.1234567890.class
=> Float
```

The result of a calculation involving a float results in a float. See Listing 2-31.

Listing 2-31. Doing Floating Calculations

```
>> monthly_salary1 = 10_000_000
>> monthly_salary2 = 10_000_000.0
>> monthly_salary1 / 31.0
=> 322580.6451612903
>> monthly_salary2 / 31
=> 322580.6451612903
```

Although we can represent a decimal number with a float, that does not mean we should use it for monetary calculations, or any calculation when exact precision is needed. That is because a float's precision can float (no pun intended). See Listing 2-32.

Listing 2-32. Floating-Point Calculations

```
>> 0.1 * 0.2
=> 0.020000000000000004
```

That floating can happen as some decimal calculations may not be terminating. In our base-10 world, a notable example is 1/3, which is equal to 0.333, with never-ending 3s.

Since the computer is a base-2 system, any rational having a denominator other than a prime factor of 2 will have an infinite binary expansion. In the previous example, the decimal number 0.1 cannot have finite precision. Instead, it yields a sequence of 1100 repeating endlessly. That is the reason that monetary calculations are usually done in cents to remove the needs of using `Float`.

Ruby has the `BigDecimal` class, which helps us do precise decimal calculations. See Listing 2-33.

Listing 2-33. Precise Calculation Using BigDecimal

```
>> require "bigdecimal"
=> true
>> (BigDecimal("0.1") * BigDecimal("0.2")).to_f
=> 0.02
```

BigDecimal also has a large scale that it is theoretically possible to calculate the value of π (pi) up to 2 billion decimal places. If BigDecimal is practically so much better, why then there is a float?

That is because while a float can be understood and calculated directly by the processor's arithmetic logic unit (ALU), BigDecimal cannot. In other words, there's an overhead when using BigDecimal.

String

String is used to represent a text. String in Ruby is UTF-8 compliant by default, which means we can also store an emoji, Arabic letters, Japanese letters, and basically all letters in the world, in addition to the Anglo-Latin alphabets. See Listing 2-34.

Listing 2-34. Expressing a String Text with Various Characters

```
>> puts "大丈夫ですか?"
大丈夫ですか?
=> nil
>> puts "¡Si estoy bien! ¿Qué hay de tí?"
¡Si estoy bien! ¿Qué hay de tí?
=> nil
>> puts "בוט ינא וכ"
בוט ינא וכ
=> nil
>> puts "Good to know that you are okay! ☺"
Good to know that you are okay! ☺
=> nil
```

Another quite common encoding is ASCII. ASCII can only encode a character into one byte, so it can represent a maximum of 256 characters. Although very limiting, a lot of older (*ancient*?) computers may only support ASCII encoding.

We can encode a `String` from UTF-8 to ASCII as shown in Listing 2-35, which by default will replace an unencodable character with a question mark.

Listing 2-35. Encoding a String

```
>> str = "¡Si estoy bien! ¿Qué hay de tí?"
>> str.encode("ASCII", "UTF-8", undef: :replace)
=> "?Si estoy bien! ?Qu? hay de t??"
```

We may also specify the character to be used for replacement. See Listing 2-36.

Listing 2-36. Specifying a Replacement Character

```
>> str.encode("ASCII", "UTF-8", undef: :replace, replace: "")
=> "Si estoy bien! Qu hay de t?"
```

Encoding aside, `String` in Ruby can be interpolated. See Listing 2-37.

Listing 2-37. String Interpolation

```
>> puts "The log10 of 10 is #{Math.log10(10)}"
The log10 of 10 is 1.0
```

Other than using a double quote to create a `String`, we can also use a single quote, or a %Q. However, a single-quoted string cannot do interpolations, and it won't escape characters. See Listing 2-38.

Listing 2-38. Different Ways to Express a String

```
>> %Q{PI: #{Math::PI}}
=> "PI: 3.141592653589793"
>> 'PI: #{Math::PI}'
=> "PI: \#{Math::PI}"
```

`String` may also span multiple lines. See Listing 2-39.

Listing 2-39. Multiline String

```
"> a = "ruby
"> is
>> awesome"
>> a
=> "ruby\nis\nawesome"
```

The \n is one of the escape characters, which, when printed, will move the cursor to a new line. Table 2-1 lists some of the most used escape characters in Ruby.

Table 2-1. *List of Escape Characters*

Character	Form
\n	Newline
\t	Horizontal tab
\s	Space
\r	Carriage return
\\	The backslash (\) character
\"	The double quote character
\'	The single quote character
\unnnn	Unicode character where n is a hexadecimal digit (0–9, a–f)

A string may also be concatenated with another string by using the plus (+) operator, or the in-place append (<<) operator. See Listing 2-40.

Listing 2-40. Various Ways of Concatenating a String with Another String

```
>> str1 = "Hello"
>> str2 = "World"
>> puts str1 + ", " + str2
Hello, World
=> nil
```

```
>> str3 = ""
>> str3 << str1
=> "Hello"
>> str3 += ", " << str2
>> str3
=> "Hello, World"
```

A `String` may also be separated word for word based on a space or based on any given string. The return of this operation is an array, which we will talk about in detail later. For now, we can think of it as a collection that can hold any objects. See Listing 2-41.

Listing 2-41. Splitting a String

```
>> colors = "blue green red".split
>> colors
=> ["blue", "green", "red"]

>> tsv = "blue\tgreen\tred"
=> "blue\tgreen\tred"
>> tsv.split("\t")
=> ["blue", "green", "red"]

>> "Rick and Morty".split("")
=> ["R", "i", "c", "k", " ", "a", "n", "d", " ", "M", "o", "r", "t", "y"]
```

Conversely, we can make a string from an array by using `Array#join`. See Listing 2-42.

Listing 2-42. Making a String from an Array

```
>> errors = ["email is taken", "name cannot be blank"]
>> "There are errors: " + errors.join(", ")
=> "There are errors: email is taken, name cannot be blank"
```

We can also get a substring by using `String#[]`. The `[]` function requires us to specify the index, which is an integer from 0, the beginning of the string, until the length of the string minus one (since it's indexed from 0). We can also use a range. See Listing 2-43.

Listing 2-43. Using the [] to Get a Substring

```
>> colors = "blue green red"
>> colors[0..3]
=> "blue"

>> colors[5..9]
=> "green"

>> colors[11..-1]
=> "red"
```

If a positive index is calculated from the first character, a negative index is reversed: the index runs from the leftmost character in the string.

Finally, to get the length of a string, we can use String#length or String#size. See Listing 2-44.

Listing 2-44. Getting the Length of a String

```
>> colors.length
=> 14
>> colors.size
=> 14
```

Now, let's put into practice what we have learned by creating a simple program. The simple program will generate an email address out of a user's full name. We will define a new method to do that. We will discuss methods in detail in the following chapter, but for now, we can think of them as a way to group statements into one functioning body that we can reuse simply by calling the name of the method. See Listing 2-45.

Listing 2-45. A Method to Generate an Email from a Full Name

```
?> def generate_an_email
?>   print "Full name: "
?>   name = gets.chomp.downcase
?>
?>   names = name.split
?>   email = ""
?>
```

```
?>    names.each do |name|
?>      email << name[0..rand(4)]
?>    end
?>    email << "@example.com"
?>
?>    email
>> end
=> :generate_an_email
>> generate_an_email
Full name: Sam Yamashita
=> "sayama@example.com"
```

Neat!

There are many other useful methods in the String class, such as
String#capitalize, String#downcase, and String#upcase, that you may want to
explore from Ruby's documentation.

Array

An array is an integer-indexed collection of any object. An array can contain any data in
it. It can grow and shrink as data is inserted into it or removed from it.

Being a dynamic language, it's effortless to declare an array in Ruby. For instance,
let's declare a variable holding an array of odd numbers. See Listing 2-46.

Listing 2-46. Declaring an Array Associated to the Variable odds

```
>> odds = []
```

To insert an element into an array, we can use Array#<< or Array#push. See Listing 2-47.

Listing 2-47. Pushing an Element into an Array

```
>> odds << 1
=> [1]
>> odds << 3
=> [1, 3]
>> odds.push 5
=> [1, 3, 5]
```

We can also declare and initiate an array at the same time. See Listing 2-48.

Listing 2-48. Declaring and Initiating an Array

```
>> even = [2,4,6]
```

To combine two arrays, we can use the `Array#+` operator. See Listing 2-49.

Listing 2-49. Combing Two Arrays

```
>> odds + even
=> [1, 3, 5, 2, 4, 6]
```

Please note that `Array#+` produces a new array instead of modifying the operands. Therefore, we need to assign the returned `Array` into a variable if we would like to access it later. See Listing 2-50.

Listing 2-50. Combining an Array and Storing the Result in a Variable

```
>> numbers = odds + even
>> numbers
=> [1, 3, 5, 2, 4, 6]
```

Otherwise, we can also use the += operator to merge an array into the left operand. See Listing 2-51.

Listing 2-51. Combining an Array in Place to the Left Operand

```
>> numbers = []
>> numbers += odds
>> numbers
=> [1, 3, 5]
```

Array also has `Array#length`, `Array#size`, and `Array#count`, which all do the same thing: determine how many objects/items are in the array. See Listing 2-52.

Listing 2-52. Checking How Many Objects Are in the Array

```
>> [numbers.length, numbers.size, numbers.count]
=> [3, 3, 3]
```

To check whether an array contains some object, we can use `Array#include?`. See Listing 2-53.

Listing 2-53. Checking Whether an Object Is in an Array

```
>> odds.include? 1
=> true
>> odds.include? 2
=> false
```

We can retrieve an item from an array using the square brackets ([ ]) method. This is the same method we have used in the previous section for accessing a substring within a string. See Listing 2-54.

Listing 2-54. Accessing an Object of an Array

```
>> numbers
=> [1, 3, 5, 7]
>> numbers[0]
=> 1
>> numbers[1]
=> 3
>> numbers[-1]
=> 7
>> numbers[-2]
=> 5
```

Just like the way substrings are indexed, items in an array are indexed beginning from 0. We can also get the element starting from the rear side by using a negative index.

In Ruby, it is customary for an enumerable data structure to feature an each method that we can use to iterate each item in the collection. See Listing 2-55.

Listing 2-55. Using Each to Iterate Each Item in an Array

```
>> numbers = odds + even
>> primes = []
>> require 'prime'
=> true
```

```
?> numbers.each do |number|
?>   primes << number if Prime.prime?(number)
>> end
=> [1, 3, 5, 2, 4, 6]
>> primes
=> [3, 5, 2]
```

The previous code can be simplified if we use `Array#select` for filtering the items of an array. See Listing 2-56.

Listing 2-56. Filtering Items Using Array#select

```
>> primes2 = numbers.select { |n| Prime.prime?(n) }
>> primes2
=> [3, 5, 2]
```

There are many other useful methods in the array class, for example, `Array#sort`. There is also `Array#each_with_index`, which yields not only an item, but also its index. See Listing 2-57.

Listing 2-57. Using Array#each_with_index

```
?> primes2.each_with_index do |prime, idx|
?>   puts "#{prime} is at position #{idx}"
>> end
3 is at position 0
5 is at position 1
2 is at position 2
```

An array may contain another array as its element. Such an array is known as a *multidimensional array*. Listing 2-58 shows an example of a two-dimensional array.

Listing 2-58. An Identity Matrix Expressed As an Array

```
?> identity_matrix = [
?>   [1, 0, 0],
?>   [0, 1, 0],
?>   [0, 0, 1]
>> ]
```

Symbol

Symbol is a part of Ruby that hardly has any doppelganger in another language. It is mostly used to represent keys in a well-structured hash, or constant values in code.

Every symbol refers to the same object throughout a Ruby program; hence, it has the same object ID. This is how symbols are different from strings: two strings with the same contents are two different objects, but for any given name there is only one symbol for the identifier. This makes symbols very efficient in terms of time and space. See Listing 2-59.

Listing 2-59. Using Symbols

```
>> a = :name
>> b = :name
>> a.object_id
=> 71068
>> b.object_id
=> 71068
>> "name".object_id
=> 180
>> "name".object_id
=> 200
```

The identifier of a symbol may also be quoted, essentially blurring the line between a string and a symbol. See Listing 2-60.

Listing 2-60. A Symbol Identifier in Between a Double Quote

```
>> :"this is a symbol".class
=> Symbol
```

However, we must remember that symbols may not be garbage collected, unlike strings or other objects. Therefore, the memory may run out of space if we use symbols liberally.

Symbol is also immutable. Once it is created, it is final! There is no append operator for a symbol. In contrast, we can append a string to another string.

Listing 2-61 proves that a string is mutable; that is, even if we change its value, the object_id remains the same.

Listing 2-61. Proving That a String Is, by Default, Mutable

```
>> s = "1"
>> s.object_id
=> 280
>> s << "1"
=> "11"
>> s.object_id
=> 280
```

It is safe to imagine that a symbol is similar to an integer. When we evaluate 1 + 1, Ruby doesn't change the value of 1 by increasing it to become 2. In fact, Ruby represents 2 entirely separate from 1, and both of them have a different object ID. Thus, integers are immutable. See Listing 2-62.

Listing 2-62. Proving That Integer Is Immutable

```
>> n = 1
>> n.object_id
=> 3
>> n = n + 1
>> n.object_id
=> 5
>> 1.object_id
=> 3
```

To reiterate, symbols in concept are simply names. They shouldn't be treated as our users' values. If we define a method called sort, a symbol :sort is automatically created. Such is the usage of symbols as they are originally conceived in Ruby: to hold names for instance variables, classes, and methods. We will see how we can use symbols to define keys in a hash, shortly.

Hash

Hash organizes data in key-value pairs. Hash is so fast that it has an O(1) constant lookup time characteristic. Meaning, the time to look up for the value associated to a key is constant regardless of the collection's size.

Hash is created using curly braces, as we can see in Listing 2-63. Notice how the keys name and age are each a symbol.

Listing 2-63. Creating a Hash

```
>> bio = {}
>> bio.class
=> Hash
>> bio[:name] = "Adam"
>> bio[:age] = 27
>> bio
=> {:name=>"Adam", :age=>27}
```

We can also initialize a hash when creating it. Again, the keys are each a symbol. See Listing 2-64.

Listing 2-64. Creating and Initializing a Hash

```
>> bio = {name: "Adam", age: 27}
>> bio
=> {:name=>"Adam", :age=>27}
```

To get the value of a hash, we can use the [ ] (bracket) operator and then specify the key. If the value does not exist, nil is returned. See Listing 2-65.

Listing 2-65. Retrieving a Value from a Hash by Using Its Key

```
>> bio[:name]
=> "Adam"
>> bio[:age]
=> 27
>> bio[:email]
=> nil
```

We can instantiate hash using the older notation (key => value) instead of the new one (key: value). With the old notation, we can use any class of object as the key, not just Symbol. See Listing 2-66.

Listing 2-66. Defining a Symbol Using Older Notation

```
?> mixups = {
?>    true => "Yes!",
?>    false => "No!",
?>    1 => "Yes!",
?>    0 => "No!",
?>    "y" => "Yes!",
?>    "n" => "No!",
?>    :y => "Yes!",
?>    :n => "No!"
>> }
>> [mixups[false], mixups[1], mixups["n"], mixups[:y]]
=> ["No!", "Yes!", "No!", "Yes!"]
```

Initiating a hash in this way feels like something from the past. It's normally preferred to use the new notation, especially if all the keys are symbols.

Sometimes, we may want to assign a value only when the key is not associated yet. To do that, we can use the conditional assignment operator (||=), as shown in Listing 2-67.

Listing 2-67. Using a Conditional Assignment Operator

```
>> bio
=> {:name=>"Adam", :age=>27}
>> bio[:age] ||= 55
>> bio
=> {:name=>"Adam", :age=>27}
>> bio[:email] ||= "adam.pahlevi@gmail.com"
>> bio
=> {:name=>"Adam", :age=>27, :email=>"adam.pahlevi@gmail.com"}
```

To delete a mapping in a hash, we use the Hash#delete method. On top of that, invoking Hash#delete also returns the associated value. See Listing 2-68.

Listing 2-68. Deleting a Key in a Hash

```
>> bio
=> {:name=>"Adam", :age=>27, :email=>"adam.pahlevi@gmail.com"}
>> bio.delete :email
=> "adam.pahlevi@gmail.com"
>> bio
=> {:name=>"Adam", :age=>27}
>> bio.delete :nothing
=> nil
```

To merge a hash with another one, we can use the Hash#merge method. This method returns a new hash instead of modifying in place. See Listing 2-69.

Listing 2-69. Using Merge to Merge Two Hashes

```
>> bio
=> {:name=>"Adam", :age=>27}
>> bio.merge(email: "adam.pahlevi@gmail.com")
=> {:name=>"Adam", :age=>27, :email=>"adam.pahlevi@gmail.com"}
```

If we want to modify in place, we can use Hash#merge! (with the exclamation mark). See Listing 2-70.

Listing 2-70. Modifying the has in Place Using merge!

```
>> bio.merge!(email: "adam.pahlevi@gmail.com")
=> {:name=>"Adam", :age=>27, :email=>"adam.pahlevi@gmail.com"}
```

In Ruby, methods that end with the exclamation mark such as this merge! are known as *bang methods* (or *dangerous methods*). They are so called because they perform an action that may change the object in place or raise an exception if there's an issue.

Arrays and hashes are best friends, so we can easily construct a hash from an array, and vice versa. See Listing 2-71.

Listing 2-71. Converting a Hash to an Array, and Vice Versa

```
>> bio = [[:name, "Adam"], [:age, 27]].to_h
=> {:name=>"Adam", :age=>27}
>> bio.to_a
=> [[:name, "Adam"], [:age, 27]]
```

Just like an array, a hash is enumerable. As such, it has the each method to iterate its key-value pair. See Listing 2-72.

Listing 2-72. Iterating the Key-Value Pair in a Hash

```
?> bio.each do |key, value|
?>   puts "#{key.capitalize}: #{value}"
>> end
Name: Adam
Age: 27
=> {:name=>"Adam", :age=>27}
```

Summary

In this chapter, you learned a lot of fundamentals of Ruby programming, from nil all the way to the hash. That definitely is not a small feat!

In the next chapter, we will venture into the more advanced topics such as regular expressions and metaprogramming. After that, you should be able to proceed comfortably into what lies ahead in the rest of this book.

CHAPTER 3

Advanced Ruby

In the previous chapter, we learned some fundamental programming techniques every Ruby engineers need to know about. For instance, we learned how to express a float.

Being true to the object-oriented paradigm, in Ruby, every object has a class. Understanding how Ruby works is necessary to becoming a productive Ruby and Rails engineer.

In this chapter, we will explore more advanced topics in Ruby programming, such as how to create our own class and how a class is different from a module.

We will also discuss methods, blocks, lambdas, and everything in between. With metaprogramming, we will learn how to create methods on-demand, a knowledge that is essential to help us see how Rails works internally. Finally, you will learn about exception handling, regular expression, and the gemfile.

Methods

Methods help us to create boundaries to organize code into smaller executable units. They are simply a set of statements and/or expressions, given a name. See Listing 3-1.

Listing 3-1. The score_grade Method

```
?> def score_grade(score)
?>    if score > 90
?>      return "A+"
?>  elsif score > 80
?>      return "A"
?>  elsif score > 70
?>      return "B"
?>  elsif score > 60
?>      return "C"
```

© Adam Notodikromo 2021
A. Notodikromo, *Learn Rails 6*, https://doi.org/10.1007/978-1-4842-6026-5_3

```
?>    elsif score > 50
?>       return "D"
?>    else
?>       return "F"
?>    end
>> end
=> :score_grade
>> score_grade(91)
=> "A+"
>> score_grade(85)
=> "A"
>> score_grade(70)
=> "C"
>> score_grade(15)
=> "F"
```

Unlike other programming languages, the return statement in Ruby is entirely optional. Simply said, the last value expressed within the block of a method is returned, if there's no return statement evaluated up to that point. Let's look at the method thanks_msg shown in Listing 3-2.

Listing 3-2. The thanks_msg Method

```
?> def thanks_msg(*items)
?>   if items.count >= 3
?>     "Thank you so so so mmuch!"
?>   elsif items.count > 1
?>     "Thank you sooo much!"
?>   else
?>     "Thank you"
?>   end
>> end
=> :thanks_msg
>> thanks_msg("1 pizza", "1 soda", "3 boba tea")
=> "Thank you so so so mmuch!"
>> thanks_msg("1 pencil")
=> "Thank you"
```

Clearly, there's no single `return` statement written there, and yet, the method is able to return a string to the caller.

However, the `return` statement is still useful when we want to return from the method midway. See Listing 3-3.

Listing 3-3. The delete! Method That Returns Midway If Not Possible

```
?> def delete!
?>    return unless possible?
?>
?>    file = find_the_file
?>    file.delete!
>> end
=> :delete!
```

A method that does not need to return anything may return `nil`. The `nil` is also implied if we don't specify what value to return. Observe the call to `Kernel#puts` shown in Listing 3-4 that returns `nil`.

Listing 3-4. Kernel#puts Returns nil

```
>> puts "I am returning nil"
I am returning nil
=> nil
```

A method can accept any arguments. The `score_grade` method accepts one argument, whereas the `delete!` method accepts no argument. The `thanks_msg` method, in contrast, accepts an infinite number of arguments by using the splat operator. See Listing 3-5.

Listing 3-5. Defining the Items Argument with a Splat Operator

```
?> def thanks_msg(*items)
?>    if items.count >= 3
?>       ...
```

The *splat operator* allows us to work with an undefined number of arguments. A parameter (or argument) with the splat operator will coerce the value into an array.

The Ruby community adopted a convention for naming a method. Quite simply, a method having identifier ending with a question mark is expected to return a Boolean. See Listing 3-6.

Listing 3-6. A pass? Method That Is Expected to Return a Boolean

```
?> def pass?(score)
?>   return score > 75
>> end
=> :pass?
>> pass? 70
=> false
>> pass? 80
=> true
>> pass? 100
=> true
```

A method's identifier that ends with a bang (!) indicates that it can modify an object it is called on, delete some files, raise an error, or do something dangerous—as you may remember from the previous chapter. See Listing 3-7.

Listing 3-7. Defining aaaargh! That Substitutes Substrings in Place

```
?> def aaaargh!(str)
?>   str.gsub!(/[aA]/, "arrgh!")
>> end
=> :aaaargh!
>> str = "abcda"
>> aaaargh!(str)
=> "arrgh!bcdarrgh!"
>> str
=> "arrgh!bcdarrgh!"
```

Although a method may take more than one argument, it is considered a best practice to limit it to three.

Note A zero-argument method is called *niladic*; a one-argument method is monadic, two is dyadic, three arguments is triadic, and more than that is polyadic. This does not need to be memorized. A triadic or polyadic method indicates a method that is doing too much or where the arguments are a subset of some data structure.

For example, instead of having a method accepting the arguments name, age, email, address, and phone_number, it may be better to create a Person class and pass its instance as an argument to the method. One sign of good engineering is avoiding getting into the habit of writing triadic or polyadic methods like the plague.

Another important point is that a method can have default arguments. To do so, we should put those arguments at the end, after any parameters that have no default value, or those known as the required arguments. See Listing 3-8.

Listing 3-8. The greet Methods with One Default Argument

```
?> def greet(name, language = "Ruby")
?>   "#{name}, the great #{language} engineer!"
>> end
=> :greet
>> greet("Sam")
=> "Sam, the great Ruby engineer!"
>> greet("Sam", "JavaScript")
=> "Sam, the great JavaScript engineer!"
```

We can also make use of keyword arguments, some of which can have default values. If no value is specified for a said keyword, the keyword is treated as a required argument. See Listing 3-9.

Listing 3-9. The greet Method with Keyword Arguments

```
?> def greet(name:, language: "Ruby")
?>   "#{name}, the great #{language} engineer!"
>> end
=> :greet
>> greet(name: "Sam")
```

91

```
=> "Sam, the great Ruby engineer!"
>> greet(language: "JavaScript", name: "Sam")
=> "Sam, the great JavaScript engineer!"
```

Classes

A class is like a blueprint in that every object is an instance of a class. As a blueprint, a class groups together its data and behaviors into a single entity, a technique known as *encapsulation.*

In a non-object-oriented language such as C and Pascal, the data and methods cannot cohabit within the same structure. So, instead of having Array#each, a function might be called Array_each. In those languages, methods need to receive the structure it operates on as there's no encapsulation.

Let's see how awesome encapsulation is. Let's create a simple Student class, as shown in Listing 3-10.

Listing 3-10. Simple Student Class

```
?> class Student
>> end
=> nil
>> s = Student.new
>> s
=> #<Student:0x00007fffda956000>
```

Using Student.new, we created an instance of Student. The process of creating an object from a class is known as instantiation. For now, the Student object is pretty much useless. It doesn't have data or any specific methods. Let's try defining some instance variables to represent some data, as shown in Listing 3-11.

Listing 3-11. Student Class with an @name Instance Variable

```
?> class Student
?>   def initialize(name)
?>     @name = name
?>   end
>> end
```

```
=> :initialize
>>
>> s = Student.new("Adam")
>> s
=> #<Student:0x00007fffda8c8b60 @name="Adam">
```

An instance variable is an internal variable of an instance. We can create and refer to an instance variable by using an at sign followed by an identifier, such as the @name instance variable in Listing 3-11.

Since @name is an instance variable, we need to create a method known as a *getter method* (or, also known as a reader method) to read and return the instance variable. See Listing 3-12.

Listing 3-12. Defining the name Getter

```
?> class Student
?>    def initialize(name)
?>       @name = name
?>    end
?>
?>    def name
?>       @name
?>    end
>> end
=> :name
```

Now we can access the value of the name, as shown in Listing 3-13.

Listing 3-13. Accessing a Student's Name Using Student#name

```
>> s = Student.new("Adam")
>> s.name
=> "Adam"
```

However, we can't change the name yet. To allow us to change the instance variable, we need to create a method known as a *setter method* or *writer method*. See Listing 3-14.

Listing 3-14. Defining the Student#name= Writer Method

```
?> class Student
?>   def initialize(name)
?>     self.name = name
?>   end
?>
?>   def name
?>     @name
?>   end
?>
?>   def name=(name)
?>     @name = name
?>   end
>> end
=> :name=
```

Now we can change the student's name, as shown in Listing 3-15.

Listing 3-15. Changing a Student's Name

```
>> s = Student.new("Adam Notodikromo")
>> s.name
=> "Adam Notodikromo"

>> s.name = "Sam Yamashita"
>> s.name
=> "Sam Yamashita"
```

We just learned a good pattern for managing data in a class, that is, by defining a getter and a setter to read and change the value of an instance variable. But, why is this a good pattern?

Using the getter-setter pattern is important because our data can be `dirty`. With a getter-setter, we can do custom actions before returning or writing the data.

In that sense, by having a getter and a setter, we cleanly separate between the data and the behavior. If we later found out that a last name must be capitalized, for instance, we can implement this requirement easily into the setter method. See Listing 3-16.

Listing 3-16. Custom Logic on the Setter

```
?> class Student
?>   def name=(name)
?>     @name = name.split.map(&:capitalize).join(" ")
>>   end
?> end
```

This getter-and-setter pattern is so prevalent that Ruby has a handy keyword to help us define both: `attr_accessor`. We can use this especially if we don't need to define custom logic on the getter and setter methods. See Listing 3-17.

Listing 3-17. Using attr_accessor to Define the Getter and Setter for the Name

```
?> class Student
?>   attr_accessor :name
?>   def initialize(name)
?>     self.name = name
?>   end
>> end
=> :initialize
>> s = Student.new("Sam Harton")
>> s.name
=> "Sam Harton"
>> s.name = "Sam Yamashita"
>> s
=> #<Student:0x00007fffda929ac8 @name="Sam Yamashita">
```

Ruby also has `attr_reader` to define just the getter method, and it has `attr_writer` to define just the setter method.

In an object-oriented world, a class may inherit from another class in a process called *subclassing*. To inherit a class, we use the < operator. By inheriting a class, we get all of the parent class's attributes and methods for free! See Listing 3-18.

Listing 3-18. Creating a User and an Admin Class That Inherits from User

```
?> class User
?>   def initialize
?>     @is_admin = false
?>   end
?>
?>   def admin?
?>     @is_admin
?>   end
>> end
=> :admin?
>>
?> class Admin < User
?>   def initialize
?>     @is_admin = true
?>   end
>> end
```

Notice that although the Admin class does not *formally* define an admin? method, since Admin inherits from User, Admin has all the data and the behavior of a User. See Listing 3-19.

Listing 3-19. Calling an Inherited admin? Method

```
>> u = User.new
>> a = Admin.new
>> u.admin?
=> false
>> a.admin?
=> true
```

In fact, an Admin is also a User! See Listing 3-20.

Listing 3-20. An Admin Is a User

```
>> a.is_a? Admin
=> true
>> a.is_a? User
=> true
```

However, a User is not (necessarily) an Admin! See Listing 3-21.

Listing 3-21. A User Instance Is Not an Admin Instance

```
>> u.is_a?(Admin)
=> false
>> u.is_a?(User)
=> true
```

An inherited class may override a method from the parent class. It can also call the parent's method implementation by using the super keyword. See Listing 3-22.

Listing 3-22. Using super to Call Inherited Function from the Superclass

```
?> class User
?>   attr_accessor :name
?>
?>   def initialize(name)
?>     @is_admin = false
?>     self.name = name
?>   end
?>
?>   def admin?
?>     @is_admin
?>   end
>> end
=> :admin?
>>
?> class Admin < User
?>   def initialize(name)
?>     super
?>     @is_admin = true
?>   end
>> end
=> :initialize
```

An example of inheritence in the Ruby's standard library is the Numeric class, from which Float and Integer inherit.

97

We have learned that an instance variable is private to the instance. Sometimes we also need methods that shouldn't be accessible from outside. These methods usually do some internal processes or calculations, so they don't need to be accessible from outside.

For example, imagine a class named Image in a common photo-sharing social media app. To download an image, we first need to authorize such a request, especially as not all users set their account as public. See Listing 3-23.

Listing 3-23. An Imaginary Download Function

```
def download(downloader)
  return unless authenticated? downloader

  file = create_file
  # the name refers to an attribute in the Image class
  file.write fetch_from_server(name)
end
```

In this case, it is sensible to mark both `authenticated?` and `fetch_from_server` as private. By doing so, we make the instance much simpler to work with as it has fewer public methods.

To make methods private, we can state `private`, and any methods defined under the statement become private methods as a result.

Let's try make a class with a private method, as shown in Listing 3-24.

Listing 3-24. Defining Private Method Greeting

```
?> class Greeter
?>   attr_reader :lang
?>
?>   def initialize(lang)
?>     @lang = lang
?>   end
?>
?>   def greet(name)
?>     puts "#{greeting}, #{name}"
?>   end
?>
```

```
?>    private
?>
?>    def greeting
?>      case lang
?>      when "English" then "Hi"
?>      when "Cool English" then "Yo!"
?>      end
?>    end
>> end
=> :greeter
```

Let's instantiate an instance and call the Greeter#greet on it. See Listing 3-25.

Listing 3-25. Instantiating a greet Instance to Greet Adam

```
>> g = Greeter.new("Cool English")
>> g.greet("Adam")
Yo!, Adam
=> nil
```

Great! Let's see what happens when we try to access the private method greeter. See Listing 3-26.

Listing 3-26. Accessing a Private Method Greeting Raises an Exception

```
>> g.greeting
Traceback (most recent call last):
  ...
NoMethodError (private method `greeting' called for ...)
Did you mean?  greet
```

Ruby complains! That's the behavior that we want. A totally unrelated outsider shouldn't need to have access to the greet method. When we define methods as private, we consider them to be implementation details; that is, the engineers who created them reverse the right to modify them in anyway, or even delete them, without having to provide alternatives. That is why private methods are usually not documented.

It's also important to remember that privacy in Ruby is about objects, instead of classes. Meaning, private methods in Ruby can be called by the same object (the self) regardless of where those methods come from. Let's observe this behavior; see Listing 3-27.

Listing 3-27. Calling a Private Method from a Subclass

```
>> class A
>>   private def hi
>>     puts "hi"
>>   end
>> end
=> A

>> class B < A
>>   def say_hi
>>     hi
>>   end
>> end
=> :say_hi

>> B.new.say_hi
hi
=> nil
```

In the previous code, we have two classes: A and B. B is a subclass of A. As we can see, within B, we can call hi, which is defined as a private method in A.

If you come from Java, this behavior might come as a surprise since, well, hi is a private method of A. Even if A is inherited by B, B shouldn't have access to A#hi. However, method privacy in Ruby is about the object rather than the class it is defined at. Since say_hi and hi belongs to the same self, say_hi can send the message hi to itself just fine. With this behavior, private in Ruby is similar to Java's protected.

However, if we call hi explicitly with self, an error will occur! Let's observe these interesting bits in Listing 3-28.

Listing 3-28. Calling a Private Method via self

```
class A
  private def hi
    puts "hi"
  end
end
```

```
class B < A
  def say_hi
    self.hi
  end
end
```

There's nothing different from the previous snippet other than adding `self` to `hi`. This call, however, will fail! See Listing 3-29.

Listing 3-29. Failure on Calling B#say_hi

```
>> B.new.hi
Traceback (most recent call last):
        ...
NoMethodError (private method `hi' called for #<B:...>)
```

In other words, a private method must not be called with a `self`. However, there is an exception. If the method is an assignment method, we can call `self` on it to access the method. This is to avoid the interpreter thinking we are defining a new variable. Let's observe that behavior; see Listing 3-30.

Listing 3-30. Using self When Accessing a Private Assignment Method

```
>> class C
>>   attr_reader :name
>>
>>   private def name=(name)
>>     @name = name
>>   end
>>
>>   def initialize
>>     self.name = "Ruby"
>>   end
>> end
>> c = C.new
=> #<C:0x0000558217ba1a28 @name="Ruby">
>> c.name
=> "Ruby"
```

In the previous snippet, we call the name= method by using self even though name= is a private method. This is the only exception where self can be used explicitly on a private method.

Back to the A and B class example: if we would like to be able to call A#hi from B through self, then we can either make A#hi a public method or make it a protected method. A protected method can be called with an implicit receiver, like a private one, and it can also be called with an explicit receiver only if the receiver is self or an object of the same class.

Listing 3-31 shows an object of the same class.

Listing 3-31. Changing Visibility of A#hi from private to protected

```ruby
class A
  privateprotected def hi
    puts "hi"
  end
end

class B < A
  def say_hi
    self.hi
  end
end
```

With the previous definition, we can run the code in Listing 3-32 just fine, which is not possible had A#hi been defined as a private method.

Listing 3-32. Calling B#say_hi That Calls Protected A#hi Explicitly

```ruby
>> B.new.say_hi
hi
=> nil
```

Public methods are obvious: anyone can call them. But, when some privacy is needed, choosing which one to use between protected and private visibility might be confusing for newcomers. In that case, perhaps defaulting to protected is sensible if the class is inheritable. Otherwise, as most classes we are going to write ourselves are not inheritable, when we want to restrict the visibility of certain methods, setting them as private is a sensible choice.

At the end of the day, when we make a method `private`, we send a strong message that we reserve the right to even remove the method without prior notice. It is because of this reasoning that `private` methods are not printed in documentation.

We can also define constants in a class (and a module). A constant indicates a value that should never change. Constants are usually expected to be highly reused over and over. Hence, rather than writing the value manually, we extract it as a constant.

Declaring a constant is similar to declaring a variable; however, uppercase letters are used. See Listing 3-33.

Listing 3-33. Creating a Book Class Having a Constant STATUS Array

```
?> class Book
?>   STATUS = [:draft, :reviewed, :published].freeze
?>
?>   attr_reader :status
?>
?>   def status=(status)
?>     unless STATUS.include?(status)
?>       raise "Please specify status correctly"
?>     end
?>   end
>> end
```

In the previous example class, we defined a constant named STATUS. A constant's value is usually `frozen` if possible to indicate that the value is final or immutable, as many data structures in Ruby are mutable by default. That being said, a constant's reference can be redefined later, even if we should never do this. The interpreter will print a warning if we reassign a new object to a constant. See Listing 3-34.

Listing 3-34. Reassigning a Constant Prints a Warning

```
>> STATUS = [:draft, :reviewed, :published].freeze
=> [:draft, :reviewed, :published]
>> STATUS = [:reassigned]
(irb):2: warning: already initialized constant STATUS
(irb):1: warning: previous definition of STATUS was here
=> [:reassigned]
```

To refer to the constant outside of the class's scope, we use the class's namespace. See Listing 3-35.

Listing 3-35. Accessing a Constant as an Outsider

```
>> Book::STATUS
=> [:draft, :reviewed, :published]
```

Last but not least, a class can define class methods, also known as *static methods*. Simply, a class method is a method belonging to a class, not its instances. An example of a class method is the new method we used to instantiate a class. We can define a class method using the self keyword. See Listing 3-36.

Listing 3-36. Defining a Class Method

```
>> require "date"
=> false
?> class Calculations
?>   def self.age(born_year)
?>     Date.today.year - born_year
?>   end
>> end
=> :age
>> Calculations.age(1992)
=> 28
```

In the previous case, we made a static method called age that belongs to the class, instead of its instances. Therefore, we access it by specifying the class's identifier.

To reiterate, a class is like a blueprint for an object. A class is responsible for launching an object into existence. Yet, shortly after, an object is an independent entity from the class. In fact, it is possible, although not advisable, to change or add a new behavior in the instance distinct from the class.

Modules

A module is like a class, minus the ability to instantiate an object. In Ruby, a module is primarily used to

1. Write library codes

2. Write functions that can be shared to avoid repetition of writing such functions again and again

3. Provide namespacing

First, where can we place methods that don't belong to the concept of a class? Not everything needs instantiation. The Calculations class in the previous section, for instance, is more appropriate to be treated as a module instead of a blueprint for an object. Calculations shouldn't be a class!

Observe the code in Listing 3-37 that creates a Calculations module. You may want to restart the irb console by terminating it and then calling it again, since Calculations was already defined as a class from the previous section and redeclaring it as a module is not allowed (and vice versa). See Listing 3-37.

Listing 3-37. Declaring a Calculations Module

```
>> require "date"
=> true
?> module Calculations
?>   extend self
?>
?>   def age(born_year)
?>     Date.today.year - born_year
?>   end
>> end
=> :age
>> Calculations.age(1992)
=> 28
```

Second, a module relieves the need for multiple inheritance. With a module, we can share common methods that can later be included in different classes. See Listing 3-38.

Listing 3-38. Module as a Way to Extract Common Methods

```
?> module Quack
?>   def quack
?>     puts "Quack quack"
?>   end
>> end
=> :quack

?> class Duck
?>   include Quack
>> end
=> Duck

?> class RoboticDuck
?>   include Quack
>> end
=> RoboticDuck

>> Duck.new.quack
Quack quack
=> nil

>> RoboticDuck.new.quack
Quack quack
=> nil
```

Unlike C++ and Python that have multiple inheritance, Ruby seems to want to create a better way to help us structure our program. Multiple inheritance is known to be more difficult to reason about, and it can create a host of issues such as the deadly diamond of death.

In this case, modules are usually used to model characteristics that can be included in classes. In that sense, class names tend to be nouns, whereas module names are adjectives. See Listing 3-39.

Listing 3-39. Modules Help Us Organize Common Characteristics

```ruby
class User
  include UniqueIdGenerator
  include Authenticatable
  include Rememberable
  include Trackable
end

class Post
  include UniqueIdGenerator
end
```

The previous example is the correct way of how modules are used to define common characteristics. The code in Listing 3-40, however, is frowned upon.

Listing 3-40. A Bad Design

```ruby
module User
end

class Authenticatable
end

class RealUser < Authenticatable
  include User
end
```

A module is also the preferred way for namespacing in Ruby. Without namespacing, we can have only one class named `Connection`, for example, since the name is scoped globally. See Listing 3-41.

Listing 3-41. Namespacing the Connection Class

```ruby
?> module Http
?>   class Connection
?>     def type
?>       "Http Connection!"
?>     end
?>   end
```

```
>> end
=> :what_am_i?

?> module Https
?>   class Connection
?>     def type
?>       "Http Secure Connection!"
?>     end
?>   end
>> end
=> :what_am_i?

>> Http::Connection.new.what_am_i?
=> "Http Connection!"
>> Https::Connection.new.what_am_i?
=> "Http Secure Connection!"
```

Although we can do namespacing by using a class, that would be quite weird as the namespace can be instantiated. In fact, it is rare to see a class containing another class or another module.

Lambdas and Blocks

Lambdas and blocks are what are formally known as *closures*. They are a block of code that has its own scope, having access to variables bounded in time when the closure is created.

In Ruby, lambda and block are the closest things to represent code as an object. A block is, in fact, used countless times in Ruby. The Array#each method, for instance, accepts a block that yields one item at a time. See Listing 3-42.

Listing 3-42. Passing a Block to Array#each

```
>> [1, 2, 3].each { |x| puts x }
1
2
3
=> [1, 2, 3]
```

Block can be declared using curly braces as in the example of `Array#each` in Listing 3-42 or, quite equivalently, using the do-end keyword. See Listing 3-43.

Listing 3-43. Passing a do-end Block to Array#each

```
?> [1, 2, 3].each do |x|
?>   puts x
>> end
1
2
3
=> [1, 2, 3]
```

There is an essential difference between a do-end block and a curly-braces block in that a curly-braces block has higher precedence than a do-end block. Therefore, check out Listing 3-44.

Listing 3-44. Passing a do-end Block to a Method Call Without Parentheses

```
task :something => arg do
  send_email
end
```

This will be interpreted as shown in Listing 3-45.

Listing 3-45. An Equivalent Way of Expressing the Previous do-end Block

```
task(:something => arg) { send_email }
```

This is intended! By contrast, see Listing 3-46.

Listing 3-46. Passing a Curly-Braces Block to a Method Call Without Parentheses

```
task :something => arg {
  send_email
}
```

This will be interpreted, unfortunately, as shown in Listing 3-47.

Listing 3-47. Curly Braces Have Higher Precedence

```
task {:something => (arg { send_email })}
```

In the previous code, the `arg` is regarded as a function, instead of a variable. And the hash that is passed as an argument to the `task` method is a hash containing the key `something` to the method call of `arg` with a block passed to it.

If we are to refer a block by giving it an identifier, we end up with a proc. A *proc* is an object that encapsulates a code block. There are two types of procs in Ruby: a lambda and a proc (yes, quite confusingly, but hold on).

Why are there two different types of proc? Basically, although they are of the same class, that is, `Proc`, they behave quite a little bit differently.

First, a lambda is stricter than a proc when it comes to its specified arguments. When a lambda defines three arguments, it strictly needs to receive three arguments; otherwise, an exception will be raised. See Listing 3-48.

Listing 3-48. A Lambda Is a Stricter Proc

```
>> greeter1 = lambda { |name| puts "Hello, #{name}" }
>> greeter2 = proc { |name| puts "Hello, #{name}" }
>> greeter1.call()
Traceback (most recent call last):
        ...
        1: from (irb):27:in `block in irb_binding'
ArgumentError (wrong number of arguments (given 0, expected 1))
>> greeter2.call()
Hello,
```

Other than using the keyword `lambda`, it is also possible to define a lambda using the arrow notation, as shown in Listing 3-49.

Listing 3-49. Using Arrow Notation to Define a Lambda

```
>> hi = -> { puts "Hi!" }
>> hi.lambda?
=> true
>> hi.call
Hi!
=> nil
```

Second, a `return` statement inside a proc is taken to mean returning from the whole method, instead of from within the block! See Listing 3-50.

Listing 3-50. A Proc Returns Immediately to the Caller

```
?> def call_with_lambda
?>   lambda { return "from the block" }.call
?>   return "from the method"
>> end
=> :call_with_lambda

?> def call_with_proc
?>   proc { return "from the block" }.call
?>   return "from the method"
>> end
=> :call_with_proc

>> call_with_lambda
=> "from the method"

>> call_with_proc
=> "from the block"
```

With a proc/lambda, we can transfer it to a method accepting a block. That way, we don't need to pass a block, although this is rarely done. See Listing 3-51.

Listing 3-51. Passing a Proc to a Method

```
>> hi_proc = proc { puts "Hi!" }
>> hi_lambda = lambda { |_| puts "Hi!" }
>> 2.times(&hi_proc)
Hi!
Hi!
=> 2
>> 2.times(&hi_lambda)
Hi!
Hi!
=> 2
```

When calling a method, the unary & (ampersand) operator shown previously converts a proc/lambda into a block, since `Integer#times` accepts a block.

The unary ampersand operator can also work with a symbol. When a symbol is used, we don't need to create a block or a proc, yet we can send a method having the same name as the symbol onto the object. This is usually used on a map function. It's easier to illustrate this by observing the behavior shown in Listing 3-52.

Listing 3-52. Using the Unary Ampersand Operator to Create a Block

```
>> ["1", "2", "3"].map(&:to_i)
=> [1, 2, 3]
>> ["1", "2", "3"].map { |x| x.to_i }
=> [1, 2, 3]
```

The previous code is equivalent to one another. What happens is that `Symbol#to_proc` is called to create a block not unlike the second call and then passes the block into the `Array#map` function.

In fact, this behavior of the ampersand method can be used on any object, not just a symbol. That is, if an ampersand method meets anything other than a proc or a block, a `to_proc` method is called on that object. See Listing 3-53.

Listing 3-53. Passing a Class with a to_proc Method Defined on It

```
>> class Greeter
>>   def self.to_proc
>>     lambda { |name| puts "Hi, #{name}" }
>>   end
>> end
=> :to_proc
>> ["adam", "sam"].each &Greeter
Hi, adam
Hi, sam
=> [nil, nil]
```

However, many Ruby engineers are not aware of this power of the ampersand operator. In fact, this way of using the ampersand operator is rarely used on anything other than a symbol.

We just learned how the unary ampersand operator works when used for calling a method. In this case, an ampersand operator converts a proc to a block if a proc is given. If another object is given, a `to_proc` method is called on that object.

When defining a method, we can use the ampersand operator to accept a block. The operator will convert the block into a `Proc` object. This is just another advanced concept that is usually employed by makers of third-party libraries or frameworks. See Listing 3-54.

Listing 3-54. Using the Ampersand Operator to Convert a Block to a Proc

```
>> class Configuration
>>   attr_accessor :name, :url
>> end
=> nil
>>
>> class App
>>   attr_reader :configuration
>>
>>   def initialize
>>     @configuration = Configuration.new
>>   end
>>
>>   def name
>>     configuration.name
>>   end
>>
>>   def config &config_block
>>     config_block.call(configuration)
>>   end
>> end
=> :config
>>
>> app = App.new
=> #<App:0x00005646b03b9de8 @configuration=#<Configuration:0x00005646b03b9f00>>
>> app.config do |c|
?>   c.name = "Cool app"
```

113

```
>> end
=> "Cool app"
>>
>> puts app.name
Cool app
=> nil
```

However, there is still a performance penalty for converting a block into a `Proc`. With a method like the previous one, it will be better to use `yield` to pass the `Configuration` object to the caller, and it will behave the same way. See Listing 3-55.

Listing 3-55. Using yield Instead of Converting and Calling a Block

```
class App
  ...

  def config
    yield configuration
  end
end
```

To sum up, there are two kinds of code blocks in Ruby: blocks and procs. Blocks are always related to a method call, and they cannot be defined outside of that context. In contrast, a proc is an addressable object that has a block. There is a mechanism to convert between a block and a proc by using the ampersand operator, which can also convert an object to a proc.

Metaprogramming

The C programming language has no keyword for the `true` and `false` of the Boolean data type. Some C developers try to augment them by using a macro, which is a form of metaprogramming. In Ruby, the metaprogramming is much more powerful than that.

First, let's learn about the basics of singleton methods. We will have a string define new functionality on the fly. See Listing 3-56.

Listing 3-56. Defining a Function on the Fly on a String Instance

```
>> name = "Adam"
?> def name.greet
?>   puts "Hello #{self}!"
>> end
=> :greet

>> name.greet
Hello Adam!
=> nil
```

Wow! The string name for sure did not have the greet method initially. If we try to invoke the custom greet method on another string, a NoMethodError exception is raised. See Listing 3-57.

Listing 3-57. Calling greet on Another String Instance

```
>> "World".greet
Traceback (most recent call last):
    ...
    1: from (irb):6
NoMethodError (undefined method `greet' for "World":String)
```

If we want to make greet available on all instances of String, we can crack open the String class and define the method. This technique is called *monkey patching*. See Listing 3-58

Listing 3-58. Monkey Patching the String Class

```
?> class String
?>   def greet
?>     puts "Hello #{self}!"
?>   end
>> end
=> :greet
>>
>> "World".greet
Hello World!
=> nil
```

With nonkey patching, Ruby allowed us to open a class or a module and add a new definition or redeclare existing ones!

In the previous case, we know that we want to name our method greet. What if the method's name is known only at runtime? Imagine a model class, which defines an association as shown in Listing 3-59.

Listing 3-59. A Transaction Class

```
class Transaction
  belongs_to :account
end
```

When the Rails engineers were developing Rails, they certainly could not account for all the possible relationships between models. They, for instance, would not know that the Transaction model in Listing 3-59 will have a relationship to an account. Despite this lack of knowledge, using the belongs_to declaration, Rails defines a handful of methods related to Account for us, as shown in Listing 3-60.

Listing 3-60. Rails Defines the Account Setter Function and Other Helpful Functions for Us

```
class Transaction
  belongs_to :account
end

# these two methods are defined by Rails for us
transaction.account = my_account
Transaction.find_by_account(my_account)
```

But, how is that possible? Yes! Metaprogramming!

To define an instance method on demand, we can use define_method. There is also define_singleton_method for defining a static method on the class. Let's observe the code in Listing 3-61 where we create a Transaction class that can define methods on demand by calling belongs_to.

Listing 3-61. Using define_method to Define a Method on Demand

```
?> class Transaction
?>   def self.belongs_to(owner)
?>     define_method "#{owner}=" do |val|
?>       @owner = val
?>     end
?>
?>     define_method owner do
?>       @owner
?>     end
?>
?>     define_singleton_method "find_by_#{owner}" do |arg|
?>       t = Transaction.new
?>       t.send("#{owner}=", arg)
?>       t
?>     end
?>   end
?>
?>   belongs_to :account
>> end
```

In the previous code, we defined a `Transaction` class that has a class method `belongs_to`. We then use `belongs_to` to define some association.

Let's now create a simple `Account` class and instantiate an `Account` object. See Listing 3-62.

Listing 3-62. Creating and Instantiating a Simple Account Class

```
?> class Account
>> end
=> nil
>> a = Account.new
```

Let's remember that in the `Transaction` class, we have never *formally* defined any getter and setter for `account`, yet the code shown in Listing 3-63 works.

117

Listing 3-63. Associating an Account to a Transaction

```
>> t = Transaction.new
>> t.account = a
>> t.account == a
=> true
```

That is, because the getter and setter are defined through metaprogramming, we can prove it by calling methods on the Transaction object to check defined methods on the object. See Listing 3-64.

Listing 3-64. Checking Whether Account and Other Methods Are Defined

```
>> t.methods.sort
=> [...:account, :account=, :class, ...]
>> t.methods.include? :account=
=> true
```

We also have never defined the Transaction.find_by_account method, and yet, the code works in Listing 3-65 too.

Listing 3-65. Calling the Dynamically Defined find_by_account

```
>> t2 = Transaction.find_by_account(a)
>> t2.account == t.account
=> true
```

We have seen how powerful metaprogramming is in Ruby. Realizing that, we must use it only sparingly, if at all. Normally, this feature of Ruby is used by library makers.

Although understanding metaprogramming offered us some rough idea as to what Rails does behind the scenes, mastering all of it is usually unnecessary.

Exception Handling

An exception is when something unexpected occurred during the runtime of a program. For example, when a program tries to read a nonexistent file, an exception is raised at that point in time.

Exception handling revolves upon three keywords.

- **rescue**: An attempt to rescue from exceptions

- **ensure**: A block to be executed regardless of whether the program raises an exception

- **raise**: A deliberate attempt to throw an exception

Let's try to write a method that expects a user to enter a numerical value. See Listing 3-66.

Listing 3-66. An ask_number Method

```
?> def ask_number(question)
?>   puts question
?>   Integer(gets.chomp)
>> end
=> :ask_number
>> ask_number("Please enter your postal code: ")
Please enter your postal code:
101110
=> 101110
```

The method ask_number shown in Listing 3-66 assumes that users enter a postcode in a particular format: a string of six decimal numbers. When we invoke it with an invalid input, such as when the input contains a dash, it can crash due to an exception. See Listing 3-67.

Listing 3-67. An Exception Causes the Program to Crash

```
>> question = "Please enter your postal code: "
>> ask_number(question)
Please enter your postal code:
101-110
Traceback (most recent call last):
      ...
ArgumentError (invalid value for Integer(): "101-110")
```

However, since we run the previous code within irb, and it is in irb's interest to catch exceptions and display the error for us, the exception is handled, and the program does not get terminated.

119

In that light, exceptions provide a way to transfer control from one part of a program to another higher up the stack, until the exception is handled. Uncaught exceptions will terminate the program abruptly.

To let ask_number handle an exception, we can use inlined rescue, as shown in Listing 3-68.

Listing 3-68. Using Rescue Inline

```
?> def ask_number(question)
?>   puts question
?>   Integer(gets.chomp) rescue nil
>> end
=> :ask_number
>> ask_number("Please enter your postal code: ")
Please enter your postal code:
101-110
=> nil
```

rescue can also be used when we are in a block. See Listing 3-69.

Listing 3-69. Rescuing an Exception in a begin-end Block

```
?> begin
?>   raise "an error"
?> rescue => e
?>   puts "Error class: #{e.class}, message: #{e.message}"
>> end
Error class: RuntimeError, message: an error
=> nil
```

We can also handle specific exceptions. See Listing 3-70.

Listing 3-70. Rescuing Specific Exceptions

```
>> require "json"
=> true
?> def extract_number(json, key)
?>   data = JSON.parse(json)
?>   Integer(data[key])
```

```
?> rescue ArgumentError
?>   puts "Data must be a number!"
?> rescue JSON::ParserError
?>   puts "Please give a correct JSON document"
>> end
=> :extract_number
```

If we invoke extract_number with sensible arguments, everything will go smoothly. See Listing 3-71.

Listing 3-71. Passing Sensible Arguments to extract_number

```
>> extract_number('{"postcode": "101110"}', "postcode")
=> 101110
```

If predicted exceptions occur, the error handler can handle them. See Listing 3-72.

Listing 3-72. Handled Exceptions

```
>> extract_number('{"postcode": "101-110"}', "postcode")
Data must be a number!
=> nil
>> extract_number('not_a_json_data', "postcode")
Please give a correct JSON document
=> nil
```

Now, of course, it is possible to catch a specific error, at the same time allowing StandardError to catch the rest of sensible errors happening inside the function. When catching StandardError, it is not required to spell out the class name. See Listing 3-73.

Listing 3-73. Catching the Rest of the Exception Using StandardError

```
?> def extract_number(json, key)
?>   data = JSON.parse(json)
?>   Integer(data[key])
?> rescue JSON::ParserError
?>   puts "Please give a correct JSON document"
?> rescue => e
?>   puts "I have a problem: #{e.message}"
>> end
```

Then, let's test it as shown in Listing 3-74.

Listing 3-74. Error Rescued by the StandardError Block

```
>> extract_number(1, 2)
I have a problem: no implicit conversion of Integer into String
=> nil
```

We can also use the rescue block in any begin-end block such as in Listing 3-75.

Listing 3-75. Using Rescue in a begin-end Block

```ruby
require "net/http"

begin
  uri = URI("https://tandibi.com")
  http = Net::HTTP.new(uri.host, uri.port)
  http.use_ssl = true
  http.read_timeout = 0.1 # second
  http.get("/")
rescue => e
  puts "Error occurred: #{e.message}"
  puts "Backtrace: #{e.backtrace.join("\n")}"
end
```

The previous code is bound to raise an exception as we assign a value too low for the timeout circuit breaker, at just 0.1 second. The previous code also demonstrated the use of backtrace to get the step-by-step execution trace, which may prove useful when debugging.

If we execute the previous code, we will see logs similar to the code shown in Listing 3-76 in the terminal.

Listing 3-76. Output Log with Backtrace

```
Error occurred: Net::ReadTimeout with #<TCPSocket:(closed)>
Backtrace:
/.../net/protocol.rb:217:in `rbuf_fill'
/.../net/protocol.rb:191:in `readuntil'
/.../net/protocol.rb:201:in `readline'
...
```

Regular Expressions

A regular expression, also known as *regex*, is a notation used to find substrings in a string. The substrings can be extracted, replaced, removed, or just found to indicate that the data is valid.

The code in Listing 3-77 searches for any sequence of numbers in a string. It returns the starting index of the first matching pattern. Notice that the regular expression is the pattern in between a slash (/).

Listing 3-77. Finding a Substring Using a Regular Expression

```
>> h = "Call ADAM at 3953672"
>> h =~ /[0-9]+/
=> 13
```

The regular expression in Listing 3-77 means a pattern consisting of a number from 0, 1, 2 ... all the way to 9. Such a pattern must be at least one character in length.

We can find a matching substring using `String#match`. See Listing 3-78.

Listing 3-78. Using String#match to Find a Matching Substring

```
>> h.match(/[0-9]+/)
=> #<MatchData "3953672">
```

There is also `String#scan` to return all matching substrings as an array. We can also use `%r{}` to express a regular expression. See Listing 3-79.

Listing 3-79. Using String#scan to Retrieve Matching Substrings

```
>> str = "Call ADAM at 3953672 12391812 1"
=> "Call ADAM at 3953672 12391812 1"
>> str.scan(%r{[0-9]+})
=> ["3953672", "12391812", "1"]
```

We can use `String#gsub` (global substitute) to replace a matching substring with the data we want. See Listing 3-80.

Listing 3-80. Using String#gsub to Replace Matching Substrings

```
>> h.gsub(/[0-9]+/, "{PHONE}")
=> "Call ADAM at {PHONE}"
```

Regexes may look exotic, and it can take a whole book to discuss how to form the pattern. Fortunately, most things about a regex is not too difficult to understand. However, the general rule is that, thanks to its exotic grammar, deep thinkers recommend that if we can avoid using a regex, we should. There's a famous quote:

> *Some people, when confronted with a problem, think "I know, I'll use regular expressions." Now they have two problems.*

Bundler and Gemfiles

As a software engineer, unless we are part of a big team, we will waste a tremendous amount of time if we have to invent everything by ourselves. The Ruby community has a software tool that makes it easy to share frameworks or library code. It is known as Bundler, and those libraries are known as *Ruby gems*.

Bundler is a package management tools, not unlike that of Maven in Java or NPM in the JavaScript community. It sets up a consistent environment for our Ruby applications by tracking and installing the exact gems and versions that our applications need. It ensures that the gems are present in the same version in development, staging, and production.

Third-party software libraries are called *gems*; hence, the gemfile is the file to specify those gems our app depends on.

To start our adventure, let's create a new folder called `coolprint` and create a new file named `gemfile` within the `coolprint` folder. See Listing 3-81.

Listing 3-81. The Directory Structure for coolprint

```
.
└── coolprint
    └── Gemfile
```

The file should have the content shown in Listing 3-82.

Listing 3-82. Gemfile for the coolprint App

```
source "https://rubygems.org"
ruby 2.6.5
```

Next let's run the commands shown in Listing 3-83 in the terminal.

Listing 3-83. Installing App Dependencies

```
$ cd coolprint
$ bundle
The Gemfile specifies no dependencies
Resolving dependencies...
Bundle complete! 0 Gemfile dependencies, 1 gem now installed.
Use `bundle info [gemname]` to see where a bundled gem is installed.
```

By executing bundle, we request that Bundler find the gems that satisfy our declarations. It then creates or updates a file known as Gemfile.lock, which is a generated file that records the exact version of the gems. The Gemfile.lock file ensures that all of our dependencies are in harmony, in other words, that they can work together by using the exact version at the time a gem was installed. See Listing 3-84.

Listing 3-84. Example of a Content of a Gemfile.lock

```
GEM
  remote: https://rubygems.org/
  specs:

PLATFORMS
  ruby

DEPENDENCIES

RUBY VERSION
   ruby 2.6.5p114

BUNDLED WITH
   2.1.4
```

There is really nothing to worry about if the content of Gemfile.lock in your local machine is different than the previous one!

Now, let's add a gem. See Listing 3-85.

Listing 3-85. Adding colorize into a Gemfile

```
gem "colorize"
```

The previous line tells Bundler to obtain a copy of colorize from the gems server when we run the bundle command.

Now, let's bundle it. See Listing 3-86.

Listing 3-86. Running bundle to Install Gem Dependencies

```
$ bundle
Fetching gem metadata from https://rubygems.org/.
Resolving dependencies...
Using bundler 2.1.2
Fetching colorize 0.8.1
Installing colorize 0.8.1
Bundle complete! 1 Gemfile dependency, 2 gems now installed.
Use `bundle info [gemname]` to see where a bundled gem is installed.
```

With a simple command, Bundle fetched colorize version 0.8.1 for us. That's great! We don't need to hunt down software libraries manually and copy the source codes by hand, unlike what's normally done in a language like C.

Now, it's possible that in your case, Bundler may download colorize version 0.8.2 or 0.9.0 if such a version becomes available since Bundler will always fetch the latest release.

We can tell Bundler to download a specific version exactly, such as in Listing 3-87.

Listing 3-87. Specifying an Exact Version for colorize in the Gemfile

```
gem "colorize", "0.8.1"
```

This versioning is called *semantic versioning*. The number represents, from left to right, the following:

- MAJOR denotes incompatible API changes between different releases. (For example, Ruby 2.0.0 is not compatible with Ruby 1.0.0, Ruby 3.0.0, Ruby 4.0.0, etc.)

- MINOR denotes backward-compatible added functionalities. (For example, software written for Ruby 2.0.0 can be upgraded seamlessly to Ruby 2.1.0, Ruby 2.2.0, etc.)

- PATCH denotes backward-compatible bug/security/design patches. (For example, Ruby 2.7.0 can be upgraded painlessly to Ruby 2.7.1.)

- Optional: revision/alpha/beta/release-candidate marker. Example: *6.0.3.rc1.*

A revision number might be used to fix a security hole in a previously released gem. In the case of Rails 6.0.2.1, the gem has the same underlying source code with 6.0.2, but the newer revision fixed a security issue in Rack, one of Rails' dependency. This part of the version string may also be used to indicate an alpha, beta, or release candidate of the gem.

Specifying our dependency with strict, exact versioning can be trouble as we add more gems. Such as when more than one gem depends on a gem with a different version, using exact versioning in that case can prevent successful bundling. Therefore, exact versioning is often rarely used.

Instead, we can set the gem's version so that Bundler has more leeway when resolving versioning differences. See Table 3-1.

Table 3-1. *The Meaning of Symbol in Semantic Versioning*

Version	Meaning
>= 1.0.0	Accept any version bigger or equal to 1.0.0.
~> 1.0.0	Accept any version from 1.0.0 to anything below 1.1.
~> 1.0	Accept any version from 1.0 to anything below 2.0.

Now let's put colorize to the same use! Let's create a new file called app.rb in the same folder where our gemfile is located. See Listing 3-88.

Listing 3-88. Content of app.rb

```
require 'rubygems'
require 'bundler/setup'
require "colorize"

puts "Hello ".colorize(:red)
puts "World".colorize(:blue)
```

Then, run the command in Listing 3-89 in the terminal.

Listing 3-89. Running app.rb

```
$ ruby app.rb
Hello
World
```

We should see that "Hello" and "World" get printed in red and blue accordingly (see Figure 3-1).

Figure 3-1. *Result of executing app.rb*

Summary

In this chapter, you learned more than enough Ruby skills required to be an awesome Rails engineers. Congratulations! Next, let's start building our social network startup!

Let's go for it!

CHAPTER 4

Modeling the Models

I am so excited I do not even have a cup of coffee with me right now. This chapter takes us into a new adventure where Active Record (AR) is the focal point. This chapter will cover AR in an in-depth and pragmatic method.

Specifically, the chapter is categorized into three sections. First, you will learn how to create, save, update, and destroy an AR instance. Next up is the domain logic, where we will make our model smarter—so that it is capable of validating itself, it knows how to relate to other models, it knows what to do at a certain point in its lifecycle, and so on. The last section, "Enrichment," discusses techniques that professionals use in their day-to-day Active Record programming.

What Is a Database?

First, what is a database? Is it like a spreadsheet? An Excel file? Yeah...but only to a degree. Saying a database is similar to a spreadsheet file will draw ire from someone, yet that's a good starting point.

A database is designed to handle highly concurrent requests in the thousands. A spreadsheet program would be in chaos under the same load. In addition, a database can handle petabytes (1 million gigabytes) worth of data, whereas many spreadsheet programs can grind to halt when handling just 0.6 gigabytes of data.

Even if we manage to write code to alleviate those problems, we would be writing only part of a database system. A full-blown relational database management system (RDBMS) is comprised mainly of these four engines:

- Transport system

- Query processor

- Execution system

- Storage engine

© Adam Notodikromo 2021
A. Notodikromo, *Learn Rails 6*, https://doi.org/10.1007/978-1-4842-6026-5_4

The transport system is to accept requests (or queries) for further processing to get the best execution plan. The plan is then fed into the execution system, which merges and sorts the results of the operations happening both locally and remotely, as a database can be spread into clusters scattered the world over.

The storage engine isn't a simple system either, as it is a mix of data organizer, transaction manager, lock manager, cache manager, and recovery system.

While a database looks frightening from the inside, it is not that complicated from the outside, thanks to SQL (pronounced "sequel"; Structured Query Language), which abstracts away complexities involved with data manipulation, management, and retrieval.

Let's say we want to retrieve all female students from a database; all that is required is to send the SQL query shown in Listing 4-1.

Listing 4-1. An Example of a SQL Query

```
SELECT * FROM students
WHERE gender = "female"
```

Initializing Tandibi

Let's initialize a new social media project, code-named Tandibi. The database we will use is PostgreSQL 11, and we will pass -T because we want to install our own testing framework of choice: RSpec. See Listing 4-2.

Listing 4-2. Initializing a New Project

```
$ rails new tandibi -d postgresql -T
```

After that, let's always ensure that we are in the project's directory. To do that, we can use the cd command for Linux and macOS users. See Listing 4-3.

Listing 4-3. Changing the Current Directory to tandibi

```
$ cd tandibi
```

Then, let's add rspec-rails into the gemfile, within the development and test groups. See Listing 4-4.

Listing 4-4. Adding rspec-rails to the Project

```
group :development, :test do
  ...
  gem 'rspec-rails', '~> 3.9'
end
```

Then, run the commands in Listing 4-5 in the project's root directory.

Listing 4-5. Installing RSpec

```
$ bundle install
$ rails generate rspec:install
```

The previous command generates files necessary to integrate RSpec into our Rails app.

Note   To avoid repetition, going forward, unless stated otherwise, every command needs to be executed at the project's root directory.

Listing 4-6 shows an example of running an RSpec test command.

Listing 4-6. The Output for Running Rspec Locally

```
$ bundle exec rspec
No examples found.

Finished in 0.00242 seconds (files took 0.10296 seconds to load)
0 examples, 0 failures
```

Next, let's install Factory Bot. Factory Bot and RSpec are a match made in heaven, as we will later see. For now, let's add Factory Bot to the same group as `rspec-rails`, and then let's run `bundle install`. See Listing 4-7.

Listing 4-7. Adding factory_bot_rails into the Project

```
gem 'factory_bot_rails', '~> 5'
```

Then, let's make RSpec load all the files in the `spec/support` folder. To do so, uncomment the code in Listing 4-8 in `spec/rails_helper.rb`.

Listing 4-8. Code to Load All Support Files for RSpec

```
Dir[Rails.root.join('spec', 'support', '**', '*.rb')].each { |f| require f }
```

The spec/support folder doesn't exist by default. So, we need to create the directory by using the command in Listing 4-9.

Listing 4-9. Code to Create Nested Directory

```
$ mkdir -p spec/support
```

Then, make a new file spec/support/factory_bot.rb, and write the code in Listing 4-10.

Listing 4-10. Code to Make Factory Bot Helper Methods Available

```
RSpec.configure do |config|
  config.include FactoryBot::Syntax::Methods
end
```

Last but not least, let's add the super helpful annotate gem. It helps with writing the schema description of our models. See Listing 4-11.

Listing 4-11. Adding the annotate Gem

```
group :development do
  gem 'annotate', '~> 3'
  ...
end
```

After that, let's run the commands in Listing 4-12.

Listing 4-12. Installing annotate

```
$ bundle install
$ rails g annotate:install
```

Note   From now on, please run bundle install after adding new gems; otherwise, we won't be able to use them.

That's that. Our project is initialized!

Welcoming Our Models

The best way to start working on an app is probably by modeling or sketching the use cases and deriving the entities that make up the application.

Let's think about what a user can do in Tandibi, a social media app.

First, they definitely can sign up. Then, they can follow other users. They would be happy if they also could post their pictures, their status updates, and so on. Right?

The use case diagram shown in Figure 4-1 captures all of those requirements and more. A use case diagram represents a user's possible interactions with the system.

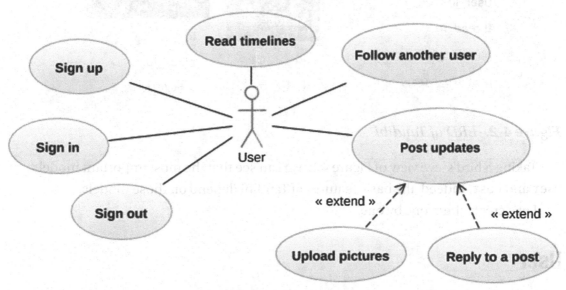

Figure 4-1. *The use cases for Tandibi*

Now, we should be able to imagine the kind of entities we need to have in order to support all of the features in the following entity-relationship diagram (ERD) shown in Figure 4-2. The ERD diagram shows the connections of things in a specific domain of knowledge and how they are interrelated.

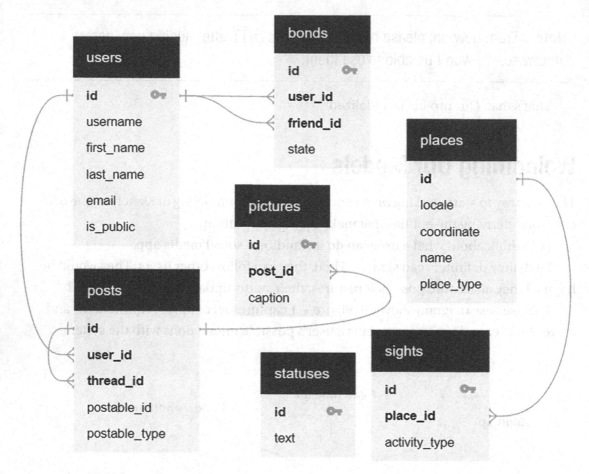

Figure 4-2. *ERD of Tandibi*

Taking a bird's-eye view of Figure 4-2, we can see that the most important models are
User and Post. Indeed, the basic features of Tandibi depend on those models.

Let's create them one by one.

User

Table 4-1 shows the schema of our User model.

Table 4-1. *User Schema*

Column	Data Type	Options
id	bigint	Primary key
username	string	Unique, non-null
first_name	string	Non-null
last_name	string	
email	string	Unique, non-null
is_public	boolean	Non-null, default: true

The command in Listing 4-13 generates a model and a migration for the model.

Listing 4-13. Command to Generate the Model and Its Migration

```
$ rails g model user username:uniq first_name \
    last_name email:uniq is_public:boolean
```

The previous command will create a migration file within the db/migrate folder. All migration files are always located there. The filename for the previous migration will be different, but it will always have the same pattern of date_class_name.rb, such as db/migrate/20200224103334_create_users.rb.

Note   By default, fields are of the string data type. Also, we don't need to list id since a model by convention always has an id.

The uniq marks that the field must be unique. So, if there is a user registered under adam@example.com, another user is prohibited from signing up with the same e-mail address.

We also want the username, first_name, email, and is_public fields to be non-nullable fields, effectively prohibiting leaving those fields blank. To do that, we add null: false to each of those fields. Let's open the newly created migration file for creating the users table in the db/migrate folder. See Listing 4-14.

Listing 4-14. Specifying Non-Nullable Fields

```
create_table :users do |t|
  t.string :username, null: false
  t.string :first_name, null: false
  t.string :last_name
  t.string :email, null: false
  t.boolean :is_public, null: false, default: true
  ...
end
```

The `is_public` field also has a `default` option. If a record is inserted into the table with this field left blank, the database assigns to it its `default` value.

Now, let's create the database and run the migration! See Listing 4-15.

Listing 4-15. Running the Migration Command

```
$ rails db:create # if the database is not yet created
$ rails db:migrate
...
Annotated (3): app/models/user.rb, spec/models/user_spec.rb, spec/
factories/users.rb
```

As we see from the previous output, some files get annotated automatically by the annotate gem. Listing 4-16 shows a snippet of the annotations.

Listing 4-16. User Model Annotated with Its Schema

```
# == Schema Information
#
# Table name: users
#
#  id     :bigint not null, primary key
#  email  :string not null
```

Nice! That way, we can check quickly what fields are in the model. Please don't forget to commit the changes to the version control system.

Bond

We use the model Bond to indicate a connection between one user and another. It has the state field to indicate the state of the connection.

Table 4-2 shows the table's schema.

Table 4-2. *Schema of Bond*

Column	Data Type	Options
id	bigint	Primary key, non-null
user_id	bigint	Foreign key (users), non-null
friend_id	bigint	Foreign key (users), non-null
state	string	Non-null

Table 4-3 shows the possible state values.

Table 4-3. *Possible Values for state*

State	Description
requesting	When a user sends a follow request to another user (which will be accepted automatically if it is a public account)
following	When a user is following another user
blocking	When a user is blocked another user

The command in Listing 4-17 generates the model and its migration for us.

Listing 4-17. Command to Scaffold Bond

```
$ rails g model bond user_id:bigint friend_id:bigint state
```

After that, let's enforce non-null constraints as shown in Listing 4-18. The file that contains this migration should be located in the same db/migrate folder. The filename should be something like {timestamp}_create_bonds.rb.

137

Listing 4-18. Setting Non-Null Constraints on Bond

```
create_table :bonds do |t|
  t.bigint :user_id, null: false
  t.bigint :friend_id, null: false
  t.string :state, null: false

  t.timestamps
end
```

Next, let's make user_id and friend_id a unique combination. This way, there is no way the table can have multiple bond records between the same user A and the same user B for those fields, respectively. See Listing 4-19.

Listing 4-19. Adding a Unique Index to bonds

```
def change
  create_table :bonds do |t|
    ...
  end

  add_index :bonds, [:user_id, :friend_id], unique: true
end
```

When a column refers to another column, it is considered a good practice to apply a *foreign key* to enforce referential integrity between the two columns.

If we look at the schema, we have both bonds.user_id and bonds.friend_id referencing users.id. So, let's add a foreign key for each of them. See Listing 4-20.

Listing 4-20. Adding Foreign Key Constraints

```
add_foreign_key :bonds,
  :users,
  column: :user_id
add_foreign_key :bonds, :users, column: :friend_id
```

After that, let's migrate and commit.

Note Any constraints, be they indexes or foreign keys, should be added after the `create_table` block.

Post

As per the use case diagram, a user can post updates in the timelines. The model `Post` represents any such updates. Table 4-4 shows the schema for the table.

Table 4-4. *Table Schema for the Post Model*

Column	Data Type	Options
id	bigint	Primary key, non-null
user_id	bigint	Foreign key (users), non-null
thread_id	bigint	Foreign key (posts)
postable_id	string	Non-null
postable_type	string	Non-null

Let's scaffold it!

```
$ rails g model post user_id:bigint thread_id:bigint \
    postable:references{polymorphic}
```

Here, we are playing around with a new toy: a polymorphic reference! For now, it suffices to say that a post can be either a *status* or a *sight* update and, therefore, polymorphic. We will talk about this in detail later in the chapter.

Last but not least, let's add foreign key constraints to the model. The file in the db/migrate folder that should contain this code is `{timestamp}_create_posts.rb`. See Listing 4-21.

Listing 4-21. Defining Foreign Key Constraints for Post

```
add_foreign_key :posts, :users, column: :user_id
add_foreign_key :posts, :posts, column: :thread_id
```

Picture

The Picture model models a picture. It stores a picture and its caption and also a pointer to the file. Its schema is as shown in Table 4-5.

Table 4-5. *Schema for Picture*

Column	Data Type	Options
id	bigint	Primary key, non-null
post_id	bigint	Foreign key (posts), non-null
caption	string	

Let's scaffold the Picture model via the command in Listing 4-22.

Listing 4-22. Command to Scaffold Picture

```
$ rails g model picture post_id:bigint caption
```

Let's not forget to add the necessary constraints in the created migration file, as shown in Listing 4-23.

Listing 4-23. Constraints for the Pictures Table

```
create_table :pictures do |t|
  ...
  t.string :caption
  t.bigint :post_id, null: false
end

add_foreign_key :pictures, :posts
```

Note As we have seen so far, we always use migrations to modify our database. Indeed, it should be the only way our schema evolves.

Status

A status is a specific type of Post. It has the schema shown in Table 4-6.

Table 4-6. *The Schema of Model Status*

Column	Data Type	Options
id	bigint	Primary key, non-null
text	string	Non-null

Listing 4-24 shows the generator command.

Listing 4-24. Command to Scaffold Status

```
$ rails g model status text
```

We also need to add a non-null constraint to the text field. See Listing 4-25.

Listing 4-25. A Non-Null Constraint on the Model Status

```
t.string :text, null: false
```

Place

Just as the name suggests, this table exists to map a coordinate to a place. We also record the locale field so that it's possible to localize the same geographical point. In this way, we can have both "Hachiko Square" and ハチ公前広場 (*Hachiko-mae Hiroba*) in the database.

Table 4-7 shows the schema for the table.

Table 4-7. *Place Schema*

Column	Data Type	Options
id	Integer	Primary key, non-null
locale	String	Non-null
coordinate	st_point	Non-null, z-coordinate geographic
name	String	Non-null
place_type	String	Non-null

Table 4-8 shows the possible values for place_type.

Table 4-8. *Enumerated Values for place_type*

Place Type	Description
restaurant	A restaurant for eating/dining
coffee_shop	A coffee shop to chill and relax
mall	A mall
hotel	A hotel
other	Other kinds of place, a generic placeholder

We are going to use PostGIS's st_point as the data type for coordinate. To do that, let's make sure Rails understands it.

Let's add activerecord-postgis-adapter into our gemfile. See Listing 4-26.

Listing 4-26. Adding activerecord-postgis-adapter

```
...
gem 'pg', '>= 0.18', '< 2.0'
gem 'activerecord-postgis-adapter', '~> 6'
...
```

Then, let's change the database from adapter to postgis. This configuration can be found in config/database.yml. See Listing 4-27.

Listing 4-27. Setting the Database adapter to use postgis

```
default: &default
  adapter: postgis
  encoding: unicode
...
```

After that, let's run the command in Listing 4-28 to set it up.

Listing 4-28. Command to Set Up the Gem

```
$ bundle install
$ bundle exec rake db:gis:setup
```

That's it. Now, let's start scaffolding the model by using the command shown in Listing 4-29.

Listing 4-29. Command to Scaffold Place

```
$ rails g model Place locale coordinate:st_point name place_type
```

Note   PostGIS seems to be the tool of choice in the community for managing spatial and geographical data. Other than using PostGIS, we may use PostgreSQL's own point data type, or even primitively store the points manually as different columns.

Then, let's add necessary constraints for the model. We also need to change something for the coordinate. See Listing 4-30.

Listing 4-30. Adding Constraints

```
create_table :places do |t|
  t.string :locale, null: false
  t.st_point :coordinate,
    geographic: true,
    has_z: true,
    null: false
  t.string :name, null: false
  t.string :place_type, null: false

  t.timestamps
end

add_index :places, :locale
add_index :places, :coordinate, using: :gist
add_index :places, [:locale, :coordinate], unique: true
```

Certain users might encounter an error when running a migration for the places table. The error is most likely because the PostGIS extension is not yet created on the database. To create the extension, let's run the command in Listing 4-31 on psql, the PostgreSQL terminal console.

Listing 4-31. Command to Create PostGIS Extension on the Database

```
$ psql tandibi_development
tandibi_development=# create extension Postgis;
tandibi_development=# \q
```

The migration file specifies a has_z option for the coordinate field. This option allows use to store the *z*-coordinate (the altitude), which is actually an optional component by default of a coordinate data type. What is a *z-coordinate*? See Figure 4-3.[1]

---

[1]Figure taken from lecture notes by Jim Lambers of the University of Southern Mississippi, https://www.math.usm.edu/lambers/mat169/fall09/lecture17.pdf

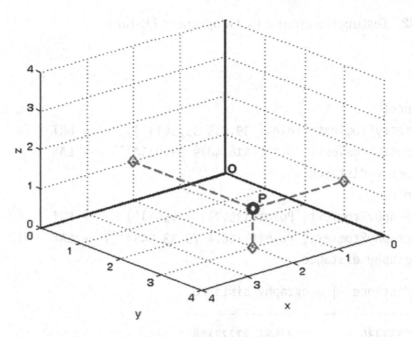

Figure 4-3. *A three-dimensional Cartesian space*

In a 3D-space Cartesian plane, we have three points in the space: the X (longitude), the Y (latitude), and the Z (altitude). Some call the *z* the *levitation* or the *elevation*. The has_z option allows us to store such an elevation point usually in meters. So, with the *z* recorded, the coordinate for point P in the space above is point (2, 3, 1), projected from the base *o*.

The geographic option is also interesting here. First, geographic coordinates are not plotted linearly unlike geometric coordinates in a Cartesian space. Rather, these spherical coordinates describe angular coordinates, and as such, their units are given in degrees.

Note   A geographic point is specified by the angle of rotation from the prime meridian (longitude, or the vertical lines on the globe) and the angle from the equator (latitude, or the horizontal lines/the parallels).

Treating geographic data as geometric can, at times, give a disturbing result. If we calculate the distance between Los Angeles to Tokyo geometrically, both cities are only 258 meters/0.16 miles apart (how inaccurate!). But, if we calculate it in geographical points, those two cities are 8,817.6 km/5,479 miles apart from each other. See Listing 4-32.

Listing 4-32. Testing Geometric vs. Geographic Distance

```
$ rails db

SELECT
  ST_Distance(
    ST_GeometryFromText('Point(139.733 35.567)'),    -- NRT
    ST_GeometryFromText('Point(-118.4079 33.9434)')  -- LAX
  ) AS geometry_distance,
  ST_Distance(
    ST_GeographyFromText('Point(139.733 35.567)'),    -- NRT
    ST_GeographyFromText('Point(-118.4079 33.9434)')  -- LAX
  ) AS geography_distance;

 geometry_distance  | geography_distance
--------------------+--------------------
 258.14600583733613 |    8833954.77277118
```

Miscalculations are not the only problem. The approximate results from indexes and true/false tests (e.g., intersections) can also suffer.

Therefore, we are using geography here so that we can accurately map points in our ellipsoidal Earth. That's not saying we cannot use geometry, though. If and only if Tandibi is used in a geographically constrained location (e.g., a city), representing the point as geometry may be preferred, since geometrical calculations are faster and simpler than their geographical equivalences.

Sight

The Sight model has an activity_type field to record whether it's checked in or checked out.

Its schema is as follows:

Column	Data Type	Options
id	Bigint	Primary key, non-null
place_id	bigint	Non-null
activity_type	string	Non-null

146

Here are the possible values for `activity_type`:

Activity Type	Description
checkin	When a user checks in on a place of interest
checkout	When a user checks out from a place of interest

Let's now scaffold the model. See Listing 4-33.

Listing 4-33. Command to Scaffold Sight

```
$ rails g model Sight place:references activity_type
```

As you can see, we can define a referential type with `references`. Doing so freed us from adding a *foreign key* constraint manually. Also, the model will have a `belongs_to` relationship written for us.

However, we still need to ensure that `activity_type` is not-nullable. See Listing 4-34.

Listing 4-34. Constraint to Ensure activity_type Is Not Nullable

```
t.string :activity_type, null: false
```

Fundamental Techniques

In this section, we are going to learn the most fundamental techniques one needs to know when working with Active Record, arguably one of the best things since sliced bread. Active Record allows us to laconically communicate with the database using pure Ruby.

Defining a Model

Active Record maps a table to a class, a row to an object, and a column to an attribute with as little code as possible, making them what is known as a *model*.

To define a model, we just need to create a Ruby class named after the singular name of the table we want to map, as the table is always in plural noun. After that, the class needs to inherit from the `ActiveRecord::Base` class.

Let's say we have a users table. We can create a model for that table as shown in Listing 4-35.

Listing 4-35. A Simple Model Class

```
class User < ActiveRecord::Base
end
```

The User class immediately gains a lot of ability without us having to write any other code. Those with the most fundamental capabilities are going to be demonstrated in this section.

Initializing a Record

We can initialize an AR model the same way we initialize any Ruby class: by using new. See Listing 4-36.

Listing 4-36. Initializing a Model

```
irb(main):001:0> user = User.new
=> #<User id: nil, username: nil, first_name: nil, last_name: nil, email:
nil, is_public: true, created_at: nil, updated_at: nil>
```

We can also pass a hash when initializing. See Listing 4-37.

Listing 4-37. Initializing with an Initial Value

```
irb(main):002:0> user = User.new(first_name: "Scott")
=> #<User id: nil, username: nil, first_name: "Scott", last_name: nil,
email: nil, is_public: true, created_at: nil, updated_at: nil>
```

To differentiate whether an instance has been saved or not, we can call new_record?. See Listing 4-38.

Listing 4-38. Checking If the Instance Is Still Newish

```
irb(main):003:0> user.new_record?
=> true
```

Saving and Updating Data

save is used to persist the data, either by creating it or by updating it. See Listing 4-39.

Listing 4-39. Inserting a New Record Using Save

```
irb(main):001:0> user = User.new(
irb(main):002:1* username: "scott12",
irb(main):003:1* first_name: "Scott",
irb(main):004:1* email: "scott@example.com")
=> #<User id: nil, username: "scott12", first_name: "Scott", last_name:
nil, email: "scott@example.com", is_public: true, created_at: nil, updated_
at: nil>
irb(main):005:0> user.save
  (0.1ms)  BEGIN
  User Create (11.9ms)  INSERT INTO "users" ("username", "first_name",
  "email", "created_at", "updated_at") VALUES ($1, $2, $3, $4, $5)
  RETURNING "id"  [["username", "scott12"], ["first_name", "Scott"],
  ["email", "scott@example.com"], ["created_at", "2020-02-26
  00:30:02.652262"], ["updated_at", "2020-02-26 00:30:02.652262"]]
  (2.0ms)  COMMIT
=> true
```

save returns true if saving is successful. Otherwise, it returns false.

We can also send it a save! method (a save variant with a bang), which, instead of returning a Boolean, it raises an error if saving fails. See Listing 4-40.

Listing 4-40. Calling save! on an Invalid Record

```
irb(main):006:0> User.new.save!
  (0.3ms) BEGIN
  User Create (1.2ms) INSERT INTO "users" ("created_at", "updated_at")
  VALUES ($1, $2) RETURNING "id" [["created_at", "2020-02-26
  00:34:07.581390"], ["updated_at", "2020-02-26 00:34:07.581390"]]
  (0.2ms) ROLLBACK
```

```
Traceback (most recent call last):
        1: from (irb):6
ActiveRecord::NotNullViolation (PG::NotNullViolation: ERROR: null value in
column "username" violates not-null constraint)
DETAIL: Failing row contains (3, null, null, null, null, t, 2020-02-26
00:34:07.58139, 2020-02-26 00:34:07.58139).
```

As shown in the previous snippet, we were unable to save! a record since the
username was nil.

On top of save, there's also a method for initializing and saving at once, which is
called create (and create!). See Listing 4-41.

Listing 4-41. Using create! to Initialize and Save a Record

```
irb(main):007:0> user = User.create!(
irb(main):008:1* username: "saveav",
irb(main):009:1* first_name: "Adam",
irb(main):010:1* email: "adam@example.com"
irb(main):011:1> )
...
=> #<User id: 4, username: "saveav", first_name: "Adam", last_name: nil,
email: "adam@example.com", is_public: true, created_at: "2020-02-26
00:37:58", updated_at: "2020-02-26 00:37:58">
```

As shown in the previous code, we don't need to call new and save to create the
record. It returns the object with an id to indicate that it's persisted.

All persisted objects will respond true to a persisted? call. See Listing 4-42.

Listing 4-42. Checking Whether an Instance Is Persisted

```
irb(main):012:0> user.persisted?
=> true
```

If we call save on a persisted record, instead of sending an INSERT statement, an
UPDATE query is going to be sent. See Listing 4-43.

Listing 4-43. Updating a Record by Calling Save

```
irb(main):013:0> user.last_name
=> nil
irb(main):014:0> user.last_name = "Smith"
=> "Smith"
irb(main):015:0> user.save
  (0.2ms)  BEGIN
  User Update (3.1ms)  UPDATE "users" SET "last_name" = $1, "updated_at" =
  $2 WHERE "users"."id" = $3  [["last_name", "Smith"], ["updated_at",
  "2020-02-26 00:41:08.089457"], ["id", 4]]
  (3.0ms)  COMMIT
=> true
irb(main):016:0> user.last_name
=> "Smith"
```

So far, we have been saving a pretty simple model. Some model, however, has relationships with other models. But don't worry, saving such a model is just as easy.

Let's demonstrate persisting a `Sight` instance, which has a relationship with a `Place`. Let's first create a `Place` record. See Listing 4-44.

Listing 4-44. Creating a Place Record

```
irb(main):017:0> place = Place.new(locale: "en", name: "Wall Street",
place_type: "other")
=> #<Place id: nil, locale: "en", coordinate: nil, name: "Wall Street",
place_type: "other", created_at: nil, updated_at: nil>
irb(main):018:0> place.coordinate = "POINT (40.706005 -74.008827 0)"
=> "POINT (40.706005 -74.008827 0)"
irb(main):019:0> place.save
```

Then, let's initialize a new Sight record. See Listing 4-45.

Listing 4-45. Initializing a New Sight

```
irb(main):019:0> sight = Sight.new(activity_type: "check_in")
=> #<Sight id: nil, place_id: nil, activity_type: "check_in", created_at:
nil, updated_at: nil>
```

Then, we assign place with the Place instance we just created earlier. Notice that there's nothing special with the assignment here—same old same old. See Listing 4-46.

Listing 4-46. Assigning the Place

```
irb(main):020:0> sight.place = place
=> #<Place id: 2, locale: "en", coordinate: #<RGeo::Geographic::Spherical
PointImpl ...>
```

To save the record, we just need to send the same save method on the object. See Listing 4-47.

Listing 4-47. Saving an Instance Having an Association with Another Nodel

```
irb(main):021:0> sight.save
  (0.2ms)  BEGIN
  Sight Create (6.6ms)  INSERT INTO "sights" ...
  (1.2ms)  COMMIT
=> true
```

That's it! There's really no differences at all between saving a simple object and saving one that has relationships to other models.

As we can see, save can be used both to insert a new record or to update existing ones. Whether a record is plain and simple or it holds relationships, save, for the record (no pun intended), can save it just fine.

Rails also has an update method that we can use against a persisted record to change its attributes' values and then save the record. This way, we don't have to manually assign the field. Let's see the code in Listing 4-48 for comparison.

Listing 4-48. Updating a Place's Name Using Save

```
irb(main):022:0> place.name = "Wall St."
=> "Wall St."
irb(main):023:0> place.save
=> true
```

Listing 4-49 shows the equivalent code using the update method.

Listing 4-49. Updating a Record Using the Update Method

```
irb(main):024:0> place.update name: "Wall St."
=> true
```

Note   The POINT (120 120) format is known as *well-known text* (WKT). Internally, the database stores geometry data in a *well-known binary* (WKB) format, which is comprised of hex digits. For example, the WKT representation shown previously is represented in WKB as 01010000000000000000005E400000000000005E40. In PostGIS, we can use ST_AsText and ST_GeomFromText to convert between the two formats.

Finding Data

First, there are two ways to retrieve data from the database: find and where. We can find an exact match using find, by giving it an argument that is the record's ID. See Listing 4-50.

Listing 4-50. Retrieving a Record by Passing the Record's ID

```
irb(main):001:0> User.find(1)
  User Load (0.7ms)  SELECT "users".* FROM "users" ...
=> #<User id: 1, username: "scott12", first_name: "Scott", last_name:
nil, email: "scott@example.com", is_public: true, created_at: "2020-02-26
00:30:02", updated_at: "2020-02-26 00:30:02">
```

We can also find a record based on other fields. See Listing 4-51.

Listing 4-51. Finding a Record Based on the User's E-mail Address

```
irb(main):002:0> User.find_by_email("scott@example.com")
=> #<User id: 1, username: "scott12", first_name: "Scott", last_name: nil,
email: "scott@example.com" ...>
```

We may also pass in a hash instead. See Listing 4-52.

Listing 4-52. Finding a Record Through Filters Defined in a Hash

```
irb(main):003:0> User.find_by(email: "scott@example.com")
=> #
irb(main):004:0> User.find_by(email: "scott@example.com", is_public: false)
=> nil
```

find_by and the find_by_{field_name} variant return nil if the record couldn't be found, which is in stark contrast to find, which raises an error instead. See Listing 4-53.

Listing 4-53. find_by Does Not Raises an Error If the Record Is Missing

```
irb(main):005:0> User.find_by_id(666)
=> nil
irb(main):006:0> User.find(666)
Traceback (most recent call last):
        1: from (irb):11
ActiveRecord::RecordNotFound (Couldn't find User with 'id'=666)
```

Unlike find, where always returns an enumerable object (an ActiveRecord::Relation instance to be precise). If no record is found, an empty collection is returned instead of nil. See Listing 4-54.

Listing 4-54. Retrieving a Collection of Records Using where

```
irb(main):007:0> User.where(is_public: false)
=> #<ActiveRecord::Relation []>
```

We can pass in an array as the filtering value, which returns records satisfying any of the array's values. See Listing 4-55.

Listing 4-55. Retrieving Records with an id of Either 1 or 4

```
irb(main):008:0> User.where(id: [1, 4])
=> #<ActiveRecord::Relation [#<User id: 1 ...>, #<User id: 4 ...>]>
```

We can even provide a range. See Listing 4-56.

Listing 4-56. Retrieving Records Within the Range

```
irb(main):009:0> User.where(created_at: 1.day.ago..Time.current)
=> #<ActiveRecord::Relation [#<User id: 1 ...>, #<User id: 4 ...>]>
```

Of course, we can also use multiple variables to filter. See Listing 4-57.

Listing 4-57. Selecting Data Using Multiple Variables

```
irb(main):010:0> User.where(is_public: true, created_at: 1.day.ago..Time.
current)
=> #<ActiveRecord::Relation [#<User id: 1 ...>, #<User id: 4 ...>]>
```

As we can see over and over again, where returns an `ActiveRecord::Relation`. This instance is a collection, so it responds to each, map, and those methods commonly found in an enumerable class. But, the most important thing is that this instance allows us to chain queries together to form a complex query, as we will see throughout this book.

As an enumerable type, we can iterate, map, and peek into the `ActiveRecord::Relation` instance in the same way as if we were dealing with an array. See Listing 4-58.

Listing 4-58. Fetching Data on a Specific Index in the Collection

```
irb(main):011:0> users = User.where(is_public: true, created_at: 1.day.
ago..Time.current)
=> #<ActiveRecord::Relation [#<User id: 1 ...>, #<User id: 4 ...>]>
irb(main):012:0> users[0] == users.first
=> true
irb(main):013:0> users[-1] == users.last
=> true
```

Sometimes, we may want to use a logical or instead of the default logical and. See Listing 4-59.

Listing 4-59. Selecting Data Using Logical or

```
irb(main):014:0> User.where(first_name: "Adam").or(User.where(first_name:
"Scott"))
=> #<ActiveRecord::Relation [#<User id: 1 ...>, #<User id: 4 ...>]>
```

We can also send a query using `where.not`, which retrieves a collection of data not matching the query. See Listing 4-60.

Listing 4-60. Using where.not to Filter Data

```
irb(main):015:0> User.where.not(first_name: "Adam")
=> #<ActiveRecord::Relation [#<User id: 1 ...>]>
```

There are times when we need to write SQL code, such as when the query is very database-specific. In that case, we can pass in a string as an argument to `where`. See Listing 4-61.

Listing 4-61. Using SQL to Fetch the Data

```
irb(main):016:0> User.where("first_name ILIKE :search AND is_public = :is_
public", {search: '%scott%', is_public: true})
=> #<ActiveRecord::Relation [#<User id: 1 ...>]>
```

However, we must be extremely careful in doing so, as this opens the door to SQL injection attacks. SQL injection is a code injection technique used by hackers to manipulate a query, resulting in them being able to access or steal data.

To avoid a SQL injection attack, we should put in placeholders instead of interpolating the values in the string. The actual values are then given as a hash for the second argument, which AR will sanitize, ensuring that those values won't compromise the database system.

Finally, the return value of `where` can be chained with another `where` or with AR scopes for further filtering. We will talk about *scope* in the "Enrichment" section. See Listing 4-62.

Listing 4-62. ActiveRecord::Relation Can Be Chained for Further Filtering

```
irb(main):017:0> User.where(is_public: true).where(created_at: 5.days.ago..
Time.current    )
```

Deleting Data

There are two ways to delete records from a table. The first is by using `delete`, and the second one is by using `destroy`.

The delete method removes a row immediately, without performing any callbacks on the object they are deleting, unlike destroy. So, delete can be dangerous and should be used seldomly. We will talk about callback shortly, but for now, we can think of it as code that gets called automatically when a certain event happens, for example, data deletion. See Listing 4-63.

Listing 4-63. Deleting a Record Using Delete

```
irb(main):001:0> data = {first_name: "Finn", username: "f", email:
"f@e.org"}
=> {:first_name=>"Finn", :username=>"f", :email=>"f@e.org"}
irb(main):002:0> user = User.create(data)
=> #<User id: 6, username: "f" ...>
irb(main):003:0> user.delete
  User Destroy (17.6ms)  DELETE FROM "users" WHERE "users"."id" =
  $1  [["id", 6]]
=> #<User id: 6, username: "f" ...>
irb(main):004:0> user.persisted?
=> false
```

To use destroy, just change delete to destroy. See Listing 4-64.

Listing 4-64. Deleting a Record Using destroy

```
irb(main):005:0> user = User.create(data)
=> #<User id: 7, username: "f" ...>
irb(main):006:0> user.destroy
=> #<User id: 7, username: "f" ...>
irb(main):007:0> user.persisted?
=> false
```

There is also delete_all and destroy_all that can be called on an Active Record collection to delete all the records in that collection. To reiterate, it's usually preferable to use destroy rather than delete.

Detecting Changes

We can ask an instance for fields that have been modified from its initial value. Just call the changes method. See Listing 4-65.

Listing 4-65. Tracking the Changed Fields

```
irb(main):001:0> data = {first_name: "Finn", username: "f", email:
"f@e.org"}
irb(main):002:0> user = User.create(data)
irb(main):003:0> user.last_name = "Firing"
=> "Firing"
irb(main):004:0> user.changes
=> {"last_name"=>[nil, "Firing"]}
```

We can also check whether a specific field has been changed. See Listing 4-66.

Listing 4-66. Detecting Changes on the Field using the _changed? Method

```
irb(main):005:0> user.username = "thefinn"
=> "thefinn"
irb(main):006:0> user.username_changed?
=> true
irb(main):007:0> user.email_changed?
=> false
```

We can also ask for the original value using {field}_was. See Listing 4-67.

Listing 4-67. Finding Out the Original Value of a Field

```
irb(main):008:0> user.username_was
=> "f"
```

The {field}_changed? and {field}_was methods are sometimes used for data validation or when deciding whether a callback should be executed. See Listing 4-68.

Listing 4-68. Dirty Methods in Action

```
validate :some_validation, if: :balance_changed?

def some_validation
  return if balance_was > 1000 || balance > 1000
  errors.add(:balance, "too low")
end
```

Transactional Block

The term *transaction* refers to a block of SQL statements that must be executed together, or should any error occur, none at all. It effectively turns a group of statements into one atomic, irreducible operation.

For example, let's say we are writing code to transfer money from one account to another like Listing 4-69.

Listing 4-69. Code to Transfer Money from adam to bryan

```
adam.withdraw!(some_amount)
bryan.deposit!(some_amount)
```

At first glance, this might not seem like a potentially unsafe set of queries. But, what if Adam's withdrawal is successful, yet we were unable to deposit the money to Bryan's bank account? In a scenario like this, it is sensible to make those operations atomic.

To do so, we can use the `transaction` method defined in the `ActiveRecord::Transaction` module. This method takes a block that, when invoked, will run the operations within the boundary of a database transaction. The safer form of the previous code looks like Listing 4-70.

Listing 4-70. Wrapping Inside a Transaction Block for Safety

```
ActionRecord::Base.transaction do
  adam.withdraw!(some_amount)
  bryan.deposit!(some_amount)
end
```

However, we must not assume that all database systems have support for `transaction`, although popular ones such as PostgreSQL, MySQL, MS-SQL, Oracle, and various others do.

It is also important to realize that a transaction block must target the specific database connection. In a case where there are multiple databases, we must call `transaction` on the model, instead of on `ActiveRecord::Base`.

Let's suppose we have two models, `Order` and `Vendor`, connected to a different database. In some operations, as shown in Listing 4-71, it is desirable that they work together as one atomic transaction.

Listing 4-71. Nested Transactions

```
Order.transaction do
  order.secure_items!

  Vendor.transaction(requires_new: true) do
    order.vendors.each(&:order_items!)
  end

  unless order.vendors.all_secured?
    raise ActiveRecord::Rollback
  end

  user.charge
end
```

In the previous code, if an error is raised by any vendor, AR will roll back changes on both models. For that to happen, we passed in the `requires_new: true` option. Otherwise, since `ActiveRecord::Rollback` does not propagate, the supposedly rolled-back changes might get dumped to the parent transaction and get committed from there, especially if both models connect to the same database connection.

Note   Although I have seen a lot of transaction blocks, none of them has been a nested transaction.

Domain Logics

Models are one of the centerpieces of a web app. Models, therefore, are often enhanced by adding domain logic, which includes the likes of validations, associations, callbacks, and custom methods. We will talk about all of those in this section.

Validations and Errors

Invalid records are the source of many problems. Imagine what happens if a user registers using an invalid e-mail address. We wouldn't be able to send them an e-mail! Fortunately, Rails provide no-brainer data validation macros that we can use to guard against such things.

Validating Data Uniqueness

We can use the uniqueness validator to ensure that a field is unique throughout the table. Listing 4-72 shows the basic form of the validation.

Listing 4-72. Validating Uniqueness of a Given Field

```
validates :field_name, uniqueness: true
```

It looks simple enough, right?

But first, before we add a validation, let's write our first test at spec/models/user_spec.rb. RSpec is going to be the test framework we use. It is one of the most widely used frameworks for testing Ruby apps. It has the basic structures shown in Listing 4-73.

Listing 4-73. Basic Testing Code

```
RSpec.describe TheClassToTest do
  describe "#the_method_to_test" do
    it "describes the intended behavior" do
      # test codes...
    end
  end
end
```

Of course, there can be as many describe blocks as we want and as many it blocks in the file as we want. The describe block is usually used to describe a method in the class to test. If we want to describe a specific condition, we may extract it to a context block. See Listing 4-74.

Listing 4-74. Using the Context Block

```
describe "#save" do
  context "when the data is invalid" do
    it "does not save the data" do
      # test codes
    end
  end
end
```

Simple right? Now, let's write our first test code. In spec/models/user_spec.rb, let's add the code in Listing 4-75.

Listing 4-75. Spec to Check the Validity of a User Instance

```
RSpec.describe User, type: :model do
  def create_a_user(email: "#{SecureRandom.hex(4)}@example.org")
    User.create!(
      first_name: "Adam",
      email: email,
      username: SecureRandom.hex(4),
    )
  end

  describe "#valid?" do
    it "is valid when email is unique" do
      create_a_user

      user = User.new
      user.email = "adam@example.org"
      expect(user.valid?).to be true
    end
  end
end
```

Now, let's run the spec. See Listing 4-76.

Listing 4-76. Running the Spec in the Terminal

```
$ rspec spec/models/user_spec.rb
.

Finished in 0.01442 seconds (files took 1.5 seconds to load)
1 example, 0 failures
```

Woo-hoo! We just wrote our first spec! Next, we want to preclude different accounts from having the same e-mail address. Listing 4-77 shows the spec for that.

Listing 4-77. Spec to Ensure E-mail Address Is Unique

```
describe "#valid?" do
  ...
  it "is invalid if the email is taken" do
    create_a_user(email: "adam@example.org")

    user = User.new
    user.email = "adam@example.org"
    expect(user).not_to be_valid
  end
end
```

Notice that the expectation code shown previously reads more naturally than the previous one. We used be_valid instead of checking User#valid?. The be_{method} eventually calls the question mark–terminated method on the expect-ed instance. In other words, be_valid calls valid? on the object, such that the expected code is equivalent to Listing 4-78.

Listing 4-78. Alternative Writing, But May Not Be Natural to Read

```
expect(user.valid?).not_to be true
```

Now if we run our spec, we will notice that it fails a test. See Listing 4-79.

Listing 4-79. Running RSpec

```
$ rspec spec/models/user_spec.rb
.F
```

Listing 4-80 shows the error.

Listing 4-80. Expectation Errors

```
Failure/Error: expect(user).not_to be_valid
  expected # not to be valid
# ./spec/models/user_spec.rb:44:in `block (3 levels) in <top (required)>'
```

RSpec expected that the model isn't valid, but it is. Time to fix it up! Open the User model, and add the validation shown in Listing 4-81.

Listing 4-81. Adding the Necessary Uniqueness Validation for E-mail Address

```
class User < ApplicationRecord
  validates :email, uniqueness: true
end
```

Now, if we test the model again, it will all be green! See Listing 4-82.

Listing 4-82. Running RSpec

```
$ rspec spec/models/user_spec.rb
..

Finished in 0.03945 seconds (files took 1.51 seconds to load)
2 examples, 0 failures
```

This process of development is called *test-driven development* (TDD), where we begin with writing test codes and only then write the smallest amount of code necessary to make the test pass.

A good test suite should adhere to the FIRST principle:

- *Fast*: It should run quickly to enable the developer to detect problems faster.

- *Independent*: A test should not depend on another test so that we can test them in isolation.

- *Repeatable*: Not every day is Monday; a test should be able to run 24/7, in any condition, to test the same thing.

- *Self-validating*: It should avoid the need for a human to verify whether it succeeds.

- *Timely*: A test should be written about the same time as the code under test to reduce the tendency of writing code that is difficult to test or ends up too complicated.

Other than an e-mail, we should also validate that the username is unique. Please add the necessary spec and code for that. Hint: we need to add the same validator but change :email to :username.

If you would like to know how to do that, Listing 4-83 shows a snippet for the spec.

Listing 4-83. Spec for Validating Username

```
it "is invalid if the username is taken" do
  user = create(:user)
  another_user = create(:user)

  expect(another_user).to be_valid
  another_user.username = user.username
  expect(another_user).not_to be_valid
end
```

Listing 4-84 shows the validation code, to be put in the User model.

Listing 4-84. Validating Username

```
validates :email, uniqueness: true
validates :username, uniqueness: true
```

Validating Data Existence

Let's make sure our user must enter their first name. For that, we are going to use a presence *validator*. The basic form of the validation code is as follows:

```
validates :field_name, uniqueness: true
```

Let's begin by writing the spec for user_spec.rb, as shown in Listing 4-85.

Listing 4-85. Test to Validate the Presence of first_name

```
it "is invalid if user's first name is blank" do
  user = create_a_user
  expect(user).to be_valid

  user.first_name = ""
  expect(user).not_to be_valid

  user.first_name = nil
  expect(user).not_to be_valid
end
```

Now if we run the spec file, we will see a failing case. See Listing 4-86.

Listing 4-86. Running RSpec

```
$ rspec spec/models/user_spec.rb
...F

Failures:

  1) User#valid? is invalid if user's first name is blank
     Failure/Error: expect(user).not_to be_valid
```

To fix that, let's add the validation for first_name. See Listing 4-87.

Listing 4-87. Validating the Presence of first_name

```
class User < ApplicationRecord
...
  validates :first_name, presence: true
end
```

Now, if we test the spec again, we made the last test green, but we upset another test. See Listing 4-88.

Listing 4-88. Running RSpec

```
$ rspec spec/models/user_spec.rb
F...
```

Failures:

```
  1) User#valid? is valid when email is unique
     Failure/Error: expect(user.valid?).to be true

       expected true
            got false
     # ./spec/models/user_spec.rb:36:in `block (3 levels) in <top (required)>'
```

The offending line seems to be line 36. So, let's go there to check it! See Listing 4-89.

Listing 4-89. Snippet of Line 36

```
user = User.new
user.email = "adam@example.org"
expect(user.valid?).to be true
```

We can see that we initialized a User and assigned it some value, but we left out the first_name field, and because of that, the record is invalid.

Let's fix it by changing the previous code to look like Listing 4-90.

Listing 4-90. Replacement for the Failing Spec

```
user1 = create_a_user
user2 = create_a_user

expect(user2.email).not_to be user1.email
expect(user2).to be_valid
```

Now, our tests should pass!

It's safe to assume that a non-nullable column should need this kind of validation. So, let's implement the validations for the remaining non-null fields on other models. Table 4-9 lists the remaining non-nullable fields that we must validate.

Table 4-9. *Non-nullable Fields in the App*

Model	Non-nullable Field
Bond	state
Place	coordinate
	locale
	name
Sight	activity_type
Status	text
User	username

It's really is simply to validate each of those fields, just like how we did for fields we already validate for its presence so far. For example, for Sight#activity_type, we can just open the model class and add the validation in Listing 4-91.

Listing 4-91. Adding Presence Validation for activity_type

```
class Sight < ApplicationRecord
  validates :activity_type, presence: true
end
```

Now, please do the same for the rest of the fields. If you are unsure how, please feel free to consult the source code of this chapter.

Restricting Possible Value

Some fields can only be parochial in the values they can accept, and validates inclusion is used precisely for that. Listing 4-92 shows its basic usage.

Listing 4-92. Basic Usage of the inclusion Validator

```
validates :field_name, inclusion: { in: valid_values_array }
```

For example, the value of activity_type from the Sight model can either be only checkin or checkout, as shown in Table 4-10.

Table 4-10. *Acceptable Values for Sight#activity_type*

Activity Type	Description
checkin	When a user checks in at a place of interest
checkout	When a user checks out from a place of interest

A more involved example is the place_type of model Place, which is allowed to accept only one of the values shown in Table 4-11.

Table 4-11. *Acceptable place_type for Model Place*

Place Type	Description
restaurant	A restaurant for eating/dining
coffee_shop	A coffee shop to chill and relax
mall	A mall
hotel	A hotel
other	Other kind of place, a generic placeholder

For now, first let's add the necessary validation for Sight#activity_type, for which the spec file would be spec/models/sight_spec.rb. See Listing 4-93.

Listing 4-93. Spec for Validating Sight#activity_type

```
RSpec.describe Sight, type: :model do
  describe "#valid?" do
    it "should validate activity type correctly" do
      sight = Sight.new(place: Place.new)

      sight.activity_type = "unknown"
      expect(sight).not_to be_valid
```

```
    ["checkin", "checkout"].each do |type|
      sight.activity_type = type
      expect(sight).to be_valid
    end
  end
end
end
```

If we run the spec, it will fail as expected. See Listing 4-94.

Listing 4-94. Running RSpec

```
$ rspec spec/models/sight_spec.rb
F

Failures:

  1) Sight#valid? should validate activity type correctly
     Failure/Error: expect(sight).not_to be_valid
```

Let's make it pass. First, let's define a frozen array for the possible states in the Sight model. See Listing 4-95.

Listing 4-95. Possible Values for the Activity Type

```
ACTIVITY_TYPES = [
  CHECKIN = "checkin",
  CHECKOUT = "checkout"
].freeze
```

After that, we can use it to validate against `activity_type`, as shown in Listing 4-96.

Listing 4-96. Validation for the Acceptable Value for Activity Type

```
validates :activity_type, inclusion: { in: ACTIVITY_TYPES }
```

Now if we run the spec again, all is green.

Should we also implement inclusion validation for `Place#place_type` and `Bond#state`? Yes!

Listing 4-97 shows the validation for Place#place_type.

Listing 4-97. Validation for Place#place_type

```
class Place < ApplicationRecord
  PLACE_TYPES = [
    "restaurant",
    "coffee_shop",
    "mall",
    "hotel",
    "other",
  ].freeze

  ...
  validates :place_type, inclusion: { in: PLACE_TYPES }
end
```

Listing 4-98 shows the validation for Bond#bond_state.

Listing 4-98. Validation for Bond#state

```
class Bond < ApplicationRecord
  STATES = [
    REQUESTING = "requesting",
    FOLLOWING = "following",
    BLOCKING = "blocking",
  ].freeze

  validates :state, inclusion: { in: STATES }
end
```

It's simple and pretty regular. There's another related technique that is known as enum. We will talk about enum in the "Enrichment" section in this chapter.

Lastly, let's create a spec to test the validity for Bond#state as shown in Listing 4-99. The spec file is spec/models/bond_spec.rb that we need to create.

Listing 4-99. Spec for Bond

```
RSpec.describe Bond, type: :model do
  describe "#valid?" do
    it "should validate the state correctly" do
      friend = User.new
      user = User.new

      bond = Bond.new(
        user: user,
        friend: friend
      )

      expect(bond).not_to be_valid

      Bond::STATES.each do |state|
        bond.state = state
        expect(bond).to be_valid
      end
    end
  end
end
```

Validating Data Conformity

We can use the format validator to make sure a field conforms to a certain regular expression pattern. If the regex (regular expression) pattern failed to match, the validation would fail. Listing 4-100 shows its basic usage.

Listing 4-100. Basic Usage of validates Format

```
validates :field_name, format: { with: /string_pattern/ }
```

We can use this validator to check that an e-mail address at least looks valid. So, let's do that. Let's validate that our user's e-mail address at least looks valid.

Note E-mail validation using a regular expression is not 100 percent foolproof since an e-mail may look valid but the mail server might not recognize the address. There needs to be an e-mail confirmation stage, where we ensure that a given e-mail address is valid.

As is the norm so far, let's begin with writing a spec first. The file for the spec is spec/models/user_spec.rb since we are going to write a validation for User#email. See Listing 4-101.

Listing 4-101. A Spec for Validating E-mail Address

```
it "is invalid if the email looks bogus" do
  user = create_a_user
  expect(user).to be_valid

  user.email = ""
  expect(user).to be_invalid

  user.email = "foo.bar"
  expect(user).to be_invalid

  user.email = "foo.bar#example.com"
  expect(user).to be_invalid

  user.email = "f.o.o.b.a.r@example.com"
  expect(user).to be_valid

  user.email = "foo+bar@example.com"
  expect(user).to be_valid

  user.email = "foo.bar@sub.example.co.id"
  expect(user).to be_valid
end
```

Now, let's run the spec. See Listing 4-102.

Listing 4-102. Running an RSpec Test

```
$ bundle exec rspec
```

We can see the output in Listing 4-103.

Listing 4-103. Failure Report When Running the Spec

```
1) User#valid? is invalid if the email looks bogus
   Failure/Error: expect(user).to be_invalid
```

It failed. That's great! Let's make it green!

To make it green, we will make use of a regular expression (regex). An example of regular expression is \d+, which might look alien if you have never seen this expression before.

So, what is a regex?

A regular expression is a generalized way to find (and optionally, extract) patterns in a text. The previous pattern, \d+, can be used to match any digits forming the sequence of a string. The plus symbol indicates that such a sequence must be at least one character long.

Usually, we can try a regex in our IDE of choice. Let's try it! In Visual Studio Code, we can create a new file (Ctrl+N) and then add the text in Listing 4-104 to the file.

Listing 4-104. Text Containing Numbers

```
My phone number is 08012345678. I have 2 brothers. They are 10 years apart
from each other. My room number is R30.
```

After that, let's press Ctrl+F so that we can find something in the text. In the Finder dialog, click the Use Regular Expression icon that has .* on it. After that, type in this expression: \d+. See Figure 4-4.

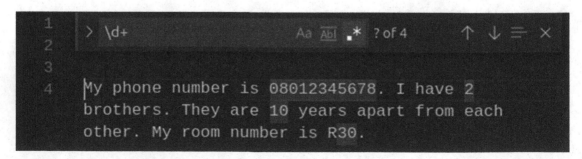

Figure 4-4. *Finding numbers in text using a regular expression*

As shown in Figure 4-4, the text editor found strings matching the regular expression. Cool, right?

Now, when validating the user's e-mail address, we will use a regular expression given by the Web Hypertext Application Technology Working Group, as shown in Listing 4-105.

Listing 4-105. Regular Expression for Validating an E-mail Address

```
/^[a-zA-Z0-9.!#$%&'*+\/=?^_`{|}~-]+@[a-zA-Z0-9](?:[a-zA-Z0-9-]{0,61}
[a-zA-Z0-9])?(?:\.[a-zA-Z0-9](?:[a-zA-Z0-9-]{0,61}[a-zA-Z0-9])?)*$/
```

Luckily, we don't have to write that regex by hand. The same value is stored as a constant called `URI::MailTo::EMAIL_REGEXP` in Ruby. So, let's use it. See Listing 4-106.

Listing 4-106. Validating the Format of an E-mail with a Given Pattern

```
validates :email, format: { with: URI::MailTo::EMAIL_REGEXP }
```

Now, if we run our spec again, everything should be green by now.

Other Validation Techniques

There are other validators that you may see from time to time, such as numericality, length, and some others, which are summarized in Appendix. But, what if a validation we want to add has specific logic that cannot be expressed by the built-in validators?

Fortunately, using the `validate` macro, we can write custom logic to validate a record. Listing 4-107 shows an example of how to write custom logic for validation. Surely, we don't need to add this code anywhere in our codebase as this is just an example of how to use validate.

Listing 4-107. Example of Custom Logic for Validation

```
validate :must_not_be_underage

def must_not_be_underage
  age = birthday.year - Time.current.year
  return if age < 18

  errors.add(:base, "must be at least 17 years old")
end
```

As we can see, we just need to write a method that does whatever is necessary for validating our record. After that, we use validate and specify the method's name as a symbol.

If the error cannot be associated with any attribute, the error should be added to the :base. Otherwise, the error can be associated with a field. See Listing 4-108.

Listing 4-108. Validating That a Password Must Not Be Recycled

```
validate :password_never_be_used_before

def password_never_be_used_before
  return if PastPassword.where(
    user: self,
    hashed_password: Digest::MD5.hexdigest(password),
  ).blank?

  errors.add(:password, "must be a new combination")
end
```

By default, validation happens before we create or update a record. We can also enforce validation only on a specific lifecycle, for example, only when the object is created for the first time, by adding an on: :create option. See Listing 4-109.

Listing 4-109. Doing Validation on a Specific Lifecycle

```
validates :first_name, presence: true, on: :create
validates :last_name, presence: true, on: :update
```

Investigating Errors

By invoking *errors* on a model's instance, we can get an ActiveModel::Errors object to investigate the invalid fields. See Listing 4-110.

Listing 4-110. Checking the Errors of an Instance

```
irb(main):001:0> u = User.new(email: "re@example.com")
irb(main):002:0> u.valid?
irb(main):003:0> u.errors
=> #<ActiveModel::Errors:0x00007fffc4890dc0 @base=#<User id: nil,
username: nil, first_name: nil, last_name: nil, email: "re@example.com",
```

is_public: true, created_at: nil, updated_at: nil>, @messages={:first_
name=>["can't be blank"], :username=>["can't be blank"]}, @details={:first_
name=>[{:error=>:blank}], :username=>[{:error=>:blank}]}>

The most commonly used method for debugging is probably full_messages, which lists the errors in a readable format. See Listing 4-111.

Listing 4-111. Finding the Errors in a Readable Format

```
irb(main):004:0> u.errors.full_messages
=> ["First name can't be blank", "Username can't be blank"]
```

The error message can also be customized.

Let's recall the time when we validated the user's e-mail address. Rails does not know that we are validating an e-mail. As a result, if the e-mail validation fails, the error message sounds very generic. See Listing 4-112.

Listing 4-112. The Error Message When the E-mail Is Invalid

```
irb(main):005:0> u.errors.full_messages
=> ["Email is invalid"]
```

To customize the message, we need to pass the message option. See Listing 4-113.

Listing 4-113. Passing the Message Option to Customize the Error Message

```
validates :email, format: {
  with: URI::MailTo::EMAIL_REGEXP,
  message: "must be a valid email address"
}
```

Now, the error message for an invalid e-mail address will be more descriptive. See Listing 4-114.

Listing 4-114. The More Descriptive Error Message When the E-mail Is Invalid

```
irb(main):001:0> u.errors.full_messages
=> ["Email must be a valid email address"]
```

177

Note   An effective error message clearly informs the user of the problem and provides a way to solve the issue.

We can also check whether a model contains any error by using any? or blank?. See Listing 4-115.

Listing 4-115. Checking Whether There Are Any Errors

```
irb(main):013:0> u.errors.any?
=> true
```

We can treat the error instance a little bit like a hash—it can respond to each, keys, [], and other hash-like messages. See Listing 4-116.

Listing 4-116. Invoking Several Methods on an ActiveModel::Errors Instance

```
irb(main):007:0> u.errors[:username]
=> ["can't be blank"]
irb(main):008:0> u.errors.keys
=> [:first_name, :username]
irb(main):012:0> u.errors.each { |k, v| puts "#{k} => #{v}" }
first_name => can't be blank
username => can't be blank
```

Or, if we really want to, we can convert it to a hash. See Listing 4-117.

Listing 4-117. Converting an Error Instance to a Hash

```
irb(main):006:0> u.errors.to_hash
=> {:first_name=>["can't be blank"], :username=>["can't be blank"]}
```

Forcing a Save

In general, we can't persist any object that failed any validations. But, as so often in life, there are exceptions. To save a record without doing data validation, we can pass validate: false to the save method.

To demonstrate, let's first create a dummy User instance and assign first_name an empty string. See Listing 4-118.

Listing 4-118. Creating a New Invalid User Instance

```
irb(main):002:0> u = User.new(username: "abc", email: "abc@example.org")
=> #<User id: nil, username: "abc", first_name: nil, last_name: nil, email:
"abc@example.org", is_public: true, created_at: nil, updated_at: nil>
irb(main):003:0> u.first_name = ""
```

We cannot save the User object because the *presence validator* doesn't like an empty string as much as it distastes a nil value. See Listing 4-119.

Listing 4-119. Failed When Saving the Object Due to Validation Errors

```
irb(main):004:0> u.save
=> false
```

But, when we pass validate: false to it, as long as the database constraints are happy, the data is going to be persisted. See Listing 4-120.

Listing 4-120. Persisting the Record by Bypassing Validations

```
irb(main):005:0> u.save(validate: false)
=> true
```

Doing this is clearly unsafe and is best avoided at all times unless it's really necessary to do. The Peter Parker principle states that with great power comes great responsibility.

Associations

Associations are a way to establish relationships between models. They are a natural construct that we encounter all the time in real-world applications. Examples of relationships are as follows:

- Articles have comments.

- An article belongs to a magazine and author.

- Magazines have subscriptions.

In this section, let's explore and establish the relationships between models in Tandibi.

One-to-One (belongs_to)

A one-to-one association connects a record to another record.

In Tandibi, we allow users to post updates. If the User and Post models live all by themselves, unconnected, Tandibi can't know who posted what. Let's make the connection.

First, let's write the spec in Listing 4-121 to test the relationship. The spec file would be spec/models/post_spec.rb since we are testing the Post model.

Listing 4-121. A Spec for Testing the Relationship Between Post and User

```ruby
RSpec.describe Post, type: :model do
  describe "#save" do
    it "belongs to a user" do
      user = User.create!(
        first_name: "Adam",
        email: "adam@example.com",
        username: "adam123"
      )

      post = Post.new(
        postable: Status.new(text: "Whohoo!"),
      )

      post.save
      expect(post).not_to be_persisted

      post.user = user
      post.save
      expect(post).to be_persisted
    end
  end
end
```

The most important behavior we are testing here is that we can't persist a post if the user (the actor) is not given.

Now if we run the spec, it will fail as expected. See Listing 4-122.

Listing 4-122. Running RSpec

```
$ rspec spec/models/post_spec.rb
F
```

Failures:

```
  1) Post#save belongs to a user
     Failure/Error: expect(post).not_to be_persisted
```

Let's fix this by adding the line in Listing 4-123 in the Post model.

Listing 4-123. A Post Belongs to a User

```
class Post < ApplicationRecord
  ...
  belongs_to :user
end
```

Let's see what happens if we run the test again. It will pass now. Sweet!

In general, if a model has a {something}_id field in it, a belongs_to relationship should be defined. If we look at the Post model, other than user_id, it also has thread_id.

thread_id intends to refer to a parent thread since a post can be a reply to another post. Thus, we can express this relationship as shown in Listing 4-124.

Listing 4-124. Connecting a Post with Itself

```
belongs_to :thread, class_name: "Post"
```

However, the catch is that a *thread* is optional—not all posts are replies! If we run the spec right now, the test is going to fail since we don't associate the *thread* to anything. Let's keep in mind that the belongs_to relationship is always mandatory, by default.

To change the relationship from mandatory to an optional one, we should pass optional: true as an option. See Listing 4-125.

Listing 4-125. Making a Thread Optional

```
belongs_to :thread, class_name: "Post", optional: true
```

And now, everything is green again!

There are other models where we should define one-to-one `belongs_to` relationships. Those models are as follows:

- `bonds.user_id` belongs to `users.id`.

- `bonds.friend_id` belongs to `users.id`.

- `pictures.post_id` belongs to `posts.id`.

For Bond, the relationships' definition would be as shown in Listing 4-126.

Listing 4-126. Relationships in Bond

```
belongs_to :user
belongs_to :friend, class_name: "User"
```

Whereby for the `Picture` model, its relationship to `Post` would be as shown in Listing 4-127.

Listing 4-127. A Picture Belongs to a Post

```
class Picture < ApplicationRecord
  belongs_to :post
end
```

It's not difficult to define a one-to-one relationship, right? What we must remember is that any `belongs_to` relationship is mandatory by default. That is, its field cannot be nullable. That's why it's not necessary to do presence validation on a one-to-one relationship field. However, if the field is optional such as in the case of the self-referencing `Post#thread_id`, we can pass in the `optional: true` argument.

One-to-Many

A one-to-many relationship is usually the reverse of `belongs_to`. If we define a model A to belong to B, sometimes we also define a relationship from many Bs to one A. See Figure 4-5.

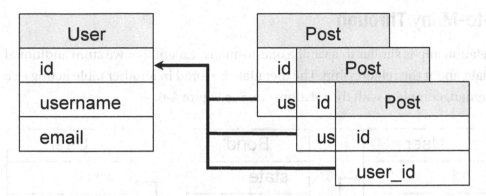

Figure 4-5. *A diagram showing a one-to-many association between a user and its posts*

For example, a newly registered user may not have any post at all to begin with. But after a while, he might post some updates. So, a post belongs to a user, and a user has many posts. It is as natural as that.

To express that, we use has_many. See Listing 4-128.

Listing 4-128. A Relationship to Allow a User to Discover Its Own Posts

```
class User < ApplicationRecord
  ...
  has_many :posts
end
```

We know that a post can have many pictures. So, let's define that relationship too. See Listing 4-129.

Listing 4-129. A Post Has Many Pictures

```
class Post < ApplicationRecord
  belongs_to :user
  belongs_to :thread, class_name: "Post", optional: true
  has_many :pictures
end
```

One-to-Many Through

This relationship is similar to a vanilla one-to-many, except that we store additional metadata about the relationship. The metadata is stored in another table acting as a middleman, complete with the relationship. See Figure 4-6.

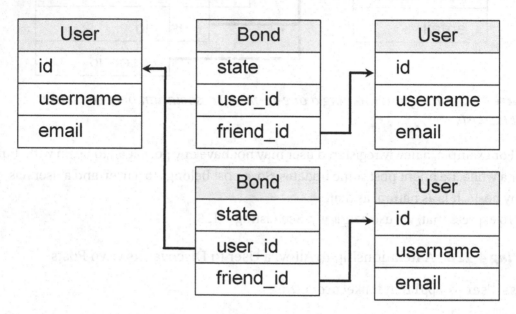

Figure 4-6. *A connection of a user and its followers through Bond*

In Tandibi, a bond expresses a connection between two users. Its state takes note of the nature of the relationship, e.g., following. In this case, state is a metadata of the relationship.

To express a relationship where a third-party model is involved, we use has_many with through.

Let's make our users aware of their relationships with other users. But, first, let's write the spec in Listing 4-130 for User. The file for the spec is spec/models/user_spec.rb.

Listing 4-130. Spec for Testing Bonds Between Users

```
RSpec.describe User, type: :model do
  describe "#valid?" do
    ...
  end
```

```
describe "#followings" do
  it "can list all of the user's followings" do
    user = create_a_user
    friend1 = create_a_user
    friend2 = create_a_user
    friend3 = create_a_user

    Bond.create user: user,
      friend: friend1,
      state: Bond::FOLLOWING
    Bond.create user: user,
      friend: friend2,
      state: Bond::FOLLOWING
    Bond.create user: user,
      friend: friend3,
      state: Bond::REQUESTING

    expect(user.followings).to include(friend1, friend2)
    expect(user.follow_requests).to include(friend3)
  end
end
end
```

The spec ensures each *bond* originating from a user knows its boundary: whether the user is following another user or the follow request is awaiting a response.

Before defining the relationship, let's ensure Bond has the correct association for friend. See Listing 4-131.

Listing 4-131. Defining the Relationship for Friend in the Bond

```
class Bond < ApplicationRecord
  ...
  belongs_to :friend, class_name: "User"
end
```

After that, we can define the relationships in User as shown in Listing 4-132.

Listing 4-132. Defining followings and follow_requests

```
has_many :bonds

has_many :followings,
  -> { where("bonds.state = ?", Bond::FOLLOWING) },
  through: :bonds,
  source: :friend

has_many :follow_requests,
  -> { where("bonds.state = ?", Bond::REQUESTING) },
  through: :bonds,
  source: :friend
```

First, we state that a user may have many bond records. This bond is defined to be a bond originating from this user, going to another user. See Listing 4-133.

Listing 4-133. Definition That States That a User Can Have Many Bonds

```
has_many :bonds
```

However, the bonds relationship obviously is going to return a collection of Bond, instead of User, of this user. But, we would like to get the User directly. So, we defined followings and follow_requests, which retrieved the Bond#friend, which is going to be a User instance for each bonds. This essentially allows us to get a list of Users without iterating and mapping the bond to a user manually.

As the scope for followings and follow_requests are not the same, we also dictated the condition in a scope.

We can simplify the previous code as shown in Listing 4-134.

Listing 4-134. Simplifying Bonds

```
has_many :bonds
has_many :friends, through: :bonds
```

If we do this, the code indeed looks simple, but we make it difficult to work with. For example, friends will be a collection that lists all users regardless of the state.

That means we will need to filter those that the user follows from those it blocks. That must be done every single time. So, let's stay away from doing that. Nevertheless, it's telling that has_many through can be as simple as that.

Apart from `followings` and `follow_requests`, it would be great if we could also get the list of `followers`. But this is trickier.

First, let's think about what it means to be a follower. A follower is someone who follows another user. Let's take a look at the simplified bonds table in Table 4-12.

Table 4-12. *Simplified bonds table*

user_id	friend_id	state
5	1	following
6	1	following
7	2	following

From Table 4-12, we can conclude that a user with ID 1 (user #1) is followed by user #5 and user #6. User #2, on the other hand, has one follower: user #7.

Let's take a look at the query made by calling `bonds`, assuming `user` is user #1. See Listing 4-135.

Listing 4-135. A Query ActiveRecord Sends to Get the Bonds

```
irb(main):001:0> puts user.bonds.to_sql
SELECT "bonds".* FROM "bonds" WHERE "bonds"."user_id" = 1
```

From the previous snippet, it's clear that we cannot express `followers` through `bonds`, because bonds is "from this user." For followers, what we need is a reversed bonds, where the linking is "from another user, to this user."

The reverse bonds, let's call it `inward_bonds`, should have something like the query in Listing 4-136 when invoked.

Listing 4-136. The Expected Query for Inward Bonds

```
SELECT "bonds".* FROM "bonds" WHERE "bonds"."friend_id" = 1
```

That way, we can get all the bonds from another user to *this* user. To do that, we set the `foreign_key` value, in this case, to `friend_id`. See Listing 4-137.

Listing 4-137. Defining inward_bonds in User

```
has_many :inward_bonds,
  class_name: "Bond",
  foreign_key: :friend_id
```

We can then define `followers`. But first, let's write the test code for it in the user spec. See Listing 4-138.

Listing 4-138. Spec for Testing Followers

```
describe "#followers" do
  it "can list all of the user's followers" do
    user1 = create_a_user
    user2 = create_a_user
    fol1 = create_a_user
    fol2 = create_a_user
    fol3 = create_a_user
    fol4 = create_a_user

    Bond.create user: fol1,
      friend: user1,
      state: Bond::FOLLOWING
    Bond.create user: fol2,
      friend: user1,
      state: Bond::FOLLOWING
    Bond.create user: fol3,
      friend: user2,
      state: Bond::FOLLOWING
    Bond.create user: fol4,
      friend: user2,
      state: Bond::REQUESTING

    expect(user1.followers).to eq([fol1, fol2])
    expect(user2.followers).to eq([fol3])
  end
end
```

Then, we can define `followers` as shown in Listing 4-139, making use of `inward_bonds`.

Listing 4-139. Definition for Followers

```
has_many :followers,
  -> { where("bonds.state = ?", Bond::FOLLOWING) },
  through: :inward_bonds,
  source: :user
```

The `source` from which we get our `User` instances is definitely `user`, since they are the ones following *this* user. If we specify `friend`, then all we get is *this* user, which is not cool.

For the previous code to work, please make sure the `user` association is defined in the Bond model. See Listing 4-140.

Listing 4-140. A User Association from Bond to User

```
class Bond < ApplicationRecord
  ...
  belongs_to :user
  belongs_to :friend, class_name: "User"
end
```

We can add a spec for `Bond#save` as shown in Listing 4-141. The spec file is `spec/models/bond_spec.rb`.

Listing 4-141. Spec for Bond#save

```
describe "#valid?" do
  ...
end

describe "#save" do
  context "when complete data is given" do
    it "can be persisted" do
      user = User.create email: "e1@example.org",
        first_name: "Edwin",
        username: "e1"
```

```ruby
      friend = User.create email: "a1@example.org",
        first_name: "Adam",
        username: "a1"

      bond = Bond.new(
        user: user,
        friend: friend,
        state: Bond::REQUESTING
      )

      bond.save
      expect(bond).to be_persisted
      expect(bond.user).to eq user
      expect(bond.friend).to eq friend
    end
  end
end
```

Many-to-Many

In Tandibi, we have the Place model, which has a place_type field. It is possible to represent place_type as a separate PlaceType model so that a place can belong to many place types, and a place type can have many places: many-to-many.

For example, we can categorize a restaurant that specializes in ethnic foods, while at the same time serve a perfect café Americano, into both restaurant and coffee_shop. Each of those categories can also contain other places of interest than that restaurant.

However, let's not separate place_type into its own model because that would complicate the system. The value of place_type is known in advance, so there's no use storing it in a separate table just because we can.

A more fitting example would be a content management system such as a blog where an article can be in many categories, and a category can contain many articles. See Figure 4-7.

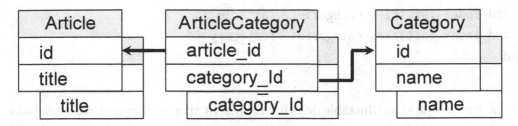

Figure 4-7. *A many-to-many relationship for both articles and categories*

In a blog system, we cannot list all the possible categories in advance. So, having a separate table is necessary to allow adding a new category on the fly. Active Record calls this kind of association between many categories and many articles has_and_belongs_to_many, often shortened to as *habtm*.

To express such a relationship, we define the model and its relationship as shown in Listing 4-142.

Listing 4-142. Modeing has_and_belongs_to_many Relationships

```
class Article < ApplicationRecord
  has_and_belongs_to_many :categories
end

class Category < ApplicationRecord
  has_and_belongs_to_many :articles
end
```

We also need to have a join table called articles_categories, which connects the two models, as shown in Listing 4-143.

Listing 4-143. Creating the Joining Table

```
class CreateArticlesCategoriesTable < ActiveRecord::Migration[6.0]
  def change
    create_table :articles_categories, id: false do |t|
      t.bigint :article_id
      t.bigint :category_id
    end
```

```
    add_index :articles_categories, :article_id
    add_index :articles_categories, :category_id
  end
end
```

Please note that since the table does not represent an actual model, we must pass id: false to the create_table method.

The has_and_belongs_to_many macro accepts an optional join_table to specify the name of the join table. If not given, Active Record assumes the name is a combination of the connected models in lexical order. So, a join between Article and Category gives the default name of articles_categories for the join table, as a outranks c in lexical ordering.

Polymorphic Association

Polymorphic means many forms. It is a rather technical word. In the case of an association, it is taken to mean that the relationship can be any model that implements the polymorphic interface.

Let's say we are creating a human resource system. The system can list both the address of branch offices and also employees' addresses.

An address is complex data in its own right. It has the country, province, city, postcode, and, finally, address fields. To avoid repetition and to make it DRY, can we model it so that both office and employee can make use of the same address class?

We can use a belongs_to association, right? See Listing 4-144.

Listing 4-144. An Address Class Implementation

```
class Address < ActiveRecord::Base
  belongs_to :employee
  belongs_to :company
end
```

Yup! But then, we will have those foreign keys where only one of them holds a value at any given time, as the same record must not belong to both a person and a company. Otherwise, if we need to change the person's address, the company's address gets inadvertently changed too. Not cool.

A cleaner way would be to use a polymorphic association, demonstrated by Listing 4-145.

Listing 4-145. Using a Polymorphic Association to Link an Address with Other Models

```
class Address < ActiveRecord::Base
  belongs_to :addressable, polymorphic: true
end

class Employee < ActiveRecord::Base
  has_one :address, as: :addressable
end

class Office < ActiveRecord::Base
  has_one :address, as: :addressable
end
```

In that situation, an address belongs to any polymorphic *addressable* model. What model that is, is only known at runtime. It can be an Employee, an Office, or something else we get to add in the future.

That is strikingly different from other relationships we have come across so far, where the model is known in advance.

In Tandibi, the Post model has a polymorphic association through an interface called postable. For now, a postable can be a status update or an activity update. But, the sky is the limit. We can add any kind of new postable models in the future, like audio voice, maybe.

Let's play around with Post a little. Let's try creating a polymorphic record. So, open up a Rails console, and let's create a user. See Listing 4-146.

Listing 4-146. Creating a User

```
irb(main):001:0> u = User.create(email: "#{SecureRandom.hex(3)}@example.org",
irb(main):002:1*   first_name: "Adam",
irb(main):003:1*   username: SecureRandom.hex(3))
=> #<User id: 1, username: "42ed5c" ...>
```

After that, let's instantiate a new post. See Listing 4-147.

Listing 4-147. Initializing a New Post

```
irb(main):004:0> post = Post.new(user: u)
=> #<Post id: nil, user_id: 1, thread_id: nil, postable_type: nil,
postable_id: nil, created_at: nil, updated_at: nil>
```

Let's imagine a user is posting a status update, so the `postable` in this case is a `Status`. See Listing 4-148.

Listing 4-148. Assignment of the Polymorphic Field postable

```
irb(main):005:0> post.postable = Status.new(text: "I love you!!!")
=> #<Status id: nil, text: "I love you!!!", created_at: nil, updated_at: nil>
```

Teenagers are always like that. Now, let's save it. See Listing 4-149.

Listing 4-149. Saving the Post

```
irb(main):006:0> post.save
=> true
```

We assume the user has just posted an update. We can check what kind of post it is by inspecting the `postable_type`. See Listing 4-150.

Listing 4-150. Checking Out the postable_type and postable_id

```
irb(main):007:0> post.postable_type
=> "Status"
irb(main):008:0> post.postable_id
=> 1
```

We can find the status by using `Status#find` and pass in 1 as the argument, or we can just access the `postable` interface. See Listing 4-151.

Listing 4-151. Retrieving the Polymorphic Instance

```
irb(main):009:0> post.postable
=> #<Status id: 1, text: "I love you!!!", created_at: "2020-03-01
09:35:07", updated_at: "2020-03-01 09:35:07">
```

Note   The -*able* suffix is commonly used for naming polymorphic associations or an interface, although it is not required. In fact, Active Storage does not use the -*able* suffix for naming its polymorphic *record* association.

There is some disadvantage of using polymorphic association. Because of its nature of being polymorphic, we cannot have the same level of security offered by database-backed foreign keys. With this setup, performance is also likely to suffer.

The problem is not a concern if we promise to always use Rails, but what if other apps write the database too or if we skip saving through the Rails stack? In those cases, we need to be extra careful.

It's also brittle if every relationship is unnecessarily polymorphic. So, it's better to be used extremely sparingly, when it is the only way. Another close contender to this technique is single-table inheritance (STI).

Single-Table Inheritance

Sometimes a possible alternative to polymorphic association is single-table inheritance. Using this technique, multiple subclasses share a single database table with the parent. The table will have a type field to indicate which subclass it actually is.

In the case of Tandibi, the `Post` model can be inherited by `Status` and `Sight`, as shown in Listing 4-152.

Listing 4-152. Single-Table Inheritance for Post

```
class Post < ActiveRecord::Base; end
class Status < Post; end
class Sight < Post; end
```

But we decided not to do that. STI is usually the right choice when the different subclasses share largely the same columns, but only have differences in behavior.

A good example for STI would be a `Student` superclass and `Graduate` and `Undergraduate` subclasses. They are almost the same and most likely share the same basic structures. This is unlike, `Post` where there will be a lot of null columns in the database if we implement the connections as STI. The table will be conceptually confusing and difficult to manage as we added different types of post.

Another good indication of STI is when we can expect to perform queries across all subclasses. In the case of Post, Status and Sight have few in common between one another. Thus, querying between subclasses is highly unlikely. However, with the Undergraduate and Graduate example that we talked about previously, we can send subqueries to detect students who deserve to receive federal aid or scholarship, for example.

We must acknowledge that polymorphic association can have performance penalties, but unless STI is an obvious knock-out choice, polymorphic association is largely the preferred way.

Callbacks

Callbacks allow us to do something at a specific point in the object's lifecycle, without having to manually invoke any code. Those lifecycles are shown in Table 4-13.

Table 4-13. *The Active Record Object Lifecycle*

Stage	Callbacks
Initialize When the object is either initialized or loaded from the database	1. `after_find` 2. `after_initialize`
Validate When a record is examined for its validity	1. `before_validation` 2. `after_validation`
Save Happening on both insert (create) and update lifecycles	1. `before_save` 2. `around_save` 3. `after_save`
Create When the object is inserted	1. `before_create` 2. `around_create` 3. `after_create`
Update When the object is updated	1. `before_update` 2. `around_update` 3. `after_update`

(continued)

Table 4-13. (*continued*)

Stage	Callbacks
Destroy When the object is removed	1. before_destroy 2. around_destroy 3. after_destroy
Commit When the transaction is committed	1. after_commit
Rollback When the transaction is rolled back	1. after_rollback

Typically, we use a callback to do automated data transformation or assignment. Let's see how we can use it to enforce strict capitalization.

First, let's write the spec as shown in Listing 4-153.

Listing 4-153. Ensuring Capitalization on Names

```
RSpec.describe User, type: :model do
  ...
  describe "#save" do
    it "capitalized the name correctly" do
      user = create_a_user

      user.first_name = "AdaM"
      user.last_name = "van der Berg"
      user.save

      expect(user.first_name).to eq "Adam"
      expect(user.last_name).to eq "van der Berg"
    end
  end
end
```

If we run the spec, it is red as expected. See Listing 4-154.

Listing 4-154. Running RSpec

```
$ rspec spec/models/user_spec.rb
.......F
Failures:

  1) User#after_save capitalized the names correctly
     Failure/Error: expect(user.first_name).to eq "Adam"

        expected: "Adam"
             got: "AdaM"

     (compared using ==)
```

Let's fix this by hooking a method to before_save to normalize the data. See Listing 4-155.

Listing 4-155. Data Normalization Before Saving

```
class User < ApplicationRecord
  ...

  before_save :ensure_proper_name_case

  private

    def ensure_proper_name_case
      self.first_name = first_name.capitalize
    end
end
```

Now if we run the spec, everything will be green and happy.

We can also run callbacks (and validations) conditionally by passing an if or unless option that accepts a proc or a method name. See Listing 4-156.

Listing 4-156. Passing Condition to before_save

```
before_save :do_something, if: :private_boolean_method?
before_save :do_something, if: -> { condition_met? }
```

Enrichment

Active Record is a wonderful framework, and its toolings are just as wonderful. If you are not convinced yet, maybe this section will add some fun.

Factory Bot: Record Maker

When working on a spec, we often need to work with an initialized model, persisted or not. Factory Bot can help prepare those instances for us. It takes inspiration from the factory pattern that deal with the problem of creating objects without having to specify the exact class of the object to be created. Let's see how it works.

First, let's define the factory for the User model. Open `spec/factories/users.rb`, or create the file if it doesn't exist. Then, let's write the code shown in Listing 4-157.

Listing 4-157. Defining a Factory for user

```
FactoryBot.define do
  factory :user do
    username { SecureRandom.hex(3) }
    first_name { ["Adam", "Sam", "Mike"].sample }
    last_name { ["Soesanto", "Yamashita", "de Flaire"].sample }
    email { "#{SecureRandom.hex(4)}@example.org" }
    is_public { true }
  end
end
```

We defined the `user` factory. This factory can produce a well-initialized user. With this, we can replace every call to `create_a_user` in `user_spec.rb` with `create(:user)`. See Listing 4-158.

Listing 4-158. Creating a User Instance Using Factory Bot

```
RSpec.describe User, type: :model do
  def create_a_user(email: "#{SecureRandom.hex(4)}@example.org")
    User.create!(
      first_name: "Adam",
      email: email,
```

```
    username: SecureRandom.hex(4),
  }
end

describe "#valid?" do
  it "is valid when email is unique" do
    user1 = create_a_user create(:user)
    ...
```

We can pass an argument to overwrite the default values! See Listing 4-159.

Listing 4-159. Specifying the E-mail When Creating a User Record

```
it "is invalid if the email is taken" do
  create_a_user(email: "adam@example.org")
  create(:user, email: "adam@example.org")
```

Unlike our `create_a_user`, `create` is made available throughout the spec files. Therefore, in `post_spec.rb`, we can replace the chunk of codes in Listing 4-160 with more succinct ones, as shown in Listing 4-161.

Listing 4-160. Old Code at post_spec.rb

```
user = User.create!(
  first_name: "Adam",
  email: "adam@example.com",
  username: "adam123"
)
```

Listing 4-161. Suggested Replacement for Creating a User

```
user = create(:user)
```

All the tests still pass!

Sometimes we don't need to work with a persisted record. A properly initialized object, albeit an unpersisted one, is sometimes more than enough. For that, we can use `build`.

Let's change the spec code for `Bond#state` as shown in Listing 4-162.

Listing 4-162. Replacing with build

```
describe "#valid?" do
  it "should validate the state correctly" do
    friend = User.new build(:user)
    user = User.new build(:user)
```

If we run the spec now, everything should still pass.

Inside a factory, we can also call another factory to *create* or *build* instances. Let's try to see how that works.

First, let's define the place factory (`factories/places.rb`, as usual; please create the file if it's nowhere to be found). See Listing 4-163.

Listing 4-163. The place Factory

```
FactoryBot.define do
  factory :place do
    locale { "en" }
    coordinate { "POINT (1 2 3)" }
    name { ["La Fantasia", "AirCoffee"].sample }
    place_type { "coffee_shop" }
  end
end
```

Then, define the `sight` factory as shown in Listing 4-164, and define another in another file (`factories/sights.rb`).

Listing 4-164. Defining the sight Factory

```
FactoryBot.define do
  factory :sight do
    place { build(:place) }
    activity_type { "checkin" }
  end
end
```

Notice that the factory shown previously uses `build` for the `place` attribute. This way, the `Sight#place` attribute is assigned to an appropriate `Place` instance.

We can change the code in Listing 4-165 in `sights_spec.rb`.

Listing 4-165. Using Build to Initialize sight

```
describe "#valid?" do
  it "should validate activity type correctly" do
    sight = Sight.new(place: Place.new)
    sight = build(:sight)
```

Well done! It's convenient, right? And every test is still green.

Automated Data Population

In Chapter 1, we briefly mentioned database seeding, which is the process of populating the database with an initial set of data. In Rails, those seeders are defined in db/seeds.rb.

Let's write some code to generate some users and other data. See Listing 4-166.

Listing 4-166. Codes to Seed Users

```
user1 = User.create!(
  first_name: "Sam",
  last_name: "Yamashita",
  email: "sam@example.org",
  username: "samsam"
)

user2 = User.create!(
  first_name: "Adam",
  last_name: "Notodikromo",
  email: "adam@example.org",
  username: "adam123",
)
```

To run the seeder, we can use the command shown in Listing 4-167.

Listing 4-167. Running Seeder

```
$ rails db:seed
```

Running the previous command subsequently will make Rails unhappy, since there is already a user with the same username. To truncate that data just before doing seeding, we execute the command in Listing 4-168.

Listing 4-168. A Command to Truncate and Seed the Database

```
$ rails db:seed:replant
```

Now, let's write some seeders for the remaining models. See Listing 4-169.

Listing 4-169. Seeders for Other Models

```
Bond.create(user: user1, friend: user2, state: Bond::FOLLOWING)
Bond.create(user: user2, friend: user1, state: Bond::FOLLOWING)

place = Place.create!(
  locale: "en",
  name: "Hotel Majapahit",
  place_type: "hotel",
  coordinate: "POINT (112.739898 -7.259836 0)"
)

post = Post.create!(user: user1, postable: Status.new(
  text: "Whohoo! I am in Surabaya!!!!"
))

Post.create!(user: user2, postable: Status.new(
  text: "Wow! Looks great! Have fun, Sam!"
), thread: post)

Post.create!(user: user1, postable: Status.new(
  text: "Ya! Ya! Ya! Are you in town?"
), thread: post)

Post.create!(user: user2, postable: Status.new(
  text: "Yups! Let's explore the city!"
), thread: post)

Post.create(user: user1, postable: Sight.new(
  place: place, activity_type: Sight::CHECKIN
))
```

Note   There are gems like Seedbank that help us to write seeders per environment.

Enumerated Values

An enum limits the assignable values to a variable to only one of the predefined constants. A common use case for an enum is to express things like state in a finite-state machine.

In Tandibi, we may express Bond#state as an enum. Let's do that. Let's open the Bond model and define the enum as shown in Listing 4-170.

Listing 4-170. Defining State Enumeration for Bond

```
class Bond < ApplicationRecord
  STATES = [
    ...
  ].freeze

  enum state: {
    requesting: REQUESTING,
    following: FOLLOWING,
    blocking: BLOCKING,
  }
```

We can also remove the inclusion validator as enum takes care of that. See Listing 4-171.

Listing 4-171. Removing the Inclusion Validation of State

```
validates :state, presence: true
validates :state, inclusion: { in: STATES }
```

If we run the spec, everything remains green.

Just for information, it's not required, but to enforce the same constraint at the database level, we could use the check constraint in PostgreSQL. See Listing 4-172.

Listing 4-172. Adding a Check Constraint for bonds.state

```
ALTER TABLE bonds
ADD CONSTRAINT allowed_state
CHECK (state in ('requesting', 'following', 'blocking'))
```

Scopes

Scope, or more appropriately *named scope*, allows us to define frequently used subqueries as a chainable method.

First, in our User model, we have the followings association defined as shown in Listing 4-173. Notice how brittle it is.

Listing 4-173. The followings Association in User

```
has_many :followings,
  -> { where("bonds.state = ?", Bond::FOLLOWING) },
  through: :bonds,
  source: :friend
```

The previous code would be easier to read had it been written as shown in Listing 4-174.

Listing 4-174. Using Named Scope for Scoping

```
has_many :followings,
  -> { Bond.following },
  through: :bonds,
  source: :friend
```

For that to work, we need to define Bond.following as a named scope. So, in the Bond model, let's define the following scope as shown in Listing 4-175.

Listing 4-175. Defining the following Scope

```
class Bond < ApplicationRecord
  ...
  scope :following, -> { where(state: FOLLOWING) }
end
```

We can also define the requesting and blocking scopes. See Listing 4-176.

Listing 4-176. Defining the requesting and blocking Scopes

```
scope :requesting, -> { where(state: REQUESTING) }
scope :blocking, -> { where(state: BLOCKING) }
```

Then, let's make use of those named scopes. See Listing 4-177.

Listing 4-177. Updating Associations to Use Named Scope

```
has_many :follow_requests,
  -> { Bond.requesting },
  through: :bonds,
  source: :friend

has_many :followers,
  -> { Bond.following },
  through: :inward_bonds,
  source: :user
```

Active Model

Active Model allows plain old Ruby objects (POROs) to gain some features normally present in an Active Record instance, without the overhead of persistence, for example.

For example, we can create a class to represent credentials data as shown in Listing 4-178.

Listing 4-178. Defining Credentials

```
class Credentials
  attr_accessor :username, :password
end
```

The class works fine, but then we need to spend time to build the initializer; otherwise, we cannot do something like shown in Listing 4-179.

Listing 4-179. Initializing the Credentials and Passing an Argument to It

```
Credentials.new(username: "adam123")
```

However, if we drop `ActiveModel::Model` into the class, suddenly the class has many capabilities, one of which causes the previous code to work. See Listing 4-180.

Listing 4-180. The Class with ActiveModel::Model Included

```
class Credentials
  include ActiveModel::Model
  ...
end
```

Not only that, we can do some validations too! See Listing 4-181.

Listing 4-181. Defining Validations for the Credentials Class

```
class Credentials
  ...
  validates_presence_of :basic_auth_password,
    :basic_auth_password
end
```

Very handy, right? This will add some fun for sure.

Summary

You learned quite a lot in this chapter. We started from the foundation and built up our knowledge to be on par with professional users of Active Record. In the process, we also learned about test-driven development.

But, we shouldn't stop our adventure here just yet. Our target is to be well-trained Rails, not just Active Record, engineers. We want to be able to produce not only working code, but readable, extensible, and scalable code.

To illustrate the point, let's say we need to display a *gravatar* image of a user, and we decide to define `gravatar_url` in the model as shown in Listing 4-182.

Listing 4-182. Adding gravatar_url to User

```
class User < ApplicationRecord
  ...

  def gravatar_url
    hash = Digest::MD5.hexdigest(email)
    "https://www.gravatar.com/avatar/#{hash}?d=wavatar"
  end

  private
  ...
end
```

The question is, do we really need that to be *in* the model?

Although it is natural to assume that a model should be intelligent, lumping every method imaginable into a model can make it *fat*.

If the method is used only in the views, maybe we can extract it out to a helper. Or into a decorator. Or into a view component?

If a method does a complicated process, maybe a service object can be of help?

How about access validations? For example, let's say some users shouldn't be allowed to visit a private account unless a follow access has been granted. How can we express and implement that kind of access validation?

The point is not to be afraid to make our models intelligent; that is exactly the power Active Record bestowed upon us. Yet it is important to apply germane engineering standards so that our app, in general, is in harmony architecturally.

The chapters to come will focus on that while at the same time building the UI!

Please take a break and see you soon. I will have my coffee when we meet in the next chapter.

CHAPTER 5

Session and Authentication

Our the next topics are session and authentication, which are fundamental concepts in any modern web application.

In this chapter, let's build features to allow our dear users to open a new account and sign in. While doing so, we will take a closer look into ERB, one of the most common templating languages powering Rails apps.

Without further ado!

First, Let's Sketch It

Wireframing is a process to produce a user interface blueprints. The blueprint, called a *wireframe*, is a quasi-prototype monochrome sketch for visualizing the page's content and functionality. The wireframing process is intended to help us realize design flaws early in the engineering process.

Alongside a wireframe, a user profiling artifact known as a *persona* is usually explored. Personas can help us when deciding how the UI and the UX should play out. So, instead of debating that the Post button should be bigger, one can argue that "since our primary persona, Sam, is always on the go, a bigger tap target might be appreciated as it reduces his eye strain," for instance.

When developing our persona, it is best to avoid two sins. First, a persona should not be *self-referential*, where it resembles its designers rather than the target audience.

Second, we must ensure that a persona is not *elastic*, or trying to represent everyone. For example, a social media app might have advertisers as a separate persona from the status updater Sam.

209

© Adam Notodikromo 2021
A. Notodikromo, *Learn Rails 6*, https://doi.org/10.1007/978-1-4842-6026-5_5

Sam, our primary persona, is an active teenager eager to share with his friends whatever he is busy doing. As a millennial, he appreciates uncluttered, minimalist design.

But before Sam can see or post an update, he needs to identify himself by signing in. Signing in is possible only if he already has an account. Otherwise, he needs to sign up. See Figure 5-1.

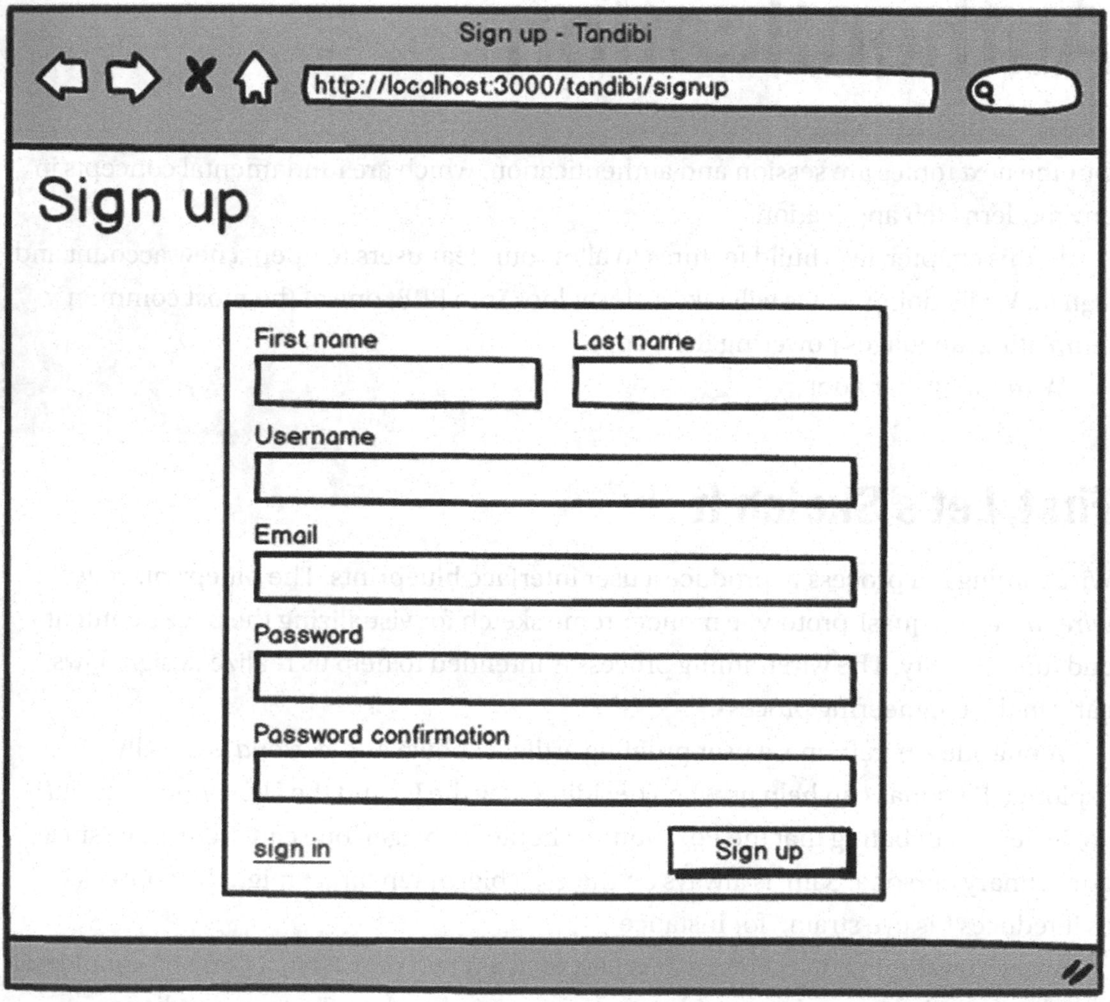

Figure 5-1. A sign-up form

To sign in, Sam needs to enter his credentials. A pair of either a username and a password, or an email and a password, will do. See Figure 5-2.

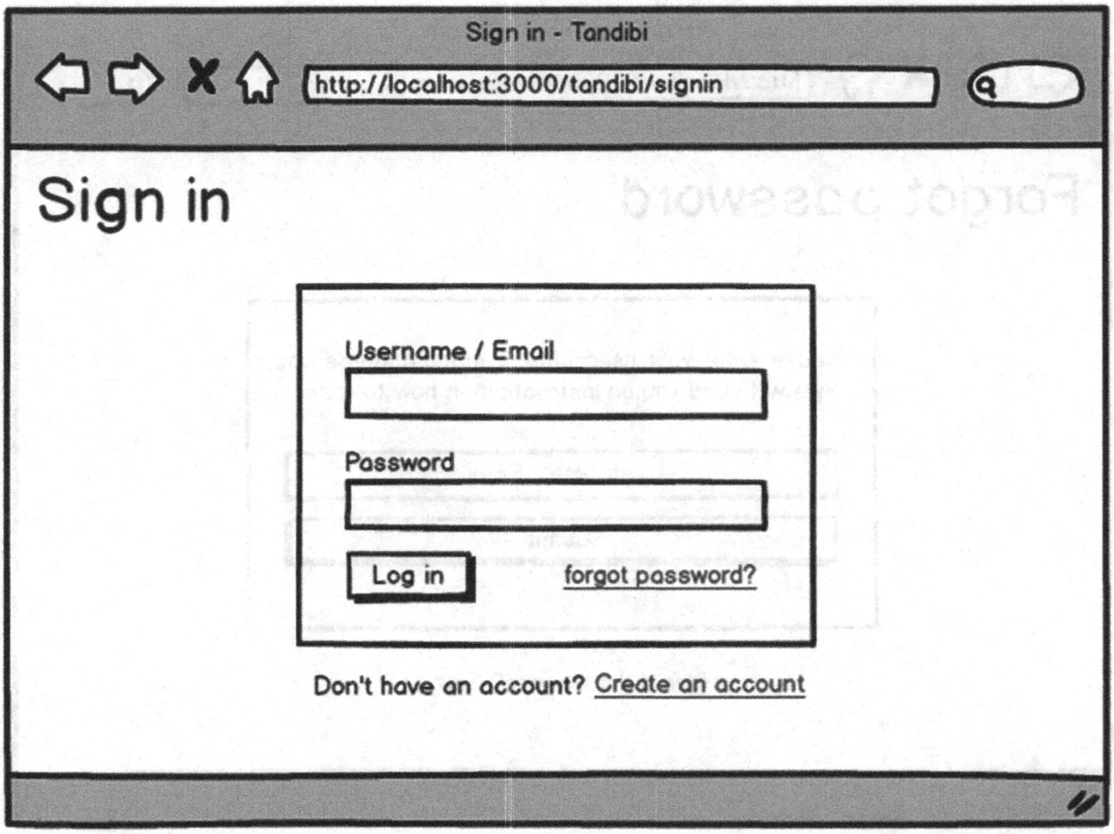

Figure 5-2. *A sign-in form*

Sam may forget his password sometimes. In that case, he can click the "forgot password?" link, which takes him to the "Forgot password" page. On that page, Sam can fill in his username or email address so that we can deliver instructions to his registered email address to reset his password. See Figure 5-3.

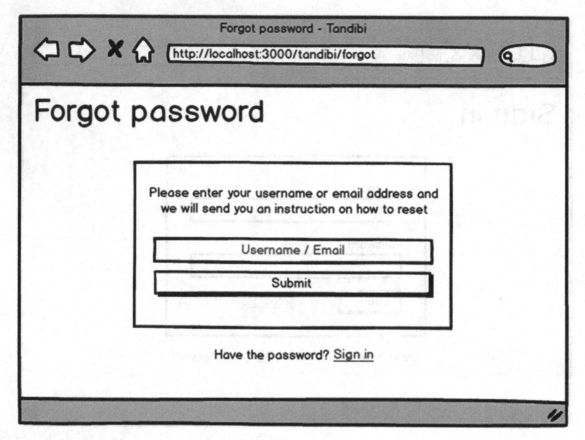

Figure 5-3. "Forgot password" page

The email will look like Figure 5-4.

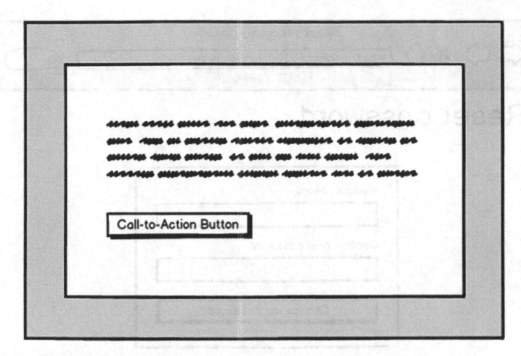

Figure 5-4. *Email template with a call-to-action button*

For a password reset email, clicking the call-to-action button takes Sam to a page where he can set a new password. See Figure 5-5.

213

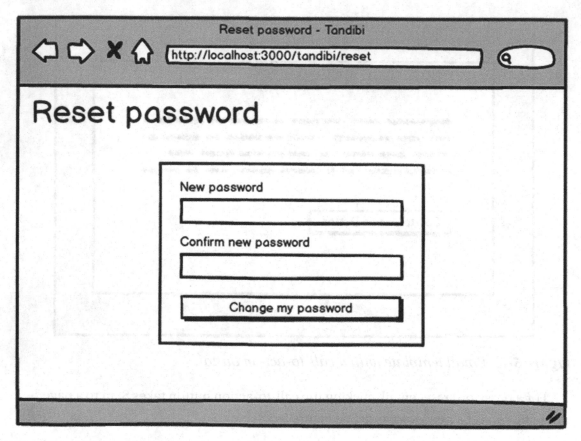

Figure 5-5. *"Reset password" page*

On the "Reset password" page, Sam needs to enter the new password twice. Only if both passwords match with each other will we set the account's password to the new one.

All of these pages are wonderful in their own right. But, without a proper home page, they are challenging to navigate for the first time. So, let's create a proper home page with a link to the sign-in page. See Figure 5-6.

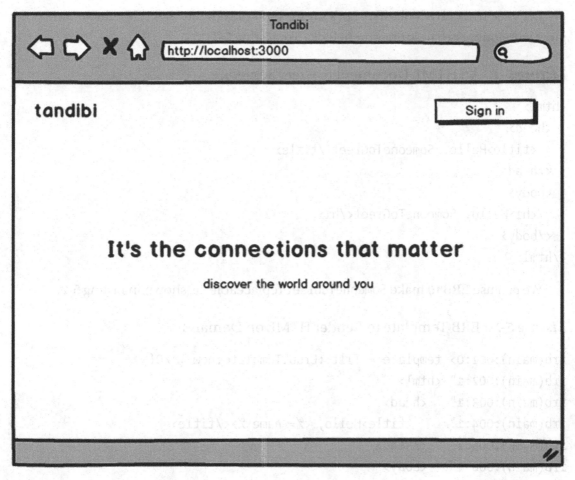

Figure 5-6. *Home page for Tandibi*

ERB Templates 101

There are many ways to generate HTML. By default, Rails uses Erubi. Erubi is an implementation of ERB, which allows us to mix Ruby with a bunch of other strings. Other alternatives, such as Slim (my favorite) and HAML, are more specialized; they can be used only for producing HTML code.

Note   There are three major implementations for ERB: Ruby's ERB, Erubis, and Erubi. Erubi is said to have an 86 percent smaller memory footprint compared to Erubis.

Let's see what ERB looks like. Let's say we want to generate an HTML document to greet someone. The static document looks like Listing 5-1.

Listing 5-1. An HTML Document to Greet Someone

```
<html>
  <head>
    <title>Hello, SomeoneToGreet</title>
  </head>
  <body>
    <h1>Hello, SomeoneToGreet</h1>
  </body>
</html>
```

We can use ERB to make SomeoneToGreet replaceable, as shown in Listing 5-2.

Listing 5-2. ERB Template to Render HTML on Demand

```
irb(main):001:0> template = Tilt::ErubiTemplate.new { %Q{
irb(main):002:1" <html>
irb(main):003:1"   <head>
irb(main):004:1"     <title>Hello, <%= name %></title>
irb(main):005:1"   </head>
irb(main):006:1"   <body>
irb(main):007:1"     <h1>Hello, <%= name %></h1>
irb(main):008:1"   </body>
irb(main):009:1" </html>
irb(main):010:1" } }
```

Then, we can render the previous template with the code shown in Listing 5-3.

Listing 5-3. Rendering the Dynamic Template

```
irb(main):011:0> template.render(Object.new, name: "Adam")
```

This produces the output shown in Listing 5-4.

Listing 5-4. Output for Executing the Template

```
<html>
  <head>
    <title>Hello, Adam</title>
  </head>
  <body>
    <h1>Hello, Adam</h1>
  </body>
</html>
```

We can think of ERB's <%= %> tag as string interpolation, where the evaluated code will supplant the tag. There's also a sister tag that evaluates the code without printing out: the <% %> tag. The version lacking an equal sign is used for iterations, variable assignment, and conditional branching, as shown in Listing 5-5.

Listing 5-5. Doing Iterations with ERB

```
irb(main):012:0> template = Tilt::ErubiTemplate.new { %Q{
irb(main):013:1" <% 5.times do %>
irb(main):014:1"    <p>Hello!</p>
irb(main):015:1" <% end %>
irb(main):016:1" } }
irb(main):017:0> puts template.render
  <p>Hello!</p>
  <p>Hello!</p>
  <p>Hello!</p>
  <p>Hello!</p>
  <p>Hello!</p>
```

That's the basic of ERB; it really is that simple.

Setting Up tailwind.css

We are going to use Tailwind in this book. Tailwind is a front-end CSS framework for building a responsive web page. Its utility classes are like Lego blocks, making it trivial to build something complex by combining small pieces.

To begin using it, let's first install it using the commands shown in Listing 5-6.

Listing 5-6. Adding Tailwind as a Development Dependency

```
$ npm install tailwindcss@1.2.0 --save-dev
$ mkdir -p app/javascript/css
$ npx tailwindcss init app/javascript/css/tailwind.js

   tailwindcss 1.2.0

   ✓ Created Tailwind config file: app/javascript/css/tailwind.js

Done in 0.45s.
```

Note   NPX makes it easy to use executables that come with a package. It comes bundled with NPM version 5.2+.

After that, let's create app/javascript/css/application.css, as shown in Listing 5-7.

Listing 5-7. Content of app/javascript/css/application.css

```
@import "tailwindcss/base";
@import "tailwindcss/components";
@import "tailwindcss/utilities";
```

Then, let's import the previous file into app/javascript/packs/application.js, as shown in Listing 5-8.

Listing 5-8. Importing application.css into application.js

```
require("@rails/ujs").start()
...

import '../css/application'
```

Although Tailwind is a CSS framework, it uniquely has directives such as @apply that require backend processing to transpile. For that reason, let's add the processor into postcss.config.js found in the root folder of our app, as shown in Listing 5-9.

Listing 5-9. Adding Tailwind into postcss.config.js

```
module.exports = {
  plugins: [
    require('postcss-import'),
    require('postcss-flexbugs-fixes'),
    require('tailwindcss')('./app/javascript/css/tailwind.js'),
    require('autoprefixer'),
    require('postcss-preset-env')({
      autoprefixer: {
        flexbox: 'no-2009'
      },
      stage: 3
    })
  ]
}
```

Authentication with Devise

Authentication is a way to allow users to obtain an identification and to get identified. It also covers cases such as when the user has forgotten their password or when they would like to sign in through third-party providers. Although that all sounds time-consuming, if not complicated, Devise is here to help.

Integrating Devise

Devise provides us with a full gamut of features that are easy to integrate with. Let's see it for ourselves. First, let's add Devise into our gemfile, as shown in Listing 5-10.

Listing 5-10. Adding Devise to the Gemfile

```
gem 'turbolinks', '~> 5'
gem 'jbuilder', '~> 2.7'
gem 'devise', '~> 4.7'
```

Then, let's execute the command in Listing 5-11 to bootstrap it. But, let's not forget to do bundle install first to download the gem.

Listing 5-11. Command to Bootstrap Devise

```
$ bundle install
$ rails generate devise:install
```

We then need to write the code in Listing 5-12 in development.rb. This code configures the default host and port for Action Mailer, a module responsible for sending out emails.

Listing 5-12. Configuring the Default URL Options for Action Mailer

```
config.action_mailer.default_url_options = {
  host: 'localhost',
  port: 3000
}
```

Also, let's change the e-mail's sender to no-reply@example.com for any emails sent by Devise. This can be done by changing the value of mailer_sender defined in initializers/devise.rb, as shown in Listing 5-13.

Listing 5-13. The mailer_sender Setting

```
config.mailer_sender = 'no-reply@example.com'
```

Then, let's define the root page for our application. To do that, let's generate HomeController and use its index page as the home page, as shown in Listing 5-14.

Listing 5-14. Command to Scaffold HomeController

```
$ rails g controller home index
```

We may change the content for app/views/home/index.html.erb, as shown in Listing 5-15.

Listing 5-15. Code for Our Home Page

```
<p>Home page</p>
```

Now, let's set the index action in HomeController to the root, or home page, of our app. To do that, let's edit the config/routes.rb file, as shown in Listing 5-16.

Listing 5-16. Defining the Root (/) Route in config/routes.rb

```
Rails.application.routes.draw do
  root to: 'home#index'
end
```

In Chapter 1, we used a flash message to display a notice to the user when a record is created or updated. Let's do the same for Tandibi. When a user signs in, for instance, we will let them know that they have successfully signed in.

For our flash message to be able to be displayed on any page in our app, let's add the code in Listing 5-17 to app/views/layouts/application.html.erb.

Listing 5-17. **Rendering** Flash Messages

```
<body>
  <p class="notice"><%= notice %></p>
  <p class="alert"><%= alert %></p>
  ...
```

The notice method prints the string assigned to flash[:notice] at the time the controller is rendering the page. The alert notice is similar; however, it fetches a message associated with flash[:alert], as shown in Listing 5-18.

Listing 5-18. Code to Assign Notice Message

```
class ExampleController < ApplicationController
  def index
    flash[:notice] = "Hi, there!"
  end
end
```

We will modify the notice and alert messages by applying some styles later, but for now, this is enough.

Because we want to customize many session pages, rather than following Devise's default templates, let's execute the command shown in Listing 5-19 to copy all of Devise's views into our own app/views folder so that we can customize them conveniently.

Listing 5-19. Command to Copy All of Devise's Views into app/views

```
$ rails g devise:views
```

Last but not least, let's generate the supporting fields for our User model. Those fields are required by Devise to support various features that come with Devise, as shown in Listing 5-20.

Listing 5-20. Adding Devise-Specific Fields for the User Model

```
$ rails g devise user
Running via Spring preloader in process 30609
      invoke  active_record
      create    db/migrate/20200315232037_add_devise_to_users.rb
      insert    app/models/user.rb
       route  devise_for :users
```

As the User model already has the email field, let's delete the code in Listing 5-21 in the migration file that Devise just generated for us. Otherwise, there will be issues when running the migration.

Listing 5-21. Commenting Out the Email Field and Its Index

```
t.string :email,               null: false, default: ""
...
add_index :users, :email,                  unique: true
```

Now, let's not forget to run the migration, as shown in Listing 5-22.

Listing 5-22. Applying the Recent Migration

```
$ rails db:migrate
```

Setting Up the Layout

A layout sets the general architecture and looks and feel of a template. An application usually contains from one to four different layouts. Each layout represents specifically themed pages such as one for the home page and its related pages (e.g., Contact US page), another one for the session-related pages, and the remaining ones for parts of the application accessible only for signed-in users.

So, let's create a new layout for the session within the views/layouts folder. Let's name the layout session.html.erb. We will refer to this layout simply as the session layout. The layout should contain the code shown in Listing 5-23.

Listing 5-23. A Template for the Session Layout

```
<!DOCTYPE html>
<html>
  <head>
    <title><%= yield :page_title %></title>
    <%= csrf_meta_tags %>
    <%= csp_meta_tag %>

    <%= stylesheet_link_tag 'application', media: 'all' %>
    <%= javascript_pack_tag 'application' %>

    <meta name="viewport"
      content="width=device-width, initial-scale=1.0">
    <meta http-equiv="X-UA-Compatible"
      content="ie=edge">
  </head>

  <body class="body-session">
    <h1 class="title hidden md:block absolute mb-6 mt-2 ml-2">
      <%= content_for(:page_title) %>
    </h1>

    <main class="container">
      <div class="m-auto w-84 md:w-96">
        <%= render "layouts/alert" %>

        <h1 class="title md:hidden mb-6">
          <%= content_for(:page_title) %>
        </h1>
        <%= yield %>
      </div>
    </main>
  </body>
</html>
```

The `viewport` meta tag instructs the browser on how to scale the view. The `width=device-width` part sets the width of the page to follow the device's screen width. Combined with `initial-scale`, it ensures that the page looks crisp and fit when rendered on any devices, mobile or desktop, as long as the page is responsive.

To design a responsive page is to use HTML and CSS techniques so that the page and its elements can be set as visible, hidden, shrunk, or enlarged automatically depending on the screen sizes.

How is that possible? Let's take a look at Listing 5-24 to start.

Listing 5-24. A Responsive h1 Element Found in the Session Layout

```
<h1 class="title hidden md:block absolute mb-6 mt-2 ml-2">
  <%= content_for(:page_title) %>
</h1>
```

Notice the `md:` code among the tag's utility classes. It is used to apply a particular styling, in this case `block`, only when the screen size fits the `md` breakpoint.

To elucidate, initially the `h1` element is hidden as we apply the `hidden` class on it without any breakpoint marker. However, when the viewpoint is bigger or equal to a tablet (an `md`), the element interprets the `block` class, effectively making it visible.

Those capabilities are given to us if we are using Tailwind CSS. Different CSS frameworks have their own ways to make the page responsive. Under the hood, however, they utilize what is known as *media queries*.

The `mb` class stands for `margin-bottom`, where the 6 denotes the "level" (not the pixel). With the same token, `mt` is short for `margin-top`, and `ml` is short for `margin-left`.

Note   We will come across `sm`, `md`, `lg`, and `xl` quite frequently in Tailwind. Those breakpoints each correspond to common device resolutions as follows:

- `sm` (small) for mobile phones. Minimum width: 640px.

- `md` (medium) for tablets. Minimum width: 768px.

- `lg` (large) for laptops. Minimum width: 1024px.

- `xl` (extra large) for desktop. Minimum width: 1280px.

It is in your interest to explore Tailwind if you think it's a good fit for you. Luckily, it has excellent documentation and tutorials. In general, you can learn Tailwind later and focus more on the Rails side as some concepts unique to Tailwind are also discussed in this book.

The `session` layout makes use of several custom classes, which we will define shortly hereafter. For now, let's create a `layouts/_alert.html.erb` partial template, as shown in Listing 5-25.

Listing 5-25. The Alert Partial Template

```erb
<% if notice && notice.present? %>
  <div class=" bg-blue-500 alert" role="alert">
    <%= notice %>
  </div>
<% end %>

<% if alert && alert.present? %>
  <div class=" bg-red-500 alert" role="alert">
    <%= alert %>
  </div>
<% end %>
```

A *partial*, or subtemplate, is a view template that can be included in another template or a layout. A partial template filename always starts with an underscore, but we must omit the underscore when rendering it.

Since we already have the `alert` partial, let's use it. Let's replace the code in Listing 5-26 in the `application` layout in favor of the partial.

Listing 5-26. Rendering the Partial in the Application Layout

```erb
<body>
  <p class="notice"><%= notice %></p>
  <p class="alert"><%= alert %></p>
  <%= render "layouts/alert" %>
```

Now, let's define the styles for the alert. But first, let's extend the Tailwind width definitions by adding `w-84` and `w-96`.

225

Let's open `css/tailwind.js` and add the new definitions, as shown in Listing 5-27.

Listing 5-27. Adding New Width Definitions

```
module.exports = {
  theme: {
    extend: {
      spacing: {
        '72': '18rem',
        '84': '21rem',
        '96': '24rem',
      }
    },
  },
  ...
```

Note   The value is calculated as follows for the width: 72 / 4 = 18; hence, *72* is mapped with `18rem`.

Then, let's create a file to hold common styles, `app/javascript/css/common.css`, as shown in Listing 5-28.

Listing 5-28. common.css File to Hold Common Styles

```
.alert {
  @apply text-white text-sm text-center font-medium px-4 py--3;
}
```

After that, let's create another CSS file for holding styles specific to the `session` layout. The file is `app/javascript/css/session.css`, as shown in Listing 5-29.

Listing 5-29. A CSS File to Hold Styles Specific to the session Layout

```
.body-session {
  @apply bg-gray-100 font-sans h-screen w-screen;
}
```

```
.body-session
h1.title {
  @apply font-hairline text-center text-4xl;
}

.body-session
.container {
  @apply mx-auto flex h-full items-center;
}

.body-session
a {
  @apply no-underline font-bold text-sm text-blue-400;
}

.body-session
a:hover {
  @apply text-blue-500;
}

.body-session
.alert {
  @apply mb-4;
}
```

Note   @apply is a Tailwind directive for mixing utility classes into our own class. Breakpoints, however, cannot be used with @apply, but they can be used with @screen, which we will see later.

Lastly, let's not forget to import it into css/application.css, as shown in Listing 5-30.

Listing 5-30. Importing Common and Session into application.css

...

```
@import "common";
@import "session";
```

Now, let's tell Rails to use the session layout for any Devise-rendered pages by adding the code in Listing 5-31 into ApplicationController.

Listing 5-31. Choosing a Layout Based on the Rendering Controller

```
class ApplicationController < ActionController::Base
  layout :layout_by_resource

  private

    def layout_by_resource
      devise_controller? ? "session" : "application"
    end
```

Now we are done. We already have the session layout. Next, let's customize the various session templates to match with our wireframes.

Customizing the Sign-Up Page

Let's translate our sign-up wireframe into a real page that looks like Figure 5-7.

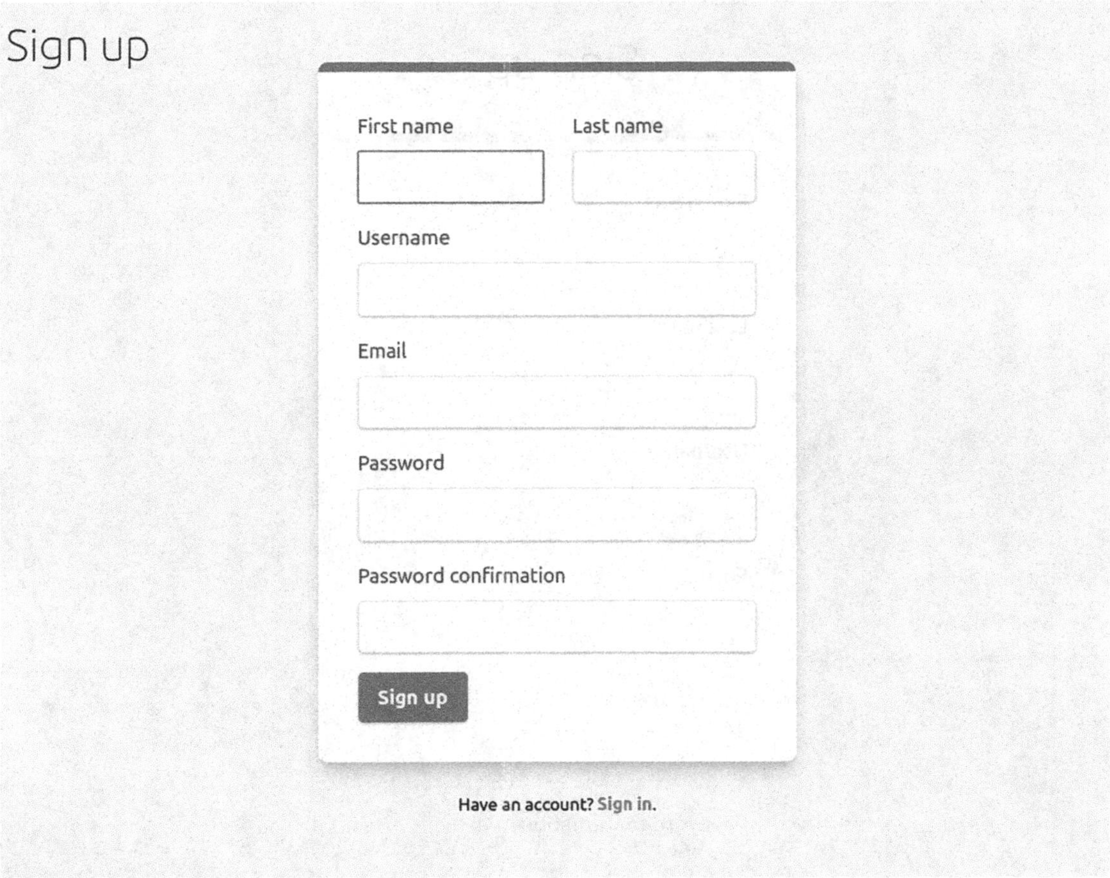

Figure 5-7. *Sign-up page on desktop*

For smartphone users, the page will look like Figure 5-8.

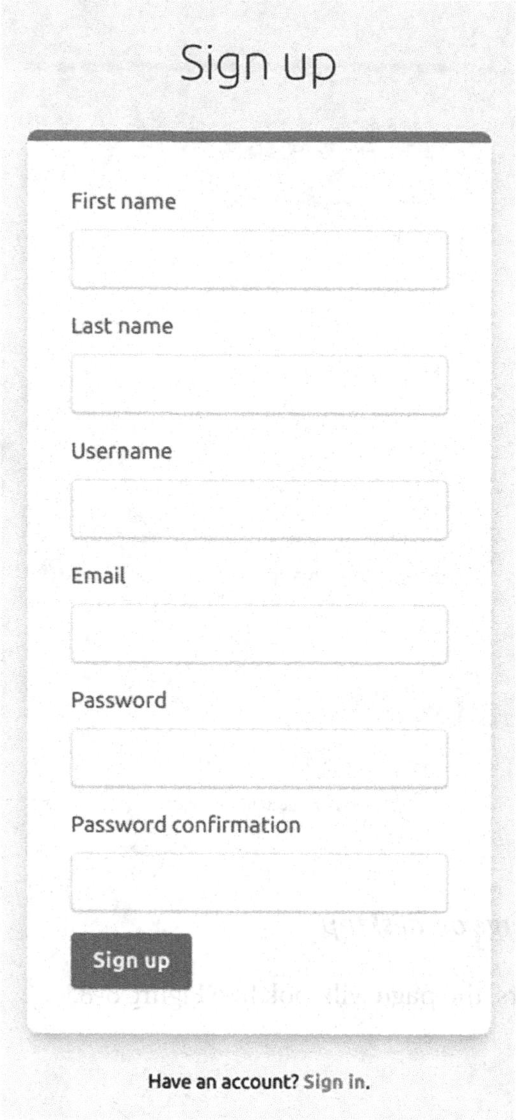

Figure 5-8. *The sign-up page rendered on a mobile phone*

Notice that on a mobile phone, the "First name" and "Last name" fields are rendered on their own rows. On the desktop, they are rendered side by side. To do that, let's use the syntax shown in Listing 5-32.

Listing 5-32. Responsive Code for the Name Fields

```
<div class="flex flex-wrap -mx-3 mb-0 md:mb-4">
  <div class="w-full md:w-1/2 px-3 mb-4 md:mb-0">
    ... First name
  </div>
  <div class="w-full md:w-1/2 px-3 mb-4 md:mb-0">
    ... Last name
  </div>
</div>
```

The previous code is another example of how breakpoints can be used to make the elements responsive. First, the browser always renders them in full due to the w-full class.

However, when the screen's width is equal to or larger than a tablet, both fields assume half of the width (w-1/2) of its container tag. At this point, the browser renders them in juxtaposition.

Listing 5-33 shows the full code for registrations/new.html.erb.

Listing 5-33. Full Source Code for registrations/new.html.erb

```
<% content_for(:page_title, "Sign up") %>

<%= form_for(resource,
  as: resource_name,
  url: registration_path(resource_name)) do |f| %>

  <div class="form-group">
    <%= render "devise/shared/error_messages",
      resource: resource %>

    <div class="flex flex-wrap -mx-3 mb-0 md:mb-4">
      <div class="w-full md:w-1/2 px-3 mb-4 md:mb-0">
        <%= f.label :first_name %>
        <%= f.text_field :first_name,
          autofocus: true,
          required: true %>
      </div>
```

```erb
    <div class="w-full md:w-1/2 px-3 mb-4 md:mb-0">
      <%= f.label :last_name %>
      <%= f.text_field :last_name %>
    </div>
  </div>

  <div class="mb-4">
    <%= f.label :username %>
    <%= f.text_field :username, required: true %>
  </div>

  <div class="mb-4">
    <%= f.label :email %>
    <%= f.email_field :email, required: true %>
  </div>

  <div class="mb-4">
    <%= f.label :password %>
    <%= f.password_field :password, required: true %>
  </div>

  <div class="mb-4">
    <%= f.label :password_confirmation %>
    <%= f.password_field :password_confirmation, required: true %>
  </div>

  <%= f.submit "Sign up", class: "cta-btn" %>
  </div>
<% end %>

<div class="text-center">
  <p class="text-grey-500 text-sm">
    Have an account?
    <%= link_to "Sign in", new_user_session_path %>.
  </p>
</div>
```

Let's check another interesting point in the previous code, as shown in Listing 5-34.

Listing 5-34. Setting the Content for page_title

```
<% content_for(:page_title, "Sign up") %>
```

The previous code replaces any `yield`-ing toward `page_title` with a given string, resulting in the page having "Sign up" in the top-left corner, as well as in the page's title. This is the intended effect when we wrote the code shown in Listing 5-35 in the `session` layout.

Listing 5-35. Excerpt from session.html.erb

```
<html>
  <head>
    <title><%= yield :page_title %></title>
```

As we have other fields on the form, let's whitelist those additional fields for Devise by adding the code shown in Listing 5-36 to `ApplicationController`.

Listing 5-36. Permitting the Necessary Fields for Signing Up

```
class ApplicationController < ActionController::Base
  before_action :config_devise_params, if: :devise_controller?

  ...

  protected

    def config_devise_params
      devise_parameter_sanitizer.permit(:sign_up, keys: [
        :first_name,
        :last_name,
        :username,
        :email,
        :password,
        :password_confirmation
      ])
    end
```

233

As in the previous snippet, we defined `config_devise_params` as a protected method. We discussed the differences between private and protected visibility in Chapter 3 if you would like to see why we do this. Yes, `ApplicationController` is inherited a lot of times.

With regard to the password field, Devise won't store the password as clear plain text. Instead, it will be cryptographically hashed. The hashed form of a strong password is of little use to a hacker as it is difficult to decipher a cryptographically secure hash back into plain text. This way, our password field is arguably secure as no one can readily know what is the real password of the user unless they perform cryptanalysis, a branch of science in the area of computer security, as shown in Listing 5-37.

Listing 5-37. Example of Hashing a Password Using the MD5 Algorithm

```
irb(main):001:0> Digest::MD5.hexdigest("mypassword")
=> "34819d7beeabb9260a5c854bc85b3e44"
```

Note   MD5 is considered no longer secure by today's standard, and the previous code is used only to demonstrate what a hashing algorithm can do to a string.

Next, let's add the styles in Listing 5-38 to `css/session.css`.

Listing 5-38. New Styles for Various Input and Button Elements

```
.body-session
.form-group {
  @apply border-main border-t-8 bg-white rounded-lg shadow-lg;
  @apply p-8 mb-6;
}

.body-session
.form-group label {
  @apply font-normal text-gray-600 block mb-2;
}
```

```
.body-session
.form-group input[type="text"],
.body-session
.form-group input[type="email"],
.body-session
.form-group input[type="password"] {
  @apply block appearance-none w-full bg-white;
  @apply border border-gray-200;
  @apply rounded shadow;
  @apply px-2 py-2;
}

.body-session
.form-group input[type="text"]:hover,
.body-session
.form-group input[type="email"]:hover,
.body-session
.form-group input[type="password"]:hover {
  @apply border-gray-300;
}

.body-session
.cta-btn {
  @apply select-none bg-main text-white font-bold;
  @apply rounded shadow;
  @apply py-2 px-4;
}

.body-session
.cta-btn:hover {
  @apply bg-main-500;
}
```

As our styles use another custom utility, bg-main, let's define it in css/tailwind.js, as shown in Listing 5-39.

Listing 5-39. Defining the Main Color

```
module.exports = {
  theme: {
    extend: {
      colors: {
        main: {
          default: "#60b0e2",
          "500": "#41a1dd",
        }
      },
      ...
```

Now, let's try registering a new user by opening the registration page at http://localhost:3000/users/sign_up and then filling in the form.

For the sake of a demo, let's input **abc** as the password and **def** as the password confirmation. Upon clicking the "Sign up" button, we will get the error messages shown in Figure 5-9.

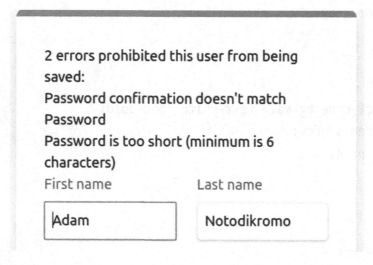

Figure 5-9. *Error messages*

Let's style the error messages to make them more pleasant. To do that, let's define the styles shown in Listing 5-40 in session.css.

Listing 5-40. Styles for an Error Box

```
.body-session
.error-box {
  @apply bg-red-100 border-t-4 border-red-500
    rounded-b text-red-900 px-4 py-3 mb-3 shadow-md;
}

.body-session
.error-box ul {
  @apply pl-4;
  list-style: disc;
}
```

Then, let's replace devise/shared/_error_messages.html.erb with the code shown in Listing 5-41.

Listing 5-41. A New error_messages.html.erb

```erb
<% if resource.errors.any? %>
  <div class="error-box" role="alert">
    <div class="flex">
      <div class="py-1"><svg class="fill-current h-6 w-6 text-red-500 mr-4"
      xmlns="http://www.w3.org/2000/svg" viewBox="0 0 20 20"><path d="M2.93
      17.07A10 10 0 1 1 17.07 2.93 10 10 0 0 1 2.93 17.07zm12.73-1.41A8
      8 0 1 0 4.34 4.34a8 8 0 0 0 11.32 11.32zM9 11V9h2v6H9v-4zm0-
      6h2v2H9V5z"/></svg></div>
      <div>
        <p class="font-bold">Request's errors</p>
        <ul>
          <% resource.errors.full_messages.each do |message| %>
            <li class="text-sm"><%= message %></li>
          <% end %>
        </ul>
      </div>
    </div>
  </div>
<% end %>
```

Now, the error messages are rendered within a stylish box. Neat! See Figure 5-10.

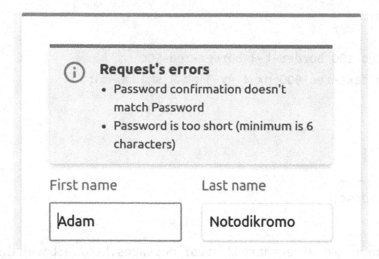

Figure 5-10. *Well-styled error messages*

Customizing the Sign-in Page

By default, Devise uses an email-password pair for authentication. However, as in the wireframe, Adam can sign in by using his username or his email address.

To do that, let's override the find_for_database_authentication method defined by Devise on the User model. To override it, we need to define our own version in the User model with the code shown in Listing 5-42.

Listing 5-42. Overriding find_for_database_authentication

```
def self.find_authenticatable(login)
  where("username = :value OR email = :value", value: login).first
end

def self.find_for_database_authentication(conditions)
  conditions = conditions.dup
  login = conditions.delete(:login).downcase
  find_authenticatable(login)
end
```

After that, let's define the authentication_keys to use login instead of the default email, as shown in Listing 5-43.

Listing 5-43. Specifying authentication_keys

```
class User < ApplicationRecord
  devise :database_authenticatable,
    :registerable,
    :recoverable,
    :rememberable,
    :validatable,
    authentication_keys: [:login]
```

Since `login` is not a database field, let's define a getter and setter for it, as shown in Listing 5-44.

Listing 5-44. Defining the Login Getter and Setter

```
class User < ApplicationRecord
  devise ...
  attr_writer :login

  validates_uniqueness_of :email
  ...

  def login
    @login || username || email
  end

  def self.find_authenticatable(login)
  ...

  private

    def ensure_proper_name_case
      self.first_name = first_name.capitalize
    end

end
```

After that, we can replace `sessions/new.html.erb` with the template shown in Listing 5-45.

Listing 5-45. Template for the Sign-in Page

```
<% content_for(:page_title, "Sign in") %>

<%= form_for(resource,
  as: resource_name,
  url: session_path(resource_name)) do |f| %>

  <div class="form-group">
    <div class="mb-4">
      <%= f.label :login, "Username / Email" %>
      <%= f.text_field :login, autofocus: true %>
    </div>

    <div class="mb-4">
      <%= f.label :password %>
      <%= f.password_field :password %>
    </div>

    <div class="flex items-center justify-between">
      <%= f.submit "Log in", class: "cta-btn" %>

      <%= link_to "Forgot password?",
        new_password_path(resource_name),
        class: "inline-block" %>
    </div>
  </div>
<% end %>

<div class="text-center">
  <p class="text-grey-500 text-sm">
    Don't have an account?
    <%= link_to "Create an Account",
      new_user_registration_path %>.
  </p>
</div>
```

Now, we can try signing in through http://localhost:3000/users/sign_in, which renders the page shown in Figure 5-11.

Sign in

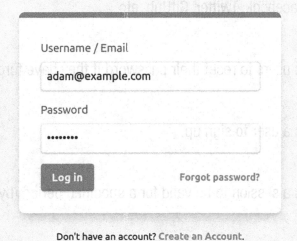

Figure 5-11. *Sign-in page*

Note   Devise has ten ready-to-use modules for authentication.

1. confirmable

Force the users to confirm that their email is valid by visiting a generated link before they are allowed to sign in for the first time.

2. database_authenticatable

This method hashes the password before saving it into the database.

3. lockable

This method blocks the user after failed login attempts.

4. omniauthable

This method adds support for logging in from third-party Omniauth providers such as Google, Apple, Facebook, Twitter, GitHub, etc.

5. recoverable

This method allows users to reset their password if they have forgotten it.

6. registerable

This method allows a user to sign up.

7. rememberable

This method allows a session to be valid for a specified period (by default two weeks).

8. trackable

This method allows you to do some basic tracking such as tracking the user's IP address, the last time they signed in, how many times they have signed in, and when was the last time they signed in.

9. timeoutable

This method allows you to log the user out after showing inactivity for a certain amount of time.

10. validatable

This method performs validations on the email and password fields, for example, by ensuring that the password meets specific security criteria.

Customizing the Forgot Password Page

The "Forgot password" page is a simple one, as shown in Figure 5-12.

Forgot password

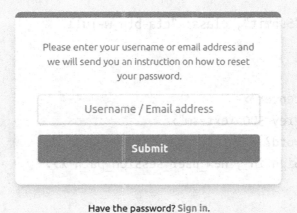

Figure 5-12. *"Forgot password" page*

The template for the page is located at app/views/devise/passwords/new.html.erb. Listing 5-46 shows the code for the template.

Listing 5-46. The Code for the Templates

```
<% content_for(:page_title, "Forgot password") %>

<%= form_for(resource,
  as: resource_name,
  url: password_path(resource_name)) do |f| %>
  <div class="form-group">
    <%= render "devise/shared/error_messages",
      resource: resource %>

    <p class="font-light text-sm text-center text-gray-600 mb-4">
      Please enter your email address and we will send
      an instruction on how to reset your password.
    </p>
```

```
  <div class="mb-4">
    <%= f.label :login, "Username / Email", class: "text-center" %>
    <%= f.text_field :login,
      autofocus: true,
      required: true %>
  </div>

  <%= f.submit "Submit", class: "cta-btn w-full" %>
  </div>
<% end %>

<div class="text-center">
  <p class="text-grey-500 text-sm">
    Have the password?
    <%= link_to "Sign in", new_user_session_path %>.
  </p>
</div>
```

However, since we use an unorthodox field, we need to override the way Devise finds the User record.

First, let's define revise_password_keys, as shown in Listing 5-47.

Listing 5-47. Use the Login Field to Retrieve the User's Account

```
devise :database_authenticatable,
  :registerable,
  :recoverable,
  :rememberable,
  :validatable,
  authentication_keys: [:login],
  reset_password_keys: [:login]
```

After that, let's define send_reset_password_instructions in the User model, as shown in Listing 5-48, to override the method with the same name that Devise has defined for us.

Listing 5-48. Overriding send_reset_password_instructions

```
def self.send_reset_password_instructions(conditions)
  recoverable = find_recoverable_or_init_with_errors(conditions)

  if recoverable.persisted?
    recoverable.send_reset_password_instructions
  end

  recoverable
end

def self.find_recoverable_or_init_with_errors(conditions)
  conditions = conditions.dup
  login = conditions.delete(:login).downcase
  recoverable = find_authenticatable(login)

  unless recoverable
    recoverable = new(login: login)
    recoverable.errors.add(:login, login.present? ? :not_found : :blank)
  end

  recoverable
end
```

That's it—our forgot password page now is usable with styles.

Customizing the Reset Password Page

Let's conclude our customization efforts with the reset password page. Let's begin by installing letter_opener. letter_opener is a gem allowing us to receive outbound emails sent by our application. As such, we can receive the reset password instruction emails, for example.

So, let's add the letter_opener within the development group in our gemfile, as shown in Listing 5-49.

Listing 5-49. Adding letter_opener_web into the Gemfile

```
gem 'letter_opener_web', '~> 1.0'
```

After that, let's register its web interface in our routes.rb file, as shown in Listing 5-50.

Listing 5-50. Registering the letter_opener's Web Interface

```
if Rails.env.development?
  mount LetterOpenerWeb::Engine, at: "/letter_opener"
end
```

After that, let's configure Action Mailer to deliver emails using letter_opener in the development environment. Let's add the code in Listing 5-51 into development.rb.

Listing 5-51. Setting the Action Mailer's delivery_method

```
config.action_mailer.delivery_method = :letter_opener_web
```

Now, let's try the "Forgot password" page. On the page, type in a registered user's email address or username. After that, let's open our mailbox at http://localhost:3000/letter_opener. There will be an email with instructions on how to reset the account's password, as shown in Figure 5-13.

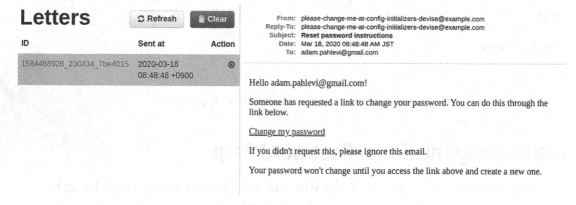

Figure 5-13. *A reset password instruction email in our inbox*

If we click the link, we can see that the page is quite rustic for now. Let's customize it! Change the view for passwords/edit.html.erb to the code shown in Listing 5-52.

Listing 5-52. New View Template for the Reset Password Page

```erb
<% content_for(:page_title, "Reset password") %>

<%= form_for(resource,
  as: resource_name,
  url: password_path(resource_name),
  html: { method: :put }) do |f| %>

  <div class="form-group">
    <%= render "devise/shared/error_messages",
      resource: resource %>

    <%= f.hidden_field :reset_password_token %>

    <div class="mb-4">
      <%= f.label :password, "New password" %>
      <%= f.password_field :password, autofocus: true %>
    </div>

    <div class="mb-4">
      <%= f.label :password_confirmation,
        "Confirm new password" %>
      <%= f.password_field :password_confirmation %>
    </div>

    <%= f.submit "Change my password", class: "cta-btn w-full" %>
  </div>
<% end %>
```

The rendered page now looks very stylish, as shown in Figure 5-14.

Figure 5-14. "*Reset password*" *page rendered for mobile screen size*

Proper Home Page

Something is missing: a proper home page! Let's create a new one that looks just as nice as in the wireframe. Not only that, in this section, you will also learn how to make a partial template that accepts an optional argument.

First, let's add evil_icons into the gemfile, as shown in Listing 5-53.

Listing 5-53. Adding evil_icons into the Gemfile

```
gem 'evil_icons', '~> 1.10'
```

After that, add the code in Listing 5-54 into stylesheets/application.css.

Listing 5-54. Adding evil-icons to application.css

```
...
*= require_tree .
*= require_self
*= require evil-icons
```

Then, let's add the icons sprite into our application.html.erb layout, as shown in Listing 5-55.

Listing 5-55. Adding the Icons Sprite into the Application Layout

```
...
  <%= evil_icons_sprite %>
</head>
```

We would like to have a home page that looks like Figure 5-15.

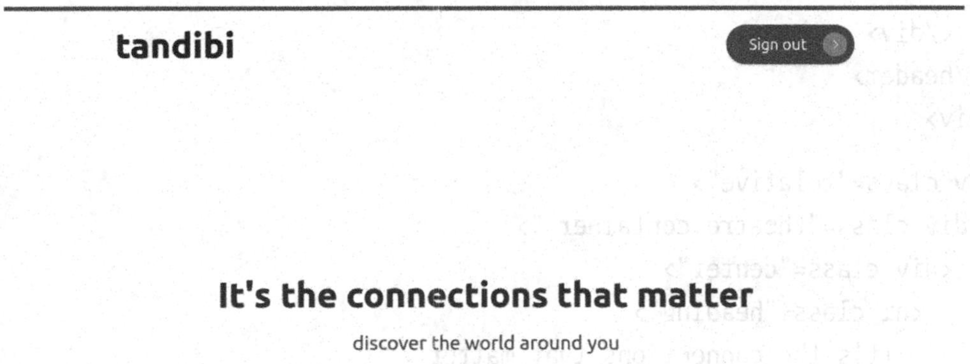

tandibi

It's the connections that matter

discover the world around you

Figure 5-15. *The new, clean home page*

So, let's replace home/index.html.erb with the code shown in Listing 5-56.

Listing 5-56. The New Code for Our Home Page

```
<div class="home">
  <div class="bg-indigo-700 h-1"></div>
  <div class="container mx-auto">
    <header>
      <div class="flex items-center flex-shrink-0">
        <h1 class="title">tandibi</h1>
```

```
      </div>
      <div class="actions">
        <div class="relative">
          <% if current_user %>
            <%= render "action_button",
              caption: "Sign out",
              icon: "ei-chevron-right",
              link: destroy_user_session_path,
              method: :delete %>
          <% else %>
            <%= render "action_button",
              caption: "Sign in",
              icon: "ei-chevron-right",
              link: new_user_session_path %>
          <% end %>
        </div>
      </div>
    </header>
  </div>

  <div class="relative">
    <div class="theatre container ">
      <div class="center">
        <h1 class="heading">
          It's the connections that matter
        </h1>
        <p class="text-gray-700 text-xl md:pb-4">
          <% unless current_user %>
            <%= link_to "Let's join", new_user_registration_path %>
          <% end %>
          discover the world around you
        </p>
      </div>
    </div>
  </div>
</div>
```

From the previous code, we can see that we are rendering `action_button` twice, depending on whether the user is logged in or not.

Note   We can also use the `user_signed_in?` helper method to check whether a user has signed in or not.

If the user is logged in, we pass in the `method` variable so that clicking the link performs a `DELETE` request, as shown in Listing 5-57.

Listing 5-57. Snippet for Rendering action_button Conditionally

```
<% if current_user %>
  <%= render "action_button",
    ...
    method: :delete %>
<% else %>
  <%= render "action_button",
    caption: "Sign in",
    icon: "ei-chevron-right",
    link: new_user_session_path %>
<% end %>
```

We can see from the previous snippet that the `method` variable is optional. The code for `views/home/_action_button.html.erb` in Listing 5-58 reveals how to do that.

Listing 5-58. Code for the action_button Partial

```
<% method = local_assigns.fetch(:method, :get) %>

<%= link_to link, class: "action", method: method do %>
  <span class="mr-4"><%= caption %></span>
  <%= evil_icon icon, size: :s, class: "arrow" %>
<% end %>
```

It turns out that we can use `local_assigns` to help us define an optional variable. The `local_assigns` itself is just a hash, so we can just use `Hash#fetch` at any time.

Note   We may use `defined?` to check whether a variable has been defined or not, but, in general, using `defined?` is quite discouraged. To see why, in this case, for example, `method` is also a valid function. So, instead of being firm that the partial does not receive it as a local variable, the system confuses it with a valid identifier of an existing `Kernel#method` function. Luckily, an unrecognized value for `link_to`'s method argument is interpreted as get—and this is a subtle bug.

Now, we need to do some more styling. Let's add the code shown in Listing 5-59 in `common.css`.

Listing 5-59.   Common CSS Style for the Link

```
a {
  @apply no-underline text-blue-400;
}

a:hover {
  @apply text-blue-500;
}
```

After that, let's create `home.css` within the `app/javascript/css` folder. The code looks like Listing 5-60.

Listing 5-60.   Code for home.css

```
.home
header {
  @apply w-full p-2 flex items-center justify-between flex-wrap;
}

.home
header .title {
  @apply font-extrabold text-2xl;
}
```

```
.home
.heading {
  @apply font-semibold text-gray-900 text-4xl pt-8;
}

.home
.actions {
  @apply w-auto flex items-center justify-end;
}

.home
.action {
  @apply flex flex-row rounded-full py-2 pl-6 pr-2;
  @apply bg-indigo-700 text-white shadow;
  @apply items-center justify-center text-base;
}

.home
.action .arrow {
  @apply flex items-center justify-center;
  @apply bg-teal-500 rounded-full w-6 h-6 text-xs;
}

.home
.theatre {
  @apply m-auto pt-8 pb-16;
}

.home
.theatre .center {
  @apply flex flex-col justify-center items-center text-center px-4;
}

@screen md {
  .home
  .header {
    @apply px-0;
  }
```

```
.home
header .title {
  @apply text-4xl;
}

.home
.heading {
  @apply pt-16 pb-2;
}

.home
.theatre {
  @apply  pt-32 pb-32;
}
}
```

After that, let's import home.css from app/javascript/css/application.css, as shown in Listing 5-61.

Listing 5-61. Importing Home Css Within application.css

```
@import "common";
@import "home";
@import "session";
```

Email Makeover

As we saw earlier in the reset password email, our email looks so unpolished. Our users might think that a site with that kind of email is bogus. So, let's do a makeover. The makeover is going to transform our email to look like Figure 5-16.

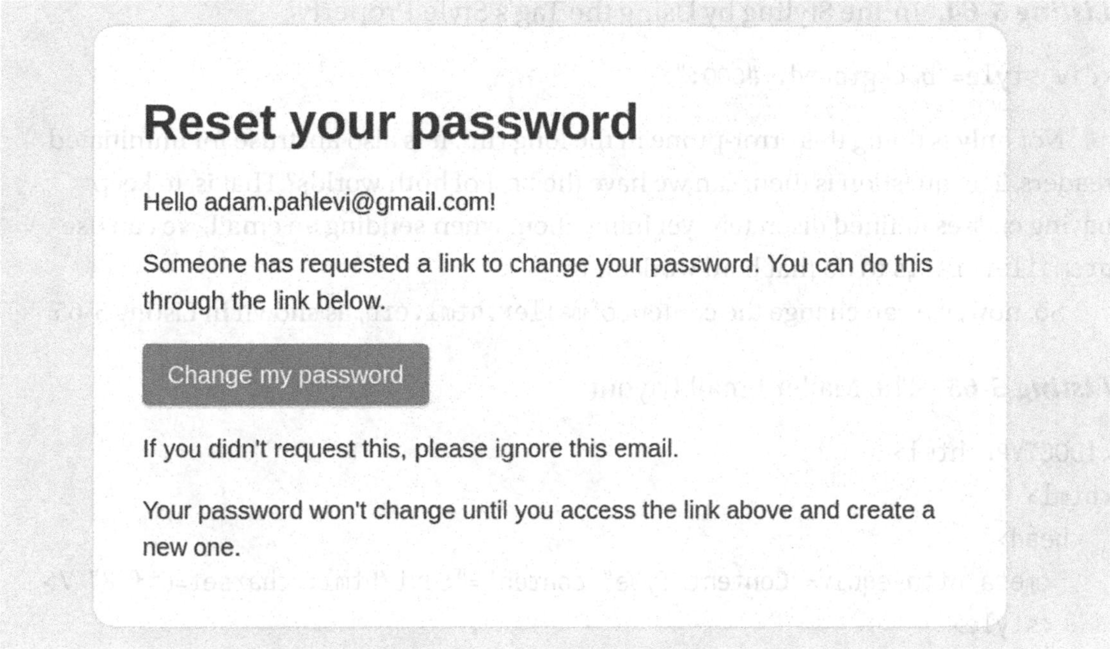

Reset your password

Hello adam.pahlevi@gmail.com!

Someone has requested a link to change your password. You can do this through the link below.

Change my password

If you didn't request this, please ignore this email.

Your password won't change until you access the link above and create a new one.

Figure 5-16. *A neater email layout*

First, let's add `premailer-rails` into our gemfile, as shown in Listing 5-62.

Listing 5-62. Adding premailer-rails into the Gemfile

```
gem 'premailer-rails', '~> 1.11'
```

The problem that `premailer-rails` solves is related to the way styling works for emails. The fact is, email clients are conservative. Many of them ignore the `<style>` tag, let alone any JavaScript code.

The workaround is to write all the CSS styles inline, that is, using the `style` attribute to style the element. So, instead of using the code in Listing 5-63, we must do something like Listing 5-64.

Listing 5-63. Styling by Using CSS Classes

```
<style>
  .card-inset { background: #000; }
</style>

<div class="card-inset">
```

Listing 5-64. Inline Styling by Using the Tag's Style Property

```
<div style="background: #000;">
```

Not only is doing this error-prone in the long run, it is also abstruse for uninitiated readers. The question is then: can we have the best of both worlds? That is, to keep having classes defined discretely, yet inline them when sending an email, we can use `premailer-rails` to do that hard work for us.

So, now, we can change the content of `mailer.html.erb`, as shown in Listing 5-65.

Listing 5-65. The Mailer Email Layout

```
<!DOCTYPE html>
<html>
  <head>
    <meta http-equiv="Content-Type" content="text/html; charset=utf-8" />
    <style>
      body {
        font-family: 'Lato','Helvetica Neue',Helvetica,Arial,sans-serif;
      }

      .content {
        background: #f4f4f4;
        text-align: center;
        width: 100%;
        padding: 24px 0 16px 0;
      }

      .container {
        text-align: left;
        display: inline-block;
        width: 70%;
        max-width: 600px;
        min-width: 280px;
      }
```

```
    .line {
      padding: 0;
      display: block;
      height: 2px;
    }
    .top.line { background: #f6f6f6; }
    .bottom.line { background: #eaeaea; }

    .card-outset {
      border: 1px solid #f0f0f0;
      border-radius: 15px;
    }

    .card-inset {
      border: 1px solid #eaeaea;
      border-radius: 15px;
      padding: 24px 32px 24px 32px;
      color: #444;
      background:#fff;
    }

    .button {
      display: inline-block;
      background: #60b0e2;
      color: #fafafa;
      font-weight: 500;
      border-radius: 0.25rem;
      box-shadow: 0 1px 3px 0 rgba(0, 0, 0, 0.1), 0 1px 2px 0 rgba(0, 0,
      0, 0.06);
      padding: 0.5rem 1rem;
      text-decoration: none;
    }

    p {
      line-height: 24px;
    }
  </style>
</head>
```

```
  <body>
    <div class="content">
      <div class="container">
        <div class="card-outset">
          <div class="card-inset">
            <%= yield %>
          </div>
        </div>
      </div>
    </div>
  </body>
</html>
```

After that, let's tell Devise to use the polished layout by adding the code shown in Listing 5-66 to `config/application.rb`.

Listing 5-66. Telling Devise to Use the Mailer Template

```
module Tandibi
  class Application < Rails::Application
    ...
    config.to_prepare do
      Devise::Mailer.layout "mailer"
    end
  end
end
```

Then, let's change the email template a little bit. First, let's add the heading shown in Listing 5-67 to `mailer/password_change.html.erb`.

Listing 5-67. Adding a Title Heading into password_change.html.erb

```
<h1>Password changed</h1>
...
```

Second, for `reset_password_instructions.html.erb`, use the code shown in Listing 5-68.

Listing 5-68. Adding a Relevant Heading for the Reset Instruction Email

```
<h1>Reset your password</h1>
...
```

Also, let's append a `button` class for the action link to render it as a proper call-to-action button, as shown in Listing 5-69.

Listing 5-69. Making the Link Looks Like a Call to Action Button

```
<p>
  <%= link_to 'Change my password',
    edit_password_url(@resource, reset_password_token: @token),
    class: "button" %>
</p>
```

That's it! Let's restart our server before testing the new layout as we have changed something in the `config` folder.

Summary

In this chapter, we got straight to business by building neat, responsive authentication pages. We used the increasingly popular Tailwind CSS, and for handling authentication, we made use of the battle-tested Devise gem. In fact, it is hard to meet a customer-facing Rails app where Devise is not used. Devise saved us a lot of time and headaches.

In the next chapter, we will focus our attention on how to test our views and learn about performing code in the background, while at the same time building the timelines.

CHAPTER 6

Building the Timeline

Timelines are newish inventions. According to the dictionary, a *timeline* is "a collection of online posts or updates associated with a specific social media account." And that is what we will build in this chapter. See Figure 6-1.

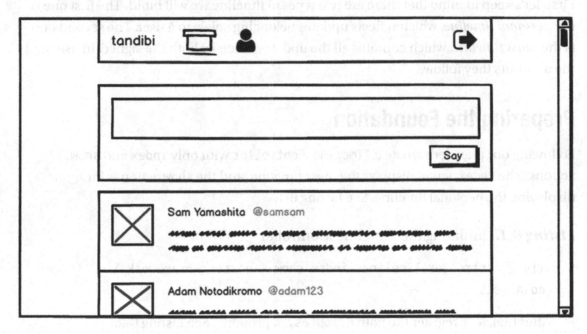

Figure 6-1. *Timeline*

The timeline is a fundamental part of any social media app. There, users can see anyone's updates (an activity known as *stalking*), reply to any of them (*commenting*), or post an update themselves (*posting*). In addition, we will skin the timeline dark because the dark mode is currently the trend. No one uses social media that doesn't follow the trend, right?

© Adam Notodikromo 2021
A. Notodikromo, *Learn Rails 6*, https://doi.org/10.1007/978-1-4842-6026-5_6

While building our timeline, you will also learn how to test our views à la carte (that's a cool way no one used to say *unit testing*). You will also learn how to do request testing, where we test all the way down from the router to rendering the view.

Indeed, testing is something the previous chapter skipped. But don't worry, being the good software engineers that we are, we will consider testing a first-class citizen. So, this chapter will cover all the necessary testing techniques commonly employed by software engineers.

Let's Build the Timeline

First, let's keep in mind that there are two types of timeline we will build. The first one is the *personal timeline*, which reflects updates belonging solely to a user. The second one is the *mass timeline*, which contains all the updates made by both the signed-in user and the accounts they follow.

Preparing the Foundation

Following our plan, let's create a `TimelinesController` with only `index` and `show` actions. The `index` action displays the mass timeline, and the `show` action is for displaying the personal timeline. See Listing 6-1.

Listing 6-1. Initiating the TimelinesController

```
$ rails g controller Timelines index show --no-test-framework \
  --no-assets
```

After that, let's register the path in `routes.rb` properly. See Listing 6-2.

Listing 6-2. Registering the Paths of the TimelinesController

```
Rails.application.routes.draw do
  get 'timelines/index'
  get 'timelines/show'
  ...
```

```
authenticate :user do
  resources :timelines,
    only: [:index, :show]
  end
end
```

With that, we are done preparing the controller and the router.

Preparing the Layout

If we look back at our home page, we can see that a navigation bar is attached to the top of the page. However, it is in the template instead of in the layout. If we are to use the same application layout for the timeline, a navbar needs to be manually rendered on both the index and show pages, which doesn't feel so DRY.

Our timeline will also use a dark mode skin, which requires a different design altogether. Using the application layout, how can we alter the coloring? Using yield and content_for to specify additional classes on the body tag feels quite indecorous, doesn't it? See Figure 6-2.

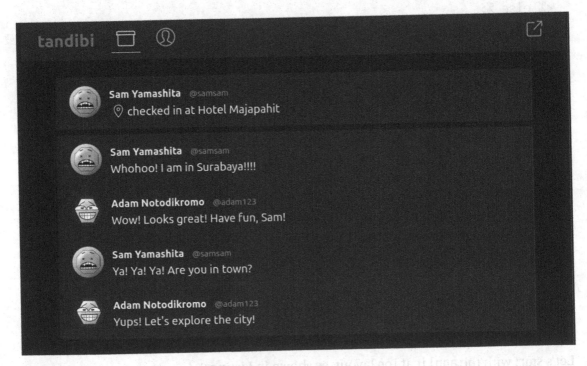

Figure 6-2. Our timeline in dark mode

Instead, let's create a new template. Let's call it member, which is used only for rendering pages mainly for logged-in users—which is why it's named member.

We could name the layout timeline, but what if in the future we wanted to use it to render any nontimeline page such as a settings page to use the same look and feel? It's essential to name a layout as inclusively as possible.

Note   There are only two hard things in computer science: cache invalidation and naming things.

Let's start making the layout. First, considering that all of our layouts currently have repeating head tags, let's DRY them out. Let's create the layouts/_header.html.erb partial and add the code shown in Listing 6-3.

Listing 6-3. DRY-ing the Head Tag in the application Layout

```
<head>
  <% if content_for?(:page_title) %>
    <title>Tandibi - <%= yield :page_title %></title>
  <% else %>
    <title>Tandibi</title>
  <% end %>

  <%= csrf_meta_tags %>
  <%= csp_meta_tag %>

  <%= stylesheet_link_tag 'application', media: 'all' %>
  <%= javascript_pack_tag 'application' %>

  <meta name="viewport"
    content="width=device-width, initial-scale=1.0">
  <meta http-equiv="X-UA-Compatible"
    content="ie=edge">

  <%= evil_icons_sprite %>
</head>
```

Then, let's replace entirely any head block with the code to render the header partial. Let's start with the application layout, as shown in Listing 6-4.

Listing 6-4. The application Layout

```
<!DOCTYPE html>
<html>
  <head>
    <title>Tandibi</title>
    <%= csrf_meta_tags %>
    <%= csp_meta_tag %>

    <%= stylesheet_link_tag 'application' ...%>
    <%= javascript_pack_tag 'application' ... %>
    <%= evil_icons_sprite %>
  </head>
  <%= render "layouts/header" %>

  <body>
    <%= render "layouts/alert" %>

    <%= yield %>
  </body>
</html>
```

After that, let's do the same for the session layout, as shown in Listing 6-5.

Listing 6-5. DRY-ing the Head Tag in the session Layout

```
<!DOCTYPE html>
<html>
  <head>
    <title><%= yield :page_title %></title>
    <%= csrf_meta_tags %>
    <%= csp_meta_tag %>

    <%= stylesheet_link_tag 'application', media: 'all' %>
    <%= javascript_pack_tag 'application' %>

    <meta name="viewport"
      content="width=device-width, initial-scale=1.0">
    <meta http-equiv="X-UA-Compatible"
      content="ie=edge">
```

265

```
</head>
<%= render "layouts/header" %>

<body class="body-session">
...
```

Now, let's create a navbar partial at layouts/member/_navbar.html.erb, and add
the code shown in Listing 6-6.

Listing 6-6. Code for the Navigation Bar

```erb
<nav class="topnav">
  <div class="flex items-center flex-shrink-0">
    <%= link_to timelines_path do %>
      <h1>tandibi</h1>
    <% end %>
  </div>
  <div class="block flex-grow flex items-center w-auto">
    <div class="text-sm flex-grow">
      <%= link_to timelines_path,
        class: "linked-icon #{"active" if on_bunch?}" do %>
        <%= evil_icon "ei-timeline" %>
      <% end %>

      <%= link_to timeline_path(current_user),
        class: "linked-icon #{"active" if on_self?}" do %>
        <%= evil_icon "ei-user" %>
      <% end %>
    </div>
    <div>
      <%= link_to destroy_user_session_path,
        class: "linked-icon sign-out",
        method: :delete do %>
        <%= evil_icon "ei-external-link" %>
      <% end %>
    </div>
  </div>
</nav>
```

In the previous code, we use `timeline_path(current_user)` to generate the link to a user's timeline. Typically, the `show` action uses the `id` of a resource. So, it spells out a path such as `/timelines/1` or `/timelines/2`. Notice the use of an ID, such as 1 and 2, which looks unfriendly and antisocial to our friendly, sociable users.

So that the path gets spelled with a username, rather than an ID, let's add the code shown in Listing 6-7 to the `User` model.

Listing 6-7. Use the User Record's Username for the Path

```
class User < ApplicationRecord
  ...
  before_save :ensure_proper_name_case

  def to_param
    username
  end

  def login
  ...
end
```

After that, let's tell the router to call the identifier as a username instead of an ID. To do that, let's add the code shown in Listing 6-8 to `config/router.rb`.

Listing 6-8. Specifying a Username As the Identifier

```
Rails.application.routes.draw do
  devise_for :users
  root to: 'home#index'
  # For details on the DSL available within this file, see https://guides.
  rubyonrails.org/routing.html

  if Rails.env.development?
    mount LetterOpenerWeb::Engine, at: "/letter_opener"
  end
```

```
  authenticate :user do
    resources :timelines,
      only: [:index, :show],
      param: :username
  end
end
```

If we look back at the code for the navbar, we can see that certain classes are to be applied conditionally, such as in Listing 6-9, where we added active only if on_bunch? returns true.

Listing 6-9. Snippet for active Class

```
<%= link_to timelines_path,
  class: "linked-icon #{"active" if on_bunch?}" do %>
```

The active class gives an underline effect on a specific icon on the navbar, but only when the user is at a certain page. For instance, if the user is on the mass timeline page, the first icon is underlined, as shown in Figure 6-3.

Figure 6-3. *An underline for the page our user is browsing*

To do this, we apply the active class conditionally by using helper methods such as on_bunch?, which we should define in TimelinesHelper as shown in Listing 6-10. Let's create a new file for TimelinesHelper at app/helpers/timelines_helper.rb.

Listing 6-10. Code for TimelinesHelper

```
module TimelinesHelper
  def on_timeline?
    controller_path == "timelines"
  end

  def on_bunch?
    on_timeline? && action_name == "index"
  end
```

```
def on_self?
  on_timeline? && action_name == "show" &&
    params[:username] == current_user.username
end
end
```

The `controller_path` method returns the snake-cased full name of the rendering controller without the word `controller`. The `action_name` returns the name of the rendering action.

For the timeline icon, we use `ei-timeline`, which is not shipped with the Evil Icons, so we need to define it ourselves. Let's add the code shown in Listing 6-11 in the `app/views/layouts/_header.html.erb` partial for the `ei-timeline` icon. Let's add it near the end of the file.

Listing 6-11. SVG Code for ei-timeline-icon

```
...
<svg xmlns="http://www.w3.org/2000/svg" style="display: none;">
  <symbol id="ei-timeline-icon" viewBox="0 0 50 50">
  <path d="M42 20h-2v-5c0-.6-.4-1-1-1H11c-.6
    0-1 .4-1 1v5H8v-5c0-1.7 1.3-3 3-3h28c1.7
    0 3 1.3 3 3v5z"/>
  <path d="M37 40H13c-1.7 0-3-1.3-3-3V20h2v17c0
    .6.4 1 1 1h24c.6 0 1-.4 1-1V20h2v17c0
    1.7-1.3 3-3 3z"/>
  <path d="M8 18h34v2H8z"/>
  </symbol>
</svg>
</head>
```

Last but not least is the styling. Before doing that, let's extend Tailwind by adding the highlighted code in Listing 6-12 to `css/tailwind.js`.

Listing 6-12. Code to Extend Tailwind.js

```
colors: {
  main: {
    default: "#60b0e2",
    "200": "#6cc1ff",
    "500": "#41a1dd",
    "800": "#04609a",
  },
  dark: {
    "400": "#8a8a8a",
    "600": "#343538",
    "700": "#2a2b2d",
    "800": "#18191a"
  }
},
spacing: {
  '14': '3.5rem',
  '72': '18rem',
  '84': '21rem',
  '96': '24rem',
  '168': '42rem',
  '192': '48rem',
}
```

Listing 6-13 shows the stylesheet for the navbar and should be saved as app/javascript/css/member/nav.css.

Listing 6-13. Stylesheet for the Navbar

```
.body-member
nav.topnav {
  @apply flex flex-wrap items-center justify-between;
  @apply pl-6 pr-6 pt-1 pb-1;
  @apply bg-dark-700;
}
```

```
.body-member
nav.topnav h1 {
  @apply font-semibold text-2xl text-dark-400;
  @apply mr-6;
}

.body-member
a.linked-icon {
  @apply inline-block mt-0 mr-3 text-main-200;
}

.body-member
a.linked-icon:hover, a.linked-icon.active {
  @apply text-teal-200;
}

.body-member
a.linked-icon.active .icon {
  @apply border-teal-200 !important;
  border-bottom: 1px solid;
}

.body-member
a.linked-icon .icon,
.body-member
nav.topnav h1 {
  @apply border-dark-700 !important;
  border-bottom: 1px solid;
}

.body-member
a.linked-icon .icon {
  width: 40px;
  height: 40px;
}
```

```
.body-member
a.linked-icon.sign-out {
  @apply mr-0;
}
```

Next, let's create the member layout. Let's create app/views/layouts/member.html. erb and then add the code shown in Listing 6-14.

Listing 6-14. Code for layouts/member.html.erb

```
<!DOCTYPE html>
<html>
  <%= render "layouts/header" %>

  <body class="body-member dark">
    <main class="container sm:w-full sm:max-w-full">
      <div class="m-auto w-full md:w-192">
        <%= render "layouts/member/navbar" %>
        <%= render "layouts/alert" %>

        <div class="container p-6 md:pr-0 md:pl-0">
          <div class="m-auto w-full md:w-168">
            <%= yield %>
          </div>
        </div>
      </div>
    </main>
  </body>
</html>
```

Listing 6-15 shows the stylesheet code for the layout and should be saved as app/ javascript/css/member.css.

Listing 6-15. Code for the Member Layout

```
@import "member/nav";

.body-member {
  @apply bg-gray-100 font-sans;
}
```

```
.body-member
.container {
  @apply mx-auto;
}

.body-member.dark {
  @apply bg-dark-800;
  @apply text-gray-100;
}
```

Then, let's import the `member` stylesheet into `css/application.css` and we are done. See Listing 6-16.

Listing 6-16. Importing the Member Stylesheet into the Main Application Stylesheet

```
...
@import "session";
@import "member";
```

After that, let's open `app/controllers/application_controller.rb`, and then let's change the `layout_by_resource` method to use the member layout when necessary, as shown here:

```
class ApplicationController < ActionController::Base
  ...

  private

    def member_controller?
      return false if controller_path == "home"

      true
    end

    def layout_by_resource
      case
      when devise_controller? then "session"
      when member_controller? then "member"
```

```
    else "application"
    end
  end

  def layout_by_resource
    devise_controller? ? "session" : "application"
  end
```

We have defined a lot of new styles and created a new layout that we will use as our foundation on which to build Tandibi.

Working on the Mass Timeline

The plan is to use @posts to hold all the posts to be displayed in the timeline. To make things DRY, we create a line partial to render each post. As you will soon see, the line partial is the crème de la crème of the whole timeline architecture.

Let's start with TimelinesController. Open app/controllers/timelines_controller.rb and then let's redefine the index action as shown in Listing 6-17.

Listing 6-17. Creating the @posts Instance Variable

```
class TimelinesController < ApplicationController
  def index
    @posts = Post.not_reply.where(user_id: [
      current_user.id,
      *current_user.followings.pluck(:id)
    ]).includes(postable: [:place]).order("created_at DESC")
  end
  ...
end
```

As you can see in the previous code, we call not_reply on the Post model. We should define not_reply soon as a scope at the Post model. But first, let's understand why we need to do this.

We know that a user's timeline consists of a lot of posted messages. Each of those pieces may have any number of replies. Yet, it might be better to display those replies if the user expands, or clicks, the post where those replies were made. This is what not_reply will do, which will filter out posts that are replies to another post.

So, let's define the not_reply scope in the Post model, as shown in Listing 6-18.

Listing 6-18. not_reply scope Defined in the Post Model

```
scope :not_reply, -> { where(thread_id: nil) }
```

Now, let's create the line partial, which should be saved as views/timelines/
_line.html.erb with the code shown in Listing 6-19.

Listing 6-19. Code for the line Partial

```erb
<% user = post.user %>
<% postable = post.postable %>

<div class="line flex">
  <div class="profile-container">
    <%= image_tag user.profile_picture_url %>
  </div>

  <div class="content">
    <div class="identifier">
      <%= link_to timeline_path(user) do %>
        <span class="name"><%= user.name %></span>
        <span class="username">@<%= user.username %></span>
      <% end %>
    </div>

    <% if postable.is_a?(Status) %>
      <%= simple_format post.postable.text %>
    <% elsif postable.is_a?(Sight) %>
      <div class="flex items-center">
        <%= evil_icon "ei-location" %>
        <p>
          <%= humanized_activity_type(postable) %>
          <%= postable.place.name %>
        </p>
      </div>
    <% end %>
  </div>
</div>
```

```
<% if post.replies.any? %>
  <div class="replies">
    <% post.replies.each do |reply| %>
      <%= render "timelines/line", post: reply %>
    <% end %>
  </div>
<% end %>
```

Next, let's define the `replies` association in the `Post` model, as shown in Listing 6-20.

Listing 6-20. Defining the Replies on the Post Model

```
class Post < ApplicationRecord
  belongs_to :postable, polymorphic: true
  belongs_to :user
  belongs_to :thread, class_name: "Post", optional: true
  has_many :replies, class_name: "Post", foreign_key: :thread_id
```

Now let's create an `all` partial to represent the timeline as a whole. Let's save the file as app/views/timelines/_all.html.erb. See Listing 6-21.

Listing 6-21. The all Partial

```
<div class="timeline">
  <% @posts.each do |post| %>
    <div class="line-group">
      <%= render "timelines/line", post: post %>
    </div>
  <% end %>
</div>
```

Let's define the missing methods that the `line` partial uses—first, the `humanized_activity_type`, which we should define in `TimelinesHelper`. This method will allow us to display more human-friendly text when the app encounter a `Sight` activity.

Let's remember that a user can post either a status or an activity such as a check-in or a checkout. Without using `humanized_activity_type`, the user interface will not be so user-friendly, since the activity type is not meant to be displayed to humans. See Listing 6-22.

276

Listing 6-22. Defining humanized_activity_type Within TimelinesHelper

```
def humanized_activity_type(sight)
  case sight.activity_type
  when Sight::CHECKIN then "checked in at"
  when Sight::CHECKOUT then "checked out from"
  end
end
```

After that, let's define both the name and profile_picture_url methods within the User model. See Listing 6-23.

Listing 6-23. Adding New Methods into the User Model

```
def name
  if last_name
    "#{first_name} #{last_name}"
  else
    first_name
  end
end

def profile_picture_url
  @profile_picture_url ||= begin
    hash = Digest::MD5.hexdigest(email)
    "https://www.gravatar.com/avatar/#{hash}?d=wavatar"
  end
end
```

Now, let's render the all partial for the timeline. To do that, let's create a new file called app/views/timelines/index.html.erb and add the code shown in Listing 6-24.

Listing 6-24. Replacing the Index with the all Partial

```
<h1>Timelines#index</h1>
<p>Find me in app/views/timelines/index.html.erb</p>
<%= render "timelines/all" %>
```

After this, we can create the `css/member/timeline.css` file with the code shown in Listing 6-25.

Listing 6-25. Stylesheet for the Timeline

```
.body-member
.timeline .line-group {
  @apply mb-2;
  @apply rounded overflow-hidden;
}

.body-member
.timeline .line {
  @apply p-3;
  @apply bg-dark-700;
}

.body-member
.timeline .line .profile-container {
  @apply w-14;
}

.body-member
.timeline .line .profile-container img {
  @apply float-right;
  @apply rounded-full;
  height: 44px;
  width: 44px;
}

.body-member
.timeline .line .content {
  @apply w--full;
  @apply pr-3 pl-3;
}
```

```
.body-member
.timeline .line .identifier {
  @apply flex items-center w-full;
}

.body-member
.timeline .line .identifier a {
  @apply text-gray-100;
}

.body-member
.timeline .line .identifier a:hover .name {
  @apply underline;
}

.body-member
.timeline .line .username {
  @apply text-xs;
  @apply ml-2;
  @apply text-gray-500;
  @apply no-underline;
}

.body-member
.timeline .line .name {
  @apply font-bold;
  @apply text-sm;
}

.body-member
.timeline .line .name:hover {
  @apply underline;
}
```

This then needs to be imported into css/member.css. See Listing 6-26.

Listing 6-26. Importing Member/Timeline into css/member.css

```
@import "member/nav";
@import "member/timeline";
...
```

All is done! If we visit `http://localhost:3000/timelines`, we can see the page as shown in Figure 6-4. Please ensure to log in before visiting the page.

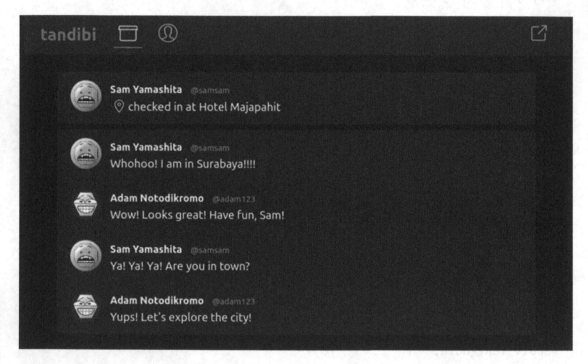

Figure 6-4. *Our timeline*

This has one catch! If a user is signed in and they visit the root URL `http://localhost:3000/`, our app renders the home page for the user. It would be nicer if a signed-in user is redirected to the timeline page directly. To do that, let's add the code shown in Listing 6-27 to `HomeController`.

Listing 6-27. Code to Redirect Signed-in User to the Timeline Page

```
class HomeController < ApplicationController
  def index
    redirect_to(timelines_path) if user_signed_in?
  end
end
```

And we are done.

Using the Decorator Pattern

Rails engineers usually reach for the decorator pattern to help make a model slimmer. However, making a model slimmer is usually just a side effect of applying the decorator pattern. The pattern is primarily here to enhance an object's capability when extending the class is either not possible or not desired, which results in a better object-oriented design overall.

Let's get into practice. First, let's add the active_decorator gem into the gemfile, and then let's run bundle install. See Listing 6-28.

Listing 6-28. Adding active_decorator into the Gemfile

```
gem 'premailer-rails', '~> 1.11'
gem 'active_decorator', '~> 1.3'
```

After that, let's run the command in Listing 6-29 to generate a decorator for the User model.

Listing 6-29. Command to Generate a Decorator for the User Model

```
$ rails g decorator User
```

Then, let's move name and profile_picture_url out from the User model and into decorators/user_decorator.rb. See Listing 6-30.

Listing 6-30. Code for UserDecorator

```
# frozen_string_literal: true

module UserDecorator
  def name
    if last_name
      "#{first_name} #{last_name}"
    else
      first_name
    end
  end

  def profile_picture_url
    @profile_picture_url ||= begin
      hash = Digest::MD5.hexdigest(email)
      "https://www.gravatar.com/avatar/#{hash}?d=wavatar"
    end
  end
end
```

Even if our User model lacked the name method, our views would still work just fine when calling name on any User instances. That is because we have defined them in the decorator module, which active_decorator uses to decorate any User instances on the view.

Using this pattern benefits us in two ways. First, it helps us make our models focus only on the basic building blocks. For example, they don't need to know view-related logic.

Second, it precludes us from defining that view logic as helpers. As we know, helpers are globally namespaced. As such, those functions should be extremely reusable instead of making them tied to a particular data type. Isn't it uncanny if we are working with an object-oriented language but we have procedures highly tied to a specific class?

Based on the second argument, let's remove humanized_activity_type from TimelinesHelper and define a similar function within a newly created app/decorators/ sight_decorator.rb file. See Listing 6-31.

Listing 6-31. Code for SightDecorator

```ruby
# frozen_string_literal: true

module SightDecorator
  def humanized_activity_type(sight)
    case activity_type
    when Sight::CHECKIN then "checked in at"
    when Sight::CHECKOUT then "checked out from"
    end
  end
end
```

Then, let's change the code shown in Listing 6-32 within the app/views/ timelines/_line.html.erb partial.

Listing 6-32. Changing the Way humanized_activity_type Is Called

```erb
<% elsif postable.is_a?(Sight) %>
  <div class="flex items-center">
    <%= evil_icon "ei-location" %>
    <p>
      <%= humanized_activity_type(postable) %>
      <%= postable.humanized_activity_type %>
      <%= postable.place.name %>
    </p>
```

We can unit test our decorators too! Let's add the code shown in Listing 6-33 into spec/decorators/user_decorator_spec.rb to test our UserDecorator.

Listing 6-33. Unit Testing UserDecorator

```ruby
# frozen_string_literal: true

require 'rails_helper'

RSpec.describe UserDecorator do
  let(:user) { create(:user).extend UserDecorator }
  subject { user }
```

```
describe "#name" do
  it "returns a full name" do
    expect(user.name).to eq "#{user.first_name} #{user.last_name}"
  end
end

describe "#profile_picture_url" do
  it "returns a gravatar URL" do
    expect(user.profile_picture_url)
      .to start_with("https://www.gravatar.com")
  end
end
end
```

One thing that a decorator function shouldn't do is to change/modify the underlying data of the object it decorates. It's a "decorator" after all.

Unit Testing a View

It's also possible to unit test a view. Just like any other unit testing, this simple testing procedure ignores architectural interactions outside the unit in question.

In this section, let's see how we can unit test our line partial. In addition, you'll learn how to do simple debugging by using the pry-byebug gem.

First, let's add pry-byebug into the development and test groups. See Listing 6-34.

Listing 6-34. Adding pry-byebug into the Gemfile

```
group :development, :test do
  gem 'byebug', platforms: [:mri, :mingw, :x64_mingw]
  gem 'pry-byebug', platforms: [:mri, :mingw, :x64_mingw]
  ...
end
```

Then, let's add a new trait for the post factory at factories/posts.rb, and let's set up the relationship properly. See Listing 6-35.

Listing 6-35. Defining the Post Factory

```
FactoryBot.define do
  factory :post do
        actor_id { "" }
    thread_id { "" }
    postable { nil }
    user { create(:user) }
    postable { create(:status) }

    trait :with_replies do
      replies { [
        create(:post),
        create(:post)
      ] }
    end
  end
end
```

It's the first time we are using a *trait*. We can use a trait to bundle field modifications that are applied only if the trait is specified when the record is constructed, for example, such as in Listing 6-36.

Listing 6-36. Creating a Post Instance with a Trait

```
let(:post) { create(:post, :with_replies) }
```

Note   It's possible to define and apply as many traits as we want.

After that, let's create `spec/views/timelines/_line.html.erb_spec.rb` and add the code shown in Listing 6-37.

Listing 6-37. Unit Testing Code for the Line Partial

```
require 'rails_helper'

RSpec.describe "timelines/_line.html.erb" do
  let(:post) { create(:post) }
```

```
before do
  render "timelines/line", post: post
end

subject { Nokogiri::HTML(rendered) }

it "can be rendered" do
  binding.pry
end
end
```

Now if we run the previous code with the command shown in Listing 6-38, the execution is paused on the line where binding.pry is evaluated.

Listing 6-38. Command to Run the Spec File

```
$ bundle exec rspec spec/views/timelines/_line.html.erb_spec.rb
```

We now are in an interactive mode, where we have access to all defined variables and methods. See Listing 6-39.

Listing 6-39. Experimenting with Our Own Code in an Interactive Environment

```
[1] pry> rendered
=> "\n<div class=\"line flex\">\n  <div class=\...
```

By calling RSpec's rendered method, we get the HTML string of the rendered partial.

Let's do some more inspection. Let's check how many line partials are rendered. See Listing 6-40.

Listing 6-40. Checking How Many Posts Are Rendered

```
[2] pry> subject.css(".line").count
=> 1
```

Let's also check whether we have the identifier element complete with the name and the username as we would expect. See Listing 6-41.

Listing 6-41. Checking the Content of an Element with the Identifier Class

```
[3] pry> subject.css(".line .identifier").text.strip.squeeze
=> "Mike de Flaire\n @d98d7"
```

Yep, it's all there! It is so handy to do this to inspect what's on the page and then use the knowledge to write the spec or do something interesting. Now, let's add the test case shown in Listing 6-42.

Listing 6-42. Code for the Rendering Test

```
it "can be rendered" do
  binding.pry
  expect(subject.css(".line").count).to eq 1
  expect(subject.css(".replies")).to be_empty
  expect(subject.css(".line .identifier"))
    .not_to be_empty
end
```

Let's also test the case when the post has some replies. This time, we use the `with_replies` trait we defined recently. See Listing 6-43.

Listing 6-43. Half-Baked Test Code

```
it "can be rendered" do
  ...
end

context "when there are replies" do
  let(:post) { create(:post, :with_replies) }

  it "can be rendered" do
    binding.pry
  end
end
```

Let's run the spec and check how many replies we have for the `post`. See Listing 6-44.

Listing 6-44. Check How Many Replies We Have

```
[1] pry> post.replies.count
=> 2
```

Great! We have two replies as expected! What about the number of replies rendered in the view. How many are there? See Listing 6-45.

Listing 6-45. Checking How Many Replies Are Rendered

```
[2] pry> subject.css(".replies .line").count
=> 2
```

There are two replies rendered, which sounds right! Capitalizing on our knowledge, we can complete our test by writing the case shown in Listing 6-46.

Listing 6-46. Code to Ensure That Replies Are Rendered by the line Partial

```
it "can be rendered" do
  ...
end

context "when there are replies" do
  let(:post) { create(:post, :with_replies) }

  it "can be rendered" do
    binding.pry
    expect(subject.css(".replies .line").count)
      .to eq post.replies.count
  end
end
```

Indeed, there are many places where we can drop in binding.pry, such as within a controller or a model. Anywhere the interpreter sees binding.pry, the execution flow is halted so that we can do some debugging or finding out.

Building the User's Timeline

Thanks to our highly reusable components architecture, rendering the personal timeline simply means rendering the all partial in the show, with @posts set to a user's posts.

First, let's change timelines/show.html.erb, as shown in Listing 6-47.

Listing 6-47. Rendering the all Partial

```
<h1>Timelines#show</h1>
<p>Find me in app/views/timelines/show.html.erb</p>
<%= render "timelines/all" %>
```

After that, let's assign @posts for the show action. See Listing 6-48.

Listing 6-48. Assigning the Posts for the show Action

```
class TimelinesController < ApplicationController
  ...

  def show
    @posts = Post.written_by(params[:username])
      .not_reply
      .order("created_at DESC")
  end
end
```

Then, let's define the written_by scope in the Post model as shown in Listing 6-49. We will use this to fetch all posts written by a specific user.

Listing 6-49. The written_by Scope for the Post Model

```
scope :written_by, -> (username) {
  poster = User.find_by_username(username)
  where(user: poster)
}
```

Notice that we look up the user record and join off a primary key, instead of joining and scanning the username, which is never going to be very performant, especially if there is no index defined for the username field. The code in Listing 6-50 is a pattern that should be avoided.

Listing 6-50. A Not Performant Alternative of the Previous Code

```
scope :written_by, -> (username) {
  joins(:user).where(users: {username: username})
}
```

That's that! Now we have a fully functioning personal timeline. For example, if we click a username, let's say Sam's, we will then be directed to Sam's personal timeline page. See Figure 6-5.

Figure 6-5. Sam's personal timeline page

Say Something

Let's allow our users to post a status or write some replies. We will also learn a new design pattern known as *service object*, and let's also learn how to do request testing.

Preparing the User Interface

First, let's prepare the user interface. Let's create a new `PostsController` by running the command shown in Listing 6-51.

Listing 6-51. Creating a New Controller

```
$ rails g controller Posts create --no-test-framework --no-assets
```

We pass in the `no-test-framework` option because we are not going to do any controller testing, but instead, we will do some request testing, which is more comprehensive in scope than just controller testing.

Since Rails 5, the official recommendation of the Rails team and the RSpec core team is to write request specs instead of controller specs, since the speed of running such tests has improved.

First, let's define the routing for the controller, as shown in Listing 6-52.

Listing 6-52. Defining the Routing for the Posts Controller

```
Rails.application.routes.draw do
  get 'posts/create'
  ...
```

```
authenticate :user do
  ...
  resources :posts, only: [:create, :show]
  end
end
```

Also, let's delete posts/create.html.erb since no template needs to be rendered.

After that, let's now create a form partial. The file should be saved as app/views/posts/_form.html.erb; then add the code shown in Listing 6-53.

Listing 6-53. Code for the Post's Form Partial

```erb
<% form_id = "poster-#{SecureRandom.hex(3)}" %>

<div class="poster flex p-3">
  <%= form_for Post.new, html: { id: form_id } do |f| %>
    <%= f.hidden_field :postable_type, value: "Status" %>
    <%= f.text_area :status_text,
      required: true,
      placeholder: "What's happening?"  %>

    <%= f.submit "Say", class: "submit-btn" %>
  <% end %>
</div>

<script type="text/javascript">
  var clickHandler = (evt) => {
    var formElm = evt.target.closest("form")
    var textareaElm = formElm.querySelector("textarea")
    textareaElm.focus()
  }

  document.querySelector("#<%= form_id %>")
    .addEventListener("click", clickHandler, false)
</script>
```

Let's have the form rendered on both timelines. So, let's add the code shown in Listing 6-54 to timelines/index.html.erb.

Listing 6-54. Rendering the Form Partial at the Mass Timeline Page

```
<%= render("posts/form")  %>
```

```
<%= render "timelines/all" %>
```

Then, in `timelines/show.html.erb`, let's add the code shown in Listing 6-55.

Listing 6-55. Rendering the Form Partial on the User's Personal Timeline

```
<% if on_self? %>
  <%= render("posts/form")  %>
<% end %>
```

```
<%= render "timelines/all" %>
```

Then, let's define a new attribute called `status_text`, which our form uses, on the Post model. See Listing 6-56.

Listing 6-56. Defining status_text Accessor at the Post Model

```
class Post < ApplicationRecord
  ...
  ## for the forms
  attr_accessor :status_text
end
```

Since `Post` is polymorphic, we don't know what it represents in advance. Still, it is much simpler for the form to work with the polymorphic `Post` model, rather than with the concrete `Status` or `Sight`. As such, we need to store the data both on the `Post` model, as well as one of the concrete model—with both of the data related to one another.

We may arguably use a pattern known as a *form object* in this case. But, the form is currently so simple that doing so feels like over-engineering.

Note   A form object is another pattern aimed to match the form of the form, no pun intended.

For example, imagine a form that ask for the following data:

- Full name (of User)
- Company name (of Company)

– Phone number (of Company)

– Email (of User)

While we can lump this data together into the User model so that we can render the form, it makes the User model take on responsibilities it doesn't have to. Not only that, but a lot of logic *must* also be lumped together on the controller for handling the record creation for each class of data, as shown here:

```ruby
def create
  @user = User.new(user_params)

  ActiveRecord::Base.transaction do
    if @user.valid?
      @user.save!
      @company = Company.new(
        name: @user.company_name,
        phone: @user.phone
      )
      @company.users << @user
      @company.save!
    end
  end

  if @user.persisted?
    redirect_to users_path
  else
    render :new
  end
end
```

It looks chaotic over there. To avoid that, we can use the form object pattern, which knows all the data it needs and how to create, update, or validate it as used in the form.

Let's explore this a little bit. We know that, in practice, a software engineering problem can have many solutions, each with its pros and cons.

If we are to use the form object now, that means we better replicate the validation logic both in the model and in the form object. Can we afford to do that now? How much repetitive code will that produce? Will it make it easier to maintain in the long run? Is it safe to move the validation responsibilities entirely to the form object, or can we force ourselves to always work with the form object? Is it worth it now?

Those questions are challenging to answer without knowing the context; they ought to be evaluated on a case-by-case basis. But, if we are not sure, solving a problem using techniques just for some abstract benefits is usually premature.

For our case, let's keep it simple and agile. Let's not introduce significant boilerplate code. But also, let's have an open-minded attitude toward the form object pattern because sometimes it is a gift to the world.

Note   A time when the form object pattern shines is when the form has become too involved that it's unclear in which model we should define the transient attributes.

Imagine a checkout form where there can easily be four different models taking part: `Item`, `Order`, `OrderItem`, and `Coupon`. In this case, having a `TransactionForm` makes things simple and agile.

Although we keep the `status_text` on the model, we will separate the logic to handle data insertion into a service object, which we will create later.

For now, as far as the UI is concerned, we just need to add some styling. Let's create a `css/member/poster.css` file with the content shown in Listing 6-57.

Listing 6-57. Style Code for the Post's Form

```
.body-member
.poster {
  @apply bg-dark-700;
}

.body-member
.poster form {
  @apply w-full;
}
```

```
.body-member.dark
.poster form textarea {
  @apply bg-dark-700 w-full;
  @apply resize-none;
  @apply outline-none;
}

.body-member
.poster .submit-btn {
  @apply rounded-full p-2 w-full float-right;
  @apply bg-indigo-800 text-white shadow;
  color: #828d9f;
  cursor: pointer;
}

@screen md {
  .body-member
  .poster .submit-btn {
    @apply w-16;
  }
}

.body-member
.poster .submit-btn:hover {
  @apply bg-indigo-700 text-white;
}

.body-member
.poster form:focus-within > .submit-btn,
.body-member
.poster form:active > .submit-btn {
  @apply bg-indigo-700 text-white;
}
```

Then, let's import the file into css/member.css. See Listing 6-58.

Listing 6-58. Importing member/poster into member.css

```
@import "member/nav";
@import "member/timeline";
@import "member/poster";
```

Let's add a top margin to create some space between the form and the timeline. To do that, add the code shown in Listing 6-59 to `timeline.css`. See Figure 6-6.

Listing 6-59. Adding a Top Margin for the Timeline

```
.body-member
.timeline {
  @apply mt-2;
}

.body-member
.timeline .line-group {
  @apply mb-2;
  @apply rounded overflow-hidden;
}

...
```

Figure 6-6. *The rendered status form*

Now that our form is ready, let's work on the backend.

Doing the Backend Work

We know that we will receive two fields from the form: postable_type and status_text. So, let's permit those fields by defining the callable sanitizer function shown in Listing 6-60 to the PostsController.

Listing 6-60. Defining permitted_params

```
class PostsController < ApplicationController
  def create
  end

  private

    def permitted_params
      params.require(:post).permit(
        :postable_type,
        :status_text
      )
    end

end
```

The permitted_params filters out unwanted params, giving us only the parameters we know are what we want.

Then, let's define the create action. See Listing 6-61.

Listing 6-61. Code for the Create Action

```
class PostsController < ApplicationController
  def create
    is_posted = Post::Creator.call(
      current_user,
      permitted_params
    )

    unless is_posted
      flash[:alert] = "Something went wrong"
    end
```

297

```
    redirect_back fallback_location: timelines_path
end
...
```

The create action simply delegates a Post to a service object called Post::Creator that we will create soon.

If the creation is successful, we redirect the user to the page. Otherwise, we let the user know that there's an issue. That is a kind of commonly seen pattern in a create or update action.

Let's now create the service. First, let's create an ApplicationService class inside app/services/application_service.rb, and yes, the services folder within the app folder needs to be created as well. See Listing 6-62.

Listing 6-62. Code for the ApplicationService

```
class ApplicationService
  def self.call(*args)
    new(*args).call
  end
end
```

Rails uses Spring in the development environment to keep our app running on the background so that we can restart the server or spawn a rails console command faster.

However, since it's caching some information about our Rails project, at some point it fails to detect a newly added folder (and the files it contains). For instance, if we now execute rails console and try to access ApplicationService, an error will be raised.

Note   Spring is currently not supported on Windows, so Windows users may not encounter this issue.

What we need to do is to stop Spring from running and run rails c to start a Rails console to boot up Spring again.

```
$ spring stop
$ rails c
```

Ensure that the service class can be called upon.

Now, the constant missing issue should have been gone away. See Listing 6-63.

Listing 6-63. ApplicationService Is Now Accessible

```
irb(main):001:0> ApplicationService
=> ApplicationService
```

Having the `ApplicationService` at hand, we are now ready to create the service object. But what exactly is a service object?

A *service object* is a class to represent a specific, actionable work. It mostly reflects what a user can do to the application. Inspecting the `services` folder must give us a glimpse of what the application does, which is not always apparent by looking at controllers, models, or somewhere else.

A service object has several conventions, which although not enforced by Rails, are usually adopted by the community. Those conventions are as follows:

- Service objects should go under the `app/services` directory. They can be subcategorized further per model. For instance, `Post::Creator` is a service object for the `Post` model.

- Services should end with an actor, for example, `Post::Creator`, `Newsletter::Sender`, `Scenario::Exporter`.

- A service object should have only one public method. The method might be named `call` to imitate `Proc#call`. Identifying it with another verb may make it inconsistent between services, for example, `Transaction::Approver#approve` versus `Newsletter::Sender#send`. Another possible naming includes `execute` and `perform`.

The `Post::Creator` service object is responsible for creating a new post. The file should be saved as `app/services/post/creator.rb` with the code shown in Listing 6-64.

Listing 6-64. Code for the Post::Creator Service Object

```
class Post::Creator < ApplicationService
  attr_accessor :creator, :params, :post
  private :creator, :params, :post
```

```ruby
  def initialize(creator, params)
    @creator = creator
    @params = params
    @post = Post.new
  end

  def call
    case postable_type
    when "Status" then create_a_status_update
    else false
    end
  rescue
    false
  end

  private

    def postable_type
      @postable_type ||= params.fetch(:postable_type)
    end

    def status_text
      @status_text ||= params.fetch(:status_text)
    end

    def create_a_status_update
      status = Status.new(text: status_text)
      post.postable = status
      post.user = creator
      post.save

      post.persisted?
    end

end
```

Now, let's write the spec for the service. The spec file should be saved as spec/
services/post/creator_spec.rb. Yes, let's create any missing folders too. Then, let's
add the code in Listing 6-65 to the creator_spec.rb file.

Listing 6-65. Code for spec/services/post/creator_spec.rb

```ruby
require "rails_helper"

describe Post::Creator do
  let(:user) { create(:user) }
  let(:permitted_params) { {} }

  subject { described_class.new(user, permitted_params) }

  describe "#call" do
    context "when creating a status" do
      let(:postable_type) { "Status" }
      let(:status_text) { "Howdy!" }

      let(:permitted_params) { {
        postable_type: postable_type,
        status_text: status_text,
      } }

      it "can post successfully" do
        expect {
          subject.call
        }.to change {
          user.posts.reload.count
        }.from(0).to(1)

        post = user.posts.first
        expect(post.postable).to be_a Status
        expect(post.postable.text).to eq "Howdy!"
      end

      context "when the user is not known" do
        let(:user) { nil }

        it "cannot be posted" do
          expect(subject.call).to be_falsey
        end
      end
```

```
      context "when the status text is empty" do
        let(:status_text) { "" }

        it "cannot be posted" do
          expect(subject.call).to be_falsey
        end
      end

      context "when the postable type is empty" do
        let(:postable_type) { "" }

        it "cannot be posted" do
          expect(subject.call).to be_falsey
        end
      end
    end
  end
end
```

Note   You can create a folder at your discretion, and RSpec can just pick it up.

Now let's try posting a new status by going to a timeline page. If we have a Rails server previously running, it's advisable to stop and relaunch the server, since the program might use an older copy of our app as cached by Spring before we added the service folder. See Figure 6-7.

Figure 6-7. *Writing a new status*

So, it's October 2020, and the pandemic[1] is making life a bit harder for almost everyone. Adam is no exception. He misses his friends. So, Adam wrote a status update for fun. Upon clicking the Say button, the new status will be posted, and Adam is taken back to the page where he wrote the status. Everything works as expected! See Figure 6-8.

Figure 6-8. *Rendered status*

Performing Request Testing

Request testing is when integrated units from the router to the view are tested as a whole unit. This kind of testing is also known as *integration testing* in other languages or frameworks.

Let's create our first request spec for posting a status. Let's create a file named posts_ controller_spec.rb inside the spec/requests folder, which we also need to create. After that, add the code shown in Listing 6-66.

Listing 6-66. Request Testing for the PostsController

```
require "rails_helper"

describe PostsController do
  let(:user) { create(:user) }

  before do
    sign_in user
  end

  describe "POST /posts" do
    context "when posting a status update" do
      it "can post the status if all data is valid" do
        expect {
```

---

[1]For future readers, I mean COVID-19.

```
            post "/posts", params: {
              post: {
                postable_type: "Status",
                status_text: "Howdy!",
              }
            }
        }.to change {
          user.posts.reload.count
        }.from(0).to(1)

        expect(response).to redirect_to(timelines_path)
        follow_redirect!
        expect(response.body).to include "Howdy!"
      end
    end
  end
end
```

That's our request spec. Simple, right?

The test uses the `sign_in` method provided by Devise. To make the `sign_in` method available in our spec files, let's create the `spec/support/devise.rb` file and then add the code shown in Listing 6-67.

Listing 6-67. Including Devise::Test::IntegrationHelpers for Request Specs

```
RSpec.configure do |config|
  config.include Devise::Test::IntegrationHelpers,
    type: :request
end
```

Notice that our test case makes a POST request to the `/posts` path. Although the path was written as a string, we can also use the equivalent `posts_path` function instead.

In addition to sending a POST request, we can send a GET request using `get`. Similarly, there are also `delete`, `patch`, `put`, as well as `head` functions for sending DELETE, PATCH, PUT, and HEAD requests, respectively.

We can also attach a request body to any of them by using `params`. And it's also possible to customize the header by specifying the values and their keys through `header`. The code shown in Listing 6-68 demonstrates an example.

Listing 6-68. Sending a POST Request with Custom Body and Header

```
headers = { "ACCEPT" => "application/json" }
post "/somepath", params: { age: 17 }, headers: headers
```

Although a request spec falls under integration testing, it's not an end-to-end test where a real browser is involved. As such, we cannot interact with elements on the page.

For instance, it is not possible to fill in a form and then click a specific button to test what is going to happen, as seen by the user's browser. To do that, we need to involve a real browser, which we will talk about it in the next chapter.

That being said, request testing is definitely much faster than an end-to-end test. Albeit, it's a bit slower than a unit test for the obvious reason that it runs all the way through the stack. Because of its nature, request testing is usually the go-to choice for testing an application's endpoints.

Posting a Comment

It would be more fun if users could reply with an update, so let's make this feature! See Figure 6-9.

Figure 6-9. *Comment pop-up*

To send a reply, users first click the bubble icon. A pop-up will then appear, inside which they type in their reply. Upon clicking the Say button, their reply will be posted.

This is a functional requirement. There are two types of requirements: functional and non-functional requirements.

A *functional requirement* describes a function that a system component must be able to perform, while the *nonfunctional requirements* elaborate on the characteristic of the system behind the scene. A nonfunctional requirement usually deals with accessibility, scalability, availability, maintainability, security, testability, and documentation.

For an example of nonfunctional requirements, let's say we want the pop-up dialog to be highly reusable. See Listing 6-69.

Listing 6-69. An Example Snippet to Make and Call a Pop-up

```
<%= render "layouts/inside_modal", title: "Send a reply",
  modal_class: "mypopup" do %>
  <%= render "posts/form", thread: post %>
<% end %>

<a class="js-modal-open" data-modal-class="mypopup">
  Open mypopup popup
</a>
```

In the previous snippet, we just need to wrap the content of a pop-up within a block that renders the `layouts/inside_modal` partial. Please note that we don't have to add any of the previous code to any file just yet. We want rendering a pop-up, its trigger, and its content to be no-brainer.

Let's work on it! Let's begin with preparing the `inside_modal` partial within the layouts folder. The file should be `app/views/layouts/_inside_modal.html.erb`, and then let's add the code shown in Listing 6-70.

Listing 6-70. Code for the inside_modal Partial

```
<div class="modal opacity-0 pointer-events-none"
  data-modal-class="<%= modal_class %>">
  <div class="modal-overlay js-modal-overlay"></div>

  <div class="modal-container">
    <div class="js-modal-close close-top-left">
      <%= evil_icon "ei-close" %>
      <span class="text-sm">(Esc)</span>
    </div>
```

```
    <div class="modal-content">
      <div class="title-bar">
        <p class="title"><%= title %></p>
        <div class="js-modal-close cursor-pointer z-50">
          <%= evil_icon "ei-close" %>
        </div>
      </div>

      <div class="modal-body">
        <%= yield %>
      </div>
    </div>
  </div>
</div>
```

After that, let's have the style defined as shown in Listing 6-71, which should be saved as css/modal.css within the app/javascript folder.

Listing 6-71. Stylesheet for the Modal

```
body.modal-active {
  @apply overflow-x-hidden;
  @apply overflow-y-visible !important;
}

.modal {
  @apply fixed w-full h-full top-0 left-0;
  @apply flex items-center justify-center;
  @apply z-10;
}

.modal
.modal-overlay {
  @apply w-full h-full;
  @apply absolute bg-gray-900 opacity-50;
}
```

```
.modal
.modal-container {
  @apply w-11/12 max-w-lg mx-auto overflow-y-auto;
  @apply bg-dark-700 rounded shadow-lg z-50;
  border: 1px solid #212121;
}

.modal
.modal-container .close-top-left {
  @apply absolute top-0 right-0;
  @apply flex flex-col items-center;
  @apply text-white text-sm;
  @apply cursor-pointer mt-4 mr-4 z-50;
}

.modal
.modal-container .modal-content {
  @apply py-4 px-6;
  @apply text-left;
}

.modal
.modal-container .title-bar {
  @apply flex justify-between items-center;
  @apply pb-3;
}

.modal
.modal-container .title-bar .title {
  @apply text-2xl font-bold;
}
```

Then, let's import the style into css/application.css. See Listing 6-72.

Listing 6-72. Importing the Modal into css/application.css

```
@import "common";
@import "modal";
@import "home";
```

Lastly, we will need JavaScript so that the model can work. Let's create app/javascript/packs/modal.js and add the code shown in Listing 6-73.

Listing 6-73. Code for javascript/packs/modal.js

```
window.toggleModal = (modalClass) => {
  const modalIdentifier = `[data-modal-class=${modalClass}]`
  const body = document.querySelector("body")
  const modal = document.querySelector(modalIdentifier)

  modal.classList.toggle("opacity-0")
  modal.classList.toggle("pointer-events-none")
  body.classList.toggle("modal-active")
}

window.closeAllModal = () => {
  document.body.classList.remove("modal-active")
  document.querySelectorAll(".modal").forEach((modal) => {
    if (!modal.classList.contains("opacity-0")) {
      modal.classList.add("opacity-0")
      modal.classList.add("pointer-events-none")
    }
  })
}

document.addEventListener("DOMContentLoaded", () => {
  document.addEventListener("click", (e) => {
    if (e.target) {
      var classes = e.target.classList
      const modalElm = e.target.closest("[data-modal-class]")

      if (!modalElm) { return }

      const modalClass = modalElm.getAttribute("data-modal-class")

      if (classes.contains("js-modal-overlay")) {
        e.preventDefault()
        window.toggleModal(modalClass)
```

309

```
      } else if (e.target.parentElement) {
        var parentClasses = e.target.parentElement.classList
        if (parentClasses.contains("js-modal-close")) {
          e.preventDefault()
          window.toggleModal(modalClass)
        } else if (parentClasses.contains("js-modal-open")) {
          e.preventDefault()
          window.closeAllModal()
          window.toggleModal(modalClass)
        }
      }
    }
  })

  document.addEventListener("keydown", (evt) => {
    evt = evt || window.event
    var key = evt.key || evt.keyCode

    if (key === "Escape" || key === "Esc" || key === 27) {
      window.closeAllModal()
    }
  })
})
```

From the previous code, we can see that there are two event listeners. The first one listens to any click event. It monitors what the user clicks so that we can open and close a pop-up.

The second one is the keydown event listener, which gets triggered anytime someone presses a key on a keyboard. If the user presses the Esc key, the modal should disappear.

Note   It is considered good practice that if an HTML element requires JavaScript interactivity, the class should start with js-. If you are using React, Vue or Angular, adding js- prefixes to some classes is not usually enforced since interactivity is built into the component.

Now, let's import the JavaScript code into packs/application.js, as shown in Listing 6-74.

Listing 6-74. Importing modal.js into application.js

```
...
import '../css/application'
import './modal'
```

Now, we are ready to work on the comment form and its backend code.

First, apart from status_text, we now need to specify thread_id on the form partial. So, let's add the code shown in Listing 6-75 to app/views/posts/_form.html.erb.

Listing 6-75. Adding a Thread into the Form

```
<% form_id = "poster-#{SecureRandom.hex(3)}" %>
<% thread = local_assigns[:thread] %>

<div class="poster flex p-3">
  <%= form_for Post.new, html: { id: form_id } do |f| %>
    <%= f.hidden_field :postable_type, value: "Status" %>
    <%= f.hidden_field :thread_id, value: thread&.id %>
    ...
```

After that, we need to permit thread_id in PostsController. See Listing 6-76.

Listing 6-76. Adding thread_id into permitted_params

```
def permitted_params
  params.require(:post).permit(
    :postable_type,
    :status_text,
    :thread_id,
  )
end
```

Then, let's make the Post::Creator service associate a post to a thread if there is a thread_id in the params. See Listing 6-77.

Listing 6-77. Making the Service Associate a Post to a Thread If Any

```
...
def thread
  @thread ||= begin
    thread_id = params[:thread_id].presence
    Post.find(thread_id) if thread_id
  end
end

def create_a_status_update
  status = Status.new(text: status_text)
  post.postable = status
  post.user = creator
  post.thread = thread
  post.save

  post.persisted?
end
...
```

The presence method will return nil if the data is blank. Only if the thread_id is not nil will thread return a Post.

Now, let's render the modal for each line. The modal has a unique class so that a link element can target and open a specific pop-up.

So, let's add the code shown in Listing 6-78 inside the line partial.

Listing 6-78. Adding Code to Render the Form Inside a Modal

```
...
...
<% postable = post.postable %>
<% show_replies = local_assigns.fetch(:show_replies, false) %>

<%= render "layouts/inside_modal",
  title: "Send a reply",
  modal_class: "comment_modal_#{post.id}" do %>
```

```erb
<%= render "posts/form", thread: post %>
<% end %>

<div class="line flex" data-post-path="<%= post_path(post) %>">
...
```

Then, let's add the link that can trigger the modal. See Listing 6-79.

Listing 6-79. Link with Comment Icon to Trigger the Modal

```erb
<div class="line flex" data-post-path="<%= post_path(post) %>">
  ...
  <div class="content">

    <div class="identifier">
      ...
    </div>

    <% if postable.is_a?(Status) %>
      ...
    <% end %>

    <div class="controls">
      <%= link_to "#" do %>
        <div class="control js-modal-open"
          data-modal-class="comment_modal_<%= post.id %>">

          <%= evil_icon "ei-comment" %>
          <% if post.replies.any? %>
            <span> <%= post.replies.count %></span>
          <% end %>

        </div>
      <% end %>
    </div>
  </div>
</div>
```

Equally important, let's style the new `controls` element we just added. Let's add the code shown in Listing 6-80 into `member/timeline.css`. See Figure 6-10.

313

Listing 6-80. Styles to Style the Controls

```
...
.body-member
.timeline .line .name:hover {
  @apply underline;
}

.body-member
.timeline .line .controls {
  @apply mt-2;
  @apply flex items-center justify-between flex-wrap;
}

.body-member
.timeline .line .control {
  @apply flex items-center flex-shrink-0;
  color: #a0aec0;
}

.body-member
.timeline .line .controls .icon {
  @apply rounded-full;
}

.body-member
.timeline .line .controls .icon:hover {
  @apply bg-teal-100;
  @apply text-dark-800;
  transition: all 0.25s ease;
}

.body-member
.timeline .line .controls .icon:focus-within {
  @apply bg-teal-100;
  @apply text-dark-800;
}
```

```
.body-member
.timeline .line .controls a:hover {
  @apply text-teal-200;
}
```

Figure 6-10. *The form with padding*

Now things are functioning as expected. We can try sending some replies. There's something a little bit off here, though. It seems like padding is not needed when we render the form inside a pop-up dialog.

So, let's apply the p-3 class conditionally. Let's add the code shown in Listing 6-81 into the post's form partial.

Listing 6-81. Applying the p-3 Padding Utility Class Conditionally

```
<% thread = local_assigns[:thread] %>

<div class="poster flex p-3 <%= "p-3" unless thread %>">
  <%= form_for Post.new, html: { id: form_id } do |f| %>
```

Now, padding is added only if the form is rendered inside a dialog box or, to be precise, whenever we assign the partial a thread local variable. See Figure 6-11.

Figure 6-11. *The form displayed without additional padding inside a pop-up*

Note   We have made some questionable design decisions in this section when we render a pop-up for every `line` partial. Doing so easily increases the file size of the HTML document.

A better solution would be to only render the dialog once for all partials and swap the form's `thread_id` automatically. Although that is doable, that would overcomplicate the point of this chapter.

Summary

In this chapter, we went through the journey of building the timeline, and you also learned how to do unit testing and integration testing.

In addition, you learned how to apply some design patterns commonly used in a Rails project, such as the service object pattern, the decorator pattern, and the form object pattern.

We have made a good progress so far in our journey, which is great. Onto the next destination: uploading pictures using Rails' Active Storage. Choo-choo!

Picturesque Storage

As the saying goes, if you don't have pictures, it didn't happen.

It's too bad no one can upload any pictures to our social media app just yet. But, by the end of this chapter, our users will be able to share their beautiful memories of sunset in Bali, serene cherry blossoms in Kyoto, or bucolic village life in a Dutch hamlet.

We will be using Active Storage to help us upload and store files. You will also learn how to use the newish File's Blob URL API on the front end. On top of that, let's see how we can utilize Capybara and RSpec to do end-to-end testing by controlling Google Chrome remotely.

Off we go!

Hitchhiker's Guide to Active Storage

Rails 5.2 comes with Active Storage which can do more than just upload files to the cloud. Since then, Active Storage has changed a lot, and it's still evolving in terms of features and capability.

Note Before Active Storage was around, we had to choose between Carrierwave, Shrine, or Paperclip to make uploading files from the user's machine to the server easier. Some projects still use these other tools.

Active Storage abstracts away the different interfaces exposed by various file storage providers. It supports storing files to the local disk, Amazon S3, Google Cloud Storage, and Microsoft Azure Storage. Those uploaded files can then be attached to a model.

In this section, let's see how we can activate Active Storage in our Rails project, and let's try uploading some files on the disk.

© Adam Notodikromo 2021
A. Notodikromo, *Learn Rails 6*, https://doi.org/10.1007/978-1-4842-6026-5_7

Setting Up Active Storage

Active Storage needs two tables for it to function: `active_storage_blobs` and `active_storage_attachments`. Let's run the command shown in Listing 7-1 to bootstrap Active Storage.

Listing 7-1. Command to Bootstrap Active Storage

```
$ rails active_storage:install
```

The previous command will generate a migration file that creates those tables. So, let's run the migration before proceeding, as always.

Note   The `active_storage_blobs` table is used to store the file, and the `attachments` table functions as a polymorphic interface between our model and the attached files. *Blob* means a binary large object or perhaps, simply, binary object.

Attaching Files

It is easy to integrate Active Storage into an Active Record model. Let's allow our `Picture` model to store a file by using the `has_one_attached` macro, as shown in Listing 7-2.

Listing 7-2. Attaching a File to the Picture Model

```
class Picture < ApplicationRecord
  belongs_to :post
  has_one_attached :file
end
```

Done! We just extend the capability of the `Picture` model to allow it to store a file. Let's try attaching some file next.

Let's execute the code shown in Listing 7-3 in a Rails console. But before that, please put copy any image file into the app's root folder, and then let's rename the file as `lgtm.png`. Otherwise, the code that tries to open the file in the snippet shown in Listing 7-3 won't work.

Listing 7-3. Code to Attach a File

```
post = FactoryBot.create(:post)
picture = Picture.new(post: post)
picture.caption = "Looks good to me!"
picture.file.attach(
  io: File.open(Rails.root.join("lgtm.png")),
  filename: "lgtm.png")
picture.save
```

As shown in the previous code, we can use `attach` to upload a file from the local file system to the server's. Since the default storage is always the local disk, the "uploaded" files will be stored locally.

To check where the file is stored, we can use the command shown in Listing 7-4.

Listing 7-4. Code to Check Where the File Is Stored

```
ActiveStorage::Blob.service.send(:path_for, picture.file.key)
```

To remove the file, we can use `purge` or, alternatively, `purge_later`. `purge_later` removes the file in the background using what's called a *background job*, a topic discussed in the next chapter. For now, it's fair to say that `purge_later` deletes the file asynchronously, in a separate execution timeline, whereby `purge` removes the file synchronously or within the same execution timeline. See Listing 7-5.

Listing 7-5. Using purge to Delete the Attached File

```
picture.file.purge
```

We are free to attach any other file.

But currently, we know how to store only one file for one record. While that's fine for the `Picture` model, can we actually store multiple files? And, do we need to name the attachment association `file`?

Of course, yes, we can attach many files at once by using `has_many_attached` instead of `has_one_attached`, and the code will remain largely the same! As for the association name, we can name it with any other sensible name: `file`, `avatar`, `reports`, and `attachments`, to name a few.

Posting the Pictures

In this section, let's build the capability to upload and display the picture. A status with pictures will have the pictures displayed inline, as shown in Figure 7-1.

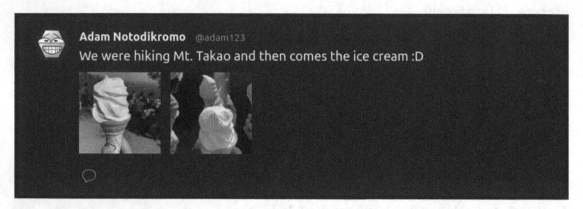

Figure 7-1. *An update with pictures*

When one of the pictures is clicked, we will display the picture at a maximum size in a modal dialog, as shown in Figure 7-2.

Figure 7-2. *Showing a picture in full size in a modal*

Our users are sure to be excited when they can post a status with pictures. So, let's do it!

Creating the Uploader Form

First, let's begin by creating a button that, when clicked, will allow our users to choose a picture to attach to the status. The button should be displayed beneath the text field, and it should have a picture icon so users will intuitively know what the button is for.

To do this, let's open the app/views/posts/_form partial and replace the submit button with the code shown in Listing 7-6.

Listing 7-6. Code for the Controls

```
<%= f.submit "Say", class: "submit-btn" %>
<div class="controls">
  <div class="options">
    <div class="option">
      <%= evil_icon "ei-image" %>
    </div>
  </div>

  <div>
    <%= f.submit "Say", class: "submit-btn" %>
  </div>
</div>
```

After that, let's add the following style into poster.css:

Listing 7-7. Adding styles into poster.css

```
...

.body-member
.poster .controls {
  @apply mt-2;
  @apply flex flex-wrap items-center justify-between;
}
```

```
.body-member
.poster .controls .options {
  @apply block flex-grow flex items-center w-auto;
}

.body-member
.poster .controls .options .option {
  @apply text-sm;
}

.body-member
.poster .controls .options .icon {
  @apply rounded-full align-middle;
  height: 31px;
  width: 31px;
  color: #a0aec0;
}

.body-member
.poster .controls .options .icon:hover {
  @apply bg-teal-100 text-dark-800;
  @apply cursor-pointer;
  transition: all 0.25s ease;
}

.body-member
.poster .controls .options .icon:focus-within {
  @apply bg-teal-100 text-dark-800;
}
```

Now, we can see the controls section rendered nicely on the form, as shown in Figure 7-3.

Figure 7-3. *The controls section with the attach pictures button*

However, now if we click the picture button, the text area will receive the focus, which is counterintuitive to say the least. Instead, let's not give it the focus if the button is clicked.

To do that, let's go back to the form partial and add the JavaScript code shown in Listing 7-8.

Listing 7-8. Code to Prevent Text Area from Receiving the Focus Unnecessarily

```
<script type="text/javascript">
  var clickHandler = (evt) => {
    var formElm = evt.target.closest("form")
    var textareaElm = formElm.querySelector("textarea")

    if (evt.target && evt.target.classList.contains("icon")) {
      return;
    }

    textareaElm.focus()
  }
...
```

Now, let's make the picture icon open a file selection window when it is clicked. Since we need to have an HTML file input tag for that to happen, we will need to add one. However, since it's quite ugly to display this file input element, we will want to hide it from the view. Instead, we will subscribe to click events on the picture icon and will click the file input programmatically so that the file dialog opens.

Note   We can have the JavaScript code execute automatically when an event happens on the page, such as when a user clicks a button. If we subscribe to such an event, then when the event does happen, our code will be executed by the event handler. You can learn about this for free in more detail in W3 Schools' JS HTML DOM tutorial.[1]

---

[1]https://www.w3schools.com/js/js_htmldom.asp

First, let's add the stylesheet for the input. Let's add the style shown in Listing 7-9 to poster.css.

Listing 7-9. Style for Hiding a File Input Field

```
.body-member
.poster .controls input[type='file'] {
  @apply invisible block;
  @apply w-0 h-0;
}
```

Then, let's change the option div for the attach pictures button in the form partial, as shown in Listing 7-10.

Listing 7-10. Adding the Input Field

```
<div class="option">
  <input type="file" multiple
    id="picture_files"
    name="post[pictures][]"
    accept="image/*">
  <%= evil_icon "ei-image" %>
</div>
```

We specify the optional accept parameter with image/*, which means only image files can be selected in the file selection dialog.

Next, let's add the JavaScript code within the form partial, as shown in Listing 7-11. The code will programmatically click the input element if the button is clicked.

Listing 7-11. JavaScript Code to Click the Input Field Programatically

```
if (evt.target && evt.target.classList.contains("icon")) {
  return
  var parentElm = evt.target.parentElement
  var parentClasses = parentElm.classList

  if (parentClasses.contains("js-pictures-uploader")) {
    var fileElm = parentElm.querySelector("input[type='file']")
    fileElm.click()
  }
```

```
    return
} else if (evt.target) {
  var parentElm = evt.target.parentElement
  var parentClasses = parentElm.classList

  if (parentClasses.contains("js-pictures-uploader")) {
    return
  }
}
...
```

Then, let's attach the `js-pictures-uploader` class in the `option` section for the upload pictures button, as shown in Listing 7-12.

Listing 7-12. Adding the js-pictures-uploader Class

```
<div class="option js-pictures-uploader">
  <input type="file" multiple
    id="picture_files"
    name="post[pictures][]"
    accept="image/*">

  <%= evil_icon "ei-image" %>
</div>
```

Great, it works! Now, if a user clicks the button, a file selection window will be displayed where the user can select multiple images at once.

Now, let's make the upload mechanism work as far as the front end is concerned. This means that after the user selects the pictures to attach, those pictures are then displayed in the form.

Let's add a new `pictures` section before the `controls` section in the `form`, as shown in Listing 7-13. The `pictures` section will contain all the selected images.

Listing 7-13. The Pictures Section Above Controls for Holding Images

```
<div class="pictures">
  <div class="picture-cont template">
    <img class="picture">
  </div>
</div>
```

```
<div class="controls">
...
```

Listing 7-14 shows the style for the `pictures` section and its children. We should add these styles into `poster.css`.

Listing 7-14. Styles for the Pictures Section

```
...
.body-member
.poster .pictures {
  @apply mt-2;
}

.body-member
.poster .pictures .picture-cont {
  @apply inline-block mr-2;
}

.body-member
.poster .pictures .picture-cont.template {
  @apply hidden;
}

.body-member
.poster .pictures .picture-cont img {
  @apply object-cover;
  height: 80px;
  width: 80px;
}
```

Now it's time to write the code to display the images. The big idea is that, for each selected file, we clone the `template` section and change its `img` element to represent the file. However, we must find a way so that we don't have to upload the image just to display it, as uploading an image takes time and the user might feel that our system is sluggish. To do that, we are going to use the File's Blob URL API.

Listing 7-15 shows the code that does this. The code should be put within the same app/views/posts/_form partial, within the same script tag, just below the clickHandler function.

Listing 7-15. Code to Display the Selected Images

```
var clickHandler = (evt) => {
}

...

var fileChangeHandler = (evt) => {
  var images = evt.target.files
  var formElm = evt.target.closest("form")
  var picturesElm = formElm.querySelector(".pictures")
  var templateElm = picturesElm.querySelector(".template")

  picturesElm.innerHTML = ''
  picturesElm.appendChild(templateElm)

  for(var i = 0; i < images.length; i++) {
    var image = images[i]
    var newPicContainerElm = templateElm.cloneNode(true)
    var newImgElm = newPicContainerElm.querySelector("img")

    if (!image.type.startsWith("image")) {
      continue
    }

    var imageUrl = URL.createObjectURL(image)
    newImgElm.setAttribute("src", imageUrl)
    newPicContainerElm.classList.remove("template")
    picturesElm.appendChild(newPicContainerElm)
  }
}
```

As we can see, we do not upload the selected images just yet at this point. But we still need to display the images, so what do we do?

327

As planned, we used `URL.createObjectURL` to create a blob URL. We can then use the generated blob URL as the `src` for the `img`. If we don't do that, we have to upload our image to the backend—a process that is never going to be an instantaneous one. However, it is important to remember that a blob URL is tied to the document in the window in which it was created; it cannot be created from the server or accessed. Hence, it is temporary/ephemeral in nature.

Compared to a base64-encoded data URL, a blob URL does not contain the actual data of the object; therefore, we don't need to be worried about exceeding the URL limit, which currently is capped at 2,048-characters long.

Not to mention, the process of making a blob URL is much more efficient both in terms of time and memory than creating a data URL.

Although a blob URL is a newish API,[2] it is supported by every modern browser, including Internet Explorer 10. If our application has to support Internet Explorer 6, we might suggest to our users that they update their browser instead; otherwise, there is no choice but to use something like direct upload (which Active Storage also supports out of the box).

If we decide to use a blob URL, it's good practice to revoke the URL when we are done with it. Otherwise, the claimed memory will be freed up only if we close the page or navigate away from it.

Revoking a blob URL is a simple process, as we just need to call the static `URL.revokeObjectURL` function for each URL we want to revoke.

Let's add a new function called `revokeImageBlobUrl` to revoke blob URLs in the DOM we are interested in. Listing 7-16 shows the code for that.

Listing 7-16. A Function to Revoke Blob URLs

```
...

var revokeImageBlobUrl = (picturesElm) => {
  var imgElms = picturesElm.querySelectorAll("img")

  for (var i = 0; i < imgElms.length; i++) {
    var imgElm = imgElms[i]
    var blobUrl = imgElm.getAttribute("src")
```

---

[2]You can find the File's Blob URL API documentation on the Mozilla Developer Network: `https://developer.mozilla.org/en-US/docs/Web/API/URL/createObjectURL`.

```
    if (blobUrl) {
      URL.revokeObjectURL(blobUrl)
    }
  }
}

var fileChangeHandler = (evt) => {
  ...
}
```

Next, let's call the function just before we empty out the DOM for the `pictures` section, as shown in Listing 7-17.

Listing 7-17. Calling the Function That Revokes Blob URLs

```
var fileChangeHandler = (evt) => {
  var images = evt.target.files
  var formElm = evt.target.closest("form")
  var picturesElm = formElm.querySelector(".pictures")
  var templateElm = picturesElm.querySelector(".template")

  revokeImageBlobUrl(picturesElm)
  picturesElm.innerHTML = ''
  ...
```

Now, let's attach the `fileChangeHandler` to the change event of the `file` input field, as shown in Listing 7-18.

Listing 7-18. Add the fileChangeHandler to the File Input Field

```
...
document.querySelector("#<%= form_id %>")
  .addEventListener("click", clickHandler, false)

document.querySelector("#<%= form_id %> input[type='file']")
  .addEventListener("change", fileChangeHandler, false)
```

Last but not least, we need to change the encoding for the form to be `multipart`, since our form by now can send binary data as well. Quite simply, without this modification, we cannot send files to our server.

329

To do that, simply add `multipart: true` to the form. While doing that, let's switch from `form_for` to `form_with`, as shown in Listing 7-19.

Listing 7-19. Make the Form Multipart and Switch to form_with

```
<%= form_for Post.new, html: { id: form_id } do |f| %>
<%= form_with model: Post.new,
  id: form_id,
  multipart: true do |f| %>
```

Note   We deliberately introduced `form_for` earlier as most Rails projects are still using `form_for`. There is also `form_tag`, which is like `form_for` but without a model. However, `form_for` and `form_tag` are soft-deprecated in favor of `form_with`. That being said, it is not yet known, at the time of this writing, when they will be removed.

There is a technique called *direct upload* that allows files to be uploaded directly to the cloud, bypassing our backend completely. It is not difficult to implement, but we are not going to use it.

Working on the Backend

The status update form can now send pictures to the backend; the backend just needs to upload it.

First, let's permit the `pictures` param in the `PostsController`, as shown in Listing 7-20.

Listing 7-20. Adding Pictures (Which Is an Array) to the List of Permitted Params

```
def permitted_params
  params.require(:post).permit(
    :postable_type,
    :status_text,
    :thread_id,
    :pictures => [],
  )
end
```

The whole => [ ] thing we added just for :pictures, and not other fields, is because we expect that pictures possibly contain a lot of data. When we want to mark fields as an array of data, we have to list them after we list other scalar (nonarray) fields. If we don't do this, we wouldn't be able to receive that data.

Now, let's create a new service object: Post::PictureAttacher. The file should be saved as services/post/picture_attacher.rb with the code shown in Listing 7-21.

Listing 7-21. A New Service Object for Attaching a Picture to a Post

```
class Post::PictureAttacher < ApplicationService
  attr_reader :post, :blob_arg
  private :post, :blob_arg

  def initialize(post, blob_arg)
    @post = post
    @blob_arg = blob_arg
  end

  def call
    if blob_arg.is_a?(ActionDispatch::Http::UploadedFile)
      handle_from_file_upload
    end
  end

  private

  def handle_from_file_upload
    picture = post.pictures.build
    picture.file.attach(blob_arg)
    picture.save!
  end
end
```

As shown in the previous snippet, the Post::PictureAttacher service is going to raise an error if it can't save a picture. We will depend upon this behavior later to abort creating a status update if there's an issue with uploading the pictures, if there are any pictures.

After that, let's change the Post::Creator service. Let's attach the pictures if a Post is persisted successfully. First, let's define the attach_pictures private method, as shown in Listing 7-22.

Listing 7-22. Defining the New attach_pictures! and pictures

...

```
def pictures
  @pictures ||= params.fetch(:pictures, [])
end

def attach_pictures!
  pictures.each do |uploaded_picture|
    Post::PictureAttacher.call(post, uploaded_picture)
  end
end

def create_a_status_update
  ...
end
```

We put a bang on attach_pictures! to indicate that this method can raise an error. Now, let's call it inside the create_a_status_update private method, as shown in Listing 7-23.

Listing 7-23. Let's Attach the Pictures If the Post Is Persisted

```
def create_a_status_update
  status = Status.new(text: status_text)
  post.postable = status
  post.user = creator
  post.thread = thread
  post.save

  if post.persisted?
    attach_pictures!
  end

  post.persisted?
end
```

Although now the pictures can be posted, we need to display the pictures on the timeline.

Showing Off the Pictures

Now it's showtime. Let's add the `pictures` section shown in Listing 7-24 before `controls` in the app/views/timelines/line partial. See Figure 7-4.

Listing 7-24. Adding the pictures Section

```
<div class="pictures">
  <% post.pictures.each do |picture| %>
    <a href="#">
      <div class="picture js-modal-open"
        data-modal-class="picture_modal_<%= picture.id %>">
        <img src="<%= rails_blob_path(picture.file) %>">
      </div>
    </a>
  <% end %>
</div>

<div class="controls">
...
```

Figure 7-4. *Pictures shown in the pictures section*

The `pictures` section contains all the pictures, if any, of a Post. If the user clicks any of those pictures, a modal will pop up to show the picture in a higher resolution.

Let's add the modal dialog definition in the same file, just after we define the modal dialog for the reply form, as shown in Listing 7-25.

333

Listing 7-25. Defining the Modal Dialogs for the Picture

```
  ...
  <%= render "posts/form", thread: post %>
<% end %>

<div class="picture-modals">
  <% post.pictures.each do |picture| %>
    <%= render "layouts/inside_modal",
      title: "",
      modal_class: "picture_modal_#{picture.id}" do %>

      <img src="<%= rails_blob_path(picture.file) %>">
    <% end %>
  <% end %>
</div>
```

The modal by default has a fixed width; however, we would like to display it in full width. Let's define some styles for the modal and append the styles shown in Listing 7-26 into `timeline.css`.

Listing 7-26. Defining Styles for the Dialog

```
.body-member
.timeline .picture-modals .modal-container {
  @apply max-w-full;
}

.body-member
.timeline .picture-modals .modal-body {
  @apply text-center;
}

.body-member
.timeline .picture-modals img {
  @apply inline-block;
}
```

Also, just as importantly, let's add the styles shown in Listing 7-27 to style the pictures section.

Listing 7-27. Defining Styles for the pictures Section

```
.body-member
.timeline .picture-modals img {
  @apply inline-block;
}

.body-member
.timeline .line .pictures {
  @apply mt-2;
}

.body-member
.timeline .line .picture {
  @apply inline-block;
}

.body-member
.timeline .line .picture img {
  @apply object-cover mr-2;
  height: 100px;
  width: 100px;
}
```

However, the app currently suffers from a problem known as the N+1 query problem. This problem occurs when the code needs to load a collection, but the queries are issued one by one per record in that collection. We can see it in the log; there will be similar queries issued one after another when rendering a post with multiple pictures, as shown in Figure 7-5.

```
  ActiveStorage::Attachment Load (0.6ms)  SELECT "active_storage_attachments".* FROM "active_storage_attachments" W
HERE "active_storage_attachments"."record_id" = $1 AND "active_storage_attachments"."record_type" = $2 AND "active_
storage_attachments"."name" = $3 LIMIT $4  [["record_id", 2], ["record_type", "Picture"], ["name", "file"], ["LIMIT
", 1]]
  ↳ app/views/timelines/_line.html.erb:19
  ActiveStorage::Blob Load (0.5ms)  SELECT "active_storage_blobs".* FROM "active_storage_blobs" WHERE "active_stora
ge_blobs"."id" = $1 LIMIT $2  [["id", 2], ["LIMIT", 1]]
  ↳ app/views/timelines/_line.html.erb:19
  Rendered layouts/_inside_modal.html.erb (Duration: 12.0ms | Allocations: 2231)
  ActiveStorage::Attachment Load (0.8ms)  SELECT "active_storage_attachments".* FROM "active_storage_attachments" W
HERE "active_storage_attachments"."record_id" = $1 AND "active_storage_attachments"."record_type" = $2 AND "active_
storage_attachments"."name" = $3 LIMIT $4  [["record_id", 3], ["record_type", "Picture"], ["name", "file"], ["LIMIT
", 1]]
  ↳ app/views/timelines/_line.html.erb:19
  ActiveStorage::Blob Load (0.8ms)  SELECT "active_storage_blobs".* FROM "active_storage_blobs" WHERE "active_stora
ge_blobs"."id" = $1 LIMIT $2  [["id", 3], ["LIMIT", 1]]
  ↳ app/views/timelines/_line.html.erb:19
  Rendered layouts/_inside_modal.html.erb (Duration: 17.0ms | Allocations: 2224)
  ActiveStorage::Attachment Load (0.7ms)  SELECT "active storage attachments".* FROM "active storage attachments" W
```

Figure 7-5. *N+1 queries issued for Active Storage*

This problem seems innocuous, but under heavy loads, it can render the page inaccessible or even take the whole system down.

In the context of Active Storage, this problem happens when we need to refer to the attachments one by one, such as in the code snippet shown in Listing 7-28.

Listing 7-28. Iterating the Files One by One

```
<% post.pictures.each do |picture| %>
  <a href="#">
    <div class="picture js-modal-open"
      data-modal-class="picture_modal_<%= picture.id %>">
      <img src="<%= rails_blob_path(picture.file) %>">
    </div>
  </a>
<% end %>
```

Most ORMs have lazy loading enabled by default, and Active Record is no exception. Therefore, the previous code will load the pictures' files one by one.

To fix that, we can use the with_attached_{association_name} scope that Active Storage has defined for us.

First, let's define a loaded pictures variable, as shown in Listing 7-29, within the app/views/timelines/_line partial.

Listing 7-29. Eager Loading the File

```
<% user = post.user %>
<% postable = post.postable %>
<% show_replies = local_assigns.fetch(:show_replies, false) %>
<% pictures = post.pictures.with_attached_file %>
```

After that, we can replace all other references to post.pictures with the eagerly loaded pictures, as shown in Listing 7-30.

Listing 7-30. Replacing post.pictures with eager-loaded Pictures

```
<% post.pictures.each do |picture| %>
<% pictures.each do |picture| %>
  ...
<% end %>
```

Now if we reload our pages, there will be no repeating queries made for fetching the pictures, as shown in Figure 7-6.

```
Rendered posts/_form.html.erb (Duration: 4.4ms | Allocations: 708)
  Rendered layouts/_inside_modal.html.erb (Duration: 7.5ms | Allocations: 1181)
  Picture Load (0.6ms)  SELECT "pictures".* FROM "pictures" WHERE "pictures"."post_id" = $1  [["post_id", 7]]
  ↳ app/views/timelines/_line.html.erb:14
  ActiveStorage::Attachment Load (1.1ms)  SELECT "active_storage_attachments".* FROM "active_storage_attachments" W
HERE "active_storage_attachments"."record_type" = $1 AND "active_storage_attachments"."name" = $2 AND "active_stora
ge_attachments"."record_id" IN ($3, $4, $5)  [["record_type", "Picture"], ["name", "file"], ["record_id", 2], ["rec
ord_id", 3], ["record_id", 4]]
  ↳ app/views/timelines/_line.html.erb:14
  ActiveStorage::Blob Load (0.9ms)  SELECT "active_storage_blobs".* FROM "active_storage_blobs" WHERE "active_stora
ge_blobs"."id" IN ($1, $2, $3)  [["id", 2], ["id", 3], ["id", 4]]
  ↳ app/views/timelines/_line.html.erb:14
  Rendered layouts/_inside_modal.html.erb (Duration: 2.5ms | Allocations: 223)
  Rendered layouts/_inside_modal.html.erb (Duration: 1.2ms | Allocations: 218)
  Rendered layouts/_inside_modal.html.erb (Duration: 1.9ms | Allocations: 218)
  Post Exists? (0.9ms)  SELECT 1 AS one FROM "posts" WHERE "posts"."thread_id" = $1 LIMIT $2  [["thread_id", 7], ["
LIMIT", 1]]
  ↳ app/views/timelines/_line.html.erb:66
  Rendered timelines/_line.html.erb (Duration: 64.0ms | Allocations: 8828)
  CACHE User Load (0.0ms)  SELECT "users".* FROM "users" WHERE "users"."id" = $1 LIMIT $2  [["id", 1], ["LIMIT", 1]
```

Figure 7-6. *No more excessive N+1 queries for a post's pictures*

Although fetching an image's URL from our database has been made much more efficient, browsers are still loading those images one by one from our backend. This is inefficient. We can make it more efficient if those pictures are stored in a way that doesn't require browsers to hit our backend.

One way we can do that is by using a cloud service provider such as Amazon S3. We then upload all our pictures onto S3. Then, we use the URL endpoints given by Amazon S3 to display each image, rather than using our own endpoints. This process is known as *hotlinking*.

However, it's important to note that hotlinking must be evaluated based on the security profile of the app. For example, if we need custom logic for who can access what, then we cannot use this technique since hotlinking means anyone with the correct link can access the file.

Note   There is a gem called *bullet* that can help us discover N+1 query issues. Many other monitoring tools, such as New Relic and Scout APM, can also report these issues for us.

Storing to Amazon S3

How to store files should not be an afterthought. For most web applications, there are two challenges we must consider when choosing how to store files: durability and space elasticity.

Durability describes the quality of our storage mechanism in terms of accessibility, redundancy, and security, while *space elasticity* makes sure we are not running out of disk space as users generate more content.

Solving those challenges is difficult if we are forced to use disks connected to a single machine. Not to mention, it is difficult enough to set up our own distributed disk storage system.

It was said that Jeff Bezos' original spec for Amazon S3 was very succinct; he wanted `malloc`[3] for the Internet.

Hence, Amazon S3 was born. Amazon S3 is an acronym for Amazon Simple Storage Service, a fully managed, highly available, distributed data store that can store objects on a whim. And since our data is distributed, the risk of losing access to our data is dramatically reduced.

---

[3]A key memory allocation function for C programs

Amazon S3, however, is not free. In general, we are billed for every gigabyte of space we use (which is roughly $0.023 USD/GB in Ohio). We also incur costs for data transfer. At the time of writing, the free tier covers 20,000 GET requests and 2,000 PUT requests.

Note   Amazon offers a free tier if we create a new AWS account. The free tier includes 12 months free of Amazon S3 with 5 GB standard storage, among other perks.

In this section, we will create a new Amazon S3 bucket[4] and learn how to use it to store uploaded pictures.

Creating an S3 Bucket

Amazon S3 offers containers with unlimited storage space. A container is known as a *bucket*. A bucket can store any kind of object, such as videos, images, or binaries, as long as the size of the object does not exceed 5 TB.

Let's create a new Amazon S3 bucket. From the dashboard, type **S3** in the search bar, as shown in Figure 7-7.

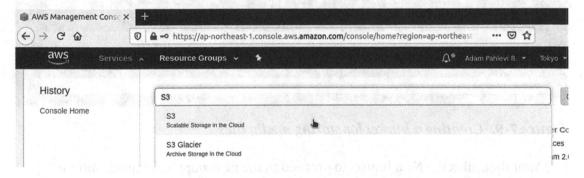

Figure 7-7.   Typing S3 in the search bar

We will be redirected to the Amazon S3 dashboard page, as shown in Figure 7-8.

---

[4]To sign up for AWS, go to https://aws.amazon.com/resources/create-account/ in your select browser. To access the AWS dashboard, go to https://console.aws.amazon.com/.

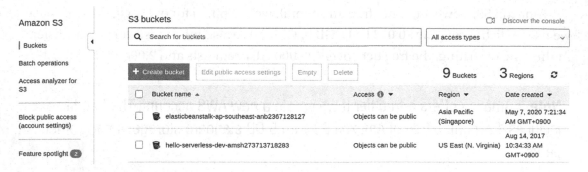

Figure 7-8. *The index page of Amazon S3*

On the index page, let's click the "Create bucket" button and fill in some unique name for it. I am going to name it `tandibi-stg-uploaded-media`, but you should pick another unique name. For this example, let's choose US East (N. Virginia) as the region, as shown in Figure 7-9. Please feel free to choose any other region.

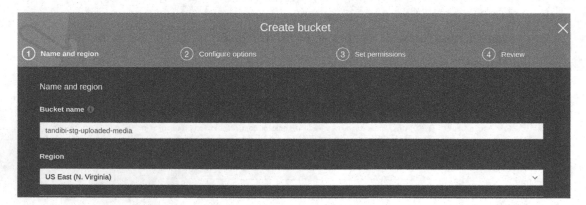

Figure 7-9. *Creating a bucket for storing media files*

After that, click the Next button to proceed to the next step: "Configure options." Then click the Next button again. At the Set permissions step, let's click Next again. Then, on the Review step, let's click the "Create bucket" button, and we are done!

Obtaining and Storing Credentials

We need an access key and secret access key pair so that we can access our bucket programmatically through API calls from our Rails app. So, let's generate those keys. As the name implies, we cannot expose those keys carelessly.

To generate the key, let's go to the My Security Credentials page, the link for which can be found under the account's pull-down menu on the navigation bar, as shown in Figure 7-10.

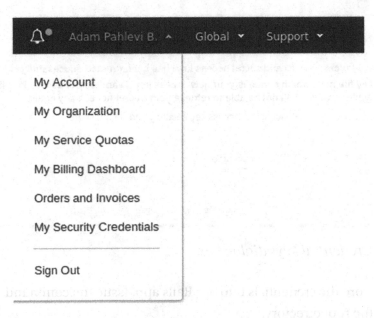

Figure 7-10. *The My Security Credentials link in the pull-down menuc*

After that, within the Your Security Credentials page, click the Create New Access Key button, as shown in Figure 7-11.

Your Security Credentials

Use this page to manage the credentials for your AWS account. To manage credentials for AWS Identity and Access Management (IAM) users, Console .

To learn more about the types of AWS credentials and how they're used, see AWS Security Credentials in AWS General Reference.

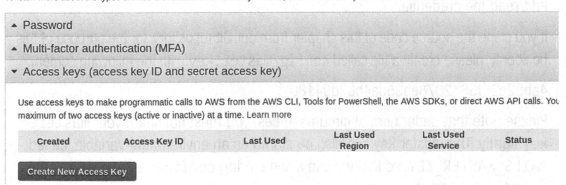

Figure 7-11. *The Create New Access Key button*

By clicking the button, a modal dialog will show up. There, we can download our key file. Again, we must keep the file carefully, as shown in Figure 7-12.

Figure 7-12. *Credential keys dialog box*

Then, let's store the credentials into our Rails app. Issue the command shown in Listing 7-31 in the root directory.

Listing 7-31. Command to Edit the Credential File

```
$ rails credentials:edit
```

Note   If you face trouble running the `rails credentials:edit` command, most likely it is because you don't have the `master.key` stored in the `config` folder. The `master.key` is used to decrypt the file, so if it is missing, we cannot edit/read the credentials.

If you clone the source code of this chapter from our Git repository, for the purpose of this book only, please create a file called `config/master.key` with the following content:

4ab82a34f5642078eb35da4b67d94180

Please note that under normal circumstances, you must not share your `master.key` lightly. The master key can also be stored as an environment variable, called `RAILS_MASTER_KEY`, so that we can avoid storing `config/master.key` in the repository but still allow our app to have access to the credentials.

Next, let's define a new section for storing our Amazon API credentials, as shown in Listing 7-32.

Listing 7-32. Storing Our Amazon Credentials

```
aws:
  access_key: YOUR ACCESS KEY
  secret_key: YOUR SECRET KEY
```

Please be sure to replace YOUR ACCESS KEY and YOUR SECRET KEY with the keys we obtained earlier.

To check whether the keys can be accessed, we can run the command shown in Listing 7-33 in a Rails console.

Listing 7-33. Code to Access the S3 Credentials We Have Defined

```
irb(main):001:0> Rails.application.credentials[:aws    ]
=> {:access_key=>"[redacted]", :secret_key=>"[redacted]"}
```

Configuring Active Storage to Use S3

First, let's add the aws-sdk-s3 gem into our gemfile, as shown in Listing 7-34, and run bundle install.

Listing 7-34. Adding the Gem into Gemfile

```
gem "aws-sdk-s3", require: false
```

After that, let's add a new entry at storage.yml, as shown in Listing 7-35.

Listing 7-35. Adding a New Storage Option

```
s3:
  service: S3
  access_key_id: <%= Rails.application.credentials.dig(
    :aws    , :access_key) %>
  secret_access_key: <%= Rails.application.credentials.dig(
    :aws    , :secret_key) %>
  region: us-east-1
  bucket: tandibi-stg-uploaded-media
```

343

We can name the storage option anything we want, such as `media_s3`, `s3_stg_media`, or something else; it doesn't have to be named `s3`. However, we must change the region and bucket accordingly. Also, please ensure that the service is S3 for Amazon S3, that is, with a capital *S*.

Table 7-1 lists the region codes. Please note that new regions might be added in the future.

Table 7-1. *Region Names and Codes*

Region Name	Region Code
US East (Ohio)	us-east-2
US East (N. Virginia)	us-east-1
US West (N. California)	us-west-1
US West (Oregon)	us-west-2
Asia Pacific (Mumbai)	ap-south-1
Asia Pacific (Seoul)	ap-northeast-2
Asia Pacific (Singapore)	ap-southeast-1
Asia Pacific (Sydney)	ap-southeast-2
Asia Pacific (Tokyo)	ap-northeast-1
Canada (Central)	ca-central-1
Europe (Frankfurt)	eu-central-1
Europe (Ireland)	eu-west-1
Europe (London)	eu-west-2
Europe (Milan)	eu-south-1
Europe (Paris)	eu-west-3
Europe (Stockholm)	eu-north-1
South America (Sao Paulo)	sa-east-1

After that, in `development.rb`, let's change the Active Storage service to use `s3` instead of `local`, and then let's restart the server, as shown in Listing 7-36. If you named the storage option with a name other than `s3`, please use that name instead.

Listing 7-36. Change to Let Active Storage Store the File in s3

```
config.active_storage.service = :local
config.active_storage.service = :s3
```

We have just configured Active Storage to use our s3 bucket. We can try writing a new status and attach some pictures, as shown in Figure 7-13.

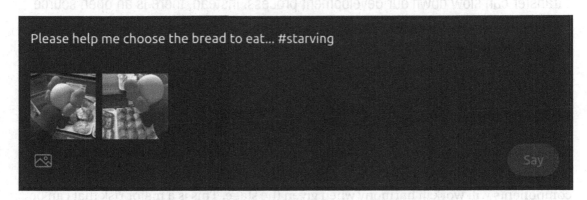

Figure 7-13. *Writing a new status update*

Upon hitting the Say button, our pictures will be uploaded to AWS S3 immediately. We can check that those files are indeed in our bucket by visiting the bucket's management page, as shown in Figure 7-14.

tandibi-stg-uploaded-media

Overview	Properties	Permissions	Management	Access points

Q Type a prefix and press Enter to search. Press ESC to clear.

⬆ Upload	➕ Create folder	Download	Actions ⌄		Asia Pacific (Singapore) ⟳

Viewing 1 to 2

☐	Name ▾	Last modified ▾	Size ▾	Storage class ▾
☐ 🗋	p5vyg9pql1qkbcwv1rzwtrmnlktq	Apr 12, 2020 10:40:47 AM GMT+0900	605.2 KB	Standard
☐ 🗋	xbdbbk1rdf144s3wvff6f0vaj2y4	Apr 12, 2020 10:40:48 AM GMT+0900	595.6 KB	Standard

Figure 7-14. *Our files on Amazon S3*

If you have prior posts with images uploaded locally, you will notice that the images are no longer displayed, since the storage mechanism has been changed. That is expected.

Note   For a development environment, normally we don't store files by uploading them directly to Amazon S3, as that will incur unnecessary cost and the network transfer can slow down our development process. Instead, there is an open source tool named Localstack that can emulate Amazon S3—the experience is extremely similar to Amazon S3 although everything is stored locally in our machine.

Integration Testing with Capybara

Nowadays, software systems are composed of various interconnected subsystems, or *features*. Sometimes, unit testing is not enough to guarantee that those small components will work in harmony when given the stage. This is a major risk that can be avoided by conducting end-to-end testing.

End-to-end testing involves ensuring that all the integrated components of our application function as designed. To do that, the entire application stack, not just a single component or a part of it, is tested. Thus, usually a real browser is involved for a web app, or a real/emulated mobile device is used instead for a mobile app.

Note   There are certain kind of tests where the only option is to do it in an end-to-end manner, such as uploading files.

For us, we can integrate Capybara with RSpec so that we can write automated tests using a real browser controlled remotely. This essentially allowed us to simulate how a real user would interact with our application under a given scenario.

We will be using a headless Chrome browser, which is a Chrome browser but without the window that shows up during the testing process. The browser will be controlled through the Chrome DevTools protocol so that we don't need to install additional software other than the Chrome browser.

All of that may sound complicated to set up, but nothing is further than the truth. Let's begin!

First, let's add the gems shown in Listing 7-37 into the new test group in our gemfile, after which let's not forget to run bundle install.

Listing 7-37. Adding Capybara, Apparition, and Launchy into the Gemfile

```
group :test do
  gem 'launchy', '~> 2.5'
  gem 'capybara', '~> 3.31'
  gem 'apparition', '~> 0.5'
end
```

Capybara will equip us with various handy syntaxes to do automated browser manipulation and interaction. Apparition provides Capybara with the driver to control Chrome.

After that, let's create spec/support/capybara.rb and add the code shown in Listing 7-38.

Listing 7-38. Code to Integrate Capybara with RSpec and Apparition

```
require "capybara/rspec"
require "capybara/apparition"

Capybara.default_driver = :apparition
Capybara.javascript_driver = :apparition
```

The setup is done. It's that easy!

Let's write our first end-to-end integration spec. Those specs are best located within the spec/features folder. Let's create posting_spec.rb in that folder and add the code shown in Listing 7-39.

Listing 7-39. Code to Simulate Posting a Status

```
require "rails_helper"

feature "Posting" do
  given(:user) { create(:user) }
  given(:status_text) { "Whohoo!" }
```

347

```
  def sign_in(user)
    visit new_user_session_path
    fill_in "Username / Email", with: user.username
    fill_in "Password", with: user.password
    click_on "Log in"
  end

  scenario "Posting a status" do
    sign_in user

    expect {
      fill_in "post_status_text", with: status_text
      click_on "Say"
    }.to change { user.reload.posts.count }.from(0).to(1)

    posted_status = user.posts.first.postable
    expect(posted_status.text).to eq status_text
    expect(page).to have_content status_text

    within(".line .content") do
      expect(page).not_to have_selector("img")
    end
  end
end
```

If we are not using Capybara, we would not have access to the new DSLs such as fill_in, click_on, within, have_selector, click_on, and visit among others.

The fill_in function helps us to fill in some text into some field. If the field has a label, we can use the label to refer to the field. Otherwise, we can pass in the field's id.

The click_on button finds a button or link on the page and then clicks it. If we want to specifically target a button, we can use click_button. In the same fashion, we use click_link if we want to specifically click a link.

The within function accepts a block that executes the given code within the context of a specific HTML node. Last but not least is the visit function, which we use to navigate to a given path or URL.

Integration testing usually use words such as `given`, `feature`, and `scenario`, instead of `let`, `describe`, and `it`. Therefore, we used those DSLs instead, which also comes from Capybara.

Now if we run the spec, everything is green as expected. That is great! But now, let's see how we can debug our code. Let's insert the mighty `binding.pry` at the very last of the scenario, as shown in Listing 7-40.

Listing 7-40. Adding binding.pry Within the Scenario

```
scenario "Posting a status" do
  ...
  binding.pry
end
```

Now if we run the spec again, the executing spec is halted at the point just as we want it. Again, we can have access to all the functions and variables defined so far. But what's interesting is, we can see what's displayed on the screen right now.

To do that, let's call `save_and_open_screenshot`, which should take a screenshot of the page and open it for us, as shown in Figure 7-15.

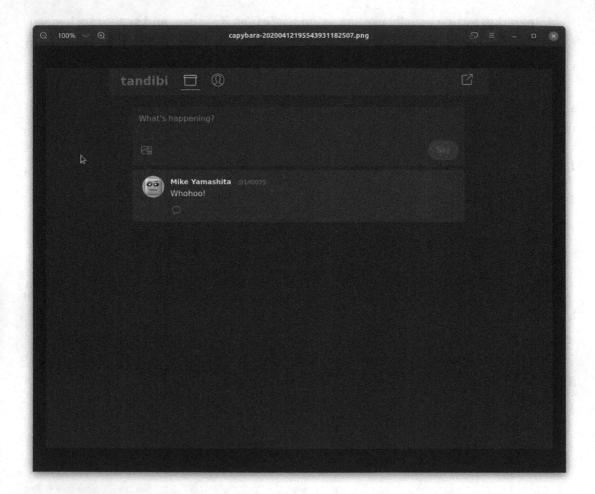

Figure 7-15. *Screenshot of the page*

We can also find out where the screenshots are located by calling `Capybara.path`. Another similarly interesting method is `save_and_open_page` to save and open the currently tested page in a separate browser.

Let's now add another scenario when the user is posting a status with a picture attached. Listing 7-41 shows the code for that.

Listing 7-41. Code to Test Posting a Status with a Picture Attached

```
scenario "Posting a status with a picture" do
  sign_in user

  expect {
    fill_in "post_status_text", with: status_text
    attach_file "picture_files", Rails.root.join("lgtm.png"), visible: false
    click_on "Say"
  }.to change { user.reload.posts.count }.from(0).to(1)

  expect(page).to have_content status_text

  within(".line .content") do
    expect(page).to have_selector(".pictures")
    expect(page).to have_selector("img", count: 1)
  end
end
```

As we can see, we use `attach_file` to attach a file (or multiple files) to an input field. Since the input field in this case, `picture_files`, is not visible to the user, we pass in the `visible: false` option.

There are three possible values for `visible` when we are interacting with an element.

- `true`, which finds only visible elements (as seen by the user)

- `false`, which finds both visible and invisible elements

- `:hidden`, which finds only invisible elements

It is good to note that Capybara has a global option `Capybara.ignore_hidden_` `elements` that determines whether Capybara should see or ignore hidden elements. It seems like it is better to keep the value `true`, which is the default value, to treat elements invisible from the user in the same way. This means we would need to use the `visible` option like the one shown previously when interacting with invisible elements.

Note   Capybara has many driver implementations, Apparition being only one of the many possible drivers. Undoubtedly, all those drivers have their own notion of "visibility."

Before we run the test again, let's ensure that we have a file named `lgtm.png` in the app's root directory. After that, if we run the spec again, everything is green as expected.

Let's add the last spec to test when multiple images are attached, as shown in Listing 7-42. This time, let's ensure we have `lgtm2.gif` in the app's root directory. Both `lgtm.png` and `lgtm2.gif` are provided in the repository[5] if you would like to use the same images we used in this book.

Listing 7-42. Code to Test Posting with Multiple Pictures

```
scenario "Posting a status with multipe pictures" do
  sign_in user

  expect {
    fill_in "post_status_text", with: status_text
    attach_file "picture_files", [
      Rails.root.join("lgtm.png"),
      Rails.root.join("lgtm2.gif")
    ], visible: false
    click_on "Say"
  }.to change { user.reload.posts.count }.from(0).to(1)

  within(".line .content") do
    expect(page).to have_selector("img", count: 2)
  end
end
```

And if we check the screenshot, it will look something like Figure 7-16.

---

[5]https://github.com/adamnoto/learn-rails-6/tree/master/chapter7/tandibi

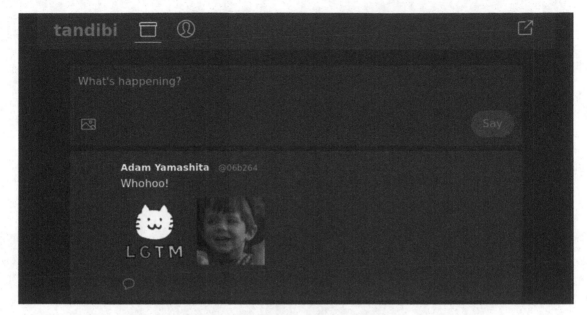

Figure 7-16. *Screenshot for the scenario of attaching multiple pictures*

Although we have covered a lot of things with Capybara, Capybara has other DOM-related interactivity functions such as `choose`, `check`, `uncheck`, `select`, and `find` among many others. We can also call `execute_script` to execute some JavaScript scripts. And, to get the path of the page currently under test, we can use `current_path`.

Actually, Rails has a built-in, full-stack testing mechanism known as *system tests* that uses Capybara and Selenium by default. Perhaps it's a matter of preference about which system to use. There are also other driver options besides Apparition, such as Poltergeist and Selenium.

Summary

Active Storage makes it easy to store and retrieve our files on the cloud. However, the framework is still relatively new compared to other frameworks within Rails, and we should expect some things to change in the future.

Some of those changes might require us to update our Active Storage schema migrations. But, in a case like that, Rails usually provides us with the tools and guidelines for seamless migration, so we probably don't need to be worried.

This chapter also covered how to store our Amazon IAM credentials securely. You learned how to do end-to-end integration testing by using Capybara and a headless Chrome browser through Apparition. In the next chapter, you'll learn about executing code in the background and various other things.

CHAPTER 8

Places and Queues

In the previous chapters, we used vanilla JavaScript to manage the UI. Truth be told, that code was highly fragile; bugs are happy to slip in as our cool startup evolves. Of course, we don't want that to happen.

In this chapter, you will learn how to integrate JavaScript frameworks seamlessly into our Rails app by using Webpacker. For those who are wondering, we will be using Vue.js for the task.

You will also learn how to build an API controller and how to serialize our data. Finally, you will learn how to run some code in the background using Active Job.

Enter Vue.js and Webpacker

It is difficult to find a web app engineer who hasn't worked with any JavaScript code, since a moderately complex web app must have used JavaScript in some way to enrich the user experience.

In the past, when working with JavaScript code, the Rails community used a module bundler known as Sprockets. It allows us to orchestrate and package our assets seamlessly. It even allows us to import and export JavaScript assets as if they were Ruby gems.

Yet, since it is a Ruby technology, our front-end teammates won't be familiar with Sprockets. It also cannot tap into NPM, a software registry for the JavaScript world not unlike RubyGems is for us. Thus, admittedly Sprockets has created a divide between the Ruby world and the JavaScript world, and whether that's necessary or not has been a subject of debate.

Nevertheless, Rails has decided to move toward Webpackers, which wraps Webpack. Webpack is a native JavaScript technology and is popular for managing and bundling JavaScript code. With it, the gap between the `.js` and the `.rb` that must exist in our app's front end keeps closing.

© Adam Notodikromo 2021
A. Notodikromo, *Learn Rails 6*, https://doi.org/10.1007/978-1-4842-6026-5_8

> **Note**   It is an understatement to say Webpacker *just* wraps Webpack. Webpack is a powerful beast, and Webpacker helps us to control it without first asking us to learn how to tame a beast, in JavaScript. No animals were harmed when Webpack was made, I sincerely believe.

In this chapter, we are going to use Vue.js to make a form for posting a check-in status. It is one of the three most commonly used front-end frameworks alongside React and AngularJS. Please be sure that no one is forced to use Vue.js or, for that matter, to adopt this style of development. So, why Vue.js?

The most prominent reason why frameworks like Vue.js are used is that it is difficult already to keep the UI and the application states in sync, let alone add interactivity on the given page. Those things are really error-prone to be handled using vanilla JavaScript.

Yeah, but why Vue.js specifically?

Vue.js is a progressive web framework for building UI components. By "progressive," I mean it doesn't attempt to take over the whole front-end stack unlike, say, Google's AngularJS. By "framework," I mean it is more than just being a UI rendering library that is Facebook's React. It is, therefore, relatively easier to set up and migrate an existing app into.

If we imagine that React and Angular as two strong forces repelling each other, distancing themselves as far as possible from one another, then there exists something around the midpoint, and that is Vue.js.

Being in the middle, it can go either direction or just stay in the middle. Being in the middle, Vue.js takes less time to set up and possibly fewer boilerplates to type. Objectively, however, if we look at the download statistics in NPM for all those three frameworks, React is leading the race. Truth be told, React is generally favored by many startups and enterprises alike. But, let's give Vue.js a try!

> **Note**   This chapter is highly opinionated. It's not that this chapter refuses to use the most popular framework out there; we are simply using Vue.js because we like the solutions Vue.js offers.

Let's start by adding Vue.js into our project. You will be surprised that integrating Vue.js into a Rails app is as simple as issuing the command shown in Listing 8-1 thanks to the Webpacker.

Listing 8-1. Integrating Vue.js into Our Rails App

```
$ rails webpacker:install:vue
```

That command asked Yarn, a package manager, to install Vue and its dependencies. Webpacker then applies some necessary changes for Webpack to be able to recognize and work with a .vue file extension.

And that's it, we are done with integrating Vue.js into our Rails app.

Note   You may want to ensure that the Vue version installed is version 2.6, as used in this book. The Vue.js team is planning to release a new major version in the near future: Vue 3.0.

Please refer to `package.json` to see which version of Vue.js is used. The whole setup for all Vue-related things in this chapter should look like the following one, with `vuex` added later in the book, so it's expected if it is missing in the definition for now.

```
{
  ...
  "dependencies": {
    ...
    "vue": "^2.6.11",
    "vue-loader": "^15.9.1",
    "vue-template-compiler": "^2.6.11",
    "vuex": "^3.1.3"
  },
  ...
}
```

However, quite unfortunately, there is a bug in Webpack that can potentially raise a syntax error. Let's upgrade Webpack to version 5.0 or newer.

Note   For details of the bug, please visit pull request ID 10424 in the webpack/webpack repository on GitHub.

First, let's change the version of Webpacker in the gemfile, as shown in Listing 8-2.

Listing 8-2. Upgrading Webpacker to Version 5.0.x

```
gem 'webpacker', '~> 4.0'
gem 'webpacker', '~> 5.0'
```

After that, let's execute the commands shown in Listing 8-3, which will upgrade our Webpacker to the latest version available in NPM.

Listing 8-3. Upgrading the Webpacker and Its Dependencies

```
bundle update webpacker
rails webpacker:binstubs
yarn upgrade @rails/webpacker --latest
yarn upgrade webpack-dev-server --latest
```

The first command, `bundle update webpacker`, is essentially a bundle update command. But, if `bundle update` attempts to update every gem in the gemfile, `bundle update webpacker` will update Webpacker and its dependencies only if necessary.

The command `rails webpacker:binstubs` will execute the `webpacker:binstubs` rake task. This task essentially copies some executable scripts into the `bin` folder. We need to run this command even if there are already executable Webpack scripts in the `bin` folder, in case some of those scripts need to be updated to keep working with the upgraded version. See Listing 8-4.

Listing 8-4. Command Output When Executing rails webpacker:binstubs

```
    exist  bin
identical  bin/webpack
identical  bin/webpack-dev-server
```

The last two commands basically upgrade the related JavaScript packages, namely, @rails/webpacker and webpack-dev-server.

The bin/webpack-dev-server is a helpful tool that we should use during development. It can detect file changes and then perform any necessary recompilation. That way, if we make some changes to our assets or front-end code, Webpack can automatically bundle and might reload the page for us. As it's advised to use this tool during development, let's launch it by executing the command shown in Listing 8-5.

Listing 8-5. Command to Run webpack-dev-server

```
$ ./bin/webpack-dev-server
```

In the case, when there is a "permission denied" error, as shown in Listing 8-6.

Listing 8-6. Error While Executing webpack-dev-server

```
zsh: permission denied: ./bin/webpack-dev-server
```

Then we need to grant the script an executable permission. The permission told the operating system that the code in the file can be executed. To do that, we run the command shown in Listing 8-7 in a Linux or macOS environment.

Listing 8-7. Granting the Executable Permission to webpack-dev-server

```
$ chmod +x ./bin/webpack-dev-server
```

Then, we can try to relaunch the script.

Google Maps and Places API

We are going to build a check-in status form that looks like Figure 8-1.

Figure 8-1. *Final appearance of the check-in poster*

As we can see, we are going to use Google Maps for the map. Behind the scenes, we will use the Google Places API to search for places. So, we must sign up[1] for the Google Cloud Platform and enable those APIs; otherwise, we wouldn't be able to proceed with the rest of the chapter.

Note   Those APIs are not free to use. However, although we are not experts in billing calculation, we incurred no cost when we were using them in the context of this book. Please take it with a grain of salt, and be careful of overusing the API lest you incur some cost.

After you have a Google Cloud Platform account, please sign in and then click the sidebar to search for *IAM & Admin*. Hover on the menu and then click Manage Resources, as shown in Figure 8-2.

---

[1]To sign up, go to https://console.cloud.google.com/getting-started.

Google Cloud Platform
Manage resources
CREATE PROJECT
DELETE
SHOW INFO PANEL
Filter tree
Name
ID
Status
Charges
Labels
Actions
No organization
0
3 RESOURCES PENDING DELETION

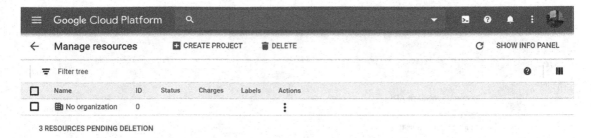

***Figure 8-2.** "Manage resources" page*

Then, click the Create Project button, which takes us into the New Project page. Type in the name of the project and then click the Create button, as shown in Figure 8-3.

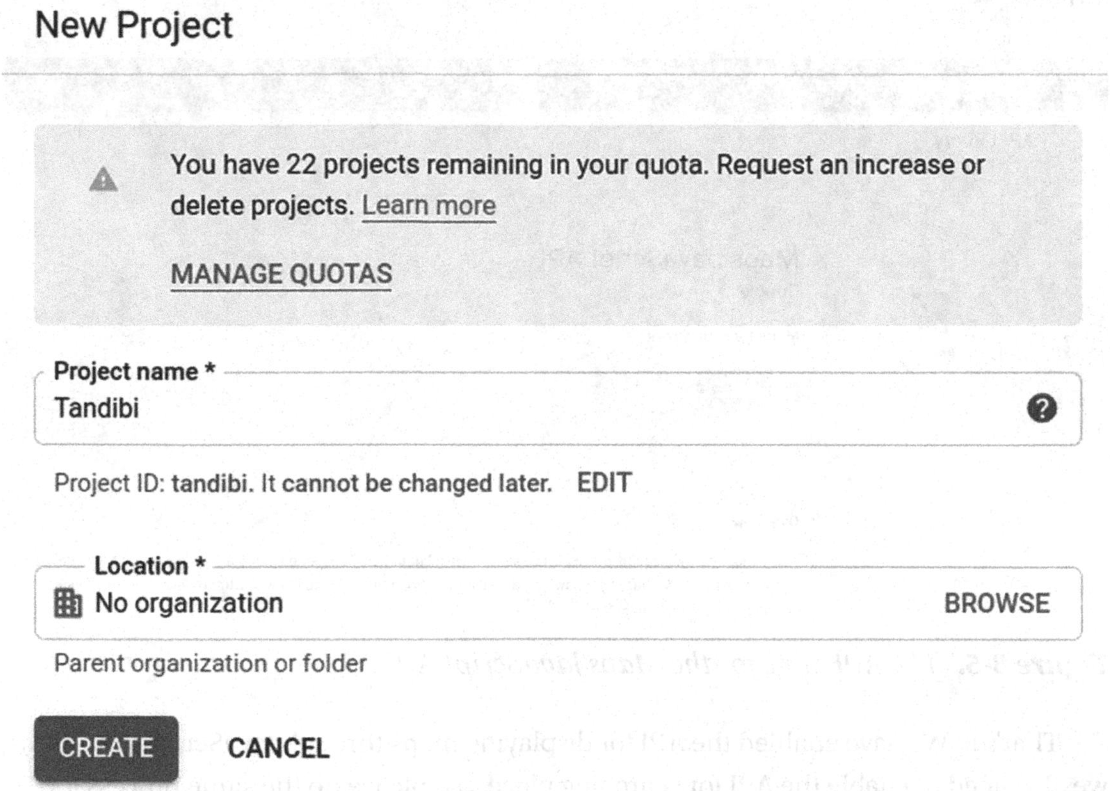

New Project
You have 22 projects remaining in your quota. Request an increase or delete projects. Learn more
MANAGE QUOTAS
Project name *
Tandibi
Project ID: tandibi. It cannot be changed later. EDIT
Location *
No organization
BROWSE
Parent organization or folder
CREATE
CANCEL

***Figure 8-3.** Creating a new project Tandibi*

Go back to the sidebar, hover over the APIs & Services menu, and then click Library. From the library page, type in **Maps JavaScript API**, and click the one that matches, as shown in Figure 8-4.

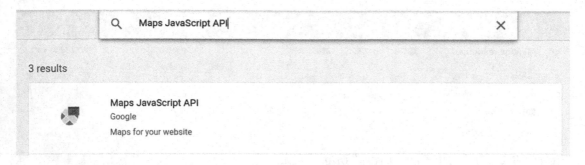

Figure 8-4. *Searching for the Maps JavaScript API*

After that, on the Maps JavaScript API page, let's click the Enable button, as shown in Figure 8-5.

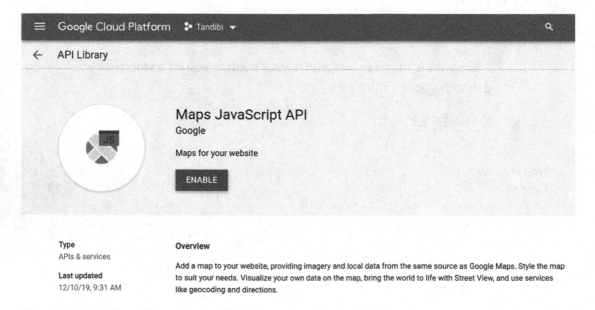

Figure 8-5. *The API page for the Maps JavaScript API*

That's it! We have enabled the API for displaying maps through JavaScript code. But, we also need to enable the API for searching places, so please do the same process for the Places API, as shown in Figure 8-6.

Google Cloud Platform
Tandibi
API Library
Places API
Google
Get detailed information about 100 million places
ENABLE

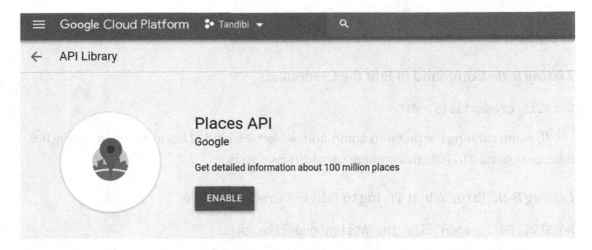

***Figure 8-6.** The API page for the Places API*

After that, let's obtain the credentials so that we can call the APIs from our system. First, hover the APIs & Services on the sidebar and then click Credentials. Then, click Create Credentials and then select API key. Please take note of the generated API key, as shown in Figure 8-7.

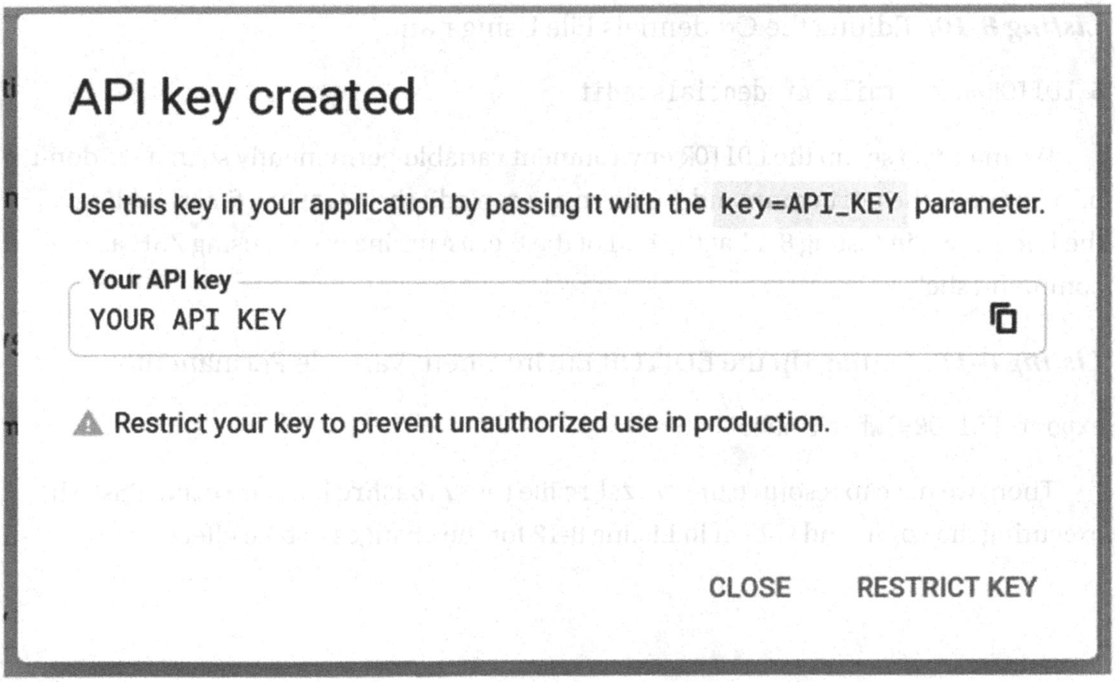

API key created
Use this key in your application by passing it with the key=API_KEY parameter.
Your API key
YOUR API KEY
Restrict your key to prevent unauthorized use in production.
CLOSE
RESTRICT KEY

***Figure 8-7.** The API key displayed on a modal dialog*

Then, let's add the API key into `credentials.yml` by executing the command shown in Listing 8-8.

Listing 8-8. Command to Edit the Credentials

```
$ rails credentials:edit
```

If, when running the previous command, we get the kind of error shown in Listing 8-9, it is because the `EDITOR` environment variable was not set.

Listing 8-9. Error When Trying to Edit the Credential File

```
No $EDITOR to open file in. Assign one like this:

EDITOR="mate --wait" bin/rails credentials:edit
```

For editors that fork and exit immediately, it's important to pass a wait flag; otherwise, the credentials will be saved immediately with no chance to edit.

Thus, Rails was not sure which editor it can use for us to edit the credentials with. Assuming that we have nano installed, which ships with most Unix-like operating systems, we can run the command shown in Listing 8-10 as an alternative.

Listing 8-10. Editing the Credentials File Using nano

```
$ EDITOR=nano rails credentials:edit
```

We may also set up the `EDITOR` environment variable permanently so that we don't have to prefix the `edit` command. To do so, we can edit the `~/.zshrc` file by adding the line shown in Listing 8-11 at the end of the file, assuming we are using ZSH as the command shell.

Listing 8-11. Setting Up the EDITOR Environment Variable Permanently

```
export EDITOR=`which nano`
```

Then, we have to resource the `~/.zshrc` file (or `~/.bashrc` if we are using Bash) by executing the command shown in Listing 8-12 for the changes to take effect.

Listing 8-12. Sourcing the ~/.zshrc File

```
source ~/.zshrc
```

Doing so, we can run `rails credentials:edit` without having to append the command by specifying the `EDITOR` value.

Now, let's add the API key into the credentials file with the structure shown in Listing 8-13.

Listing 8-13. The Credential Structure for Our APIs

```
secret_key_base: ...
google:
  credentials:
    map: XYZ123
```

That's it! We are done! We are ready to continue our adventure. It's important to note that the previous data structure is completely up to us. The way we define it won't affect anything, so long that we can get back the value by specifying some unique key.

Early User Interfaces

In this section, we will create the foundation of our check-in form. The form should look like Figure 8-8 on a mobile platform.

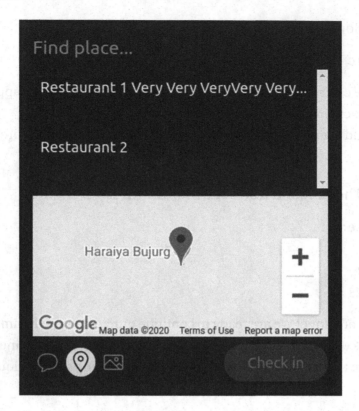

Figure 8-8. *The check-in form rendered for a mobile device*

On a desktop platform, the check-in form should be rendered as shown in Figure 8-9.

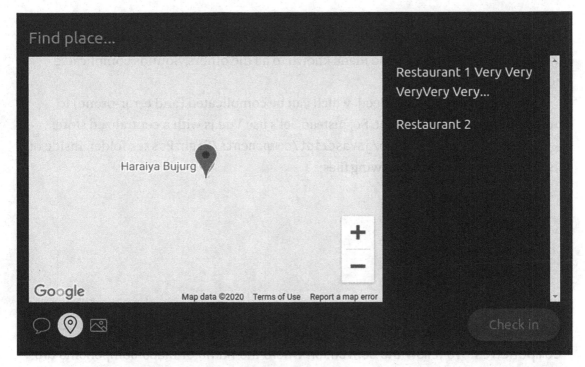

Figure 8-9. *The check-in form on the desktop*

The check-in form consists of three interdependent components: the map, the keyword input field, and the list for displaying places. Those components must work in tandem with each other, as shown in Figure 8-10.

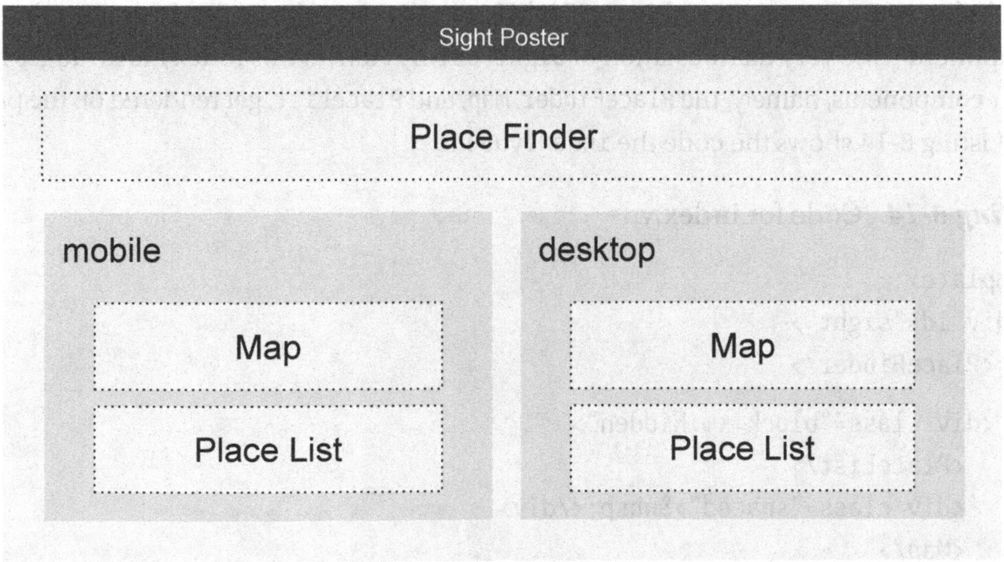

Figure 8-10. *Map and its related components*

Not only that, but for a better user experience, we render the map and the list twice depending on the screen's size. So, in total, we have five components to render, each having some states that must be made known to all the others. Sounds complicated enough, right?

This is quite ambitious indeed, which can be complicated (and error-prone) to implement in vanilla JavaScript. So, instead, let's use Vue.js with a centralized store.

To start, let's create the `app/javascript/components/SightPoster` folder. Inside of this folder, let's create the following files:

- `index.vue`
- `Map.vue`
- `PlaceFinder.vue`
- `PlaceList.vue`

Note   Vue recommends putting components under a directory called `components`. We follow the convention where the name of those components are written in CamelCase.

Adding index.vue

The `index.vue` component within the `SightPoster` folder is basically the main component—the very manifestation of `SightPoster`. Hence, this index file arranges how other components, namely, the `PlaceFinder`, `Map`, and `PlaceList`, get rendered on the page.

Listing 8-14 shows the code the `index.vue` file.

Listing 8-14. Code for index.vue

```
<template>
  <div id="sight">
    <PlaceFinder/>

    <div class="block sm:hidden">
      <PlaceList/>
      <div class="spaced"> </div>
      <Map/>
    </div>
```

```
    <div class="hidden sm:flex">
      <div class="w-2/3">
        <Map/>
      </div>

      <div class="w-1/3">
        <PlaceList/>
      </div>
    </div>
  </div>
</template>

<script>
  import Map from "./Map"
  import PlaceFinder from "./PlaceFinder"
  import PlaceList from "./PlaceList"

  export default {
    components: {
      Map,
      PlaceFinder,
      PlaceList
    },
  }
</script>

<style scoped>
  .spaced {
    @apply mt-1 mb-1;
    font-size: 0;
  }
</style>
```

In general, a vue file can contain any of template, script, and style tags. The template tag contains HTML-like notations representing the user interface.

The `style` is where we put our CSS styles, and yes, we can use our beloved TailwindCSS too in this place, thanks to Webpack. We can make the `style` tag be `scoped` so that classes defined therein wouldn't affect components from different files that by chance use classes with the same name.

The `script` tag is where we make the template come alive. We can define custom functions and interactivities here. This is also the place where we define custom components that the `template` can use. If we use any custom components in the `layout` that we don't export from here, Vue will complain. That is why we use the code shown in Listing 8-15.

Listing 8-15. Custom Components That the Layout Uses

```
export default {
  components: {
    Map,
    PlaceFinder,
    PlaceList
  },
```

Now, let's create a new pack for bundling our Vue code. Let's create the vue_application.js within app/javascript/packs folder and add the code shown in Listing 8-16.

Listing 8-16. Code for the vue_application Pack

```
import Vue from 'vue'
import SightPoster from '../components/SightPoster'
import { truncate } from "../lib/filters"

Vue.filter("truncate", truncate)

function renderSight() {
  const sightPoster = new Vue({
    render: h => h(SightPoster)
  }).$mount()

  document.querySelector(".js-sight-poster")
    .appendChild(sightPoster.$el)
}
```

```
document.addEventListener('turbolinks:load', () => {
  if (document.querySelector(".js-sight-poster")) {
    renderSight()
  }
})
```

The packs folder is a special directory made for Webpack's entry files. So, we should not put anything in this folder that we won't link in our views.

In our vue_application we just wrote, we import the truncate function from filters. We need to define this custom function ourselves. So, let's create the app/javascript/lib/filters.js file and then add the truncate function, as shown in Listing 8-17. The app/javascript/lib folder needs to be created as well, since it doesn't exist initially.

Listing 8-17. Code for the truncate Filter

```
export function truncate(text, length) {
  const clamp = "..."
  if (text.length <= length) {
    return text
  } else {
    let subString = text.substr(0, length-1)
    let lastSpaceIdx = subString.lastIndexOf(' ')
    subString = subString.substr(0, lastSpaceIdx)
    return subString + clamp
  }
}
```

After that, let's add the pack into our app/views/layouts/_header partial, as shown in Listing 8-18.

Listing 8-18. Adding the vue_application Pack into the Header Partial

```
...
<%= stylesheet_link_tag 'application', media: 'all' %>
<%= javascript_pack_tag 'application' %>
<%= javascript_pack_tag 'vue_application' %>
```

Now, let's update our poster form at posts/_form.html.erb. Let's wrap status_text inside a new div section, which we can later toggle the visibility of according to the user: whether they want to post a status or post a location update. So, let's wrap the input field as shown in Listing 8-19.

Listing 8-19. Wrapping the Status Text Area into Its Own Section

```
<%= f.text_area :status_text,
  required: true,
  placeholder: "What's happening?"  %>

<div class="poster js-status-poster">
  <%= f.text_area :status_text,
    required: true,
    placeholder: "What's happening?"  %>
</div>
```

After that, just below the js-status-poster, let's add a new div section that contains the check-in form. By default, this section should be hidden, so we added the hidden class in its class. And, since the elements will be rendered by Vue, its content is empty. See Listing 8-20.

Listing 8-20. Adding the Section for the Check-in Form

```
<div class="poster js-status-poster">
  ...
</div>

<% unless thread %>
  <div class="poster js-sight-poster hidden"></div>
<% end %>
```

And yes, we don't want to render the check-in from on a reply thread. Therefore, we specify the unless thread before adding the section.

Now let's check how our timeline looks by visiting http://localhost:3000/timelines. It should look like Figure 8-11.

Figure 8-11. *The timeline page*

Note   If when reloading the page you get a "Webpacker can't find vue_application" error, or something similar to that, stop `webpack-dev-server` and relaunch it.

Nothing has changed much, since we haven't added anything in the `PlaceFinder`, or in `PlaceList` or `Map`. Let's work on them soon.

Adding Post Switcher

But wait, before working on various `SightPoster` subcomponents, how about adding the switch buttons? That should be a good idea so that we can switch between each poster, rather than displaying both at the same time, which would be aesthetically disturbing.

So, let's open `app/views/posts/_form` and then add the new switchers within the options div, as shown in Listing 8-21.

Listing 8-21. Switch Buttons to Switch Between the Forms

```
<div class="options">
  <div class="switch option js-status-poster-switch active">
    <%= evil_icon "ei-comment"%>
  </div>

  <div class="switch option js-sight-poster-switch">
    <%= evil_icon "ei-location" %>
  </div>

  <div class="option js-pictures-uploader">
    ...
```

If we reload the timeline page, we can see that we now have the switch buttons in the form, as shown in Figure 8-12.

Figure 8-12. *Switch buttons to switch between different poster forms*

But now, if we click any of those buttons, the poster form doesn't change at all. Let's make it work. Let's add a new `switchActivePoster` function in the poster form, before the `clickHandler` function we have defined within the page's `script` tag, as shown in Listing 8-22.

Listing 8-22. Code for the switchActivePoster

```
<script type="text/javascript">
  var switchActivePoster = (formElm, postableType) => {
    var postersElm = formElm.querySelectorAll(".poster")
    var switchesElm = formElm.querySelectorAll(".switch")
    var postTypeHiddenElm = formElm.querySelector(
      "[name='post[postable_type]']")

    postersElm.forEach((elm) => elm.classList.add("hidden"))
    switchesElm.forEach((elm) => elm.classList.remove("active"))

    var posterCls = `.js-${postableType.toLowerCase()}-poster`
    var switcherCls = `${posterCls}-switch`

    formElm.querySelector(posterCls).classList.remove("hidden")
    formElm.querySelector(switcherCls).classList.add("active")
    postTypeHiddenElm.value = postableType
  }

  var clickHandler = (evt) => {
    ...
```

After that, for the switch buttons to work, let's add the `else-if` statements shown in Listing 8-23 within the `clickHandler` function in the same file.

Listing 8-23. Code for the Switch to Work

```
if (parentClasses.contains("js-pictures-uploader")) {
  ...
} else if (parentClasses.contains("js-sight-poster-switch")) {
  switchActivePoster(formElm, "Sight")

  var submiBtnElm = formElm.querySelector("[type='submit']")
  submiBtnElm.value = "Check in"
  submiBtnElm.style.width = "7rem"

  textareaElm.removeAttribute("required")
} else if (parentClasses.contains("js-status-poster-switch")) {
  switchActivePoster(formElm, "Status")

  var submiBtnElm = formElm.querySelector("[type='submit']")
  submiBtnElm.value = "Say"
  submiBtnElm.removeAttribute("style")

  textareaElm.setAttribute("required", "required")
}
```

Finally, let's add the code in Listing 8-24, which will prevent focusing on the status text field if a click occurs within the check-in form. Let's scroll to the end of the `clickHandler` function and add the code just under the `js-pictures-uploader` if condition. This is the kind of interactivity that would be easier to handle if the form were Vue in its entirety. This is why managing interactivity in plain JavaScript is error-prone even if it is easy and possible.

Listing 8-24. Adding Final Code for Escaping Unwanted Focus Request

```
  ...

} else if (evt.target) {
  ...
```

```
if (parentClasses.contains("js-pictures-uploader")) {
  return
}

if (parentElm.closest(".sight-poster")) {
  return
}
}
...
```

The last thing we need to do now is to define the style shown in Listing 8-25 in poster.css.

Listing 8-25. Adding the Style for the Active Icon for the Form's Options

```
...
.poster .controls .options .option {
  @apply text-sm mr-1;
}

...


.body-private
.poster .controls .options .icon {
  ...
}
.body-member
.poster .controls .options .active .icon {
  @apply bg-teal-200 text-dark-800;
}
```

Now, let's refresh our timeline! We will see that the status update switch button is active by default, with a light teal, rounded background, as shown in Figure 8-13.

Figure 8-13. *Status update switch highlighted by default*

Now, we can click the location switch button. Doing so, the whole form now changes to something else, supposedly the location update form. But, currently, it is blank since we haven't really defined the PlaceFinder component and friends, as shown in Figure 8-14.

Figure 8-14. *The empty location update poster*

But at least the switcher works!

Adding PlaceFinder.vue

Let's code our PlaceFinder.vue, which is downright the easiest component to code. Basically, it's just a "glorified" input field. The code for the component is as shown in Listing 8-26.

Listing 8-26. Code for the PlaceFinder.vue

```
<template>
  <div class="sight-place-finder">
    <input type="text"
      placeholder="Find place...">
  </div>
</template>

<script>
  import Vue from "vue"

  const Component = Vue.extend({
  })

  export default Component
</script>

<style scoped>
  input {
    @apply bg-dark-700 text-xl;
    @apply mb-2;
    width: 100%;
  }
</style>
```

Later, however, we will modify this component to connect it with a centralized state.

For now, if we refresh the timeline page and click the sight poster switch, we can see the form now has an input field with that helpful placeholder, as shown in Figure 8-15.

Figure 8-15. *Sight poster form with PlaceFinder*

Adding Map.vue

Now, wouldn't it be great if we could have a map on the form? Let's make this Map component, as shown in Listing 8-27.

Listing 8-27. Code for Map.vue

```
<template>
  <div class="sight-map">
    <div id="map" ref="map"></div>
  </div>
</template>

<script>
  import Vue from "vue"

  const Component = Vue.extend({
    data() {
      return {
        map: null,
        coordinates: {
          lat: 35.6804,
          lng: 139.7690,
        },
      }
    },

    methods: {
      redraw() {
        const coordinates = this.coordinates

        if (!window.google) {
          setTimeout(function() {
            this.redraw()
          }.bind(this), 1000)
          return
        }
```

```
      if (coordinates.lat && coordinates.lng) {
        this.map = new window.google.maps.Map(
          this.$refs["map"], {
            center: this.coordinates,
            zoom: 18,
            disableDefaultUI: true,
            zoomControl: true,
          }
        )

        new window.google.maps.Marker({
          position: this.coordinates,
          map: this.map
        })
      }
    }
  },

  mounted() {
    if (navigator.geolocation) {
      navigator.geolocation.getCurrentPosition((pos) => {
        const coords = pos.coords
        this.coordinates.lat = coords.latitude
        this.coordinates.lng = coords.longitude

        this.redraw()
      })
    }
  },

})

export default Component
</script>

<style scoped>
  #map {
    height: 150px;
```

```
  }
  @screen sm {
    #map {
      height: 300px;
    }
  }
}
</style>
```

We used `navigator.geolocation.getCurrentPosition` to get the user's current longitude and latitude from the browser. However, we can obtain that data only if the user gave their consent, as the browser will ask for their approval first. In this book, we assume that our users will always give their permission.

Next, let's add the code in Listing 8-28 into `_header.html.erb` so that `Map.vue` can resolve `window.google.maps.Map`.

Listing 8-28. Adding the Script Tag for Google Maps API

```
...
<%= csp_meta_tag %>
<script async defer src="<%= google_map_api_url %>"></script>
```

Then, let's define `google_map_api_url` within `app/helpers/application_helper. rb`. See Listing 8-29.

Listing 8-29. Defining the google_map_api_url Helper Method

```
module ApplicationHelper
  def google_map_api_url
    credentials = Rails.application.credentials
    key = credentials.dig(:google, :credentials, :map)

    "https://maps.googleapis.com/maps/api/js?key=" + key
  end
end
```

Now, if we refresh the timeline page and switch to the sight poster, we can see now we have a map under the finder field. Great! It's taking shape. See Figure 8-16.

Figure 8-16. *Form complete with the Map component*

Adding PlaceList.vue

We are done with `PlaceFinder.vue` and `Map.vue`, so let's make our `PlaceList.vue`. Let's add the code in Listing 8-30 into `PlaceList.vue`.

Listing 8-30. Code for PlaceList.vue

```
<template>
  <div class="places">
    <div v-for="place in places"
      class="place"
      :key="place.id">
      <p>{{ place.name | truncate(40) }}</p>
    </div>
  </div>
</template>
```

```
<script>
  import Vue from "vue"

  const Component = Vue.extend({
    data() {
      return {
        places: [
          {
            id: "1",
            locale: "en",
            name: "Restaurant 1 Very Very Very" +
              "Very Very Ultimately Very " +
              "Very Long Name",
            place_type: "restaurant",
            coordinates: { lng: 1, lat: 1 }
          },
          {
            id: "2",
            locale: "en",
            name: "Restaurant 2",
            place_type: "restaurant",
            coordinates: { lng: 1, lat: 1 }
          }
        ]
      }
    }
  })

  export default Component
</script>

<style scoped>
  .places {
    @apply overflow-x-hidden overflow-y-scroll;
    height: 8em;
```

```
    min-height: 8em;
    max-height: 8em;
  }

  .place {
    @apply p-2 overflow-hidden;
    @apply cursor-pointer;
    min-height: 4em;
    height: 4em;
  }

  .place:hover {
    @apply bg-dark-600;
    @apply transition duration-100 ease-in;
  }

  @screen sm {
    .places {
      height: 300px;
      max-height: 300px;
      min-height: 300px;
    }

    .place {
      @apply ml-2;
    }
  }
</style>
```

Let's see how it gets rendered on the page by refreshing the timeline page and switching to the sight poster, as shown in Figure 8-17.

Figure 8-17. *Complete sight poster form*

There we go! We have a complete sight poster form. Granted, all those components are working independently of each other. They don't share data. In fact, the PlaceList component displays dummy data since it doesn't know yet the current position at the map, so it cannot suggest nearby places of interest.

In the next part of this chapter, let's make a centralized store to share our Vue app's states. That way, we can fetch places based on the entered text in the finder field and then display suggested places on the form for the user to select. The map would also point to the correct location. Learning how to centralize the data is our next adventure.

Centralizing States via the Vuex Store

A front-end app sufficiently complex enough will definitely have some states. For a simple case, we can use props (properties) to share, or pass, states from one component to another, as shown in Listing 8-31.

Listing 8-31. Passing States to a Hypothetical Phone Through the name and os Props

```
<template>
  <p>Select your phone:</p>
  <PhonesChoice>
    <Phone name="iPhone" os="iOS 14"/>
    <Phone name="Galaxy S20" os="Android 10"/>
  <PhonesChoice>
</template>
```

Another way to share state is by using a centralized store. But why do we need a centralized store when we can pass state through props?

At times, data must be accessible by components that are quite abstract that they don't really fulfill a parent-child relationship. In that case, it feels quite not right to use props for sharing data.

For example, although our `SightPoster` has the three children `PlaceFinder`, `Map`, and `PlaceList`, all those components are quite abstract from one another. Their relationship with the parent is not like that of `PhonesChoice`, which acts as a list, and its Phone items.

In fact, `PlaceFinder`, `Map`, and `PlaceList` are grouped into `SightPoster` only to abstract away the implementation detail of our `SightPoster`. It should be obvious that those subcomponents don't share the same kind of parent-child relationship as would `PhonesChoice` and `Phone`.

In another case, when data is exchanged between various components and when passing them in props would only increase complexity, using centralized state makes sense.

Vuex is a state management library for Vue. The core of Vuex is a store that keeps states in a central place; thus, it is known as a *centralized store*. Each component in an application can retrieve data as needed from that central store.

Vuex adopts Flux, an architecture/pattern, that was developed by Facebook; it is composed of four unidirectional parts. Those four parts are laid out in Figure 8-18.

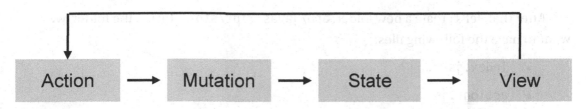

Figure 8-18. *The flux pattern in a diagram*

The actions, mutations, and states are lumped together into something known as *store* that the view is reactive to. The view may re-render itself when any of the states it depends on have changed.

The state, however, cannot change by itself. For changing any value, there must be explicit mutation dispatched as a result of an action.

An action can be anything, from a click on a button to a keypress on an input field. However, it can also be more complicated than that, such as fetching data from a server.

Indeed, using Vuex means introducing certain architectural overhead. But, is it justified?

In any nontrivial app, almost always yes! The separation of concerns helps us to frame user interactivity and lay out changes into organized entities that are easy to reason about.

For example, if we want to know who changed a particular state, we only need to find which actions dispatch the mutation. All will be revealed in an organized, unidirectional flow, which is relatively easy to wrap our head around.

Again, the naming conventions are still to be respected here. For example, actions are normally spelled in lower camelCase, such as `fetchData` or `redrawMap`. While mutations are in an upper-case SNAKE_CASE, such as `SET_COORDINATES` or `SET_USER`.

Note   At times, we may see projects that do not adhere to these naming conventions. However, it would be great if we could follow them here.

Now let's add vuex into our project by executing the command shown in Listing 8-32.

Listing 8-32. Adding vuex into the Repertoire

```
$ yarn add vuex@^3.1.3
```

After that, let's create a new folder: `app/javascript/store`. Inside the folder, we want to have the following files:

- `index.js`
- `actions.js`
- `mutations.js`

Let's add the code shown in Listing 8-33 into the `index.js` file.

Listing 8-33. Code for store/index.js

```
import Vue from "vue"
import Vuex from "vuex"
import actions from "./actions"
import mutations from "./mutations"

Vue.use(Vuex)

const isDev = process.env.NODE_ENV !== "production"

const store = new Vuex.Store({
  state: {
    error: null,
  },

  // the only way to change the state
  mutations,

  // perform async actions
  actions,

  // values derived from the state
  getters: {
    hasError: state => state.error ? true : false
  },

  // raise an error if a state is unlawfully mutated
  strict: isDev
})

store.commit("RESET")
export default store
```

Then for `mutations.js`, use the code shown in Listing 8-34.

Listing 8-34. Code for store/mutations.js

```
const mutations = {
  SET_ERROR(state, error) {
    state.error = error
  },

  RESET(state) {
    state.error = null
  }
}

export default mutations
```

Then for `actions.js`, use the code shown in Listing 8-35.

Listing 8-35. Code for store/actions.js

```
function handleError(commit, error) {
  const message = error.message || error.info.error_description
  commit('setError', message)
}

const actions = {

}

export default actions
```

After that, let's tell our Vue application that they have a store. Let's make these changes in `packs/vue_application.js`, as shown in Listing 8-36.

Listing 8-36. Registering the Store into the Vue Application

```
...
import store from "../store"
import SightPoster from '../components/SightPoster'
...
```

```
function renderSight() {
  const sightPoster = new Vue({
    store,
    render: h => h(SightPoster)
  }).$mount()
...
```

We are done! Our components now have access to the central store by virtue of `this.$store`, they can also subscribe or unsubscribe for mutations, and they can also call an action or dispatch a mutation, as we will soon see.

Working on the Backend

Before we can work further on the front-end side, we need our backend side ready to answer API requests.

Place Finder and Crawler

We will have two new service classes for the `Place` model: `Place::Finder` and `Place::Crawler`. We use `Place::Finder` for searching places from within our own database. On the other hand, we use the crawler service to fetch places from Google Places through its API and then save the data into our database.

Listing 8-37 shows the code for `services/place/finder.rb`.

Listing 8-37. Code for Place::Finder

```
class Place::Finder < ApplicationService
  attr_reader :keyword, :lat, :lng
  private :keyword, :lat, :lng

  DISTANCE_RADIUS_IN_METRES = 200_000

  def initialize(keyword, lat:, lng:)
    @keyword = keyword
    @lat = lat
    @lng = lng
  end
```

```
def call
  result = sort_by_distance(search_keyword_within_radius)

  if result.empty?
    result = sort_by_distance(search_by_keyword)
  end

  result
end

private

  def base_point
    point = "POINT(#{lng} #{lat})"
    @base_point ||= "ST_GeographyFromText('#{point}')"
  end

  def search_by_keyword
    Place.where("name ILIKE ?", "%#{keyword}%")
  end

  def search_keyword_within_radius
    search_by_keyword
      .where("ST_DWITHIN(#{base_point}, coordinate,
        #{DISTANCE_RADIUS_IN_METRES}, true)")
  end

  def sort_by_distance(relation)
    relation.order("ST_DISTANCE(#{base_point}, coordinate)")
  end
end
```

As we can observe from the previous code, we are using SQL extensions such as ST_DWITHIN to search places within the specified distance of one another using geographical, rather than geometrical, calculations. We then sort the results using ST_DISTANCE, which also performs calculations in geographical terms.

Notice how we break down those works into smaller, laser-focused methods. Those smaller methods handle generic parts of the use case, which then get glued to handle the entire use case.

When we approach coding in this way, we help make our software more flexible as it has become easier to reuse those APIs later to solve other problems.

Note   ST stands for *spatial type*, which is used to namespace PostGIS functions as suggested by the SQL/MM convention. The MM in SQL/MM means *multimedia*, or in full terms: SQL Multimedia and Application Packages. People think SQL/MMAPP just doesn't make the cut.

The standard requires SQL extensions to namespace their keywords to avoid collisions. For example, the keyword CONTAINS behaves differently for a full-text search and a spatial search. Therefore, it should be namespaced accordingly, such as FT_CONTAINS and ST_CONTAINS, where FT stands for *full-text*.

If one ever experienced a "Cannot find SRID (4326) in spatial_ref_sys" error, it means the internal table used by PostGIS to store information about different projections was missing (sometimes as a result of truncation). Re-creating the database using the migration files should help fix the problem.

For the crawler, we will use faraday to make the API calls, instead of Ruby's own HTTP library: Net::HTTP. This is because faraday is an adapter that wraps other HTTP libraries so that we can switch from Net::HTTP to Excon, Typhoeus, Patron, or EventMachine easily without changing more than a line or two of the configuration. See Listing 8-38.

Listing 8-38. Adding faraday into the Gemfile

```
gem 'faraday', '~> 1.0'
```

Now, after having faraday bundled, let's add the code shown in Listing 8-39 for the crawler. The file should be saved as services/place/crawler.rb.

Listing 8-39. Code for Place::Crawler

```ruby
class Place::Crawler < ApplicationService
  attr_reader :keyword, :lat, :lng
  private :keyword, :lat, :lng

  API_KEY = Rails.application.credentials.dig(
    :google, :credentials, :map)
  ENDPOINT = "https://maps.googleapis.com".freeze

  def initialize(keyword, lat:, lng:)
    @keyword = keyword
    @lat = lat
    @lng = lng
  end

  def call
    crawled_places.each do |place_data|
      coordinates = place_data["geometry"]["location"]
      lat, lng = coordinates["lat"], coordinates["lng"]

      # possible N+1, would you find a way to fix it?
      next if exists?("en", lng, lat)

      Place.create(
        name: place_data["name"],
        coordinate: geo.point(lng, lat),
        locale: "en",
        place_type: place_type(place_data["types"])
      )
    end
  rescue Faraday::ConnectionFailed => e
    # actually, we should report this error
    # to a centralized error notification service
    puts e.message
  end
```

```ruby
  private

    def connection
      @connection ||= Faraday.new(
        ENDPOINT,
        request: {
          timeout: 7.seconds
        }
      )
    end

    def crawled_places
      @crawled_places ||= begin
        response = connection.get do |req|
          req.url "/maps/api/place/textsearch/json"
          req.params["query"] = keyword
          req.params["radius"] = 2000
          req.params["language"] = "en"
          req.params["location"] = "#{lat},#{lng}"
          req.params["key"] = API_KEY
        end

        response = JSON.parse(response.body)
        response["results"]
      end
    end

    def place_type(google_types)
      types = Place::PLACE_TYPES.dup
      intersect = google_types & types
      intersect.first || "other"
    end

    def geo
      @geo ||= RGeo::Geographic::Factory.new(
        "Spherical",
        has_z_coordinate: true,
        srid: 4326,
```

```
        )
    end

    def exists?(locale, lng, lat)
        point = geo.point(lng, lat)

        place = Place.where(
            coordinate: point,
            locale: "en",
        ).exists?
    end
end
```

Observe how we specify the `timeout` in the `connection` method. This is a common pattern for circuit-breaking in case the other server is taking too much time to process our request. When that happens, we time out ourselves so that our system can keep being responsive.

However, this is a kind of error that we shouldn't ignore. Instead of `puts`, we should properly log the error to a centralized error management system, which we will discuss in a later chapter.

The Place Controller API

Now we are ready to build our API controller. Nowadays, modern APIs communicate using JSON documents. In other words, the client sends data in JSON format, and the server responds by giving back a JSON document. JSON is a shorthand for JavaScript Object Notation, as shown in Listing 8-40.

Listing 8-40. An Example of a JSON Document

```
{
  "author": {
    "name": "Adam Notodikromo",
    "age": 27,
    "favorites": {
      "foods": ["Soto", "Burger", "Ramen"],
    }
  }
}
```

There is a popular gem that we can use to help us serialize our record instances into JSON. The gem is called `active_model_serializers`. Let's add it to the gemfile, as shown in Listing 8-41.

Listing 8-41. Adding active_model_serializer into the Gemfile

```
gem 'active_model_serializers', '~> 0.10'
```

After that, we need to create the API controller for fetching places. We will use API versioning so that the path of the API will be something like `api/v1/places` instead of just `/api/places`. The `v1` indicates that the API interface for communication is version 1; this is done to minimize issues that are the result of breaking changes.

This kind of strategy should be made mandatory if:

- The API can be used in many different platforms, e.g., the web, mobile, etc.

- The API can be used by the public/general populations.

Our current strategy is known as URI versioning. There are other ways to version our API such as by specifying the version at the Accept header, versioning using a custom header (e.g., X-Accept-Version), or even specifying the version as part of the request's body.

In our case, we pick URI versioning as it's relatively simpler to use and understand. Now, let's start generating the versioned controller by issuing the command shown in Listing 8-42.

Listing 8-42. Command to Generate the Versioned API Controller

```
$ rails g controller Api::V1::PlacesController --no-assets
```

After that, let's add the code shown in Listing 8-43 into `Api::V1::PlacesController`.

Listing 8-43. Codes for the index Action

```
class Api::V1::PlacesController < ApplicationController
  def index
    keyword = params.fetch(:keyword)
    lat = params.fetch(:lat)
    lng = params.fetch(:lng)
```

```
    Place::Crawler.call(keyword, lat: lat, lng: lng)
    render json: Place::Finder.call(keyword, lat: lat, lng: lng)
  end
end
```

After that, let's create the serializer for the Place model, as shown in Listing 8-44.

Listing 8-44. Command to Generate a Serializer for the Place Model

```
$ rails g serializer Place
Running via Spring preloader in process 30417
    create  app/serializers/place_serializer.rb
```

You might experience the error shown in Listing 8-45 when running the previous command.

Listing 8-45. Error When Running the Serializer Task

```
Running via Spring preloader in process 210274
Could not find generator 'serializer'.
Run `rails generate --help` for more options.
```

This issue could happen since Spring caches our Rails application in the background, and this cached version is not aware of the existence of active_model_ serializers and its associated task. Stopping Spring from preloading our Rails app and then re-executing the previous command might help solve the issue, as shown in Listing 8-46.

Listing 8-46. Stopping Spring to Clear Off Preloaded App

```
$ spring stop
$ rails g serializer Place
```

After having the PlaceSerializer, let's add the code shown in Listing 8-47 into it.

Listing 8-47. Code for the PlaceSerializer

```
class PlaceSerializer < ActiveModel::Serializer
  attributes :id,
    :locale,
    :name,
    :place_type,
    :coordinates

  def coordinates
    coordinate = object.coordinate
    {
      lng: coordinate.longitude,
      lat: coordinate.latitude,
    }
  end
end
```

After that, let's define the routes at `config/routes.rb`, as shown in Listing 8-48.

Listing 8-48. Route for the Api::V1::PlacesController

```
Rails.application.routes.draw do
  ...
  namespace :api do
    namespace :v1 do
      resources :places, only: [:index]
    end
  end
end
```

That's it! Our backend is ready to process API calls from the front end.

Wiring Things Up

We can now send request to fetch places. First, let's define a new mutation inside `mutations.js`, as shown in Listing 8-49.

Listing 8-49. A New Mutation for Setting the Search Keyword

```
SET_ERROR(state, error) {
  state.error = error
},

SET_SIGHT_KEYWORD(state, kw) {
  state.sight.keyword = kw
},

RESET(state) {
  state.error = null
  state.sight = {
    keyword: ""
  }
}
```

After that, let's connect the input field in `PlaceFinder.vue` to the store by using a `v-model` directive, as shown in Listing 8-50.

Listing 8-50. Connecting the Input with a State in the Store

```
<template>
  <div class="sight-place-finder">
    <input type="text"
      v-model="keyword"
      placeholder="Find place...">
  </div>
</template>

...

const Component = Vue.extend({
  computed: {
    keyword: {
      get() {
        return this.$store.state.sight.keyword
      },
      set(value) {
```

```
        this.$store.commit(
          "SET_SIGHT_KEYWORD",
          value,
        )
      }
    }
  },
})
```

The v-model is a directive that we can use to mutate a state. In strict mode, doing this results in an error, as the state is mutated outside of a mutation handler. To make this work, we make a two-way computed property that knows how to alter or read the state from the store.

Next, let's work on fetching and processing the places we will get from the server after sending an API call.

Then, let's define the possible mutations shown in Listing 8-51.

Listing 8-51. Defining New Mutations

```
SET_COORDINATES(state, [lng, lat]) {
  state.coordinates.lng = lng
  state.coordinates.lat = lat
},

SET_SIGHT_KEYWORD(state, kw) {
  state.sight.keyword = kw
},

SET_SIGHT_PLACES(state, places) {
  state.sight.places = places
},

SET_SIGHT_SELECTED_PLACE(state, place) {
  state.sight.selectedPlace = place
},

RESET(state) {
  state.error = null
```

```
state.coordinates = {
  lat: null,
  lng: null,
}

state.sight = {
  keyword: "",
  places: [],
  selectedPlace: null,
}
}
```

After that, let's define the new states explicitly in `store/index.js`. Defining the root keys explicitly in the store's state is of utmost importance so that Vue can track changes in the states, as shown in Listing 8-52.

Listing 8-52. Adding New States

```
const store = new Vuex.Store({
  state: {
    error: null,
    coordinates: null,
    sight: null,
  },
  ...
```

Then, let's move out location detection from `Map.vue` into the store by adding the code shown in Listing 8-53 into `store/index.js`.

Listing 8-53. Codes for resetStore

```
store.commit("RESET")
function resetStore() {
  store.commit("RESET")

  if (navigator.geolocation) {
    navigator.geolocation.getCurrentPosition((pos) => {
      store.commit("SET_COORDINATES",
```

```
        [pos.coords.longitude, pos.coords.latitude])
    })
  }
}

resetStore()

...
```

Then, let's change Map.vue to look like Listing 8-54.

Listing 8-54. Changes for Map.vue

```
mounted() {
  this.unsubscribe = this.$store.subscribe((mutation, state) => {
    if (mutation.type === "SET_COORDINATES") {
      this.coordinates.lat = this.$store.state.coordinates.lat
      this.coordinates.lng = this.$store.state.coordinates.lng
      this.redraw()
    }
  })

  this.redraw()
},

beforeDestroy() {
  this.unsubscribe()
},
```

Next, let's modify PlaceFinder. Let's display places of interest that match with the keyword the user is typing.

However, we should use debounce in this case. *Debouncing*, in a nutshell, is a common technique to prevent doing the same thing too many times at once. It does this by grouping events together and keeps them from being fired too often. Without this, we will send way too many unnecessary requests as the user types.

First, let's add lodash as we will import debounce from it, as shown in Listing 8-55.

Listing 8-55. Adding lodash

```
$ yarn add lodash@4.17.15
```

After that, let's go to `PlaceFinder.vue` and add the code shown in Listing 8-56.

Listing 8-56. Changes for PlaceFinder.vue

```
<template>
  <div class="sight-place-finder">
    <input type="text"
      v-model="keyword"
      v-on:keyup="findPlace"
      placeholder="Find place...">
  </div>
</template>

<script>
  import Vue from "vue"
  import debounce from "lodash/debounce"

  const Component = Vue.extend({
    computed: {
    },

    methods: {
      findPlace: debounce(function() {
        this.$store.dispatch("findPlace")
      }, 300)
    }
  })

  export default Component
</script>
```

Note   Debouncing might sound like throttling, but they are different. Throttling prevents something from executing for some period of time, while debouncing clumps a series of consecutive calls into a single call to that function after a specific time when no calls are made.

Let's define the `findPlace` action inside `store/actions.js`, as shown in Listing 8-57.

Listing 8-57. Defining findPlace in store/actions.js

```
const actions = {
  async findPlace({ commit, state }) {
    try {
      const url = new URL("/api/v1/places", window.location.origin)
      url.searchParams.append("keyword", state.sight.keyword)
      url.searchParams.append("lat", state.coordinates.lat)
      url.searchParams.append("lng", state.coordinates.lng)

      const performSearch = async (isRetried) => {
        let response = await fetch(url)
        let data = await response.json()

        if (data.length === 0 && !isRetried) {
          setTimeout(() => { performSearch(true) }, 5000)
        } else {
          commit("SET_SIGHT_PLACES", data)
        }
      }

      await performSearch(false)
    } catch (error) {
      handleError(commit, error)
    }
  }
}

export default actions
```

Notice that we dispatch SET_SIGHT_PLACES to set the list of places. Yet, the list won't be updated since we always use dummy data.

Let's change PlaceList.vue to reflect the code shown in Listing 8-58.

Listing 8-58. Changes for PlaceList.vue

```
<template>
  <div class="places">
    <div v-for="place in sight.places"
```

```
    class="place"
    @click="setPlace(place)"
    :class="isSelected(place)"
    :key="place.id">
    <p>{{ place.name | truncate(40) }}</p>
  </div>
  </div>
</template>

<script>
  import Vue from "vue"
  import { mapState } from "vuex"

  const Component = Vue.extend({
    computed: {
      ...mapState(["sight"]),
    },

    methods: {
      setPlace(place) {
        this.$store.commit("SET_SIGHT_SELECTED_PLACE",
          place)
      },

      isSelected(place) {
        const placeId = place.id
        const selectedPlace = this.sight.selectedPlace
        if (selectedPlace && selectedPlace.id === placeId) {
          return "selected"
        }
      }
    }
  })

  export default Component
</script>

<style scoped>
  ...
```

```
.place.selected {
  @apply bg-indigo-800;
}

.place.selected:hover {
  @apply bg-indigo-700;
}

.place:hover {
...
</style>
```

Notice how we append a class dynamically by using the `:class` directive, which is equivalent to `v-class`. We also dispatch a mutation to change the selected place if the user clicks an item in the list.

Now, should we check how things look? Let's reload the timeline page and switch over to the sight poster. In the place finder input field, we can type any keyword, and places of interests satisfying the keyword will be displayed immediately.

Let's try *sushi*. Please note that our results are likely to be different since it takes into account the user's current geolocation, as shown in Figure 8-19.

Figure 8-19. *Finding sushi restaurants nearby*

But, if we click the list, the pointer on the map doesn't change. This is a really bad user experience, as this can potentially confuse our user. Let's change this behavior by adding the code shown in Listing 8-59 to Map.vue.

Listing 8-59. Code to Redraw the Map If the User Clicks a Place

```
mounted() {
  this.unsubscribe = this.$store.subscribe((mutation, state) => {
    if (mutation.type === "SET_COORDINATES") {
      ...
    } else if (mutation.type == "SET_SIGHT_SELECTED_PLACE") {
      const selectedPlace = this.$store.state.sight.selectedPlace
      const placeCoords = selectedPlace.coordinates
      this.coordinates.lat = placeCoords.lat
      this.coordinates.lng = placeCoords.lng
      this.redraw()
    }
  })

  this.redraw()
}
```

Now, if our user clicks any item on the list, not only is that the item highlighted, but the map will also redraw, as shown in Figure 8-20.

Figure 8-20. *Map redrawn if the user clicks any listed places of interest*

All is good! The last step we want to do is to ensure the user can post a new sight update. We will begin with adding a hidden input field that represents the selected place. Then, let's make the Post controller and also the service be able to process the form if the user clicks the form's submit button. First, let's define a new accessor sight_place_ id in the Post model, as shown in Listing 8-60.

Listing 8-60. Adding sight_place_id into Post

```
class Post < ApplicationRecord
  ...
  ## for the forms
  attr_accessor :status_text
  attr_accessor :sight_place_id
end
```

After that, let's whitelist the sight_place_id from the params. Specifically, let's add the change shown in Listing 8-61 to PostsController.

Listing 8-61. Whitelisting sight_place_id

```
def permitted_params
  params.require(:post).permit(
    :postable_type,
    :status_text,
    :sight_place_id,
    :thread_id,
    :pictures => [],
  )
end
...
```

After that, let's add the code shown in Listing 8-62 to Post::Creator.

Listing 8-62. Changes for Post::Creator Service

```
class Post::Creator < ApplicationService
  ...
```

```ruby
  def call
    case postable_type
    when "Status" then create_a_status_update
    when "Sight" then create_a_sight_update
    else false
    end
  rescue
    false
  end

  private

    ...

    def place
      @place ||= begin
        place = Place.find(params[:sight_place_id])
      end
    end

    ...

    def create_a_sight_update
      sight = Sight.new(
        place: place,
        activity_type: Sight::CHECKIN
      )

      post.postable = sight
      post.user = creator
      post.thread = thread
      post.save

      if post.persisted?
        attach_pictures!
      end

      post.persisted?
    end
end
```

Now, let's ensure that this selected place is sent along with other data from the form when the form is submitted. To do that, we need to add a hidden input field, since only input fields are sent by the browser.

Let's add the changes shown in Listing 8-63 to SightPoster/index.vue.

Listing 8-63. Changes for SightPoster/index.vue

```
<template>
  <div id="sight">
    <input type="hidden" name="post[sight_place_id]"
      :value="selectedPlace.id">

    ...
  </div>
</template>

<script>
  ...
  export default {
    ...

    computed: {
      selectedPlace() {
        return this.$store.state.sight.selectedPlace || {}
      }
    }
  }
</script>
...
```

We are done! Now we can post a check-in. See Figure 8-21.

Figure 8-21. *Checked in at Genki Sushi*

Crawling in the Background

In a large application, we usually need to spot processes that can take considerable time to process and then try to speed them up. Those processes can be everything from image manipulations to calculating billing for hundreds of clients.

There are also tasks that are actually possible to be done by other processes in the background, instead of in the controller. This way, a request can get its response as soon as possible. A classic example of such a task is sending an email.

If we don't optimize for those kinds of processes, we risk making our Rails app sit around waiting as users' requests quickly come in. The request may even time out, frustrating our users. This is a common issue where applications become unresponsive. It can also bring an app down due to a build-up of requests in the pipeline, caused by existing long-running requests.

Rails provides a way to execute task in the background by using Active Job. Active Job is a unifying interface to the many queuing backends available for us Ruby engineers. One of the most used queuing backends is Delayed::Job, a system extracted out of Shopify. Another popular worker system is Sidekiq.

In this section, you will learn how to use a background job for crawling places, instead of doing it synchronously. This way, even if Google's servers take a longer time to process our requests, it won't upset our own request-response cycle. Thus, we are stopping the domino effect where one server is down as a result of another.

First, let's install Delayed::Job by adding the gem into the gemfile and then execute `bundle install` at the root folder as usual. See Listing 8-64.

411

Listing 8-64. Adding delayed_job_active_record into the Gemfile

```
gem 'delayed_job_active_record', '~> 4.1'
```

After that, let's generate a migration for the table required by Delayed::Job to function properly. Let's run the command shown in Listing 8-65.

Listing 8-65. Command to Generate Migration for Delayed::Job

```
$ rails generate delayed_job:active_record
```

Then, let's execute the migration, as shown in Listing 8-66.

Listing 8-66. Running the Migration

```
$ rails db:migrate
```

After that, let's tell Active Job to use Delayed::Job by adding the line shown in Listing 8-67 into application.rb.

Listing 8-67. Telling Active Job Which Adapter To Use

```
...
config.generators.system_tests = nil
config.active_job.queue_adapter = :delayed_job
```

After that, let's generate a job for crawling the place with the command shown in Listing 8-68.

Listing 8-68. Command to Generate a Job

```
$ rails g job PlaceCrawler
Running via Spring preloader in process 24553
      invoke  rspec
      create    spec/jobs/place_crawler_job_spec.rb
      create  app/jobs/place_crawler_job.rb
```

After that, add the code shown in Listing 8-69 into jobs/place_crawler_job.rb.

Listing 8-69. A Job for Crawling Places

```
class PlaceCrawlerJob < ApplicationJob
  queue_as :default

  def perform(name, lat:, lng:)
    Place::Crawler.call(name, lat: lat, lng: lng)
  end
end
```

After that, we can invoke the job in Api::V1::PlacesController instead of calling the crawler service directly, as shown in Listing 8-70.

Listing 8-70. Performing Crawling in the Background

```
class Api::V1::PlacesController < ApplicationController
  def index
    keyword = params.fetch(:keyword)
    lat = params.fetch(:lat)
    lng = params.fetch(:lng)

    Place::Crawler.call(keyword, lat: lat, lng: lng)
    PlaceCrawlerJob.perform_later(keyword, lat: lat, lng: lng)
    render json: Place::Finder.call(keyword, lat: lat, lng: lng)
  end
end
```

Notice that we use perform_later to enqueue a job. If we want to execute the job synchronously, we call perform_now instead.

Now, before testing that our system still works well, we need to run the worker process by executing the command shown in Listing 8-71 in a separate terminal.

Listing 8-71. Command to Execute the Jobs

```
$ rails jobs:work
```

If we ever need to empty out the queue, we can issue the command shown in Listing 8-72.

Listing 8-72. Command to Empty Out Jobs in the Queue

```
$ rails jobs:clear
```

Everything should still work as usual. To try it, let's search for some new keyword where the crawler has never crawled before such as *eiffel*, as shown in Figure 8-22.

Figure 8-22. *Querying for eiffel still works*

But how is that possible? Since the crawling happens in the background, shouldn't the first request return an empty response? Shouldn't we need to type **eiffel** again for the second time to finally retrieve the crawled data?

Right? If we think about it, the first request should return an empty response since in our case, we have never searched for *eiffel* before. There would be no such entry for *eiffel* in our database. The crawler must search it from Google's servers, and that happens in the background. Since it happens in the background, the request returns with whatever response there is: empty data.

But, why do we see the Eiffel Tower without changing anything on the front-end side? Why does it work as if the request to the Google server is made synchronously, instead of asynchronously?

It's because, actually, we have prepared for this case. There is no magic. If we look back at `app/javascript/store/actions.js`, we can see that, inside the `performSearch` function, we actually send a search request for the second time if the first request returns empty data, as shown in Listing 8-73.

Listing 8-73. performSearch Snippet

```
const performSearch = async (isRetried) => {
  let response = await fetch(url)
  let data = await response.json()

  if (data.length === 0 && !isRetried) {
    setTimeout(() => { performSearch(true) }, 5000)
  } else {
    commit("SET_SIGHT_PLACES", data)
  }
}
```

However, as we can inspect from the previous snippet, we only send the second request after waiting for five seconds (or 5,000 milliseconds). This is to give the job some time to be successfully executed by the worker, in the hopes that the second request can return with meaningful data. Hence, we can just type **eiffel** once and still get the place even if there is no such data in the database yet as we type.

Writing the Tests

The crawler is executed in the background, so how can we test it? We also know that our test makes an HTTP call to Google's servers, so how can we test it independent of Internet connection?

It's easy! To answer the first question, we will perform_enqueued_jobs. And for the last question, we will use an external gem called VCR that can record our test's HTTP interactions and replay them for any future tests, making the test deterministic and independent of an Internet connection.

Let's add VCR into our gemfile, which allows us to record HTTP calls for later replays, as shown in Listing 8-74.

Listing 8-74. Adding VCR into the Gemfile

```
group :test do
  ...
  gem 'vcr', '~> 5.1'
end
```

After that, let's configure it. Let's create `spec/support/vcr.rb` and add the code shown in Listing 8-75.

Listing 8-75. Code to Configure VCR

```
require "vcr"

VCR.configure do |config|
  config.cassette_library_dir = "spec/fixtures/vcr_cassettes"
  config.hook_into :faraday
end
```

Now, add the code in Listing 8-76 for `places_controller_spec.rb`, which we should create inside the `spec/requests/api/v1` folder. And yes, we need to create the `api` and `v1` folders that might not have existed yet, as shown in Listing 8-76.

Listing 8-76. Code for Testing Api::V1::PlacesController

```
require "rails_helper"
describe Api::V1::PlacesController do
  let(:user) { create(:user) }

  before do
    sign_in user
  end

  describe "GET /" do
    context "when the given place is not exist yet" do
      it "can give us the list after being crawled" do
        VCR.use_cassette("api_v1_places_index_central_park") do
          perform_enqueued_jobs do
            expect(Place.all).to be_blank

            get api_v1_places_path, params: {
                keyword: "Central Park",
                lat: 40.785091,
                lng: -73.968285
              }
```

```
            expect(json_response).not_to be_blank
            expect(Place.all).not_to be_blank
          end
        end
      end
    end
  end
end
```

Notice how we wrap our test code inside perform_enqueued_jobs, which executes jobs synchronously. We also wrap code that makes HTTP calls inside VCR.use_cassette. Now, let's define json_response in spec/support/api.rb, as shown in Listing 8-77.

Listing 8-77. Code for json_response

```
def json_response
  JSON.parse response.body
end
```

After that, let's import the module that defines the perform_enqueued_jobs method. Let's create a new file called spec/support/job.rb and add the code, as shown in Listing 8-78.

Listing 8-78. Importing ActiveJob::TestHelper

```
RSpec.configure do |config|
  config.include ActiveJob::TestHelper, type: :job
  config.include ActiveJob::TestHelper, type: :request
end
```

If we execute the spec, everything will be green as expected. See Listing 8-79.

Listing 8-79. Executing the places_controller_spec.rb Spec File

```
$ bundle exec rspec spec/requests/api/v1/places_controller_spec.rb

.

Finished in 0.16401 seconds (files took 1.51 seconds to load)
1 example, 0 failures
```

417

For PlaceCrawlerJob, let's test that the crawler service is called when the job is executed. Let's add the code shown in Listing 8-80 into jobs/place_crawler_job_spec.rb.

Listing 8-80. Code to Test the Crawler Job

```
require "rails_helper"

describe PlaceCrawlerJob, type: :job do
  describe "#perform" do
    it "calls the crawler service" do
      perform_enqueued_jobs do
        expect(Place::Crawler).to receive(:call)
          .with("Central Park", lat: 1, lng: 2)

        described_class.perform_later("Central Park",
          lat: 1, lng: 2)
      end
    end
  end
end
```

Great! Now we have tested both the job and the API endpoint.

Summary

One of the most important user experience principles is probably this: don't let our users wait. That's why we are using a background job to crawl for places and return results immediately. But, that's not the only thing you learned in this chapter.

Just as importantly, we shouldn't waste our precious engineering time by using inadequate tools on the front end. There are times where pairing those "proper" front-end frameworks with Rails is a match made in heaven. Had we used vanilla JavaScript, we would probably balk at writing any of that at all.

Well, let's congratulate ourselves! The social media app is taking shape and looking better and better. See you in the next chapter, where we allow our users to connect with other users through a Follow button.

CHAPTER 9

Friendship

In earlier chapters, you learned how to use Devise for authentication. We are requiring our users to sign in before accessing several pages in our app. However, in many scenarios, authentication is not enough. We need to implement access authorization as well.

To put it simply, access authorization is concerned with who can do what, who can access what, or who can see what. For instance, a user can set their profile to private, which limits their timeline only to their followers. This is authorization.

In this chapter, let's see how we can implement access authorization using Bali. In the process, we will also build the feature to add and confirm followers. We will create a dedicated settings page too so that users can set their privacy levels.

Let's go for it.

The Settings Page

Our long journey starts with a simple settings page that, in the end, should look like the one shown in Figure 9-1.

© Adam Notodikromo 2021
A. Notodikromo, *Learn Rails 6*, https://doi.org/10.1007/978-1-4842-6026-5_9

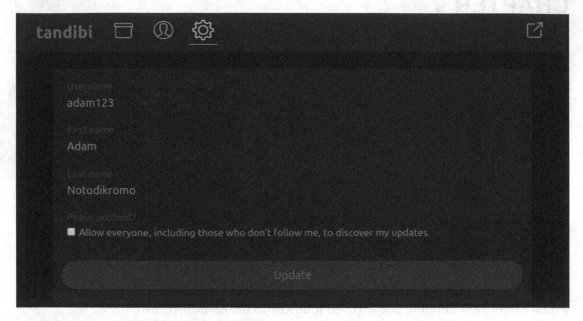

Figure 9-1. *A simple settings page for our users*

On the settings page, a user will be able to update their username, their first name, their last name, and, just as importantly, their privacy setting.

To create this page, let's generate the controller, as shown in Listing 9-1.

Listing 9-1. Command to Generate a User's Settings Controller

```
$ rails g controller Settings::Users show update --no-assets \
  --no-test-framework
```

After that, let's define the routes shown in Listing 9-2 and remove the routes defined from running the previous command.

Listing 9-2. Adding the Routes to the User Settings Page

```
Rails.application.routes.draw do
  namespace :settings do
    get 'users/show'
    get 'users/update'
  end

  ...
```

420

```
namespace :settings do
  resource :user, only: [:show, :update]
end

namespace :api do
  namespace :v1 do
    resources :places, only: [:index]
  end
end
end
```

After that, let's add the settings icon to the navigation bar. But first, let's rename helpers/timelines_helper.rb to helpers/page_type_helper.rb and then add the command shown in Listing 9-3.

Listing 9-3. Renaming and Enriching TimelinesHelper into PageTypeHelper

```
module TimelinesHelper
module PageTypeHelper

  ...

  def on_settings?
    controller_path.start_with? "settings"
  end
end
```

After that, in app/views/layouts/member/_navbar.html.erb, let's add the link to the settings page, as shown in Listing 9-4.

Listing 9-4. Adding the Link to the Settings Page

```
<div class="text-sm flex-grow">
  ...

  <%= link_to timeline_path(current_user),
    class: "linked-icon #{"active" if on_self?}" do %>
    <%= evil_icon "ei-user" %>
  <% end %>
```

```
<%= link_to settings_user_path,
  class: "linked-icon #{"active" if on_settings?}" do %>
  <%= evil_icon "ei-gear" %>
<% end %>
</div>
```

Now, to create the settings page, let's modify app/views/settings/users/show. html.erb to reflect the code shown in Listing 9-5.

Listing 9-5. Code for the Settings Page's Form

```
<div class="settings">
  <div class="setting-form">
    <%= form_with model: current_user,
      url: settings_user_path,
      method: :patch do |f| %>

      <div class="field">
        <%= f.label :username %>
        <%= f.text_field :username %>
      </div>

      <div class="field">
        <%= f.label :first_name %>
        <%= f.text_field :first_name %>
      </div>

      <div class="field">
        <%= f.label :last_name %>
        <%= f.text_field :last_name %>
      </div>

      <div class="field">
        <%= f.label :is_public, "Public account?" %>
        <div class="checkbox-unit">
          <%= f.check_box :is_public %>
          <span class="help-text">
            Allow everyone, including those who don't follow me,
            to discover my updates.
```

```
      </span>
    </div>
  </div>

  <div>
    <%= f.submit "Update", class: "submit-btn" %>
  </div>
<% end %>
  </div>
</div>
```

As shown in the previous code, we can make a setting form that users can use to set their username, first name, last name, and whether their account is a public account or not.

Then, let's make a new stylesheet file at `app/javascript/css/member/settings.css` and add the code shown in Listing 9-6.

Listing 9-6. Settings Stylesheet

```css
.settings {
  @apply p-3;
  @apply bg-dark-700;
}

.settings
.setting-form .field {
  @apply p-2 pt-0 rounded;
  @apply bg-dark-700 text-dark-600;
  @apply border-b border-solid border-dark-700;
  @apply mb-1;
}

.settings
.setting-form label {
  @apply w-full inline-block;
  @apply text-sm;
  color: #5c5c5c;
}
```

```
.settings
.setting-form .field input[type="text"] {
  @apply bg-dark-700;
  @apply w-full outline-none;
  color: #a0aec0;
}

.settings
.setting-form .field:focus-within,
.settings
.setting-form .field:focus-within input[type="text"] {
  @apply bg-dark-600;
}

.settings
.setting-form .field:focus-within {
  @apply border-b border-solid border-teal-200;
}

.settings
.setting-form .field:focus-within label {
  color: #a0aec0;
}

.settings
.setting-form .help-text {
  @apply text-sm;
  color: #a0aec0;
}

.settings
.setting-form .field .checkbox-unit {
  @apply flex flex-wrap items-center;
}

.settings
.setting-form .field .checkbox-unit .help-text {
  @apply pl-1;
}
```

```
.settings .submit-btn {
  @apply rounded-full p-2 w-full;
  @apply bg-indigo-800 text-white shadow;
  @apply mt-4 mb-2;
  color: #828d9f;
  cursor: pointer;
}

.settings
.submit-btn:hover {
  @apply bg-indigo-700 text-white;
}
```

Then, let's import the stylesheet into app/javascript/css/member.css, as shown in Listing 9-7.

Listing 9-7. Importing private/settings.css into private.css

```
@import "member/nav";
@import "member/timeline";
@import "member/poster";
@import "member/settings";
```

That's it for the form! Let's try it. First, we should see a gear icon on the navigation bar, as shown in Figure 9-2.

Figure 9-2. *Gear icon on the navigation bar*

By clicking the gear icon, we will be directed to the settings page, as shown in Figure 9-3.

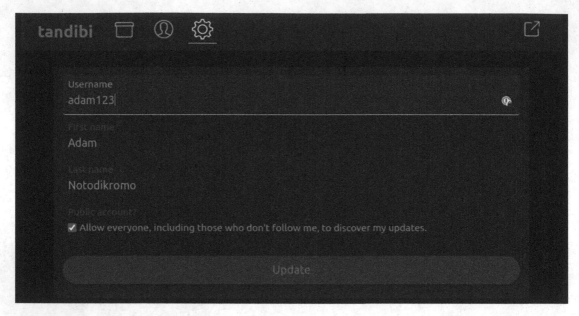

Figure 9-3. *The settings page*

However, clicking the Update button won't do anything yet for now. Let's make that work. Begin by defining permitted_params as shown in Listing 9-8 in app/controllers/settings/users_controller.rb.

Listing 9-8. Defining permitted_params

```
class Settings::UsersController < ApplicationController

  def show
  end

  def update
  end

  private

    def permitted_params
      params.require(:user).permit(
        :username,
        :first_name,
        :last_name,
        :is_public,
```

```
        )
    end
end
```

Then, the update action should take the `permitted_params` and try to update the user record accordingly, as shown in Listing 9-9.

Listing 9-9. Code for the Update Action

```
def update
  current_user.assign_attributes permitted_params
  changes = current_user.changes

  if changes.any?
    if current_user.save
      flash[:notice] = "Profile's settings updated"
    else
      flash[:alert] = "Unable to update the profile settings"
    end
  end

  redirect_to settings_user_path
end
```

Now we have a settings page where the user can adjust their profile the way they want it.

Let's try updating our profile, for example, by changing the first name to Richard. Upon clicking the Update button, we will see a flash message on the page. See Figure 9-4.

Figure 9-4.   *A flash message after doing a successful update*

Respecting Privacy Through Authorization

To secure software, among the first thing we must do is to verify the identity of a requesting entity. This process is referred as *authentication*, a precursor to authorization.

Authentication serves two purposes.

- Distinguishing entities from one another. An entity is a claimant to a verifying end. Most of the time, an entity represents a user. But, in other cases, it may represent another app, another system, or even a bot.

- Producing an audit trail so that an issue can be pinned down to a specific entity. For instance, this can help find out who made an edit to a given resource.

By default, the mere fact that a user has an account means that the user is authorized to do something. Thus, at times, the difference between authentication and authorization is subtle until we start to differentiate the two.

The term *authorization* is often used to refer to the right itself, as in "The doctor has the authorization to see the patient's health record." This statement is especially more valid if there are many doctors in the hospital and not all of them should be allowed to see the patient's health record.

In the social media app we are building, certain users prefer that only their followers be given the right to see their timelines. Currently, however, everyone can see everyone else's timelines.

So, let's implement access authorization properly. We will be using Bali to help us define access rules and authorize accesses. It is easy to set up, and its domain-specific language (DSL) makes it easier and more expressive to set up and do role-based authorization than some of the current alternatives.

So, let's add Bali into the gemfile, as shown in Listing 9-10.

Listing 9-10. Adding Bali to the Gemfile

```
...
gem 'active_model_serializers', '~> 0.10'
gem 'bali', '~> 6.0'
```

Then, let's run the `bundle` command to ensure that the gem is downloaded, ready for use, as shown in Listing 9-11.

Listing 9-11. Running bundle to Install the Newly Added Gem

```
$ bundle
```

After that, let's generate a `UserRules` class by issuing the `rails generate rules` command, as shown in Listing 9-12. This command is available only if we install Bali, as this is command is a generator provided by Bali to generate a rule class. A rule class is where we will define access rules related to a specific resource.

Listing 9-12. Command to Generate the UserRules Class

```
$ rails generate rules user
```

Having the `UserRules` class, let's now define a rule for accessing the timeline, as shown in Listing 9-13.

Listing 9-13. Defining the Rule for Seeing a Timeline of Another User

```
class UserRules < Bali::Rules
  can :see_timeline do |user, current_user|
    user.is_public? ||
      user == current_user ||
      user.followers.include?(current_user)
  end
end
```

With Bali, rules are defined through a DSL, which is a language specifically created to make it easier to program or configure a specific, complex domain.

It is not the first time we are going to use a DSL. In the past, we have used a DSL when we have written numerous spec files, when we defined factories using Factory Bot, and when we set up our app's routes. All of those files employ their own DSL, and they make their domain problems easier to solve, don't they? That's the power of a DSL: simplifying complex problems in its very specific domain through expressive syntax.

Bali also provides its own DSL to help us define authorization rules. To define a rule, we can use code like in the previous snippet. A rule may have a block, accepting two optional arguments: the resource and the entity (e.g., the current user).

In the `see_timeline` rule we defined earlier, we allow the current user entity to access the user resource only if any of these three conditions are met:

- The user account being visited is a public account.

- The user account is the current user itself.

- The user account has the current user as one of their followers.

If none of those conditions is met, we should display something else, such as a message that the timeline is private.

So, let's enforce it. To do that, let's open `app/views/timelines/show.html.erb`. We will ask for authorization through a `can?` method provided by Bali in our views, as shown in Listing 9-14.

Listing 9-14. Displaying the Content for the Timeline Accordingly

```
<%= render "timelines/all" %>
<% if can? current_user, :see_timeline, @visited_user %>
  <%= render "timelines/all" %>
<% else %>
  <p style="text-align: center">These posts are protected</p>
<% end %>
```

Let's define and then use the `@visited_user` by changing the `show` action in `app/controllers/timelines_controller.rb` to exactly match Listing 9-15.

Listing 9-15. Updated Code for TimelinesController#show

```
def show

  @visited_user = User.find_by_username!(params[:username])
  @posts = @visited_user
    .posts
    .not_reply
    .order("created_at DESC")
end
```

Done! Now, let's test it. First, let's visit our own timeline, and everything should be fine, just as before. See Figure 9-5.

Figure 9-5. *Timeline when visiting by ourselves*

However, if you see the kind of error shown in Figure 9-6, you should be able to fix it by restarting the server.

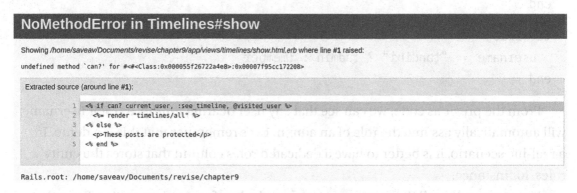

Figure 9-6. *Error when executing the can? method*

This error can happen if we have a running server that has long been loaded into memory without the gem we just installed. To solve it, we can just restart the running server process.

Let's set Sam's account to private, and then let's register a new user. Since the new user is not one of Sam's followers, the new user won't be able to see Sam's timeline at `http://localhost:3000/timelines/samsam`. See Figure 9-7.

Figure 9-7. *Nonfollower is unable to see Sam's account*

As we know it, the `see_timeline` applies for everyone regardless of role. What if we make an admin able to see anyone's timeline, private or not? Luckily, Bali makes it easy to overwrite a specific rule based on the entity's role.

Although Tandibi has no such concept of role, since every user is just a user, we can simulate it by defining a `User#role` method, as shown in Listing 9-16.

Listing 9-16. Adding a role Method to a User

```
class User < ApplicationRecord
  ...

  def login
    @login || username || email
  end

  def role
    username == "tandibi" ? :admin : :member
  end
end
```

From the previous code, we can see that any user bearing *tandibi* as their username will automatically assume the role of an admin. Let's remember that this is a demo. In a real-life scenario, it is better to have a dedicated roles column that stores the entity's roles, for instance.

Now we need to tell Bali how to extract the role data from a given entity. To do that, we use Bali's `extract_roles_from` macro, which we can readily use from within any ActiveRecord model, as shown in Listing 9-17.

Listing 9-17. Telling Bali How to Extract a Role from a User

```
class User < ApplicationRecord
  extract_roles_from :role
```

Now, we can define the rule shown in Listing 9-18 in the `UserRules`.

Listing 9-18. Defining the Rule for an Admin

```
class UserRules < Bali::Rules
  ...
```

```
role :admin do
  can :see_timeline
end
end
```

By having that rule, we allow any admin user to see anyone's timeline, including that of a private account. This demonstrates that any scoped rules will take precedence over the general ones.

To prove that everything works as expected, we can write the code shown in Listing 9-19 for spec/rules/user_rules_spec.rb.

Listing 9-19. Unit Spec to Verify the Authorization Behavior

```
require 'rails_helper'

RSpec.describe UserRules do
  let(:admin) { create(:user, :private, username: "tandibi") }
  let(:user1) { create(:user) }
  let(:user2) { create(:user, :private, followers: [user1]) }

  describe "can see_timeline?" do
    it "is possible if public profile" do
      expect(user2).to be_able_to :see_timeline, user1
    end

    context "when private profile" do
      it "is not possible" do
        expect(user1).not_to be_able_to :see_timeline, admin
        expect(user2).not_to be_able_to :see_timeline, admin
      end

      it "is possible if the viewer is a follower" do
        expect(user1).to be_able_to :see_timeline, user2
      end

      it "is possible if the viewer is an admin" do
        expect(admin).to be_able_to :see_timeline, user1
        expect(admin).to be_able_to :see_timeline, user2
      end
```

```
    it "is possible if seeing their own profile" do
      expect(admin).to be_able_to :see_timeline, admin
      expect(user1).to be_able_to :see_timeline, user1
      expect(user2).to be_able_to :see_timeline, user2
    end
  end
end
end
```

In the previous spec, we have three users.

- admin, which is a user with an admin role

- user1, a public user following user2

- user2, a private user

In the code shown in Listing 9-20, we ensure that an admin user can visit any user, private or not.

Listing 9-20. Code to Ensure That an Admin Can Visit Anyone

```
it "is possible if the viewer is an admin" do
  expect(admin).to be_able_to :see_timeline, user1
  expect(admin).to be_able_to :see_timeline, user2
end
```

With Bali, if we want to authorize an entity, we can make use of the be_able_to helper in our spec files. This is nothing short of helpful, as it helps make the spec read so much better. This kind of helper is not available in other authorization libraries.

Now, before we can run the spec, we must define some traits. First, let's add the code shown in Listing 9-21 into spec/factories/users.rb.

Listing 9-21. Additional Code for the User Factory

```
FactoryBot.define do
  factory :user do

    username { SecureRandom.hex(3) }
    first_name { ["Adam", "Sam", "Mike"].sample }
    last_name { ["Soesanto", "Yamashita", "de Flaire"].sample }
```

```
      email { "#{SecureRandom.hex(4)}@example.org" }
      is_public { true }
      password { "MyPwd123" }

      trait :private do
        is_public { false }
      end

      transient do
        followers { [] }
      end

      after(:create) do |user, evaluator|
        evaluator.followers.each do |follower|
          create(:bond, :following, user: follower, friend: user)
        end
      end
    end
end
```

Then, let's add the following trait into spec/factories/bonds.rb:

```
FactoryBot.define do
  factory :bond do
    actor_id { 1 }
    friend_id { 1 }
    state { "MyString" }
    trait :following do
      state { Bond::FOLLOWING }
      user { create(:user) }
      friend { create(:user) }
    end
  end
end
```

It's the first time we are using a transient block to define transient fields in the factory. A transient field is really just a field that won't be persisted into the database but that can be manipulated by the factory and its callers.

Those transient fields are usually used for manipulating data. In the previous case when we defined the private trait, we used the transient block to define the `followers` field. We then iterate on it to create a bond between the user and each follower.

As another example, let's say we create a transient field called `upcase`. If `upcase` is set to `true`, the user's name will be written in uppercase. Otherwise, the name is written as is. As we don't need to record `upcase` into our table, we made `upcase` as a transient field.

Let's examine the code shown in Listing 9-22, which will serve as an example. Yes, we don't need to add this code into any files. Let's see how we defined the `upcase` transient field.

Listing 9-22. Example of Defining and Using a Transient Field

```
factory :user do
  transient do
    upcase { false }
  end

  ...

  before(:create) do |user, evaluator|
    if evaluator.upcase
      user.first_name.upcase!
      user.last_name.upcase! if user.last_name
    end
  end
end
```

Then, we can set the transient field the same way as if it were just a regular field. And just like any regular field, we can set it when we are creating or building the resource through the factory. And just like any other fields, transient fields are optional, as shown in Listing 9-23.

Listing 9-23. Setting the Transient Field Upcase

```
create :user,
  first_name: "Sam",
  last_name: "Yamashita",
  upcase: true
```

436

Now, let's run our spec, and everything should be green, as shown in Listing 9-24.

Listing 9-24. Running user_rules_spec.rb

```
bundle exec rspec spec/rules/user_rules_spec.rb
.....

Finished in 0.13412 seconds (files took 1.33 seconds to load)
5 examples, 0 failures
```

Note   There are other Ruby libraries we can use for building authorization systems, such as Pundit or CanCan. Bali is written by the author of this book.

Follow Requests: Front End

In this section, let's add a profile header on top of every user's timeline page. There, we can see various information such as the username, the number of posts, the number of followers, and so on. Additionally, there will be a plus button so that a user can follow anyone they want by clicking that button. See Figure 9-8.

Figure 9-8. *The plus button to follow next to the profile's name*

When the plus button is clicked, either of these two things should take place:

- *Immediately following*: The user instantly becomes a follower of another user, if the account to follow is a public account.

- *Not instantly following*: If the account is private, the user must wait for an explicit approval from the owner of the account.

Without using Bali, it's only natural to put that kind of logic into the User model. However, let's not do that in order to prevent our model from becoming fat. Also, concentrating authorization rules in a separate file should make it easy to scan the overall rules of an application.

Note   I have reiterated multiple times how we should avoid making our models fat. However, the idea is much bigger than that. We want to avoid having a casually structured system where design is dictated by mere expediency. Architecture plays a vital role in the success of any application, and skilled software engineers are invested in the architecture of the application so that it won't turn into a big ball of mud as it grows.

Let's get going. First, let's create app/views/timelines/_profile_header.html.erb and write the code shown in Listing 9-25.

Listing 9-25. Code for the Profile Header Partial

```
<div class="profile-header">
  <div class="card">
    <div class="picture-container">
      <%= image_tag user.profile_picture_url %>
    </div>

    <div class="content">
      <p class="username">@<%= user.username %></p>
      <p class="name"><%= user.name %></p>
    </div>

    <%= render "bonds/bonding_buttons", user: user %>
  </div>
```

```
<div class="stats">
  <%= render "timelines/profile_stat",
    count: user.posts.count,
    counter: "posts",
    is_active: true %>

  <%= render "timelines/profile_stat",
    count: user.followers.count,
    counter: "followers" %>

  <%= render "timelines/profile_stat",
    count: user.followings.count,
    counter: "following" %>
</div>
</div>
```

Then, let's create a new partial at app/views/timelines/_profile_stat.html.erb and add the code shown in Listing 9-26.

Listing 9-26. Code for timelines/_profile_stat.html.erb

```
<% is_active = local_assigns.fetch(:is_active, false) %>

<%= link_to "#", class: "stat #{"active" if is_active}" do %>
  <p class="count"><%= count %></p>
  <p class="counter"><%= counter %></p>
<% end %>
```

The profile_header partial also makes use of the bonding_buttons partial. First, let's create the app/views/bonds directory. After that, within that directory, let's create a new file called _bonding_buttons.html.erb and then add the code shown in Listing 9-27.

Listing 9-27. Code for bonds/_bonding_buttons.html.erb

```
<div class="bonding-buttons">
  <% if can? :follow, user %>
    <%= link_to "#", method: :post do %>
      <%= evil_icon "ei-plus", class: "green" %>
    <% end %>
  <% end %>
```

```erb
  <% if can? :unfollow, user %>
    <%= link_to "#", method: :post do %>
      <%= evil_icon "ei-minus", class: "red" %>
    <% end %>
  <% end %>
</div>
```

Next, let's add new rules for `follow` and `unfollow` at `rules/user_rules.rb`, as shown in Listing 9-28.

Listing 9-28. Adding New Rules for follow and unfollow

```ruby
class UserRules < Bali::Rules
  ...

  can :follow do |user, current_user|
    user != current_user &&
      !user.followers.include?(current_user) &&
      !user.inward_bonds.where(
        user: current_user,
        state: Bond::REQUESTING
      ).exists?
  end

  can :unfollow do |user, current_user|
    user != current_user &&
      current_user.bonds.where(
        friend: user,
        state: [Bond::REQUESTING, Bond::FOLLOWING]
      ).exists?
  end
end
```

Now we can render the profile header at `timelines/show.html.erb`, as shown in Listing 9-29.

Listing 9-29. Rendering the Profile Header

```
<%= render "timelines/profile_header", user: @visited_user %>

<% if on_self? %>
  <%= render("posts/form")  %>
<% end %>
```

Cool! Let's check out what things look like. See Figure 9-9.

Figure 9-9. *Rendered profile header*

Yeah! Although the profile header is currently really bad to look at, it displays everything we want successfully. It has the button to follow or unfollow a user, and it displays enchanting statistics about the user as well. It's time to style this section.

First, let's define a new shade for the dark color palette. We'll add the definition shown in Listing 9-30 to `app/javascript/css/tailwind.js`.

Listing 9-30. Defining a New Shade for Dark

```
module.exports = {
  theme: {
    extend: {
      colors: {
```

441

```
    ...
    dark: {
      "400": "#8a8a8a",
      "500": "#4f4f4f",
      "600": "#343538",
```

Then, let's create these two stylesheets:

- `app/javascript/css/member/profile_header.css`

- `app/javascript/css/member/bonding_buttons.css`

Then, let's import them into `css/member.css`, as shown in Listing 9-31.

Listing 9-31. Importing New Styles into private.css

```
...
@import "private/poster";
@import "private/settings";
@import "private/profile_header";
@import "private/bonding_buttons";
```

Listing 9-32 shows the styles for `bonding_buttons.css`.

Listing 9-32. Styles for bonding_buttons.css

```
.body-member
.bonding-buttons {
  @apply self-center;
}

.body-member
.bonding-buttons,
.body-member
.bonding-buttons .icon {
  height: 42px;
  width: 42px;
}
```

```
.body-member
.bonding-buttons .icon {
  @apply rounded-full;
  color: #98a6b7;
}

.body-member
.bonding-buttons .green.icon:hover {
  @apply text-teal-200;
  @apply bg-teal-800;
}

.body-member
.bonding-buttons .red.icon:hover {
  @apply text-red-200;
  @apply bg-red-800;
}
```

Listing 9-33 shows the style for the profile header.

Listing 9-33. Styles for profile_header.css

```
.body-member
.profile-header {
  @apply mb-8;
}

.body-member
.profile-header .card {
  @apply flex;
}

.body-member
.profile-header .picture-container img {
  @apply rounded-full;
  height: 64px;
  width: 64px;
}
```

```
.body-member
.profile-header .content {
  @apply ml-4 flex-grow;
}

.body-member
.profile-header .content .username,
.body-member
.profile-header .content .name {
  @apply leading-none;
}

.body-member
.profile-header .content .username {
  @apply text-4xl;
}

.body-member
.profile-header .content .name {
  @apply pt-2;
}

.body-member
.profile-header .stats {
  @apply flex flex-wrap;
  @apply mt-4;
}

.body-member
.profile-header .stats .stat {
  @apply w-1/3;
  @apply pt-3 pb-3;
  @apply border-dark-600 border-b border-b-4 border-solid;
  @apply bg-dark-600;
}

.body-member
.profile-header .stats .stat:hover {
```

```
    @apply bg-dark-500 border-dark-500;
}

.body-member
.profile-header .stats p {
    @apply leading-none text-center;
}

.body-member
.profile-header .stats p.count {
    @apply text-gray-300 font-extrabold;
}

.body-member
.profile-header .stats p.counter {
    @apply text-gray-400;
}

.body-member
.profile-header .stats .stat.active {
    @apply bg-dark-700 border-teal-200;
}

.body-member
.profile-header .stats .stat.active:hover {
    @apply bg-dark-500;
}
```

Done! We now have a nice profile header on the show page, as shown in Figure 9-10.

Figure 9-10. *Well-styled profile header*

Processing Follow Requests

Now, let's work on the backend part. First things first, let's add a new function called visited_user into ApplicationHelper, as shown in Listing 9-34. The visited_user function will be the user resource that the current user is checking in at. Thus, it can be the current user itself or someone else.

Listing 9-34. A New Function, ApplicationHelper#visited_user

```
def visited_user
  @visited_user ||= begin
    username = params.fetch(:username)
    User.find_by_username!(username)
  end
end
```

After that, let's create a new controller called BondsController by executing the command shown in Listing 9-35 in the terminal.

Listing 9-35. Creating a New BondsController

```
$ rails g controller Bonds --no-helper --no-assets --no-test-framework
```

Then add the code shown in Listing 9-36 to the newly created BondsController at app/controllers/bonds_controller.rb.

Listing 9-36. Code for BondsController

```
class BondsController < ApplicationController
  delegate :visited_user, to: :helpers

  def follow
    unless can? :follow, visited_user
      return redirect_to timeline_path(visited_user)
    end

    bond = Bond::Follower.call(
      current_user,
      visited_user,
    )
```

```
      if bond.requesting?
        flash[:notice] = "A follow request has been sent to " +
          "@#{visited_user.username} and is pending their approval."
      end

      redirect_to timeline_path(visited_user)
    end
end
```

Notice that we delegate any call to visited_user to helpers. Using helpers, we can call any method defined in the helper modules. This way, we don't need to include a helper in our class, since helper methods are by default inaccessible from the controller—which is a good thing since we don't want to have a name clash.

Then, let's define Bond::Follower within app/services/bond/follower.rb, a newly created file, and then add the code shown in Listing 9-37.

Listing 9-37. Defining Bond::Follower

```
class Bond::Follower < ApplicationService
  attr_reader :requester, :target_user
  private :requester, :target_user

  def initialize(requester, target_user)
    @requester = requester
    @target_user = target_user
  end

  def call
    bond = requester.bonds.build(
      friend: target_user,
      state: bond_state
    )

    bond.save!
    bond
  end

  private
```

447

```
    def bond_state
      case target_user.is_public?
      when true then Bond::FOLLOWING
      when false then Bond::REQUESTING
      end
    end

end
```

Then for the `bonding_buttons` partial at app/views/bonds/_bonding_buttons. html.erb, let's change the path for the `follow` link, as shown in Listing 9-38.

Listing 9-38. Using the follow Path

```
<div class="bonding-buttons">
  <% if can? :follow, user %>
    <%= link_to follow_bond_path(user), method: :post do %>
      <%= evil_icon "ei-plus", class: "green" %>
```

Last but not least, let's register the `follow` link as shown in Listing 9-39 within routes.rb.

Listing 9-39. Routing the follow Endpoint

```
Rails.application.routes.draw do
  devise_for :users
  root to: 'home#index'
  # For details on the DSL available within this file, see https://guides.
rubyonrails.org/routing.html

  if Rails.env.development?
    mount LetterOpenerWeb::Engine, at: "/letter_opener"
  end

  authenticate :user do
    resources :timelines,
      only: [:index, :show],
      param: :username

    resources :posts, only: [:create, :show]
```

```
    resources :bonds, param: :username do
      member do
        post :follow
      end
    end
  end

  namespace :settings do
    resource :user, only: [:show, :update]
  end

  namespace :api do
    namespace :v1 do
      resources :places, only: [:index]
    end
  end
end
```

Now let's try following a user. To do that, we need to create a new user. Let's create a new user with the username *yuyuha*. We can give them any full name we fancy, but what about Graham de Sivir?

Now, if we visit Graham's account at `http://localhost:3000/timelines/yuyuha`, we can spot the plus button, which we can click to add them as our friend. See Figure 9-11.

Figure 9-11. *Visiting Graham's profile*

Now, let's smash that plus button because Graham will be more than happy to have one more friend! See Figure 9-12.

Figure 9-12. *The button on Graham's account becomes the unfollow button*

Upon clicking the follow button, it will become the unfollow button. And, its color turns to red when we hover our cursor over it. If we try to click that button, we will see an error page, since this is not yet implemented.

Our social media app definitely is taking shape now. Anyone can send a follow request, and there is a profile header, so what's not to like? Well, users cannot unfollow another user right now. So, let's work on that next!

Unfollowing

Let's begin with adding an unfollow path into bonds in routes.rb, as shown in Listing 9-40.

Listing 9-40. Adding unfollow into bonds

```
resources :bonds, param: :username do
  member do
    post :follow
    post :unfollow
  end
end
```

Then, let's add the unfollow action into BondsController, as shown in Listing 9-41.

Listing 9-41. Adding the unfollow Action into BondsController

```
def unfollow
  unless can? :unfollow, visited_user
    return redirect_to timeline_path(visited_user)
  end
```

```
  bond = Bond::Unfollower.call(
    current_user,
    visited_user,
  )

  redirect_to timeline_path(visited_user)
end
```

Then, let's create the Bond::Unfollower service. This is a new service, so we should also create the file at app/services/bond/unfollower.rb and then add the code shown in Listing 9-42.

Listing 9-42. Code for services/bond/unfollower.rb

```
class Bond::Unfollower < ApplicationService
  attr_reader :requester, :target_user
  private :requester, :target_user

  def initialize(requester, target_user)
    @requester = requester
    @target_user = target_user
  end

  def call
    bond = requester.bonds.where(friend: target_user).first
    return unless bond

    bond.destroy!
  end
end
```

Last but not least, let's update the link in the bonding_buttons partial to refer to the real path, as shown in Listing 9-43.

Listing 9-43. Sending an Unfollow Request to the unfollow Endpoint

```
<% if can? :unfollow, user %>
  <%= link_to unfollow_bond_path(user), method: :post do %>
  <%= evil_icon "ei-minus", class: "red" %>
<% end %>
```

Nice! Now, anyone will be able to follow and unfollow anyone they want. Let's try unfollowing Graham. See Figure 9-13.

Figure 9-13. *The button to unfollow a user*

Upon clicking the unfollow button, the button should become a follow button in the next rendering.

Everything is great, except that currently, private users will have no way to accept any follow requests. Let's fix it next.

Accepting and Rejecting Requests

To simulate this, let's make adam123's account private from the settings page. Let's say we have a new user: Graham. If Graham is to visit Adam's account, Graham won't be able to see Adam's timeline, since Graham has not followed Adam yet. See Figure 9-14.

Figure 9-14. *Adam's profile page as seen by Graham*

If Graham clicks that plus-to-follow button, Graham should see the notice in Figure 9-15 on the screen.

Figure 9-15. *Notice to ask Graham to wait for approval*

But, even so, Adam currently has no way to respond to Graham's request. To remedy the issue, let's create a page to display the followers list. On the followers page, Adam can see not only his followers but also all the follow requests Adam has.

First, let's add the routes shown in Listing 9-44 into `routes.rb`.

Listing 9-44. Adding Followers and Following Routes for BondsController

```
resources :bonds, param: :username do
  member do
    post :follow
    post :unfollow
    get :followers
    get :following
  end
end
```

Let's create a new file at `app/views/bonds/followers.html.erb` and then add the code shown in Listing 9-45. We will define the `users_list` partial later.

Listing 9-45. Code for bonds/followers.html.erb

```
<%= render "timelines/profile_header", user: visited_user %>

<%= render "bonds/users_list", users: @bonded_users %>
```

Then, still in the same folder, let's create a new file called `following.html.erb` and add the code shown in Listing 9-46

Listing 9-46. Code for bonds/following.html.erb

```erb
<%= render "timelines/profile_header", user: visited_user %>

<%= render "bonds/users_list",
    users: @bonded_users do |each_user| %>

  <%= render "bonds/bonding_buttons", user: each_user %>
<% end %>
```

Let's assume @bonded_users is a collection of User records. This instance variable is then passed into the users_list partial we will create soon. The partial then processes each user in the collection. We can add additional rendering code by passing a block that yields a user instance currently iterated. This way, we can add the buttons we need, by rendering *bonds/bonding_buttons* partial, for the user we are rendering a list for. See Figure 9-16.

Figure 9-16. *Adding buttons as wanted through the optional block*

Now, let's create a new file called _users_list.html.erb within the app/views/bonds directory, and add the code shown in Listing 9-47.

Listing 9-47. Code for bonds/_users_list.html.erb

```erb
<div class="users-list">
  <% users.each do |user| %>
    <div class="user">
      <%= link_to timeline_path(user), class: "profile-link" do %>
        <div class="picture-container">
          <%= image_tag user.profile_picture_url %>
        </div>

        <div class="content">
          <div class="identity">
```

```
      <p class="name"><%= user.name %></p>
      <p class="username">@<%= user.username %></p>
    </div>
  </div>
<% end %>

<%= yield user %>
    </div>
  <% end %>
</div>
```

Then, let's define @bonded_users in BondsController at app/controllers/bonds_controller.rb, as shown in Listing 9-48

Listing 9-48. Code for the followers and the following Actions

```
class BondsController < ApplicationController
  ...

  def followers
    @bonded_users = visited_user.followers
  end

  def following
    @bonded_users = visited_user.followings
  end
end
```

Then, let's create a new stylesheet for the list. Add the code shown in Listing 9-49 inside a file saved as app/javascript/css/member/users_list.css.

Listing 9-49. Styles for the User List

```
.body-member
.users-list .user {
  @apply flex;
}
```

```
.body-member
.users-list .user {
  @apply flex;
  @apply bg-dark-700;
  @apply  mb-2 pt-2 pb-2 pr-4 pl-4;
}

.body-member
.users-list .user:hover {
  @apply bg-dark-600;
  @apply transition duration-100 ease-in;
}

.body-member
.users-list .user a.profile-link {
  @apply flex flex-grow;
}

.body-member
.users-list .picture-container,
.body-member
.users-list .content {
  @apply self-center;
}

.body-member
.users-list .picture-container img {
  @apply rounded-full;
  height: 32px;
  width: 32px;
}

.body-member
.users-list .content {
  @apply ml-4 flex-grow;
}
```

```
.body-member
.users-list .content .username,
.body-member
.users-list .content .name {
  @apply leading-5;
}

.body-member
.users-list .content .username {
  @apply text-white;
}

.body-member
.users-list .content .name {
  @apply text-gray-400;
}
```

Then, let's import the style into member.css, as shown in Listing 9-50.

Listing 9-50. Importing private/users_list.css into private.css

```
...
@import "member/bonding_buttons";
@import "member/users_list";
```

We are almost there. Let's make the profile stat clickable by giving each a real link. So, in the app/views/timelines/_profile_header.html.erb partial, let's update it to match the code shown in Listing 9-51.

Listing 9-51. Updating the Link on the Profile Header

```
<div class="stats">
  <%= render "timelines/profile_stat",
    count: user.posts.count,
    counter: "posts",
    is_active: on_timeline?,
    link_to: timeline_path(user) %>
```

```
<%= render "timelines/profile_stat",
  count: user.followers.count,
  counter: "followers",
  is_active: on_follower_list?,
  link_to: followers_bond_path(user) %>

<%= render "timelines/profile_stat",
  count: user.followings.count,
  counter: "following",
  is_active: on_following_list?,
  link_to: following_bond_path(user) %>
```

Then, let's update app/views/timelines/_profile_stat.html.erb to take into account the link_to variable assigned to it, as shown in Listing 9-52.

Listing 9-52. Updating the profile_stat Partial

```
<% is_active = local_assigns.fetch(:is_active, false) %>

<%= link_to link_to, class: "stat #{"active" if is_active}" do %>
  <p class="count"><%= count %></p>
  <p class="counter"><%= counter %></p>
<% end %>
```

After that, in app/helpers/page_type_helper.rb, let's define the code shown in Listing 9-53.

Listing 9-53. New Functions to Help in Detecting the Type of Page

```
def on_following_list?
  controller_path == "bonds" && action_name == "following"
end

def on_follower_list?
  controller_path == "bonds" && action_name == "followers"
end
```

All should look good now! See Figure 9-17.

Figure 9-17.   Displaying followers list

Yes! Except, where's Graham's requests? Yeah, we haven't rendered them.

To begin with, let's start with defining the see_follower_requests rule inside UserRules, as shown in Listing 9-54

Listing 9-54. New see_follower_requests Rule

```
can :see_follower_requests do |user, current_user|
  user == current_user &&
    user.inward_bonds.where(state: Bond::REQUESTING).any?
end

role :admin do
  ...
  can :see_follower_requests
end
```

Then, let's create new endpoints called accept and reject. To do that, let's edit config/routes.rb, as shown in Listing 9-55.

Listing 9-55. Adding the accept and reject Endpoints

```
resources :bonds, param: :username do
  member do
    post :follow
    post :unfollow
    post :accept
```

```
      post :reject
      get :followers
      get :following
    end
  end
end
```

Then, let's create a new `Bond::Acceptor` service at `app/services/bond/acceptor.rb`. This service class will be used by the acceptor action we will define later. For now, let's add the code shown in Listing 9-56 to the `bond/acceptor.rb` file we just created.

Listing 9-56. Codes for Bond::Acceptor

```
class Bond::Acceptor < ApplicationService
  attr_reader :requester, :target_user
  private :requester, :target_user

  def initialize(requester, target_user)
    @requester = requester
    @target_user = target_user
  end

  def call
    bond = requester.bonds.where(friend: target_user).first
    bond.state = Bond::FOLLOWING
    bond.save!
  end
end
```

Still in the same folder, let's create `bond_rejector.rb` and add the code shown in Listing 9-57.

Listing 9-57. Code for Bond::Rejector

```
class Bond::Rejector < ApplicationService
  attr_reader :requester, :target_user
  private :requester, :target_user

  def initialize(requester, target_user)
    @requester = requester
```

```
    @target_user = target_user
  end

  def call
    requester.bonds.where(friend: target_user).destroy_all
  end
end
```

Now, it's time to use those services with their respective actions. Let's open our BondsController class at app/controllers/bonds_controller.rb and add the code shown in Listing 9-58.

Listing 9-58. The accept and reject Actions in BondsController

```
class BondsController < ApplicationController
  ...

  def accept
    Bond::Acceptor.call(visited_user, current_user)
    redirect_to timeline_path(current_user)
  end

  def reject
    Bond::Rejector.call(visited_user, current_user)
    redirect_to timeline_path(current_user)
  end
end
```

Then, let's add the code shown in Listing 9-59 to bonds/followers.html.erb.

Listing 9-59. Code for Rendering the Follower Requests

```
<%= render "timelines/profile_header", user: visited_user %>

<% if can? :see_follower_requests, visited_user %>
  <%= render "bonds/users_list",
      users: visited_user.inward_bonds.requesting
        .map(&:user) do |user| %>
```

461

```
<%= link_to accept_bond_path(user), method: :post do %>
  <div class="bonding-buttons">
    <%= evil_icon "ei-check", class: "green" %>
  </div>
<% end %>

<%= link_to reject_bond_path(user), method: :post do %>
  <div class="bonding-buttons">
    <%= evil_icon "ei-close-o", class: "red" %>
  </div>
<% end %>
<% end %>
<% end %>

...
```

For a visual effect, let's add a star after the follower counter to indicate whether there are follow requests. Let's make the edit shown in Listing 9-60 on the app/views/timelines/_profile_header.html.erb partial.

Listing 9-60. Indicator for New Followers

```
<%= render "timelines/profile_stat",
  count: user.followers.count,
  count: user.followers.count.to_s +
    "#{"*" if can? :see_follower_requests, user}",
  counter: "followers",
  is_active: on_follower_list?,
  link_to: followers_bond_path(user) %>
```

Now, Adam can respond to Graham's request. Of course, this is not limited to Adam and Graham. See Figure 9-18.

Figure 9-18. *Rendering followers and new follower requests*

Summary

In this chapter, you learned how to perform authorization by using Bali. This way, we still maintain control over our app and keep it from becoming an uncontrollable big ball of mud.

At this point, our social media app is quite ready for the world. We already have a minimum viable product (MVP). But, we can't tell our mom, friends, colleagues, or the world yet as the app is currently accessible only locally on our own machine.

Of course, we can push it to Heroku, the cloud platform we used back in the first chapter. We have gone through a long journey since then! But, let's try an alternative. In the next chapter, we are going to learn how to use AWS as our cloud platform to host Tandibi.

On to the next station, captain!

CHAPTER 10

A Well-Rounded Engineer

Congratulations! You have done a really great job at learning many things about Ruby and Rails. I hope you feel proud about your achievement, which is nothing short of awesome.

This chapter is an optional read for you. Here, we will mainly discuss things outside of our own app. They are things that will make our global users happier. We will talk about an alternative for deploying our app: Amazon AWS. Also, we will talk about a alternative to develop our app: Docker.

It's really amazing what we have achieved thus far. You can come back here again anytime you want to try something new. If you want to build your own product first, you can do that too. This chapter won't get in the way but will try to be there when you want to learn something more.

Continuous Integration

Continuous integration is a development practice where code changes are integrated into a shared repository as soon as possible. It ensures that the code runs somewhere else, not just on our own machine. It provides a common place for the code from multiple developers to be merged and verified. All of that will lead to a faster development cycle as a team.

The integration may trigger some responses, such as the following:

- Spec test (e.g., CodeShip, Travis CI, Semaphore CI)

- Code maintainability test (e.g., Codeclimate)

- Syntax style test (e.g., Hound, Rubocop)

- Automatic deployment when all tests passed

Let's try integrating CodeShip into our CI process in GitHub. If you have not created a GitHub repository for our app, please create one and push our code into it. Let's recall

© Adam Notodikromo 2021
A. Notodikromo, *Learn Rails 6*, https://doi.org/10.1007/978-1-4842-6026-5_10

that we have talked about Git and should have installed it in our machine from the first chapter. See Figure 10-1.

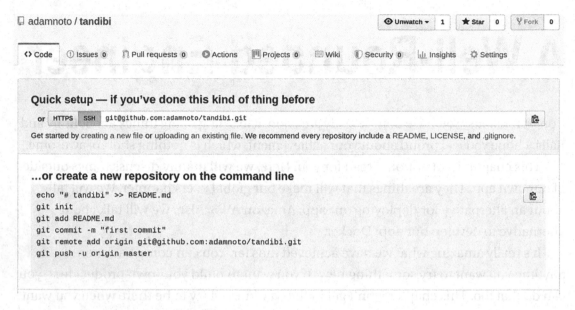

Figure 10-1. *The new tandibi repository on Github*

After that, let's go to GitHub Marketplace[1] and type **codeship** into the search field, as shown in Figure 10-2, and then hit Enter.

Extend GitHub
Add tools to help you build and grow

Explore apps

Types

Apps

Actions

Q codeship

Figure 10-2. *Typing codeship into the search field*

---

[1]github.com/marketplace

After that, we will be able to see CloudBees CodeShip on the search result page; click it. Then click "Set up a plan" button. See Figure 10-3.

Figure 10-3. *CodeShip app page on GitHub Marketplace*

Let's start with the Free plan. Then click "Install it for free." See Figure 10-4.

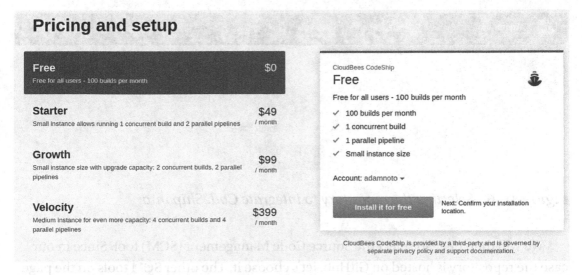

Figure 10-4. *CodeShip pricing*

On the "Review your order" page, click the "Complete order and begin installation" button. Then, let's click the Install button to authorize CodeShip to access our repositories if everything is OK with you. See Figure 10-5.

Review your order

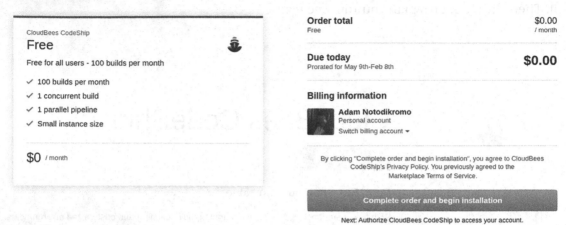

Figure 10-5. *Order review page for our choice*

Then, in CodeShip, let's click Projects and then the New Project button. See Figure 10-6.

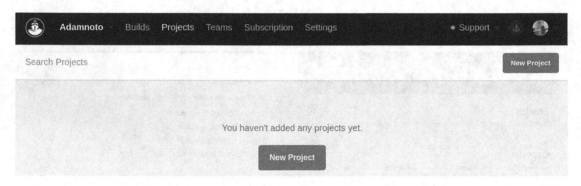

Figure 10-6. *Selecting the repository to integrate CodeShip into*

We will then need to select the Source Code Management (SCM) tool. Since in our case the repository is hosted on GitHub, let's choose it. The other SCM tools on the page are also worth trying; they offer great features. See Figure 10-7.

Figure 10-7. *Page to choose the SCM of the repo*

On the next page, select our `tandibi` repository. See Figure 10-8.

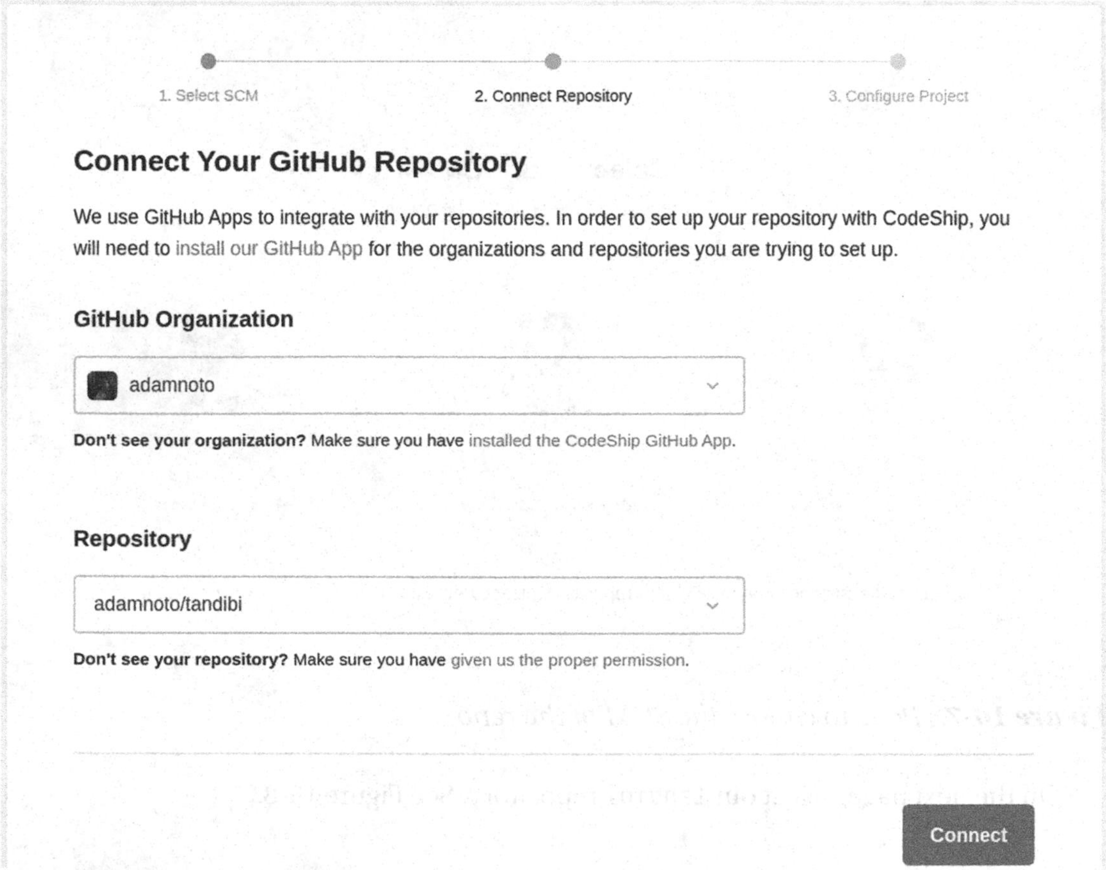

1. Select SCM   **2. Connect Repository**   3. Configure Project

Connect Your GitHub Repository

We use GitHub Apps to integrate with your repositories. In order to set up your repository with CodeShip, you will need to install our GitHub App for the organizations and repositories you are trying to set up.

GitHub Organization

adamnoto

Don't see your organization? Make sure you have installed the CodeShip GitHub App.

Repository

adamnoto/tandibi

Don't see your repository? Make sure you have given us the proper permission.

Connect

Figure 10-8. *Selecting the repository*

Now, let's select Codeship Basic for the project type. See Figure 10-9.

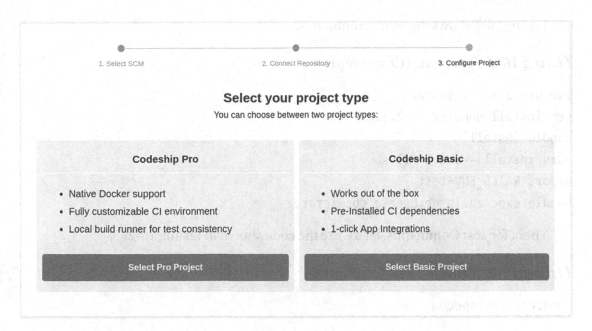

Figure 10-9. *Selecting the project type*

After that, let's fill in the setup commands, as shown in Figure 10-10.

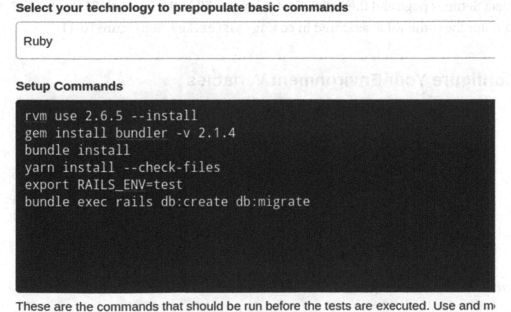

Select your technology to prepopulate basic commands

Ruby

Setup Commands

```
rvm use 2.6.5 --install
gem install bundler -v 2.1.4
bundle install
yarn install --check-files
export RAILS_ENV=test
bundle exec rails db:create db:migrate
```

These are the commands that should be run before the tests are executed. Use and m

Figure 10-10. *Configuring the setup commands*

Listing 10-1 shows the setup commands.

Listing 10-1. The Setup Commands

```
rvm use 2.6.5 --install
gem install bundler -v 2.1.4
bundle install
yarn install --check-files
export RAILS_ENV=test
bundle exec rails db:create db:migrate
```

Then, for Test Commands, let's write the code shown in Listing 10-2.

Listing 10-2. Code for Test Comamnds

```
bundle exec rspec
```

We can change those commands at anytime on the Project Settings page. We can also define environment variables on the Settings page too, instead of defining them using the export command.

Let's try defining the RAILS_MASTER_KEY as an environment variable. Let's go to the Project Settings page and then click Environment. Fill in the key with RAILS_MASTER_KEY, and enter the same value as stored in config/master.key. See Figure 10-11.

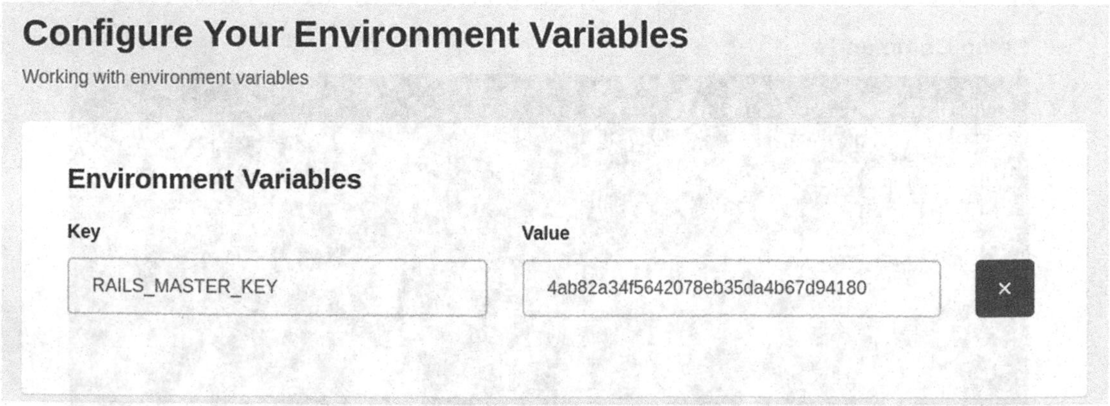

Configure Your Environment Variables

Working with environment variables

Environment Variables

Key	Value
RAILS_MASTER_KEY	4ab82a34f5642078eb35da4b67d94180

Figure 10-11. *Defining environment variables*

That's it! We are ready to push some changes into our repository, which is one way we can kick off the integration process.

For example, by now, a newer version of Rails must have been released already. Let's upgrade our project to use the newer version, for example, version 6.0.3. See Listing 10-3.

Listing 10-3. Process to Upgrade from Rails 6.0.2.1 to Rails 6.0.3

```
$ git checkout -b upgrade-rails
$ bundle update rails
$ git add Gemfile.lock
$ git commit -m "upgrade rails to v 6.0.3"
$ git push origin update-rails
```

By pushing the changes into the repository, the integration process will be triggered. If we go back to CodeShip, we can see that the build process has been started.

We can wait for it, although normally, we can just leave it since CodeShip essentially freed us to do something else while it takes care of running the test suite. See Figure 10-12.

Figure 10-12. *A CI process executed for tandibi*

We can also see the test result on GitHub. See Figure 10-13.

Upgrade rails to v 6.0.3 #2

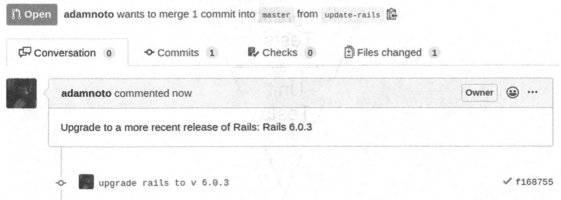

Figure 10-13. *The test result as reflected on the commit*

Continuous integration is cheaper than not integrating continuously. Without this process, we would be less productive as we must run the integration processes by hand. That is on top of time spent on being busy finding out possible problems.

We should be able to appreciate by now how important it is to write good test specs. Writing test specs is an integral part of a speedy integration process. But, just writing a test is not enough. We must ensure the test codes are lean and cover real cases.

To reiterate, we must stay clear from the ice cream cone anti-pattern, as shown in Figure 10-14, which can bring a host of problems, one of which is making testing runs much slower. As we know, the lower the layer, the faster it is to run and provide feedback, whereas the higher we go, the more time and costs that are associated with them. In addition, embracing the ice cream cone style would make it harder to point out the root cause of failures as the surface area under test has become wider.

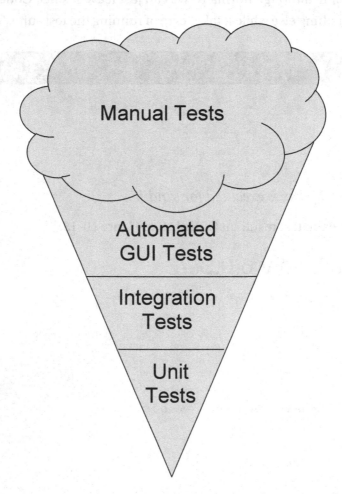

Figure 10-14. *Ice cone anti-pattern for writing test code*

Inseparable from making our test code lean is the realization that our codebase, in general, should be too. A large codebase is intimidating to work with. Multiple implementation patterns begin to emerge, and it gets difficult to reach consensus. In that way, it hurts our integration process.

I have reiterated on many occasions how important it is not to make the models fat and to make things well architected. There are probably two reasons why a codebase can become large: either it has become bloated or the architecture is monolithic in nature.

Bloated software is not equal to monolithic software. A good monolith can still be a well-architected one and less intimidating to work with. Yet, with so many people on a team pushing at the same time, the CI process for such a monolith can be hardly bearable at many times.

One way to avoid that is by adopting a microservices architecture. This style of development is not without problems of its own, though. And most early-stage startups do not need to do this.

In the end, to keep everyone happy, our software needs to be lean and readable. For our test suite, that means having just enough end-to-end testing code, whereby the rest gets covered by laser-focused unit testing and a smaller layer of integration testing.

Engineers may also integrate continuous deployment into their integration process, effectively automating the release process.

In the end, having a low-risk release process allows us to quickly adapt to business requirements and user needs, turning our release process into a business advantage that, again, makes everyone happier.

Internationalization

People in different countries speak different languages, so the ability of a software product to feel native can determine its rate of adoption in a given market.

We must remember that even the same language can have variations. Those variations, or shall we say *conventions*, govern the local rules of a language. We call them *locales*. See Table 10-1.

Table 10-1. *Code Representation for Various Locales of Some Languages*

Language	Language Code (ISO 639-1)	Country Code (ISO 3166)	Rails Locale Code
Simplified Chinese	Zh	CN	zh-CN
Traditional Chinese	Zh	TW	zh-TW
English (Australia)	En	AU	en-AU
English (US)	En	US	en
English (GB)[2]	En	GB	en-GB
Bahasa (Indonesia)	Id	ID	id
Bahasa (Malaysia)	Ms	MY	ms
Korean	Ko	KR	ko
Spanish (Spain)	Es	ES	es
Spanish (Mexico)	Es	MX	es-MX

A locale entails customization related to the following:

- Numeric

- Date and time formats

- Use of currency

- Collation and sorting

- Imagery and colors

- Legal requirements

As such, well-localized software does not only remember the language but also the locale of the user.

Imagine what happens to European users when a software product uses the rural U.S. mailbox imagery to represent the concept of an inbox. In this case, the people in Europe may have to wonder what a breadbox sitting on a pole has to do with emails. See Figure 10-15.

---

[2]en-UK is not considered a valid country code, and ISO-3166 should be used instead, although UK is reserved by the request of the United Kingdom.

Figure 10-15. *Icons representing email boxes (inbox). The right one is Google's Inbox app's icon*

To avoid those kind of problems, localization usually involves an expert team of its own. In that point of view, *localization* (l10n) is the adaptation of our product, and possibly its contents, to suit a specific region.

Internationalization (i18n) is taken to mean only the engineering efforts in making the app adaptable to those locales. The way the businesspeople see it, those two could be lumped together simply as *globalization* (g11n).

Note   All those numbers represent the number of letters in between the nonabbreviated word. Since the word *internationalization* has 18 letters in between *i* and *n*, it is commonly shortened to just i18n. The same custom applies for both *localization* and *globalization*.

Internationalization as a process is more than just concatenating strings. For example, it is not appropriate to take the code shown in Listing 10-4 seriously as an i18n effort.

Listing 10-4. Code to Display Localized Message

```
case user.language
when "id-ID"
  "Beli #{count} buku?"
else
  "Buy all #{count} books?"
end
```

While the word for *book* in Indonesian doesn't have to agree with the count, in English we need have the noun agree with the count. Of course, we can add an additional if condition, but that is still not the best strategy.

Let's learn how we can internationalize our product following acceptable practices. First, we need to store the user's preferred locale.

Let's create a migration to add `locale` into `User`, as shown in Listing 10-5.

Listing 10-5. Migration to Add a Locale Field into User

```
$ rails g migration add_locale_to_users locale:string
Running via Spring preloader in process 1130026
    invoke  active_record
    create    db/migrate/20200510232213_add_locale_to_users.rb
```

Let's open the migration file, and let's add the code shown in Listing 10-6 to make sure the field is never `nil`.

Listing 10-6. Adding the Default Value for Locale

```
class AddLocaleToUsers < ActiveRecord::Migration[6.0]
  def change
    add_column :users, :locale, :string,
      null: false,
      default: "en-US"
  end
end
```

Before we proceed, let's run the migration, as shown in Listing 10-7.

Listing 10-7. Running the Migration

```
$ rails db:migrate
```

Second, before we define the locales, let's specify what locales the app supports. Let's also define the default locale for the app. To do that, let's add the code shown in Listing 10-8 into `config/application.rb`.

Listing 10-8. Specifying Available Locales and the Default Locale

```
module Tandibi
  class Application < Rails::Application
    ...
```

```
    config.i18n.available_locales = [
      :"en-US",
      :"id"
    ]

    config.i18n.default_locale = :"en-US"
  end
end
```

We can check with `rails console` that we have set up things correctly, as shown in Listing 10-9.

Listing 10-9. Checking the Available Locales and the Default Locale

```
$ rails c
irb(main):002:0> I18n.available_locales
=> [:"en-US", :id]
irb(main):003:0> I18n.default_locale
=> :"en-US"
```

Then, let's ensure our controllers pick up the user's locale. Let's add the code shown in Listing 10-10 to `ApplicationController`.

Listing 10-10. Code to Configure the Locale for the Current Request

```
class ApplicationController < ActionController::Base
  before_action :set_locale

  private

    def set_locale
      return unless current_user
      I18n.locale = current_user.locale
    end

  ...
end
```

Note   If the user has not signed in yet, we may use HTTP header Accept-Language to try to get their preferred locales. An example of the Accept-Language header is as follows:

`Accept-Language: fr-CH, fr;q=0.9, en;q=0.8, de;q=0.7, *;q=0.5`

We can use the following code to pick the locale for our app support:

`negotiated_locales = request.env['HTTP_ACCEPT_LANGUAGE']`

`pick_locale negotiated_locales.scan(/([a-z]{2}(?:-[a-z]{2})?)/i)`

Another way is by detecting the geographic location of the user, through their IP address, and attempting to deduce the language in that way.

Next, let's hook up `rails-i18n` into our app. This gem is so helpful as it has already localized common features in many locales so we don't have to do so. For instance, it has localized various error messages, names of days and months, and more, as shown in Listing 10-11.

Listing 10-11. Adding rails-i18n into the Gemfile

```
...
gem 'bali', '~> 6.0'
gem 'rails-i18n'
```

After adding the gem, let's not forget to run `bundle install`, as shown in Listing 10-12.

Listing 10-12. Running bundle install

```
$ bundle install
```

Now that everything is configured, how do we store and use translated text? There are two ways to do that. The first option is to localize the view template. The second one is by storing translations into a locale file. Let's see how we can make use of each technique, starting with the first option.

Let's consider the `TimelinesController#show` action, which renders a notice message if a user is stalking the private account of a stranger. See Figure 10-16.

Figure 10-16. *Private account's notice message in English*

How do we localize the message? To do that, let's create both show.en-US.html.erb
and show.id.html.erb.

For the English locale, let's simply rename timelines/show.html.erb to show.en-
US.html.erb.

For the Indonesian locale, let's create timelines/show.id.html.erb and add the
command shown in Listing 10-13.

Listing 10-13. Localized View for Indonesia

```
<%= render "timelines/profile_header", user: @visited_user %>

<% if on_self? %>
  <%= render("posts/form")  %>
<% end %>

<% if can? current_user, :see_timeline, @visited_user %>
  <%= render "timelines/all" %>
<% else %>
  <p style="text-align: center">
    Post ditampilkan hanya untuk pengikut
  </p>
<% end %>
```

Let's check it to see if that works!

Let's change Adam's `locale` value to `id` by executing the code shown in Listing 10-14 in `rails console`.

Listing 10-14. Updating Adam's Preferred Locale to id (Indonesian)

```
irb(main):001:0> u = User.find_by_username("adam123")
irb(main):002:0> u.update locale: "id"
```

Now, let's visit Sam's account. Since Adam and Sam are friends, let's unfollow Sam for now. Also, let's ensure that Sam's account is set to private. Then, we can see that the notice message will be given in Indonesian, the locale that Adam has chosen. See Figure 10-17.

Figure 10-17. *Private account's notice message in Indonesian*

Although this works perfectly fine, this localization manner is more suitable if the template is significantly different for each locale.

That is not the case for this page. The template remains the same; it's just the message that was changed.

In that case, the second option of storing the localized string in a separate file is much preferred. That way, we can reduce maintenance costs, as each locale is using the same template; we just need to change the locale file. This is less time-consuming than adopting a separate template in this case.

Rails employs YAML files for storing translated strings and other localization data in the `config/locales` directory. Each file is named after a specific locale, and as such, it only hosts localizations for that locale. In our case, we need to have `en-US.yml` and `id.yml`.

First, let's create two files, en-US.yml and id.yml, within the config/locales directory. For en-US.yml, let's add the command shown in Listing 10-15.

Listing 10-15. Definitions for en-US.yml

```
en-US:
  common:
    say: Say

  posts:
   form:
     whats_happening: What's happening?
```

For id.yml, let's add the command shown in Listing 10-16.

Listing 10-16. Definitions for id.yml

```
id:
  common:
    say: Kata

  posts:
   form:
     whats_happening: Apa yang terjadi?
```

Now, how to make use of that? Rails provides the translate or t method, which we can utilize in the manner shown in Listing 10-17 in the view.

Listing 10-17. Using t to Access the Translated Data

```
<p><%= t("common.say") %></p>
```

The t methods accept multiple arguments. One of the most important arguments we must pass is the translation key.

When the page is requested, Rails attempts to render the string that corresponds to the key. If the translation cannot be found, the key will be rendered for the user in a readable form, instead of raising an error.

Now, let's use the key in our view. Let's change the post's form partial at views/posts/_form.html.erb, as shown in Listing 10-18.

Listing 10-18. Using Text from a Locale File

```
<div class="poster js-status-poster">
  <%= f.text_area :status_text,
    required: true,
    placeholder: "What's happening?"
    placeholder: t("posts.form.whats_happening")  %>
</div>

...

<div class="controls">
  ...
  <div>
    <%= f.submit "Say", class: "submit-btn" %>
    <%= f.submit t("common.say"), class: "submit-btn" %>
  </div>
</div>
```

Now let's render the page again, and we can see that it's rendered according to the user's locale: the placeholder is in Indonesian. See Figure 10-18.

Figure 10-18. *Post form rendered in Indonesian*

Let's take a look again at the code shown in Listing 10-19 that we use to render the placeholder.

Listing 10-19. The Code to Render the Placeholder Using t

```
<%= f.text_area :status_text,
  required: true,
  placeholder: t("posts.form.whats_happening")  %>
```

We pass in `posts.form.whats_happening` as the locale key. However, instead of specifying the key in full (e.g., `posts.form.whats_happening`), there exists a `lazy` form for the key (e.g., `.whats_happening`).

To use lazy lookup, we must namespace the key following the folder structure. And yes, the leading dot is necessary. Since our key already follows the path structure, let's make the key lookup more concise by using the lazy lookup, as shown in Listing 10-20.

Listing 10-20. Using the Lazy Lookup Technique for Specifying the Locale Key

```
<%= f.text_area :status_text,
  required: true,
  placeholder: t(".whats_happening")  %>
```

The t method accepts multiple arguments. We can use those optional arguments to pass data into the translated string, such as in the hypothetical way shown in Listing 10-21.

Listing 10-21. Passing Username As an Optional Argument

```
<p><%= t(".posted_by", username: current_user.username) %></p>
```

We can define the localization in this way for `posted_by`, as shown in Listing 10-22.

Listing 10-22. Defining the posted_by Key Under the posts.form Namespace

```
posted_by: Posted by @%{username}
```

If, again hypothetically, pluralization is needed, for example for the case of counting followers, we may define the key as shown in Listing 10-23.

Listing 10-23. Defining the Pluralization Rules for Followers

```
en:
  common:
    followers:
      zero: no followers
      one: 1 follower
      other: %{count} kids
```

Then, we can use the key in this way to render the counter properly, as shown in Listing 10-24.

Listing 10-24. Rendering the followers Counter

```
You have <%= t("common.followers", count: followers.count) %>
```

It must be noted that zero, one, or other subkeys for pluralization are all optional. We can use any combination that makes sense for a given locale, such as two, few, and many.

If we ever need to access the t method outside of a view or controller, we can use I18n.t, which behaves quite the same way with the t method, except that we must be aware lazy lookup is usable only in the view or controller layer.

Another thing we need to do is to rename devise.en.yml to devise.en-US.yml, and then let's change file a little bit to match Listing 10-25.

Listing 10-25. Changing en to en-US

```
en:
en-US:
  devise: ...
```

That is done because Devise assumes our English localization is stored under the en namespace, but it's actually en-US. Nevertheless, most Rails applications don't differentiate between English locales and simply use en.

With all that stuff in mind, how do we test this?

The process of testing internationalization efforts is called _enabling testing_. It is a testing methodology in which both the design decision and the source code of the software are inspected.

Some items to keep on the review checklist for enabling testing are as follows:

- Check the code for hard-coded date, currency, and number formatting that should be avoided.

- Check that no string concatenation occurs for internationalizing messages, as they should use the system-provided APIs instead (e.g., `I18n.t`).

- Check that file and directory path manipulations are using native APIs rather than manually concatenating the path (e.g., `Rails.root.join`).

- Check whether UI components have enough space for expansion for all locales that the app supports.

- Check that there is no slang or region-cultural based words/imagery (e.g., buck, error-free versus correct, henceforth, fortnight versus two weeks, etc.).

- Optionally, messages should be documented with adequate usage context that can aid localization efforts of a new language.

There exist tools such as the `i18n-tasks`[3] gem that we can use to check missing/untranslated locales when we add new keys into the locale file.

Containerization: Hypersonic Setup

Docker recently has become popular because it can improve a team's productivity and make the overall software development experience better. But, what kind of problem does it solve?

Imagine if you could share your project on a repository and any person could just run a single command to get everything up and running, provided that they have Docker running on their machines.

Or imagine yourself just reinstalling your operating system and getting your project up and running is just a command away, rather than installing all the tools, languages, frameworks, drivers, and whatnots.

That's how helpful Docker can be for us.

---

[3] https://github.com/glebm/i18n-tasks

Yet, Docker is not a virtual machine in the same sense like that of Vagrant, VMware, or VirtualBox. For starters, those systems need an entire guest operating system to operate, which takes gigabytes in size after install and takes time to boot up.

Instead, Docker use the same kernel shared by the operating system it runs on. To create a sandboxed environment, isolation is done using process grouping and resource control mechanisms. That in turn makes Docker extremely lightweight in comparison, allowing it to boot up faster and use less disk space.

A container is created from an image. A Docker image, in turns, encapsulates an application with all of its dependencies. We can use the Docker image to include our source code, system libraries, and anything else we would install on a server to get our software up and running if we weren't using Docker. And this image file (known as the Dockerfile) is portable between OSs that can run Docker.

Let's see how we can Dockerize our application. First, please ensure that Docker is installed on the operating system. For Linux users, we will want to install Docker Compose too. Docker Compose should already be bundled with Docker in Docker Desktop for macOS and Windows users.

Then, let's create a Dockerfile in the root directory. A Dockerfile is a text containing all the sequential instructions—a recipe, if you will—needed to build an image.

Consider the Dockerfile shown in Listing 10-26.

Listing 10-26. Hypothetical Dockerfile

```
FROM ubuntu:18.04
COPY . /app
WORKDIR ./app
RUN bundle install
CMD bundle exec rails s
```

Each one of those instructions creates a single layer, starting with the FROM, which creates a layer with ubuntu:18.04 as the base. Subsequent layers will be using that of ubuntu:18.04.

COPY creates another layer that adds files from the current directory into the container. Those files are available in the subsequent layers.

WORKDIR simply sets the current working directory so that we don't have to cd to execute a given command. It also created its own layer.

The RUN command will execute some command. Again, a new layer will be stacked. As we realize it, a Docker image consists of read-only layers, which itself is an instruction, stacked in order. If a layer doesn't change, Docker may not have to rebuild that part.

There is also a CMD command, but it is certainly different from the RUN command. The CMD command sets the default command when the image is running. If the container is run with a command, the default command is to be ignored. If multiple CMD instructions are defined in the Dockerfile, only the last one will be used.

When Dockerizing an application, it's important to do so in a modular manner. For example, since there is already a Docker image for PostgreSQL, we don't need to install PostgreSQL within our image. In this case, we consider PostgreSQL as a separate application.

Now, for real, let's add the code shown in Listing 10-27 into our Dockerfile.

Listing 10-27. Code for the Dockerfile

```
FROM ruby:2.6.5
RUN gem install bundler:2.1.4

ENV LANG C.UTF-8
ENV APP_ROOT /tandibi

RUN curl -sS https://dl.yarnpkg.com/debian/pubkey.gpg \
  | apt-key add -
RUN echo "deb http://dl.yarnpkg.com/debian/ stable main" \
  | tee /etc/apt/sources.list.d/yarn.list
RUN curl -sL https://deb.nodesource.com/setup_10.x | bash -
RUN apt-get update -qq
RUN apt-get install -y build-essential libpq-dev libssl1.1 \
  yarn nodejs libssl-dev postgresql-client screen

RUN mkdir -p ${APP_ROOT}
WORKDIR ${APP_ROOT}
COPY . ${APP_ROOT}

# Script to be executed every time the container starts.
COPY docker-entrypoint.sh /usr/bin/
RUN chmod +x /usr/bin/docker-entrypoint.sh
ENTRYPOINT [ "docker-entrypoint.sh" ]
```

The ENTRYPOINT command is like the CMD, except that an ENTRYPOINT is always executed. There is a way to skip its execution, but it is unlikely anyone should want to do that.

Now let's create docker-entrypoint.sh in the root directory and add the command shown in Listing 10-28.

Listing 10-28. Code for docker-entrypoint.sh

```
#!/bin/bash
set -eu

eval "bundle install -j8"
eval "yarn install --check-files"

exec "$@"
```

Many Dockerized Rails apps usually RUN the bundle install within the Dockerfile. This means the bundling process is done when the image is being built. Ours will be much freer, where adding a new gem doesn't necessitate the re-building of the image.

Now that we have an image of our application, how can we run it? The answer lies in a tool called Docker Compose.

Docker Compose is a way to orchestrate independent, self-contained apps. The orchestration is done through definitions in a YAML file.

In the YAML file, we can set containers (or *services*), their builds, their storage designs, their exposed ports, and so on. And, with a single command, we can configure, build, and run all those containers.

Let's create a docker-compose.yml file in the root directory and add the command shown in Listing 10-29,

Listing 10-29. Code for docker-compose.yml

```
version: "3"

services:
  tandibi-db:
    image: postgis/postgis:11-2.5-alpine
    volumes:
      - database:/var/lib/postgresql/data
    environment:
      POSTGRES_PASSWORD: Password01
```

```
tandibi-webpacker:
  build: .
  environment:
    NODE_ENV: development
    RAILS_ENV: development
    WEBPACKER_DEV_SERVER_HOST: 0.0.0.0
  command: ./bin/webpack-dev-server
  volumes:
    - .:/tandibi
    - bundler_gems:/usr/local/bundle
  ports:
    - "3035:3035"
tandibi-web:
  build: .
  tty: true
  stdin_open: true
  volumes:
    - .:/tandibi
    - bundler_gems:/usr/local/bundle
  ports:
    - "3000:3000"
  depends_on:
    - tandibi-db
  command:
    - /bin/sh
    - -c
    - |
      # Remove a potentially pre-existing server.pid for Rails.
      rm -f /tandibi/tmp/pids/server.pid
      # Start server
      bundle exec rails server -b 0.0.0.0 -p 3000
  environment:
    RACK_ENV: development
    RAILS_ENV: development
    WEBPACKER_DEV_SERVER_HOST: tandibi-webpacker
```

```
volumes:
  bundler_gems:
  database:
```

As we can see from our previous `docker-compose.yml` file, we define three containers to be built and run, as listed here:

- `tandibi-db`
- `tandibi-webpacker`
- `tandibi-web`

`tandibi-db` is the container responsible for hosting the database. We specify the volume so that when we have to rebuild the container, we don't lose our data. And thanks to the modularity that Docker offers, having the database up and running is as simple as declaring `image: postgis/postgis:11-2.5-alpine`. What a time-saver!

We also define some volumes that can preserve files/data. For instance, any data that we have in the database can remain even if we rebuild the container.

We also use the volume to cache downloaded gems. This ensures that we don't spend time on downloading gems again if we already did, even if we rebuild the container.

Next, let's update our `database.yml` definition to reflect the code in Listing 10-30.

Listing 10-30. Updating Our database.yml Configuration

```
default: &default
  adapter: postgis
  encoding: unicode
  # For details on connection pooling, see Rails configuration guide
  # https://guides.rubyonrails.org/configuring.html#database-pooling
  pool: <%= ENV.fetch("RAILS_MAX_THREADS") { 5 } %>
  host: tandibi-db
  username: postgres
  password: Password01
```

Now, let's build and run our containers! To build them, let's issue the command shown in Listing 10-31.

Listing 10-31. Code to Build Our Containers

```
$ docker-compose build --parallel --no-cache
```

Then, to have all those containers defined in `docker-compose.yml`, let's execute the command shown in Listing 10-32.

Listing 10-32. Running the Containers

```
$ docker-compose up
```

The first time we run our containers, it will take some time since we have to download the Docker images, gems, and Node.js dependencies that our app uses.

If those downloading and bundling process are done, we can visit our app again at `http://localhost:3000`, and everything will work as usual, but this time, from within a Docker container. See Figure 10-19.

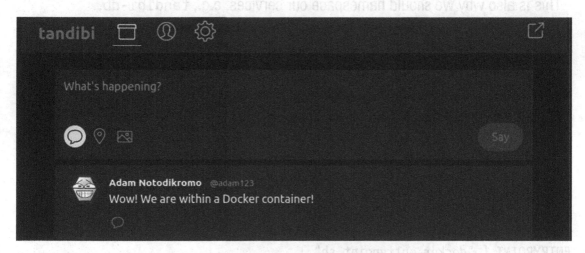

Figure 10-19. *Timeline page of containerized Tandibi*

> **Note** If we look back at our `docker-compose.yml` file, we can see that this
> file contains three definitions: the *version*, the *services*, and the *volumes*. There
> is another possible key, which is *network*. A *network* allows services of different
> `docker-compose.yml` files to communicate with each other.
>
> Here's an example of an external network definition:
>
> ```
> networks:
>   default:
>     external:
>       name: tandibi-network
> ```
>
> This way, if for example we create a User microservice, existing in its own space
> separate from Tandibi and hence having its own `docker-compose.yml`, by using
> the same network, Tandibi can communicate with the User microservice and vice
> versa.
>
> This is also why we should namespace our services, e.g., `tandibi-db`,
> `tandibi-web`, `user-db`, `user-web`, and so on, instead of just `db`, `web`, `worker`, etc.

Next, we need to install Google Chrome and do some configurations for Capybara so
that we can run our tests inside our container.

First, let's install Google Chrome in our app's container by adding the code shown in
Listing 10-33 to the Dockerfile.

Listing 10-33. Code to Install Google Chrome

```
...
RUN chmod +x /usr/bin/docker-entrypoint.sh
ENTRYPOINT [ "docker-entrypoint.sh" ]

# Install Google Chrome
RUN curl -sS -o - https://dl-ssl.google.com/\
linux/linux_signing_key.pub | apt-key add -
```

```
RUN echo "deb http://dl.google.com/\
linux/chrome/deb/ stable main" >> \
/etc/apt/sources.list.d/google-chrome.list
```

```
RUN apt-get -yqq update && \
apt-get -yqq install google-chrome-stable && \
rm -rf /var/lib/apt/lists/*
```

After that, we need to ensure that Chrome is executed in headless mode. We also want to make Chrome not write shared memory files into /dev/shm, since this space is only 64 MB in size by default. Instead, by passing disable-dev-shm-usage, Docker will write shared memory files into the /tmp folder.

Let's do this configuration by opening spec/support/capybara and adding the command shown in Listing 10-34.

Listing 10-34. Redefining Apparition Driver

```
require "capybara/rspec"
require "capybara/apparition"

Capybara.register_driver :apparition do |app|
  Capybara::Apparition::Driver.new app,
    headless: true,
    debug: true,
    browser_options: {
      "no-sandbox" => true,
      "disable-dev-shm-usage" => true
    }
end

Capybara.default_driver = :apparition
Capybara.javascript_driver = :apparition
```

After that, since Docker apps are accessed by the container's name, we must allow a connection from 127.0.0.1 and also www.example.com from within our container. To do that, let's open config/environments/test.rb and add the command shown in Listing 10-35.

Listing 10-35. Allowing Access from Some Hosts Within Docker

```
Rails.application.configure do
  ...

  # Raises error for missing translations.
  # config.action_view.raise_on_missing_translations = true

  config.hosts << "www.example.com"
  config.hosts << "127.0.0.1"
end
```

After that, since we defined RAILS_ENV to always be development in our docker-compose.yml file, we must set RAILS_ENV to test in spec/rails_helper.rb, as shown in Listing 10-36.

Listing 10-36. Setting RAILS_ENV to Test When Executing Tests

```
# This file is copied to spec/ when you run 'rails generate rspec:install'
require 'spec_helper'
ENV['RAILS_ENV'] ||= 'test'
ENV['RAILS_ENV'] = 'test'
```

That's it! Now, let's try executing our tests within our container. Everything should be green as usual, as shown in Listing 10-37.

Listing 10-37. Running rspec from Within the Container

```
$ docker-compose run --rm tandibi-web bundle exec rspec
```

Deploying to AWS Elastic Beanstalk

One of the major issue we developers have to ponder is how to share the app we build. One approach we have tried has been to use Heroku.

Heroku is easy to set up and is fully managed, true to its label as a platform-as-a-service. But, if cost is part of our justification, we must know that Heroku could be relatively more expensive as we scale up.

Let's explore a different solution: AWS Elastic Beanstalk.

Note   There is nothing wrong with using Heroku, as there is nothing wrong with using AWS. We need to judge which one to use based on various variables, which this section will simply disregard. Personally, I like both products and have used them happily.

As we already know, Amazon Web Services (AWS) is a cloud platform offered by Amazon. We have used AWS in the past to store objects using AWS S3. In this section, we will explore AWS Elastic Beanstalk and AWS RDS (Relational Database Service). Under the hood, Elastic Beanstalk is using AWS EC2, one of the core product of AWS.

With Elastic Beanstalk, however, we can quickly deploy and manage our web app without having to learn the infrastructure needed to run it. It's pretty similar to the Heroku experience. Indeed, we may say that Beanstalk is an attempt by AWS to enter the market where Heroku has reigned supreme. However, as we will soon see, setting up Beanstalk requires more effort.

Note   There is no cost in using Beanstalk; you may incur cost for using EC2 and RDS.

Installing the Command-Line Interface

First, let's install the AWS command-line tools. For macOS users, we may be able to simply install them through Homebrew, as shown in Listing 10-38.

Listing 10-38. Installing awsebcli Through Homebrew

```
$ brew update && brew install awsebcli
```

For Linux users, we will need to have Python 3 installed prior to installing the CLI. We may also need to install `libffi-dev` first, which is a dependency of `pip`, as shown in Listing 10-39.

Listing 10-39. Installing libffi-dev

```
$ sudo apt-get install libffi-dev # for Linux users
```

We can install Python almost the same way we install Ruby using asdf, as shown in Listing 10-40.

Listing 10-40. Installing Python Using asdf

```
$ asdf add python
$ asdf install python 3.7.1
$ asdf global python 3.7.1
```

Now, we can install awsebcli, as shown in Listing 10-41.

Listing 10-41. Installing awsebcli Through pip

```
$ pip install awsebcli --user
```

Installing the CLI using the previous command will put the executable in the Python's user script directory, which might not be discoverable by our system by default.

To make the executable on that folder discoverable, on Linux machines, let's add the code shown in Listing 10-42 to the terminal profile file (e.g., ~/.bash_profile).

For macOS users, if you are not installing through Homebrew, the user script directory should be ~/Library/Python/3.7/bin instead of ~/.local/bin.

Listing 10-42. Adding the Local Path to Be Discoverable

```
export PATH=~/.local/bin:$PATH
```

Then, let's resource the profile file or re-open the terminal window, and let's type in eb to check if it can be resolved. See Listing 10-43.

Listing 10-43. Executing the eb CLI

```
$ eb
```

Setting Up the Elastic Beanstalk App

Now, let's make a new application instance to host our app through Elastic Beanstalk. In the root folder of our app, let's execute the command shown in Listing 10-44.

Listing 10-44. Initializing our App for Deployment Into AWS Cloud

```
$ eb init
```

The eb init command will ask us to pick the availability zone for the application instance. We may choose us-wast-2 (Oregon), which is the default region in most cases. You are free to choose a different region, as shown in Listing 10-45.

Listing 10-45. Choosing a Region

```
Select a default region
1) us-east-1 : US East (N. Virginia)
2) us-west-1 : US West (N. California)
3) us-west-2 : US West (Oregon)
4) eu-west-1 : EU (Ireland)
5) eu-central-1 : EU (Frankfurt)
6) ap-south-1 : Asia Pacific (Mumbai)
7) ap-southeast-1 : Asia Pacific (Singapore)
8) ap-southeast-2 : Asia Pacific (Sydney)
9) ap-northeast-1 : Asia Pacific (Tokyo)
10) ap-northeast-2 : Asia Pacific (Seoul)
11) sa-east-1 : South America (Sao Paulo)
12) cn-north-1 : China (Beijing)
13) cn-northwest-1 : China (Ningxia)
14) us-east-2 : US East (Ohio)
15) ca-central-1 : Canada (Central)
16) eu-west-2 : EU (London)
17) eu-west-3 : EU (Paris)
18) eu-north-1 : EU (Stockholm)
19) eu-south-1 : EU (Milano)
20) ap-east-1 : Asia Pacific (Hong Kong)
21) me-south-1 : Middle East (Bahrain)
22) af-south-1 : Africa (Cape Town)
(default is 3): 7
```

If this is the first time we execute the command, the CLI may ask for the AWS credentials, which we need to provide, as shown in Listing 10-46.

Listing 10-46. Entering the AWS Credentials for the eb CLI

```
You have not yet set up your credentials or your credentials are incorrect
You must provide your credentials.
(aws-access-id): YOUR_ACCESS_ID
(aws-secret-key): YOUR_SECRET_KEY
```

Next, we may need to select an application. Let's choose to create a new one, as shown in Listing 10-47.

Listing 10-47. Choosing an Application to Deploy Into

```
Select an application to use
1) zenta
2) [ Create new Application ]
(default is 2): 2
```

It will then ask us to name the application; let's call it tandibi, as shown in Listing 10-48.

Listing 10-48. Naming the App

```
Enter Application Name
(default is "tandibi"): tandibi
Application tandibi has been created.
```

Once done, it may detect that we are using Docker. However, let's not deploy our app as a Docker container. So, let's type in n, as shown in Listing 10-49.

Listing 10-49. The CLI Asks If We Would Like to Use Docker

```
It appears you are using Docker. Is this correct?
(Y/n): n
```

As a consequence, the CLI will ask for the platform of the app. Let's choose Ruby, which is number 10 in the list. The numbering could be different in your platform, so please ensure the number maps to Ruby, as shown in Listing 10-50.

Listing 10-50. Choosing the Platform

```
Select a platform.
1) .NET on Windows Server
```

```
2) Docker
3) GlassFish
4) Go
5) Java
6) Node.js
7) PHP
8) Packer
9) Python
10) Ruby
11) Tomcat
(make a selection): 10
```

After that, we need to choose the exact platform. In this case, let's choose Puma with Ruby 2.6, as shown in Listing 10-51.

Listing 10-51. Choosing the Exact Platform Type

```
Select a platform branch.
1) Ruby 2.7 running on 64bit Amazon Linux 2
2) Ruby 2.6 running on 64bit Amazon Linux 2
3) Ruby 2.5 running on 64bit Amazon Linux 2
4) Puma with Ruby 2.6 running on 64bit Amazon Linux
5) Puma with Ruby 2.5 running on 64bit Amazon Linux
6) Puma with Ruby 2.4 running on 64bit Amazon Linux
...
(default is 1): 4
```

When the CLI asks if we would like to set up SSH for the instance, let's type Y, as shown in Listing 10-52.

Listing 10-52. Request to Set Up SSH to Our Tandibi Instances

```
Cannot setup CodeCommit because there is no Source Control setup,
continuing with initialization
Do you want to set up SSH for your instances?
(Y/n): Y
```

If the prompt asks whether we want to continue with CodeCommit, we can safely choose N, which is the default value.

Then, when it asked for a key pair, we can create a new one. See Listing 10-53.

Listing 10-53. Creating a New Key Pair

```
Select a keypair.
1) aws-eb
2) [ Create new KeyPair ]
(default is 1): 2
```

Then let's name our key pair and assign it a password that you like. See Listing 10-54.

Listing 10-54. Naming the Key Pair

```
Type a keypair name.
(Default is aws-eb2): aws-tandibi-eb
```

Now, let's log in to the AWS console[4] to check our app. From the Elastic Beanstalk dashboard, choose Applications. There, we can verify that our Tandibi application has been created successfully. See Figure 10-20.

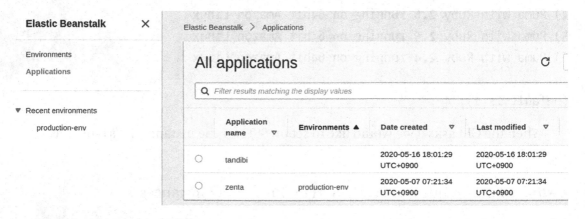

Figure 10-20. *Listing of our Elastic Beanstalk applications*

---

[4]https://console.aws.amazon.com/console/home

Next, let's create a production environment for our application. Let's click the tandibi app and click the "Create a new environment" button displayed on the page. See Figure 10-21.

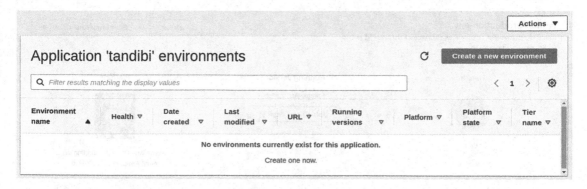

Figure 10-21. *The application page of tandibi*

On the next screen, when asked about the environment tier, let's choose "Web server environment." See Figure 10-22.

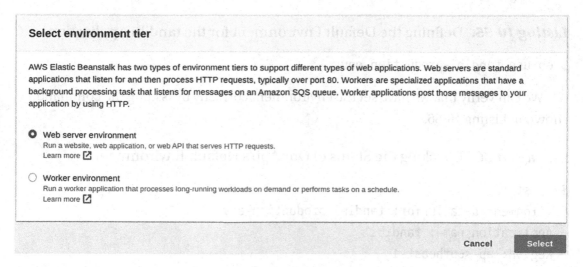

Figure 10-22. *Choosing the environment tier*

Then, let's name the environment name `tandibi-production-env`. For the platform, let's select Puma with Ruby 2.6. For the application code, let's choose Sample Application for now. Then, let's hit the Create Environment button on the page.

After a while, our application's new environment will be ready, and we will see the screen in Figure 10-23.

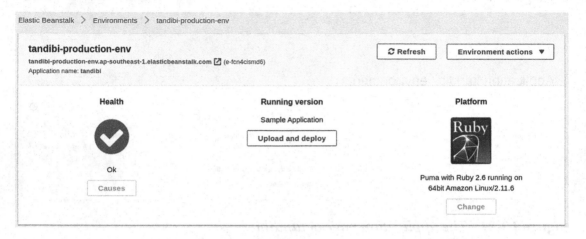

Figure 10-23. *Page for the production environment*

Back in our terminal, let's define the default environment using the command shown in Listing 10-55.

Listing 10-55. Defining the Default Environment for the tandibi Application

```
$ eb use tandibi-production-env
```

We can verify that we have set the environment correctly by issuing the command shown in Listing 10-56.

Listing 10-56. Checking the Status of Our App's Default Environment

```
$ eb status
Environment details for: tandibi-production-env
  Application name: tandibi
  Region: ap-southeast-1
  Deployed Version: Sample Application
  Environment ID: e-fcn4cismd6
  Platform: arn:aws:elasticbeanstalk:..
  Tier: WebServer-Standard-1.0
  CNAME: tandibi-production-env.ap...
```

```
Updated: 2020-05-16 10:37:37.697000+00:00
Status: Ready
Health: Green
```

Setting Up the Database

Amazon RDS allows developers to set up managed relational database in the cloud, with rich backends available to choose from: PostgreSQL, MySQL, Oracle, Microsoft SQL, and Amazon Aurora.

Let's create a Postgres database. First, from the console, search for *RDS*, and let's go to the RDS management page. On the management page, let's click "Create database."

On the database creation page, ensure Standard Create is selected when asked about the creation method. See Figure 10-24.

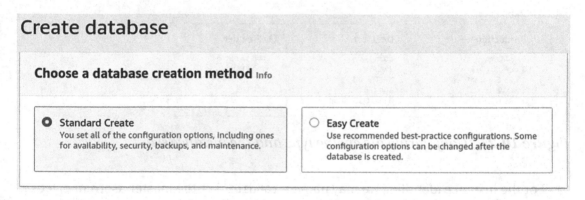

Figure 10-24. *Choosing Standard Create*

Then, for the engine type, let's choose PostgreSQL. And for the instance size, let's choose the "Free tier" option. See Figure 10-25.

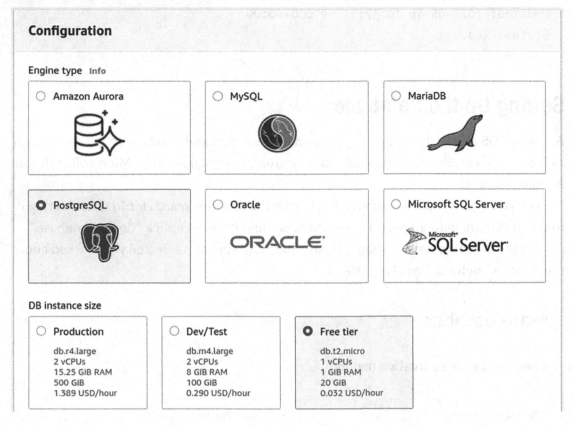

Figure 10-25. *Configuring the engine type and the instance size*

For the instance identifier, we may name it tandibi. For the master username, let's keep it as is: postgres. For the password, fill in with one you believe to be safe.

After that, scroll down to the section about connectivity, and expand the detail panel for additional connectivity configuration. See Figure 10-26.

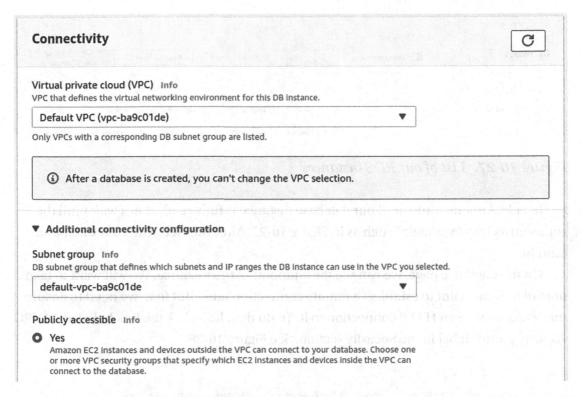

Figure 10-26. *Adjusting the connectivity settings*

There, let's ensure that our database is to be publicly available so that we don't have to set up a VPN connection to connect to it, for now. Please note that this has a security implication. To make a more secured application, we should set up a VPN connection so that the connection to our database is limited to a select few, rather than open to the public. However, this security-related topic is left to as an exercise for you to explore. Regardless, we are still going to use a username and password to authenticate ourselves to our database instance.

After that, let's click the "Create database" button, and we will be taken back to a page that lists all of our databases. See Figure 10-27.

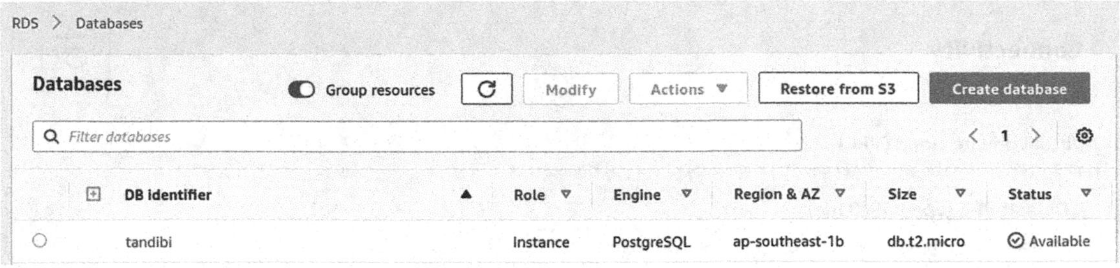

Figure 10-27. *List of our RDS instances*

It will take some time until our database instance is fully ready. Let's wait until the status turns into "Available" such as in Figure 10-27. After this, let's click our database: tandibi.

On the database page, we can see the endpoint of the instance. We will want to take note of this endpoint to establish a remote connection later. But first, we need to ensure that we can make an HTTP connection to it. To do that, let's click the link below the "VPC security group" label in the Security section. See Figure 10-28.

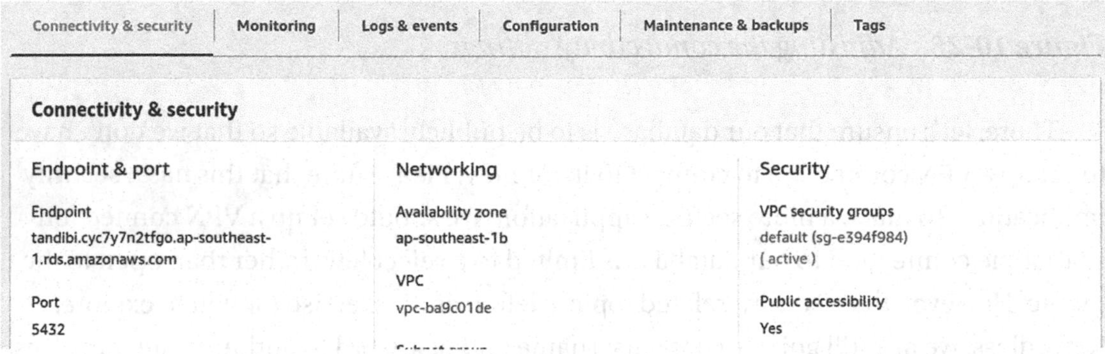

Figure 10-28. *The page that displays the database connectivity and security settings*

We will be taken to the security groups page. Let's click the link that refers to the security group ID. After that, let's click the "Edit inbound rules" button on the page. For the source, let's add `0.0.0.0/0` so that it looks like the one in Figure 10-29. After that, click the "Save rules" button at the bottom of the page.

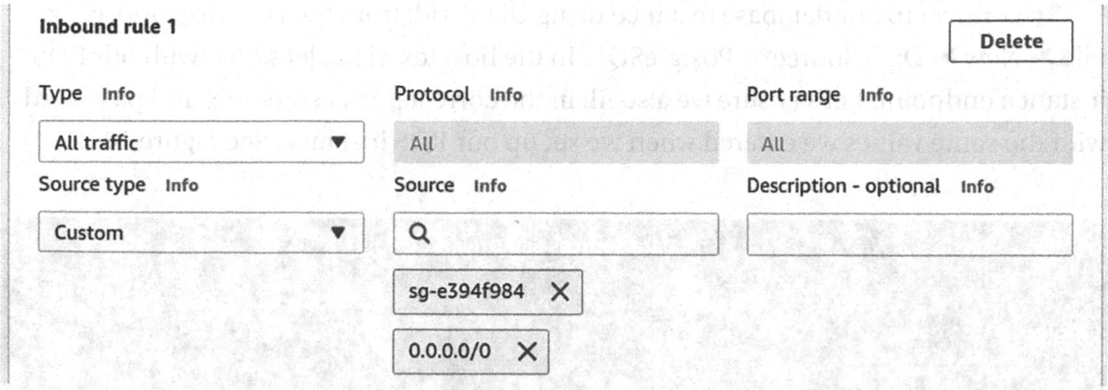

Figure 10-29. *Adjusting the inbound rules*

Let's do the same for the outbound rules. Let's ensure that 0.0.0.0/0 is set as the destination, so that our outbound setting looks like the one in Figure 10-30.

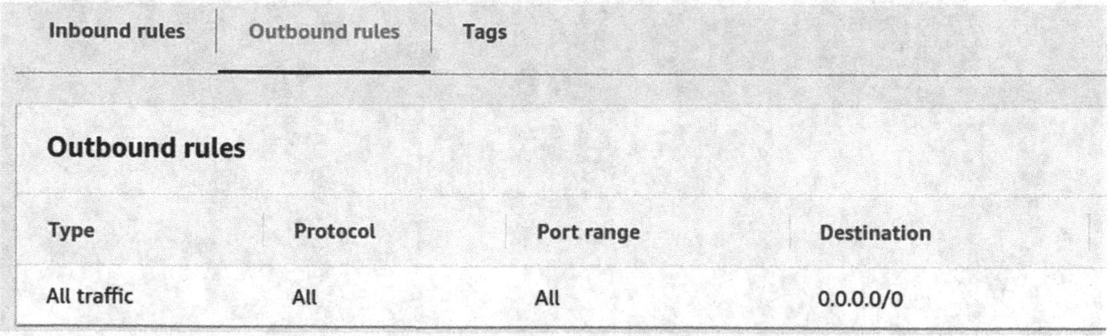

Figure 10-30. *Adjusting the outbound rules*

All is good! Let's connect to our RDS instance to create the database and install the PostGIS extension. There are many great GUI software applications that we can use to manage our database, such as DataGrip,[5] TablePlus, and Postico. If you prefer an open source alternative, Postbird is worth the try. We will be using JetBrains DataGrip for the rest of this section.

---

[5]https://www.jetbrains.com/datagrip/

To connect to our database instance using DataGrid, from the DataGrip app, click File ➤ New ➤ Data Source ➤ PostgreSQL. In the host text field, let's fill it with our RDS instance endpoint. Let's ensure we also fill in the correct port, username, and password with the same values we entered when we set up our RDS instance. See Figure 10-31.

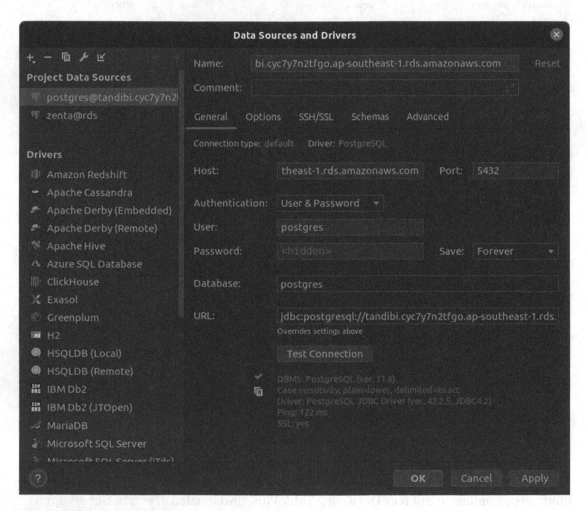

Figure 10-31. Setting up the connection on DataGrip

After that, we can check whether we will be able to connect to the instance, by hitting the Test Connection button. If all is good, let's click OK. See Figure 10-32.

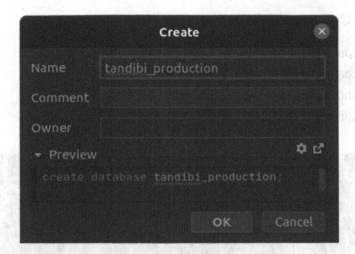

Figure 10-32. *Creating a new database*

Then, let's click File ➤ New ➤ Database, and let's name it `tandibi_production`. After that, let's enable the PostGIS extension.

In the query command section on the right side of DataGrip, let's click the schema selector option. See Figure 10-33.

Figure 10-33. *Selecting the tandibi_production to run queries on*

Among the choices, let's select `tandibi_production`. This way, all the SQL commands we are going to execute are executed against `tandibi_production`, the database our app will connect to.

Now, let's execute these SQL commands. To do that, input the command shown in Listing 10-57 into the editor, press Ctrl+A to select all the text in the editor, and then click the green triangle button that says Execute. See Figure 10-34.

Listing 10-57. Creating Extension

```
create extension postgis;
create extension fuzzystrmatch;
create extension postgis_tiger_geocoder;
create extension postgis_topology;
```

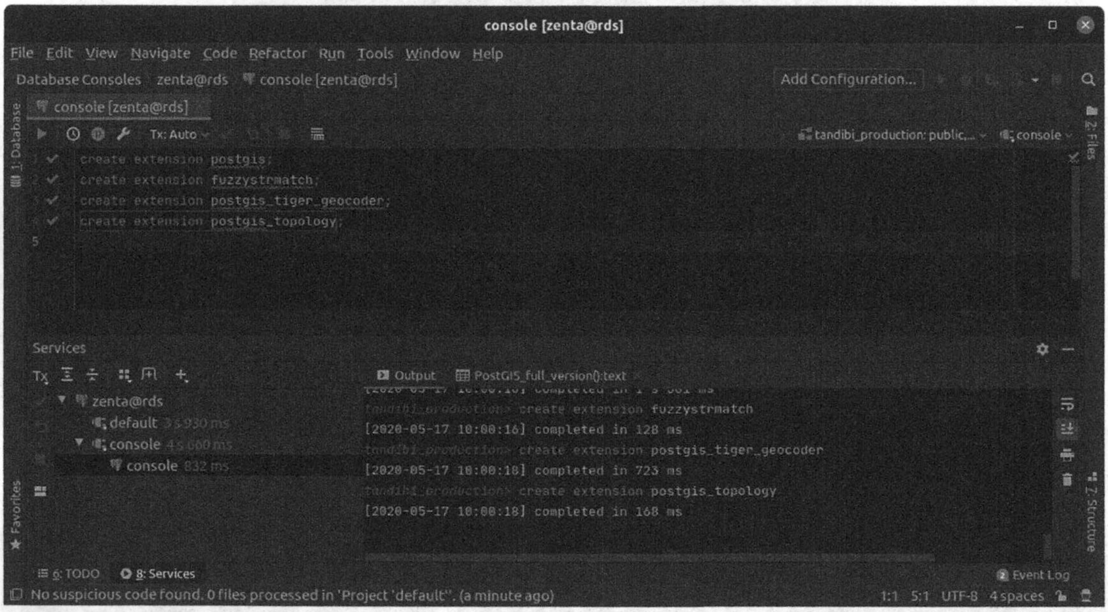

Figure 10-34. *Running queries on the database using DataGrip*

After that, let's execute the command shown in Listing 10-58 to transfer ownership of some schemas to the `rds_superuser` role.

Listing 10-58. Command to Transfer Ownership of Some Schemas

```
alter schema tiger owner to rds_superuser;
alter schema tiger_data owner to rds_superuser;
alter schema topology owner to rds_superuser;
```

After that, let's create the exec function shown in Listing 10-59 that can evaluate a string of a SQL query.

Listing 10-59. A Function to Execute a Query

```
CREATE FUNCTION
    exec(text)
    returns text
    language plpgsql volatile AS $f$
    BEGIN
        EXECUTE $1;
        RETURN $1;
    END; $f$;
```

Then, let's use the exec function we just created on the query in Listing 10-60 that will transfer ownership of PostGIS objects to the rds_superuser role, the role to which our master user system account is assigned.

We didn't need to do these steps while developing locally because in our local environment, our system account is assigned to the customarily default Postgres role. But, AWS uses the rds_superuser role instead; hence, we need to transfer the ownership.

Listing 10-60. Query to Transfer PostGIS Objects' Ownership to rds_superuser

```
SELECT exec(
    'ALTER TABLE ' ||
    quote_ident(s.nspname) ||
    '.' ||
    quote_ident(s.relname) ||
    ' OWNER TO rds_superuser;')
FROM (
    SELECT nspname, relname
    FROM pg_class c
        JOIN pg_namespace n
        ON (c.relnamespace = n.oid)
    WHERE nspname in ('tiger','topology') AND
    relkind IN ('r','S','v') ORDER BY relkind = 'S') s;
```

Next, let's try executing the query in Listing 10-61 to check if PostGIS is already installed.

Listing 10-61. Query to Check the Version of PostGIS Extension

```
SELECT PostGIS_full_version();
```

This produces the output shown in Listing 10-62.

Listing 10-62. Output from Checking the PostGIS Version

```
POSTGIS="2.5.2 r17328" [EXTENSION] PGSQL="110" GEOS="3.7.0-CAPI-1.11.0
673b9939" PROJ="Rel. 5.2.0, September 15th, 2018" GDAL="GDAL 2.3.1,
released 2018/06/22" LIBXML="2.9.1" LIBJSON="0.12" LIBPROTOBUF="1.3.0"
TOPOLOGY RASTER
```

By now, we are done setting up our database instance! We are ready to deploy our application, but we will need to do a bit more configuration on the Beanstalk part.

As information, to check the extensions enabled on our RDS database, we can execute the command shown in Listing 10-63.

Listing 10-63. Command to Check the Extensions Used by a Database

```
SHOW rds.extensions;
```

```
address_standardizer, address_standardizer_data_us, amcheck, aws_commons,
aws_s3, bloom, btree_gin, btree_gist, citext, cube, dblink, dict_int, dict_
xsyn, earthdistance, fuzzystrmatch, hll, hstore, hstore_plperl, intagg,
intarray, ip4r, isn, jsonb_plperl, log_fdw, ltree, orafce, pageinspect,
pgaudit, pgcrypto, pglogical, pgrouting, pgrowlocks, pgstattuple, pgtap,
pg_buffercache, pg_freespacemap, pg_hint_plan, pg_prewarm, pg_repack,
pg_similarity, pg_stat_statements, pg_transport, pg_trgm, pg_visibility,
plcoffee, plls, plperl, plpgsql, plprofiler, pltcl, plv8, postgis, postgis_
tiger_geocoder, postgis_topology, postgres_fdw, prefix, sslinfo, tablefunc,
test_parser, tsm_system_rows, tsm_system_time, unaccent, uuid-ossp
```

It might be interesting to check what each of those extensions do to our database. However, that's not required to proceed with our business.

Configuring the Application

In this section, we will configure our web server. We will install Yarn, if the software is not yet installed. We will also configure the Nginx web server, and finally, let's define some environment variables necessary for the app to connect to the database.

Indeed, our app installs the front-end dependencies through Yarn, and both NodeJS and Yarn are not installed by default on a Ruby platform. We need to install them independently.

Let's create a new folder called .ebextensions in the root path, and then let's create a new file: 09_yarn_install.config. Put the code shown in Listing 10-64 in the file.

Listing 10-64. Code to Install Our Front-End Dependencies Through Yarn

```
files:
  "/opt/elasticbeanstalk/hooks/appdeploy/pre/09_yarn_install.sh" :
    mode: "000775"
    owner: root
    group: users
    content: |
      #!/usr/bin/env bash

      set -xe

      EB_APP_STAGING_DIR=$(/opt/elasticbeanstalk/bin/get-config \
        container -k app_staging_dir)
      EB_APP_USER=$(/opt/elasticbeanstalk/bin/get-config \
        container -k app_user)

      if which yarn; then
        echo "Skipping installation of yarn -- yarn already installed."
        echo "yarn --version: `yarn --version`"
      else
        # Download the yarn repo, not zero, but big O
        sudo wget https://dl.yarnpkg.com/rpm/yarn.repo -O \
          /etc/yum.repos.d/yarn.repo
        file /etc/yum.repos.d/yarn.repo

        echo "Installing Node v10.x ..."
```

```
    curl --location https://rpm.nodesource.com/setup_10.x > \
      /home/ec2-user/node_install.sh
    file /home/ec2-user/node_install.sh
    sudo bash /home/ec2-user/node_install.sh
    sudo yum install -y nodejs
    node --version

    echo "Installing Yarn"
    sudo yum install -y yarn
    yarn --version
fi

echo "Change directory to $EB_APP_STAGING_DIR"
cd $EB_APP_STAGING_DIR

# yarn install
echo "Running yarn install."
yarn install
```

Next, we need to manually configure how Nginx (pronounced "Engine X") works. Otherwise, using the default configuration, our app won't be able to access assets under the packs directory. So, let's create 02_nginx.config within the .ebextensions directory on the root path and add the command shown in Listing 10-65,

Listing 10-65. Code for the nginx Configuration

```
files:
  "/etc/nginx/conf.d/02_nginx.conf":
    mode: "000644"
    owner: root
    group: root
    content: |
      # The content of this file is based on the content
      # of /etc/nginx/conf.d/webapp_healthd.conf

      # Change the name of the upstream because it can't have
      # the same name as the one defined by default in
      # /etc/nginx/conf.d/webapp_healthd.conf
      upstream new_upstream_name {
```

```
    server unix:///var/run/puma/my_app.sock;
}

# Change the name of the log_format because it can't have
# the same name as the one defined by default in
# /etc/nginx/conf.d/webapp_healthd.conf
log_format new_log_name_healthd '$msec"$uri"'
  '$status"$request_time"$upstream_response_time"'
  '$http_x_forwarded_for';

server {
  listen 80;
  server_name _ localhost;
  client_max_body_size 200M;

  if ($time_iso8601 ~ "^(\d{4})-(\d{2})-(\d{2})T(\d{2})") {
    set $year $1;
    set $month $2;
    set $day $3;
    set $hour $4;
  }

  access_log  /var/log/nginx/access.log  main;
  access_log
    /var/log/nginx/healthd/application.log.$year-$month-$day-$hour
    new_log_name_healthd;

  location / {
    # Match the name of upstream directive which is defined above
    proxy_pass http://new_upstream_name;
    proxy_set_header Host $host;
    proxy_set_header X-Forwarded-Proto
      $http_x_forwarded_proto;
    proxy_set_header X-Forwarded-For
      $proxy_add_x_forwarded_for;
    proxy_set_header X-Forwarded-Proto $scheme;

    add_header Cache-Control no-store;
```

```
    }

    set $gzipable 'text/css image/svg+xml';
    set $gzipable '${gzipable} text/javascript application/javascript';

    location /assets {
      alias /var/app/current/public/assets;
      gzip on;
      gzip_vary on;
      gzip_min_length 10240;
      gzip_proxied expired no-cache no-store private auth;
      gzip_types $gzipable;
      gzip_disable "MSIE [1-6]\.";
      expires max;
      add_header Cache-Control public;
    }

    location /public {
      alias /var/app/current/public;
      gzip on;
      gzip_vary on;
      gzip_min_length 10240;
      gzip_proxied expired no-cache no-store private auth;
      gzip_types $gzipable;
      gzip_disable "MSIE [1-6]\.";
      expires max;
      add_header Cache-Control public;
    }

    location /packs {
      alias /var/app/current/public/packs;
      gzip on;
      gzip_vary on;
      gzip_min_length 10240;
      gzip_proxied expired no-cache no-store private auth;
      gzip_types $gzipable;
```

```
    gzip_disable "MSIE [1-6]\.";
    expires max;
    add_header Cache-Control public;
  }

}
```

```
container_commands:
  01_reload_nginx:
    command: "sudo service nginx reload"
```

After that, let's create a new `container_commands.config` within the same `.ebextensions` folder. This file would later list all stand-alone commands we would like to execute. Currently, we just have one command to add. Let's add the code shown in Listing 10-66 into the file.

Listing 10-66. Code for .ebextensions/container_commands.config

```
container_commands:
  01_set_tmp_permissions:
    command: "sudo chmod -R 777 /var/app/ondeck/tmp"
```

Last but not least, since under the production environment assets are to be precompiled, we need to add the code shown in Listing 10-67 into `layouts/_header.html.erb`.

Listing 10-67. Linking Precompiled Stylesheet into the Header

```
<%= stylesheet_link_tag 'application', media: 'all' %>
<%= stylesheet_pack_tag 'application', media: 'all' %>
<%= stylesheet_pack_tag 'vue_application', media: 'all' %>

<%= javascript_pack_tag 'application' %>
```

We also need to change our `database.yml` definition for the `production` environment, as shown in Listing 10-68.

Listing 10-68. Updating database.yml Definition for the Production
Environment

```
production:
  <<: *default
  database: tandibi_production
  username: tandibi
  password: <%= ENV['TANDIBI_DATABASE_PASSWORD'] %>
  host: <%= ENV['DATABASE_HOST'] %>
  database: <%= ENV['DATABASE_NAME'] %>
  username: <%= ENV['DATABASE_USERNAME'] %>
  password: <%= ENV['DATABASE_PASSWORD'] %>
```

Then, let's head over to our tandibi application on Elastic Beanstalk. Then, click
Configuration. Then, on the "Configuration overview" page, in the Software category,
click the Edit button as we want to define some environment variables. See Figure 10-35.

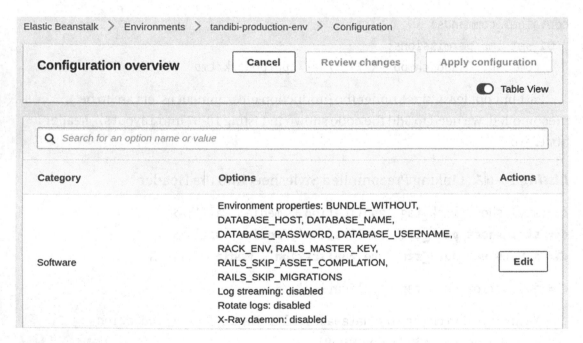

Figure 10-35. *Software category on the "Configuration overview" page*

Scroll down to the environment properties table, and let's define RAILS_MASTER_KEY, DATABASE_HOST, DATABASE_NAME, DATABASE_PASSWORD, and DATABASE_USERNAME with their corresponding values. Then, click the Apply button. See Figure 10-36.

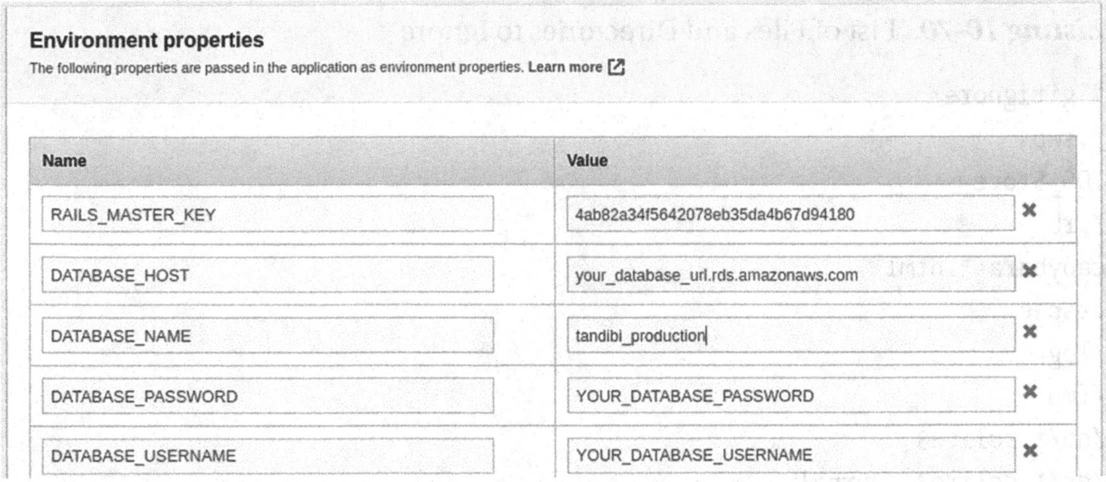

Environment properties

The following properties are passed in the application as environment properties. Learn more ⌕

Name	Value	
RAILS_MASTER_KEY	4ab82a34f5642078eb35da4b67d94180	✖
DATABASE_HOST	your_database_url.rds.amazonaws.com	✖
DATABASE_NAME	tandibi_production|	✖
DATABASE_PASSWORD	YOUR_DATABASE_PASSWORD	✖
DATABASE_USERNAME	YOUR_DATABASE_USERNAME	✖

Figure 10-36. *Configuring some environment variables for the app*

Elastic Beanstalk cannot detect the exact Ruby version that our app depends on. Instead, it will always install the latest version of the Ruby 2.6 family.

Since we specify the ruby version in the gemfile, there's a potential issue where our bundler refuses to bundle if the Ruby version doesn't match with the one defined.

Let's edit the gemfile as shown in Listing 10-69, and don't forget to rerun bundle install. Then, let's ensure that the Ruby version is no longer specified on the Gemfile.lock.

Listing 10-69. Removing Version Specification on Gemfile for Ruby

```
git_source(:github) { |repo| "https://github.com/#{repo}.git" }

ruby '2.6.5'

# Bundle edge Rails instead: gem 'rails', github: 'rails/rails'
gem 'rails', '~> 6.0.2', '>= 6.0.2.1'
...
```

That's it! We are ready for deployment.

Deployment

Before we deploy, let's create an .ebignore on the root path and add the command shown in Listing 10-70.

Listing 10-70. List of Files and Directories to Ignore

```
# gitignore
*.swp
.DS_Store
*.rbc
capybara-*.html
.rspec
/log
/tmp
/db/*.sqlite3
/db/*.sqlite3-journal
/public/system
/coverage/
/spec/tmp
*.orig
rerun.txt
pickle-email-*.html
/.idea
*.iml

# Environment normalization
/.bundle
/vendor/bundle

# Ignore encrypted secrets key file.
config/secrets.yml.key

# Generated by simplecov
coverage/
```

```
# NPM Dependency directories
node_modules/

# Generated files with Webpack
public/assets/**/*

# Elastic Beanstalk Files
.elasticbeanstalk/*
!.elasticbeanstalk/config.yml

# below is specific to .ebdeploy
.git
```

Having the .ebignore, when we deploy our app, the uploader doesn't have to bundle unnecessary files, which can slow down the deployment process.

Then, to deploy our app, simply execute the command shown in Listing 10-71.

Listing 10-71. Command to Do Deployment

```
$ eb deploy
```

If we head over to the Elastic Beanstalk console, we can see that the deployment is in progress. See Figure 10-37.

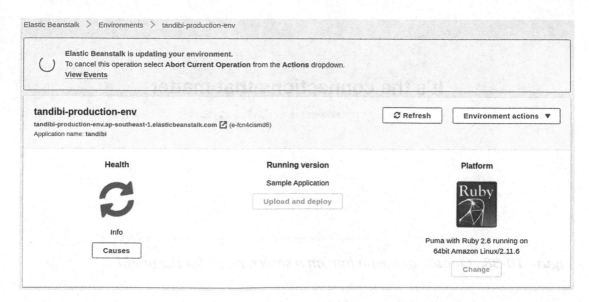

Figure 10-37. *Deployment on tandibi-production-env on progress*

And if we look at the console, we can see the progress, as shown in Listing 10-72.

Listing 10-72. Deploying to Elastic Beanstalk

```
Creating application version archive "app-200517_103206".
Uploading: [##############################] 100% Done...
2020-05-17 ..   INFO    Environment update is starting.
2020-05-17 ..   INFO    Deploying new version to instance(s).
2020-05-17 ..   INFO    New application version was deployed to ...
2020-05-17 ..   INFO    Environment update completed successfully.
```

If the deployment is done, we can check our app by clicking the link on the environment page. Or we can type **eb open** on the root path in our development machine. See Figure 10-38.

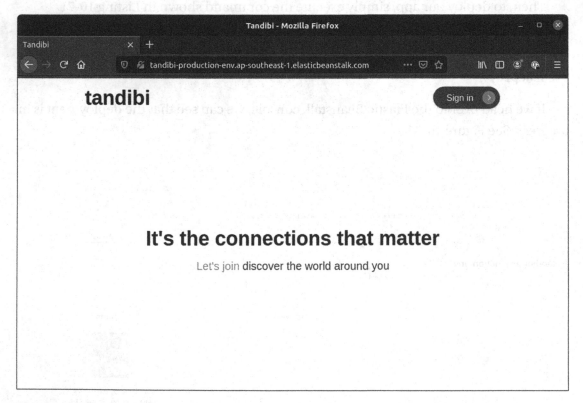

Figure 10-38. *Our social media app on a server, ready for the world*

Note   Deploying to Elastic Beanstalk feels faster than Heroku just because our deployment type and Heroku's are different. Heroku Dyno is ephemeral by design, so in every deployment, a new Dyno is set up. With our case in AWS, we don't boot up a new instance.

We can configure our Beanstalk to follow a similar deployment strategy with that of Heroku, by using immutable deployment. Immutable deployment offers such as great benefit that you should check it out, especially the possibility of having a zero-downtime deployment.

Enabling SSH

Let's enable Secure Shell (SSH) into our app so that we can log into our server's console. To do that, simply issue the command shown in Listing 10-73.

Listing 10-73. Setting Up the SSH

```
$ eb ssh --setup
To confirm, type the environment name: tandibi-production-env

Select a keypair.
1) aws-eb
2) aws-tandibi-eb
3) [ Create new KeyPair ]
(default is 2): 2

Printing Status:
2020-05-16 11:44:09   INFO   Environment update is starting.
...
```

We can then SSH to our machine by using the command shown in Listing 10-74.

Listing 10-74. Command to Connect to Our EC2 Instance

```
$ eb ssh
...
Are you sure you want to continue connecting (yes/no/[fingerprint])? yes
```

There, we can try heading to our /var/app/current folder where our app is located and initiate a rails console. If everything works as expected, we will have the console running! See Listing 10-75.

Listing 10-75. Starting a Rails Console on the Server

```
[ec2-user@ip-172-31-20-217 ~]$ cd /var/app/current/
[ec2-user@ip-172-31-20-217 current]$ rails c
Loading production environment (Rails 6.0.3)
irb(main):001:0>
```

Reflection

Deploying to AWS Elastic Beanstalk is easy and quick indeed. However, the process to set it up takes specific expertise that would be way unfamiliar for those who are new to the engineering community, compared to Heroku's.

However, AWS Elastic Beanstalk affords us more control of the instances. It also has more availability zones with affordable pricing than that offered by Heroku's. So, it's all a choice.

Choose which one makes you happier for now. Sometimes, that would mean using Heroku and then moving to Elastic Beanstalk later. Regardless, those two services are great, allowing us to focus on delivering after the system is set up.

Performance, Metrics, and Monitoring

Monitoring our app is an integral part of developing great software. There are many ways we can monitor our application.

First, for performance monitoring, Rails folks are usually going to pick New Relic. New Relic is a tool that engineers use to help detect anomalies, discover root causes of a performance issue such as N+1, and seek ways to optimize the app's performance. This kind of tool is called an *application performance monitoring* (APM) tool.

Another extremely helpful tooling in this space is Scout APM, which is a great tool to help hunt down memory issues, find long-running queries, and do some other benchmarking. However, it's way much more expensive than New Relic.

Some engineering team may set up their own in-house APM tools in addition to those two. If we need to go that way, popular choices are Prometheus and Grafana.

Another thing we need to monitor is errors. There are multiple error tracking tools we can choose from: Raygun, Bugsnag, Rollbar, Sentry, and many others. Of these, I gladly recommend Sentry, but many of them are also great, so you should check them out and evaluate them one by one by yourself.

Summary

Well-rounded engineers optimize their time and make themselves happy when on their journey of making the world a better place to live. Don't stop here. And, don't stop looking. Build something. Share your knowledge. Explore different ideas. Do something good.

APPENDIX

Validations

Validation	Purpose
acceptance	Validates that a check box, for instance, on the user interface was checked when a form was submitted. It accepts various options such as *accept*, and so forth.
confirmation	Validates that two text fields, for instance, should receive exactly the same content.
exclusion	Validates that a value is not included in a given array. It accepts various options such as *in*, and so forth.
format	Validates that a value matches with a given regular expression. It accepts various options such as *with*, and so forth.
inclusion	Validates that a value is among a given array. It accepts various options such as *in*, and so forth.
length	Validates the length of a value, for example, of a given password that should be at least eight characters long. It accepts various options such as *minimum*, *maximum*, *is*, and so forth.
numericality	Validates that a value is numerical. It accepts various options such as *only_integer*, *greater_than*, *less_than*, *other_than*, and so forth.
presence	Validates that a specified attribute's value is not empty.
absence	Validates that a specified attribute's value is absent.
uniqueness	Validates that a value is unique before the object gets saved. It accepts various options such as *scope*, *case_sensitive*, and so forth.

© Adam Notodikromo 2021
A. Notodikromo, *Learn Rails 6*, https://doi.org/10.1007/978-1-4842-6026-5

Index

© Adam Notodikromo 2021
A. Notodikromo, *Learn Rails 6*, https://doi.org/10.1007/978-1-4842-6026-5

Printed in the United States
By Bookmasters

Printed in the United States
By Bookmasters